T0335137

MIZAN SERIES 4

DECONSTRUCTING ISLAMIC STUDIES

The Mizan Series

The Mizan Series is published by the Ilex Foundation in partnership with the Center for Hellenic Studies. The series supports the central mission of the Mizan digital initiative to encourage informed public discourse and interdisciplinary scholarship on the history, culture, and religion of Muslim societies and civilizations.

www.mizanproject.org

Also in the Mizan Series

Muslim Superheroes: Comics, Islam, and Representation,
edited by A. David Lewis and Martin Lund

Muslims and US Politics Today: A Defining Moment
edited by Mohammad Hassan Khalil

The End of Middle East History and Other Conjectures
by Richard W. Bulliet

DECONSTRUCTING ISLAMIC STUDIES

Edited by
Majid Daneshgar and Aaron W. Hughes

Ilex Foundation
Boston, Massachusetts

Center for Hellenic Studies
Trustees for Harvard University
Washington, D. C.

Distributed by Harvard University Press
Cambridge, Massachusetts and London, England

Deconstructing Islamic Studies
Edited by Majid Daneshgar and Aaron W. Hughes

Published by the Ilex Foundation, Boston, Massachusetts and The Center for Hellenic Studies, Trustees for Harvard University, Washington, D.C.

Distributed by Harvard University Press, Cambridge, Massachusetts and London, England

Production editor: Christopher Dadian
Cover design: Joni Godlove
Printed in the United States of America

Library of Congress Cataloging-in-Publication Data

Names: Daneshgar, Majid, editor. | Hughes, Aaron W., 1968- editor.
Title: Deconstructing Islamic studies / edited by Majid Daneshgar and Aaron W. Hughes.
Description: Boston : Ilex Foundation, 2020. | Series: Mizan series ; 4 | Includes bibliographical references and index. | Summary: "This volume, comprising chapters by leading experts, deconstructs the ways in which classical Muslim scholarship has structured (and, indeed, continues to structure) the modern study of Islam. It explores how classical subjects have been approached traditionally, theologically, and secularly, in addition to examining some of the tensions inherent in these approaches"-- Provided by publisher.
Identifiers: LCCN 2020017154 | ISBN 9780674244689 (paperback)
Subjects: LCSH: Islam--Study and teaching. | Deconstruction.
Classification: LCC BP42 .D43 2020 | DDC 297.07--dc23
LC record available at https://lccn.loc.gov/2020017154

We would like to dedicate this volume to the memory of the victims of PS752

CONTENTS

Adab

Taṣhayyuʿ

Ismāʿīliyya

Taṣawwuf

Mashriqiyyāt

Acknowledgements

WE HAVE BEEN DISCUSSING method and theory in the study of religion in general and of Islam in particular since 2016. In that year we reached out to one another over a common concern: the fate and future of the field of Islamic studies. In this regard, we shared a worry over the increasingly apologetic and highly political posture that governs the study of Islam in both the Western and Islamic worlds. As products of those worlds, we wanted to go back and examine the ways in which classical topics in Islam have shaped our current understanding of Islam in general and Islamic studies in particular. With these concerns in mind, we invited colleagues to contribute to this task, working on the assumption that we were not alone in our concern over the fate of the study of Islam. We thank all of them for taking time out of their busy schedules to write comprehensive chapters on specific subjects. Well done friends / *eyval be hamegī*!

As with every edited volume, what we initially planned back in 2016 is not quite the same volume that has now materialized. Some contributors dropped out and others came on board rather late. Regardless, we both are of the opinion that the present volume makes an important intervention in what the shape of the study of Islam has been, is, and might be in the future.

Working with the Ilex team, Niloo Fotouhi, executive director and director of publications and media, Michael Pregill, the former Mizan series editor, and Christopher Dadian, the managing editor has been a pleasure from the beginning, and they have all accompanied us during the various stages of this project.

We also thank our families for their patience, tenderness, and love. Without them, we would be unable to do what we do.

omīdvārīm az khvāndan-e īn ketāb lezzat bebarīd!

February 2020
Editors

Contributors

Nuha Alshaar (PhD Cambridge University) is a senior research associate at the Institute of Ismaili Studies, London, where her focus has been on ethical concepts in early Qurʾān interpretation, and on the reception of the Qurʾān in classical literary traditions (adab). She is also an associate professor at the American University of Sharjah, where she teaches Islamic intellectual history as well as Arabic literature. Her publications include *Ethics in Islam (2015) and, as editor, Qurʾan and Adab* (2017) and *Sources and Approaches* (2013). Her co-authored book, *On God and the World: An Arabic Critical Edition and English Translation of Epistles 49–51 of the Brethren of Purity*, is in preparation at Oxford University Press.

Khalil Andani is assistant professor at Augustana College in Rock Island, Illinois, where he teaches courses in the study of Islam, religious studies, and Muslim-Christian interactions in the Department of Religion. He completed his PhD in Islamic studies from Harvard University's Department of Near Eastern Languages and Civilizations, with a dissertation that focused on the revelation in the Qurʾān, classical *tafsīr*, classical *kalām*, and classical Ismāʿīlī thought. Khalil's publications include articles in *Religion Compass*, the *Oxford Journal of Islamic Studies*, and the *Oxford Handbook of Islamic Philosophy*.

Mushegh Asatryan (PhD, Yale 2012) is assistant professor of Arabic and Muslim cultures at the University of Calgary, Canada. His research interests include the religious and intellectual history of the pre-modern Muslim Middle East and the history of Islamic studies in Euro-American academia in the last two centuries. He is the author of *Controversies in Formative Shiʿi Islam* (I. B. Tauris, 2017) and a number of articles. His publications explore constructions of orthodoxy and heresy in medieval Islam, antinomianism, and religious discourses and literatures among esoteric Muslim groups. His current projects include a study of medieval Muslim heresiographies.

Majid Daneshgar is research associate at the Albert-Ludwigs-Universität Freiburg, Germany. He is an alumnus of the Freiburg Institute for Advanced Studies (FRIAS) and was a Marie S. Curie Fellow in 2017–2018. He completed his PhD at the University of Malaya (UM), where he later worked as senior lecturer of Islamic studies. He also taught Islam at the University of Otago,

New Zealand, where he was nominated for the most inclusive teaching award in 2015. His main publications include two monographs, *Studying the Qurʾān in the Muslim Academy* (Oxford 2019), and *Tantawi Jawhari and the Qurʾān: Tafsir and Social Concerns in the Twentieth Century* (Routledge 2017 and 2019); and two edited volumes, *Islamic Studies Today: Essays in Honor of Andrew Rippin* (Brill 2016), co-edited with Walid A. Saleh, and *The Qurʾān in the Malay-Indonesian World: Context and Interpretation* (Routledge 2016), co-edited with Peter G. Riddell and Andrew Rippin.

Christopher A. Furlow teaches anthropology at Santa Fe College in Gainesville, Florida. He has a PhD in anthropology from the University of Florida and also has a MS in science and technology studies from Virginia Tech University. His research interests include the anthropology of science, technology, and medicine, the Islamic world, and human performance. Furlow has spent more than twenty-five years conducting research on contemporary debates about Islam and science and has conducted field research on this topic in Malaysia, Morocco, Europe, and the USA. He is past president of the General Anthropology Division of the American Anthropological Association, co-editor of the journal *General Anthropology Bulletin*, and sits on the editorial board of *Anthropology Now*.

S. M. Hadi Gerami is assistant professor of Islamic and Qurʾānic studies at the Institute for Humanities and Cultural Studies (IHCS) in Tehran. He is also an adjunct professor of the faculty of Islamic studies, culture, and communication at the Imam Sadiq University (ISU) of Tehran. His co-authored volume, *Opposition to Philosophy in Safavid Iran: Mullā Muḥammad-Ṭāhir Qummī's Ḥikmat al-ʿĀrifīn* (Brill 2017), is about less-known aspects of Safavid intellectual history. He has also published several articles in English, Persian, and Arabic, and a number of books, among others, *Nakhostīn Monāsebāt-e Fekri-ye Tashayyuʿ: Bāz-khāni-ye mafhūm-e gholovv dar Andīsha-ye jaryānhā-ye moteqaddem-e Emāmī* (The First Shīʿite Doctrinal Interactions Revisiting the Concept of Ghuluww in the Thought of Early Shīʿī Social Networks) and *Nakhostīn Andīsha-hā-ye Ḥadīthī Shīʿa* (The Earliest Shīʿī Ideas on Ḥadīth); for the latter he was awarded the Farabi International Award on the Iranian and Islamic Studies in 2018. His research expertise lies in Islamic intellectual history, history of Shīʿism, history of *ḥadīth* as well as *tafsīr*, medieval Arabic philosophy, and method and theory in the study of intellectual history.

Andreas Görke is senior lecturer in Islamic studies at the University of Edinburgh. His primary areas of research are the emergence and early history of Islam and the re-interpretation of the Islamic tradition in modern times. Amongst his publications are a monograph on the composition and transmission of Abū ʿUbayd's Kitāb al-Amwāl, a co-authored book on the earliest traditions on the life of Muḥammad, as well as a number of edited volumes and articles on Muḥammad, the early Islamic tradition, manuscript notes, and Qurʾānic exegesis.

Aaron W. Hughes is the Philip S. Bernstein Chair of Religion in the Department of Religion and Classics at the University of Rochester. He specializes in Islamic studies, Jewish studies, and method and theory in the study of religion. His publications include *Muslim Identities: An Introduction to Islam* (Columbia University Press, 2013); *Jacob Neusner: An American Jewish Iconoclast* (New York University Press, 2016); and *Shared Identities: Medieval and Modern Imaginings of Judeo-Islam* (Oxford University Press, 2017). His work has been supported by the Social Sciences Research Council of Canada (SSHRC) and the National Endowment for the Humanities (NEH).

Mahmoud Pargoo is a PhD graduate in social and political thought from the Institute for Social Justice (Australian Catholic University). He has been a visiting lecturer at the University of Sydney and his research focuses on the intersection of Shīʿī *fiqh*, secularization theories, and politics of post-revolutionary Iran.

Johanna Pink is professor of Islamic studies at the Albert-Ludwigs-Universität Freiburg, Germany. She completed her doctoral degree at the University of Bonn and taught at Freie Universität Berlin and the University of Tübingen. Her main fields of interest are the transregional history of *tafsīr*, especially in the modern period, and Qurʾān translations, with a particular focus on Indonesia. Her publications include a monograph on Sunni *tafsīr* in the modern Islamic world, a guest-edited volume of the *Journal of Qur'anic Studies* on translations of the Qurʾān in Muslim majority contexts, and a volume on *tafsīr* and Islamic intellectual history, co-edited with Andreas Görke. Her latest monograph is entitled *Muslim Qurʾānic Interpretation Today: Media, Genealogies and Interpretive Communities* (Equinox, 2019).

David S. Powers is professor of Near Eastern studies at Cornell University and author of *Muḥammad Is Not the Father of Any of Your Men: The Making of the Last Prophet*.

Mahdi Tourage (PhD 2005, University of Toronto), is currently associate professor of religious studies and social justice and peace studies in the Department of Religion and Philosophy, King's University College at Western University, Canada. His book *Rūmī and the Hermeneutics of Eroticism* was published in 2007 (Brill) and his publications have appeared in *Comparative Studies of South Asia, Africa, and the Middle East*, *Iranian Studies*, and *International Journal of Žižek Studies*. His areas of interest are Islamic religious thought, Sufism, gender and sexuality, and psychoanalysis.

Introduction

Majid Daneshgar and Aaron W. Hughes

EVER SINCE ITS EMERGENCE on the stage of world history, Islam has been approached in two competing and diametrically opposed ways, the apologetical and the polemical. The former is contingent on the preservation and propagation of religious teachings, elucidating what is imagined as proper Islamic teaching to the devout. The latter, in contrast, represents an attempt to undermine the religion or the followers of a specific tradition within it. The dialectic between these two approaches continued into the Enlightenment, and the tension between them remains into the present, and has only been exacerbated in the years after September 11, 2001.[1] The modern period, however, has also witnessed what we might call a third approach, the academic one, which is *supposed* to examine – in an ostensibly non-partisan manner – the many diverse historical, religious, legal, intellectual, and philosophical contexts in which Islam and Islamic studies has been articulated. The most important representative of this approach, of course, is the traditions associated with European Orientalism, and more recent attempts to undermine its claims and assumptions, a trend that is particularly associated with the way the study of Islam is carried out in secular departments of religious studies in the North American context. Despite all the claims and counterclaims, and the noise and vitriol they generate, there remains considerable debate as to how the academic study of Islam should be undertaken and carried out.[2]

The present volume seeks to wade through these various debates with the larger goal of demonstrating how the foundational subjects of Islam – for example, Qurʾān, *ḥadīth*, *fiqh* – have structured and indeed continue to shape our understanding of Islam into the largely secular and modern period. They are, after all, the terms that all of the three approaches mentioned in the previous paragraph share and they provide the material from which

1. In terms of the Western academy, the apologetic may be seen in the likes of the chapters included in Safi 2003 or, more recently, Rahemtulla 2017. For the polemical, see the likes of Spencer 2012. Such modern works are but the most recent iterations of approaches that date back to the early medieval period.

2. Recent attempts to do this include Ernst and Martin 2010; Hughes 2015; Hammer, et al. 2016; Sheedy 2018; and Daneshgar 2019.

all analyses must necessarily proceed. Subjects such as the aforementioned, for instance, govern the basic frameworks of the apologetic, polemical, and academic approaches to the tradition as carried out in a variety of disciplinary and institutional contexts. Depending on the historical period and the institutional framework, these subjects have: been assumed (i.e. in the apologetical approach); witnessed their truth claims undermined (i.e. in the polemical); or, as the essays below suggest, simply been carried over, taken for granted, and largely untheorized in the present academic context.

Muslims have traditionally approached their own tradition, and by extension all human knowledge, through a set of indigenous categories (*tashayyuʿ*, *taṣawwuf*, etc.) that date to the period after the death of Muḥammad and that have been developed and expanded over the centuries. The assumption, as is the case in any worldview, is that such categories simply reflect the natural world as opposed to being a set of manufactured categories that are projected onto it.[3] As a result, these categories tend not to be theorized as a set of folk taxa, which they ultimately are, but instead are largely taken for granted and assumed to be natural and discrete categories waiting to be uncovered.

Many of these terms, and their frames of analysis, subsequently helped to shape what would emerge as the Euro-American field of Islamic Studies. Within this latter context we often encounter indigenous terms that translate directly into Western academic ones (e.g. *taʾrīkh* as history).[4] Other times, the study of such terms are brought in via analogues (e.g. when the Qurʾān is envisaged as "scripture" or as "literature" along the model of biblical studies).[5] A more recent trend, particularly since the second half of the twentieth century, has witnessed approaches to Islamic data involving sociology and anthropology, both of which have attempted to create ethnographies of Muslim communities.

What, we ask, is gained and what is lost by such translations, analogues, and new approaches? Despite the appeals of many to the contrary, the contemporary study of Islam in the Western academy still relies on, continues to engage with, and otherwise works within the parameters set out by these classically constituted topics. Indeed, it seems safe to say that in the modern West, the study of Islam's relationship to the larger academic disciplines (e.g. history, religious studies, philosophy) is still being developed and their

3. In the academic study of religion, see, for example, Smith 1982, xi.

4. Like *Taʾrīkh al-Ṭabarī*, which is usually translated as the "History of al-Ṭabarī."

5. For example, Reda 2017. Or, we might also point to the "Quran and Bible" units at annual meetings associated with organizations such as the Society of Biblical Literature (SBL) or the American Academy of Religion (AAR).

intersection is not always clear or, again, is assumed or simply taken for granted. Very rarely (if at all), for example, does one find a study devoted to a non-indigenous term – such as "orality" – that makes use of traditional sources (e.g. *tajwīd*, *ḥadīth* transmission) in such a manner that the latter illumines the former and vice versa. Instead, there is a tendency to pick a topic (say, for example, *dhikr*) and then read for said topic in a specific genre and in such a manner that, appeals to the contrary, almost exclusive attention is paid to the classical tradition and its organization of knowledge. Whether we like it or not, or even whether we admit it or not, we are dependent upon particular forms of traditional Muslim epistemology that govern how the past is preserved, displayed, and disseminated. We, as editors, are neither of the opinion that this is good nor bad. We simply wish to draw attention to these tensions with the aim of thinking through the issues that they raise, including the manner in which we situate Islam in the post-Orientalist intellectual world.[6]

Indeed, one response is the development – both in the Islamic world, but also among many scholars in the West – of a set of "de-colonial," "anti-Orientalist," or "anti-Western" approaches to these classical topics. Resisting what is perceived to be the overly critical and ideologically driven study of classical Orientalism, the focus has now switched to celebrating and/or showing the superiority of non-Western – and, by extension, Islamic – forms of knowledge production. However, it is worth pointing out that even such new approaches continue to be structured by that which they seek to refute.[7] Rather than make appeals to anti-Orientalism or simply bypass the aforementioned issues, our volume aims to interrogate the tension between classical/internal and modern/external approaches to the key terms and subjects whereby the Islamic tradition itself has organized human knowledge in light of the religious sciences (*ʿulūm al-dīn*).

While some Western scholars certainly might object and argue that they operate independently of such classical and indigenous rubrics – that they engage, for example, in "cultural studies" or focus on communal praxis and self-definition – what follows aims to show just how invested the field of Islamic studies is in philology and traditional approaches. Indeed, it is our

6. We refer the interested reader to the essays collected in Ernst and Martin 2010.

7. For example, many Muslim and non-Muslim scholars have attempted to reject the so-called revisionists' scholarship (viz. anti-revisionists), like that of John Wansbrough (d. 2002), which according to them, is the continuity of nineteenth-century Orientalism. Also, in some of the so-called "anti-Orientalist" works, authors generally downgrade the contribution of Western scholars of Islam like Theodor Nöldeke (d. 1930), who was, if not the first, one of the first scholars who added the notion of the "History of the Qurʾān" (*Taʾrīkh al-Qurʾān*) into Islamic literature (Nöldeke 1860).

contention that only by grappling with the field's diverse past will it be possible to chart future trends in new and productive ways.

In order to illumine these diverse approaches to the study of Islam regardless of context, and to demonstrate how they have influenced one another into the present, our volume explores how classical Muslim scholarship has structured (and, indeed, continues to structure) the modern academic study of Islam. We have established as our goal an examination of the organizing frames and taxonomic rubrics through which Islam has been and continues to be approached in indigenous scholarship, and then to show how Western scholarship appropriates, adopts, and otherwise adapts these frames/rubrics. This will permit us (a) to understand how these classical subjects have been approached traditionally, theologically, and secularly, and (b) to examine some of the tensions inherent to and across these approaches.

To begin to address these and related issues, we have asked each contributor to address the following questions: (a) Are external/"objective"/scholarly approaches different from internal/committed/indigenous approaches? If so, how and why?; (b) How, in other words, does the insider/outsider tension manifest itself or play out in the study of each of these topics?; and (c) How might said topics be approached using different and non-indigenous analytical frames of reference?

With these questions in mind, we hope that each chapter will demonstrate the importance of its subject in the historical context of Islamic studies (signified as both *ʿulūm al-dīn* and the Western study of Islam). In addition, however, we have asked each author to articulate the fault lines (be it emic/etic, insider/outsider, critic/caretaker, scientific-academic/theological, and so on) that emerge from these contexts. Each chapter, we trust, will also make a bolder statement that will help nudge or reorient these subfields by showing their significance to the humanities (e.g. history, religious studies, literary studies) more generally.

Summary of Chapters

What follows provides a series of case studies that, when taken as a whole, will simultaneously expose and interrogate the relationship between the "insider" and the "outsider" approach to Islam and Islamic studies.

In Chapter One, David S. Powers examines the Qurʾān's legal environment from two different perspectives: the internal, which is limited to Islamic scripture, and the external, which now views qurʾānic legal aspects in the much broader non-Muslim context of the Near East on the eve of the emergence of Islam. In addition, he shows how an examination of sources both from inside and outside of Arabia help us to understand better not only the history of the Qurʾān, but also its related historical narratives. In so doing, he demonstrates the triangulation of the Qurʾān, *taʾrikh*, and *fiqh*.

In Chapter Two, Andreas Görke focuses on the second fundamental Islamic source, *ḥadīth* ("sayings" of the Prophet). In particular, he shows the manifold ways that various groups, historically and geographically, have used these prophetic traditions for their own purposes. Since the term *ḥadīth* plays such an important role in traditional Muslim scholarship, its use in contemporary Western academic scholarship has produced numerous tensions. In exposing and exploring these tensions, Görke seeks to navigate new approaches.

We have divided the category of *tafsīr* ("commentary") into two parts, one premodern and the other contemporary. In Chapter Three, Johanna Pink examines pre-modern exegetical literature, and shows how *tafsīr* was the genre responsible for drawing the boundary between legitimate and illegitimate forms of exegesis. Though the categories developed were profoundly apologetic and polemical, they fundamentally contributed to the shaping of the Western study of *tafsīr*, including the taxonomies employed. She argues further that *tafsīr* studies would benefit greatly from the application of sociological perspectives that would aid in our understanding the types of capital involved in the production of *tafsīr*.

Then, in Chapter Four, Hadi Gerami further develops the category of *tafsīr* through an examination of a less-examined side of Islamic exegetical works. He focuses on contemporary Persian Shīʿī *tafāsīr*, particularly those which have been produced before and after the Iranian Revolution of 1979. His concern is that most modern scholars have largely failed to take into account the sources produced in Iran and other non-Arab Islamic societies. In paying attention to precisely these sources, he shows their relevance for reshaping the broader category of *tafsīr*.

Chapter Five provides a re-examination of the category of *fiqh*. Therein, Mahmoud Pargoo highlights how *fiqh* (as well as *sharīʿa*) has been largely secularized during the modern period. He argues that this transformation has succeeded in creating a new secular *sharīʿa*, one that is removed from its past moral, cosmological, and ontological grounds.

Aaron W. Hughes, in the sixth chapter, examines *kalām* ("theology"). The function of *kalām*, ever since Islam's rise in the seventh century, has been about ascertaining, and subsequently defending, proper belief as if it existed in some sort of timeless vacuum. Rather than see this term and its activity as responsible for the articulation of truth claims, Hughes argues that "truth claims" are less about actual truths and more about issues of politics and ideology. *Kalām*, on his reading, is the site wherein orthodoxy is imagined, articulated, and subsequently disseminated. *Kalām* now becomes an activity that is constructed as divine in order to protect certain political or ideological interests.

In Chapter Seven, Christopher A. Furlow examines the concept of *ʿilm* ("knowledge"). He begins with an overview of the development of the concept, and shows how its meaning expanded from a narrow concept of "religious knowledge" to a much broader concept of "knowledge" or "science," which came to include non-Islamic sciences. In particular, he uses his research on contemporary debates about Islam and science over the past quarter century to illustrate some of the tensions between and among internal/committed perspectives and external/scholarly perspectives while also questioning these boundaries and distinctions.

One of the most important as well as complex but neglected concepts in Islamic studies is *adab* ("belles-lettres"). It is often used, rather imprecisely, to refer to a diverse corpus of pre-modern writings associated with numerous Arabic literary traditions. In Chapter Eight, Nuha Alshaar establishes that *adab* cannot be treated as one fixed term, and instead engages with its development, the various meanings it acquired, and how it was utilized by pre-modern scholars in different contexts. She also explores how *adab* is approached in modern scholarship, examining two main issues: the treatment of *adab* as literature or belles-lettres, and the application of the term humanism as a lens through which to study *adab*. The chapter shows that many of these modern studies have been influenced by a set of methods and theories concerning literary texts that often neglect the category's early contexts. The chapter offers a revision of the concept of *adab* and suggests that the best way to understand it is to contextualize it in its literary, religious, historical, and intellectual contexts rather than to impose Western categories on it that do not exist in the sources.

Mushegh Asatryan in Chapter Nine critically examines the category of *Tashayyuʿ* (Shīʿism) by addressing writings on the term produced in Western academia in the last century. Based on a common set of primary sources, these writings use a number of analytical categories to interpret them, and Asatryan identifies three in particular: "community," "heresy," and "thought." His main argument is that much of the surveyed scholarship uses these categories in ways that are problematic. This is because such scholarship frequently treats them as biological organisms or persons, with their own volitions and agencies, using a set of arguments that are not historical but normative and theological. The essay concludes with a discussion of how we could study the history of the early Shīʿa in a more fruitful way.

To show how other Islamic so-called minoritarian groups have been examined, Khalil Anadani, in Chapter Ten, pays particular attention to the state of academic scholarship on the *Ismāʿīliyya* in terms of theology, polemic, and academic scholarship. He presents two critical arguments on the state of the field. The first is that the earliest Western scholarship on the Ismāʿīlīs began in the eighteenth and nineteenth centuries, largely based on hostile medieval polemical accounts written by their adversaries, and, as a result, a more holistic academic approach is necessary. Second, Ismāʿīlī studies as a field takes for granted the existence of an intelligible entity called "Ismāʿīlism" that transcends history, including specific movements, communities, and theologies.

Taṣawwuf is traditionally and simply defined as "Islamic mysticism," a term that has often been romanticized in the West or denigrated in many circles in the Islamic world. In Chapter Eleven, however, Mahdi Tourage seeks to push the study of Ṣūfism beyond such parameters and instead emphasize how scholarship on Ṣūfism is itself a product and producer of specific discourses. This enables him to avoid limitations that tend to romanticize Islamic intellectual history by selectively reading premodern mystical ideas. To contest such limitations, Tourage puts Ṣūfism – especially the thirteenth-century Jalāl al-Dīn al-Rūmī (d. ca. 1278) – in counterpoint with Jacques Lacan, the late psychoanalyst. The goal of such a pairing, he suggests, shows how Lacan's theory of signification helps us to understand Rumi's understanding of the mystical enterprise.

Majid Daneshgar discusses the significance of Orientalism in the twelfth and final chapter, *Mashriqiyyāt*. First, he shows how the "Orient," "Oriental," and "Orientalism" tends to refer only to a particular group of Muslim communities. Secondly, he explores why many Western scholars of Islam no longer like to employ the term "Orientalist." To do this, the chapter addresses the use of the non-Muslim Orient (e.g. India, China) in Muslim literature and the neglect of this among Western and Muslim scholars of Islam.

The volume, when taken as a whole, will, we trust, encourage the academic study of Islam to reflect more on the indigenous terms and notions that comprise the tradition. These terms and notions, as the chapters below show in considerable detail, are not natural, nor are they static. On the contrary, they all emerged at particular times and in specific places, and often in response to distinct material and other contingent contexts. When we fail to account for the histories and genealogies of these terms, we risk simply importing them, and the discourses that surround them, into contemporary analysis. If the study of Islam is to have a place in the modern, secular academy, it needs be aware of the tensions both inherent to and between insider and outsider approaches. When we account for this tension, as the chapters below do, we maintain that an approach that is simultaneously sympathetic to tradition and in conversation with contemporary disciplines will follow.

Bibliography

Daneshgar, M. 2019. *Studying the Qurʾān in the Muslim Academy*. Oxford.

Ernst, C., and R. C. Martin, eds. 2010. *Rethinking Islamic Studies: From Orientalism to Cosmopolitanism*. Chapel Hill.

Hammer. J., et al. 2016. "Roundtable on Normativity in Islamic Studies." *Journal of the American Academy of Religion* 84.1:25-126.

Hughes, A. W. 2015. *Islam and the Tyranny of Authenticity: An Inquiry into Disciplinary Apologetics and Self-Deception.* Sheffield.

Nöldeke, Th. 1860. *Geschichte des Qorans*. Göttingen.

Reda, N. 2017. *The al-Baqara Crescendo: Understanding the Qur'an's Style, Narrative Structure and Running Themes.* Montreal and Kingston.

Rahemtulla, S. 2017. *Qur'an of the Oppressed: Liberation Theology and Gender Justice in Islam.* Oxford.

Safi, O., ed. 2003. *Progressive Muslims: On Justice, Gender and Pluralism*. Oxford.

Sheedy, M., ed. 2018. *Identity, Politics and the Study of Islam: Current Dilemmas in the Study of Religions*. Sheffield.

Smith, J. Z. 1982. *Imagining Religion: From Babylon to Jonestown*. Chicago.

Spencer, R. 2012. *Did Muhammad Exist? An Inquiry Into Islam's Obscure Origins.* New York.

1

The Qur᾿ān and Its Legal Environment

David S. Powers

Internal Perspective

ALTHOUGH NOT A LAW BOOK, strictly speaking, the Qur᾿ān does contain approximately 500 verses that treat important legal, moral, and ethical matters. These include ritual practice – prayer, alms-giving, fasting, and pilgrimage; marriage, divorce, inheritance, and adoption; trade and commerce; dress; food and drink; sexual relations; and crime and punishment. The text frequently takes the form of a verbal exchange between two figures: an authorial voice and an unidentified addressee. In some instances the authorial voice speaks in the first person plural ("we") and addresses his/her/its pronouncements to a single, male addressee ("you"); for example, "We gave her to you in marriage" (Q 33:37). In other instances, the authorial voice possesses knowledge of questions presented by an unidentified group of people to the male addressee and it provides instruction on the proper response to those questions; for example, "They ask you about wine and games of chance. Say: ..." (Q 2:219). In still other instances, the authorial voice refers, in the third person singular, to pronouncements by a divine figure to a group of men; for example, "Allāh commands you [masc. pl.] concerning your children ..." (Q 4:11). The formulation of such statements reasonably may be understood as indicating that the contents of the Qur᾿ān were transmitted by God to a prophet – universally understood by Muslims to be a man named Muḥammad. In that case, the Qur᾿ān is a written record of an ongoing series of communications between God and Muḥammad. One consequence of this assumption is the transformation of what a non-believer might regard as mundane civil matters – for instance, marriage, inheritance, and diet – into matters of sacred import.

In a number of instances, there appears to be a tension – perhaps even a contradiction – between two or more verses of these revelations. For example, one revelation states that *khamr* or red wine has both negative qualities and positive qualities ("great sin" and "benefits"; Q 2:219); another instructs believers not to approach prayer while intoxicated – leaving open the possibility of consumption at other times (Q 2:219); while a third characterizes wine as an abomination to be avoided in all circumstances (Q 5:90). Which of these three instructions should a believer follow? The tension between these three pronouncements was resolved by invoking the doctrine of *naskh* or abrogation (see Q 2:106 and 16:101): Muslim scholars teach that Q 2:219 and 4:43 were revealed *before* Q 5:90 and that the two *earlier* verses were abrogated by the chronologically *later* one.

This interest in relative chronology naturally developed into an interest in absolute chronology. Over time, the Muslim community produced detailed information about the timing and circumstances of individual revelations. This information is encoded in reports known as *asbāb nuzūl al-āyāt* or "occasions of the revelations." The reports included within this literary genre generally state that one or another revelation was sent down about this or that Companion at a specific moment in time and in connection with a specific episode that occurred in the Hijaz during the period of revelation, 610–632 CE. For example, a woman whose husband died as a martyr in a certain battle and who had no resources to support her children approached the prophet and apprised him of her situation. The prophet consulted with the divinity, who then sent down a revelation that addressed this woman's predicament. Initially, the revelation associated with the episode was inserted into a rough chronological grid; for example, one verse was revealed "at the beginning of Islam," another was revealed before – or after – the hijra, and a third was "the last verse revealed to Muḥammad." Subsequently, with the introduction of the Islamic calendar, it became possible to assign a specific date to each revelation, for example, AH 1, 5, or 11.

It follows from what precedes that the Qurʾān emerged in a local, Hijazi environment: Revelations "came down" or "were sent down" to the Prophet Muḥammad over a period of twenty-three years, beginning in Mecca (610–622) and continuing in Yathrib/Madina (622–632). If so, then the laws contained in the Qurʾān reasonably may be understood in the context of Arabian customary law which, presumably, was either confirmed, modified, or rejected by the Qurʾān. In their efforts to establish the chronology and circumstances of revelation, Muslim scholars have – perhaps unwittingly – generated a considerable body of information about Arabian customary law. Let us consider three examples:

1. In Medina Saʿd b. al-Rabīʿ and his wife Ḥabība bt. Zayd, both Helpers, were experiencing marital problems. To resolve these problems, God sent down a revelation that established a general procedure for dealing with marital disputes: it advises the families of a husband and

wife who are considering divorce to choose two *ḥakams*, or arbiters, who might reconcile the couple – one from the family of the husband and one from that of the wife. (This revelation became v. 35 of *Sūrat al-Nisā᾿*). Presumably, the *ḥakam* mentioned in this revelation was a figure familiar to the Qur᾿ān's audience. If so, then one may conclude that in Arabian customary law marital disputes – and perhaps other disputes as well – were resolved by a figure known as a *ḥakam*. In this instance, the Qur᾿ān appears to confirm an established Arabian customary practice.

2. Islamic sources report that prior to the emergence of Islam women in the Hijaz did not have the right to inherit. This situation is exemplified by a case relating to a Companion named Aws b. Thābit al-Anṣārī, who, shortly before his death at Uḥud in 3/625, appointed two of his paternal cousins as co-executors of his estate. Following the Companion's death, the two co-executors refused to share his estate with his wife, Umm Kuḥḥa, and his three daughters. Umm Kuḥḥa now approached the Prophet and appealed to his sense of justice. The Prophet instructed her to return home so that he might consult with the divinity. On the morrow, God sent down a revelation that awards specific fractional shares of the estate to females in their capacity as daughters, mothers, sisters, and wives (this revelation became vv. 11–12 of *Sūrat al-Nisā᾿*). In this instance, the Qur᾿ān appears to modify or reform Arabian customary law by raising the status of women, albeit for reasons not specified in the text.

3. Shortly before or after the Battle of the Trench in 5 AH, Muḥammad fell in love with the wife of his adopted son, a man named Zayd. According to local customary law, however, it was forbidden for a man to have sexual relations with the wife – or former wife – of his son. In order to facilitate the Prophet's marriage to this woman, God sent down a revelation in which He introduced a distinction between the wife of a biological son and that of an adopted son ("so that there should be no sin for the believers concerning the wives of their adopted sons"). This revelation became v. 37 of *Sūrat al-Aḥzāb*. Almost immediately, however, God sent down another revelation in which He abolished the institution of adoption ("call them after their [true] fathers"). This revelation became v. 5 of *Sūrat al-Aḥzāb*. In this instance, the Qur᾿ān initially endorses the institution of adoption as regulated by Arabian customary law but shortly thereafter abolishes the institution.

From examples like these, certain key features of Arabian customary law in the Hijaz in the first half of the first century AH begin to emerge. For example, arbiters played an important role in the resolution of disputes, women did not have the right to inherit, and adoption was a common practice. These are "facts" that no Muslim scholar, in my view, would dispute.

External Perspective

It must be noted that the above-mentioned key features of Arabian customary law have been "recovered" from exegetical expansions of one or another verse of the Qurʾān over the course of the second and third centuries AH. Efforts by the Muslim community to establish the chronology of revelation and the historical circumstances in which individual revelations were sent down arguably were part of a process of historicization that unfolded over several centuries. The resulting historical narrative is plausible but may not be accurate. One characteristic of this historical narrative is that it systematically excludes the possibility of any connection between qurʾānic law and the legal systems in place in the Middle East on the eve of the emergence of Islam.

Arabia is an integral part of the Mountain Arena, the series of mountain ranges – Taurus, Pontus, Caucasus, Zagros, al-Jawl, Red Sea Hills, Sinai, Nusayri, and Amanus – that circumscribe Anatolia, Mesopotamia, and Arabia. The arena created by this ring of mountain ranges includes the Hijaz, which is strategically located on the north-south axis that connects Arabia to Mesopotamia and Iran and to the Yemen and Ethiopia; and on the east-west axis that connects Egypt and the Persian Gulf. For millennia, merchants, soldiers, nomads, and others have traveled back and forth between these regions, bringing the inhabitants of Arabia into contact with the inhabitants of Egypt, the Fertile Crescent, and Iran. By ca. 500 CE, many of these people would have been monotheists of one affiliation or another – rabbinic or non-rabbinic Jews, East or West Syrian Christians, Manicheans, Mandaeans, and/or Zoroastrians. These contacts would have exposed the inhabitants of the Hijaz not only to Near Eastern social, economic, political, and religious ideas and practices but also to legal practices and institutions as well.

A non-believing historian might ask the following questions: What was the larger legal landscape or environment in which the Qurʾān emerged? What is the relationship between that legal environment and the laws and rules in the Qurʾān? What literary or documentary texts may have served as the sources of the rules and regulations found in the Qurʾān?

If we shift the focus of scholarly attention away from the Hijaz and towards the Mountain Arena, the field of investigation relevant to the legal environment of the Qurʾān becomes much wider. We may now juxtapose and compare qurʾānic law not only with Arabian customary law but also with Byzantine law, Sasanian law, Roman provincial law, Jewish law, and Christian law, keeping in mind that this list is not exhaustive. In what follows, I will attempt a brief summary of the legal environment in the Mountain Arena on the eve of the emergence of Islam in the seventh century CE and discuss a handful of examples that suggest points of contact between the Qurʾān and the wider Near Eastern legal environment.

Legal Environment

Byzantine Law

Byzantine law is based largely on earlier Roman political, cultural, and social institutions, and Roman law served as the basis of the Byzantine legal system. Law took the form of imperial enactments, and many "new laws" (*novellae*) dealing with public, private, economic, and social life were issued by emperors such as Theodosius (r. 379–395 CE) and Justinian (r. 527–565 CE). Shortly after his accession in 527, Justinian appointed a commission of jurists to compile all existing Roman law into one corpus that might be used throughout the empire – including the Greek-, Syriac-, and Aramaic-speaking provinces of the Mountain Arena. The resulting compilation, sometimes referred to as the Codex of Justinian, included three components: the Digest (533), the Code (534), and the Institutes (535). The Digest was a collection and summary of the writings of classical Roman jurists on law and justice; the Code specified the laws of the empire, based on earlier imperial pronouncements (called "constitutions") and some of Justinian's own legislation; and the Institutes, which contains a summary of the Digest, was probably designed to serve as a textbook for law students. In 556, toward the end of the emperor's reign, a group of legal scholars produced a supplement to the Code that included laws enacted after 534 as well as a summary of Justinian's imperial pronouncements. This text is known as the *Novellae Constitutiones* or *Novels*. Together, these four texts are known as the *Corpus Iuris Civilis* (CIC).

Many of the jurists who contributed to the CIC were teachers at the law school of Beirut, established ca. 200 CE. By the fifth century, the Beirut law school had developed a reputation as a preeminent center of Roman jurisprudence, and in the sixth century the centerpiece of its curriculum was the CIC. Many of the students who completed the four-year program of study went on to serve as lawyers and magistrates in the eastern provinces of the empire, where they would have been responsible for the regulation of what has been called Near Eastern provincial law.[1] The school was destroyed by a massive earthquake, tsunami, and fires that leveled Beirut in 551 – approximately twenty years before the birth of Muḥammad. It never reopened.

Sasanian Law

The Sasanian Empire (224–651 CE), called Êrānshahr by its inhabitants, was the last Iranian empire before the rise of Islam. In the third century, the king of kings invested judicial authority in the Zoroastrian high priest or supreme judge (*mowbedan mowbed*) and subordinate priest-scholars, who exercised authority over all aspects of life, both religious and secular, including the sealing of contracts, regulation of disputes, and punishment of criminals. These scholars produced a complex and sophisticated body of law that was based on the *Avesta*, cosmological thought, and other aspects of the Zoroastrian tradition. One important source for the Iranian legal tradition is the *Mādayān ī Hazār Dādestān* or *Book of a Thousand Judgments*, compiled toward the end of the reign of Husraw II (591–628) and shortly before the Arab invasion of Iran. Written for jurisprudents who had expert knowledge of the Sasanian legal system, this text arguably emerged during a period in which Sasanian law was still practiced and judges had the authority to pronounce judgment in all fields of law. It is a fundamental source for the social and institutional history of Sasanian Iran.

Syrian Orthodox Church

The early Jesus movement was spread by the Apostles, who traveled extensively throughout the Roman Empire, establishing communities in its major cities and regions. In addition, soldiers, merchants, and preachers founded church communities in North Africa, Asia Minor, Armenia, Caucasian Albania, Arabia, and Greece. By the turn of the second century CE there were more than forty such communities in Asia Minor, Greece, Italy, and India.

According to Acts 11:26, "[I]t was in Antioch that the disciples were first called 'Christians,'" and Antioch claims the honor of being the most ancient Christian church in the world. The Patriarchate of Antioch – or the Syrian Orthodox Church – was established in the year 37, with Peter as its first Bishop and the first Patriarch of the Church. From Antioch, Christianity spread to other Syrian cities and provinces, attracting both gentiles and Jews. The Bishopric of Antioch – together with the Bishoprics of Rome, Alexandria, and Jerusalem – was recognized as a Patriarchate by the First Council of Nicaea in 325.

1. See Crone 1987.

Religious treatises written by members of the Syriac Church arguably were circulating in the religious and legal zone in which the Qurʾān was produced. One such text is the *Didascalia Apostolorum* or Teaching of the Apostles, a treatise that purportedly was composed by the Twelve Apostles at the time of the Council of Jerusalem in the year 50, but likely was written ca. 230, in Greek, by a bishop in Northern Syria, perhaps near Antioch. In the late fourth century, the *Didascalia* was revised and incorporated into the Greek *Apostolic Constitutions*. A Latin palimpsest from the fifth century is extant, and the text was later translated inter alia into Syriac. Although the earliest manuscript evidence for the Syriac *Didascalia* dates only to 683, it is likely that the text was in circulation on the margins of Arabia – if not in Arabia itself – on the eve of the emergence of Islam and that it is a "document of plausible relevance for the Qurʾān's original audience."[2]

Church of the East

By the end of the fourth century CE, Aramaic-speaking Christians had established an extensive network of communities that stretched across the Iranian Empire, from Arabia to Afghanistan. These communities are known collectively as the Church of the East and its members are called East Syrians, to distinguish them from Christian communities in Byzantium or West Syrians.

In 410, a church synod announced to members of the East Syrian Church that the Sasanian king of kings Yazdagird I (r. 399–420) had issued an Edict of Toleration in which he formally recognized the bishop of Seleucia-Ctesiphon as the leader of the Church of the East, granted Christians autonomy within the empire, and promised to enforce judicial decisions made by ecclesiastical authorities. This bishop – now called catholicos – exercised jurisdiction over Christian communities in Mesopotamia, eastern Arabia, and the Iranian plateau, and the boundaries of the church were nearly identical to those of Ērānshahr. Christian religious figures who lived in the early Islamic period produced several comprehensive legal compendia, for example, the *Syndicon Orientale*, which preserves canons (*qanone*) and customary laws (*namose*) issued at synods held during the Sasanian period (although the text itself was edited only in the eleventh century). These canons and customary laws regulated the beliefs, rituals, and social and economic activities of Christian bishops, priests, and ascetics.

2. Zellentin 2013, viii. Another text of "plausible" – albeit indirect – relevance to the Qurʾān's initial audience is the ('Pseudo'-)Clementine Homilies, a fourth-century Greek text that was later translated into Latin, Syriac, and Arabic. This text endorses many ritual practices for gentile followers of Jesus that are rejected by the *Didascalia*. See Zellentin 2013, index, s.v. Clementine Homilies.

Rabbinic Law

The word *halakha* (literally, "way to walk" or "path") is used to identify the corpus of rabbinic legal texts and, by extension, the overall system of Jewish law. The starting point of *halakha* are 613 commandments (*mitzvoth*) – 248 positive and 365 negative – found in the Hebrew Bible. The manner in which these commandments are to be observed in daily practice was developed by rabbinic authorities on the basis of discussion and debate, as recorded in two texts: the Mishnah, a redaction of Jewish oral traditions undertaken by Judah the Prince at the beginning of the third century; and the Gemara, a record of rabbinical analysis of, and commentary on, the Mishnah. Together, these two texts constitute the Talmud, a massive corpus of rabbinic opinions, legislation, customs, and recommendations. In late antiquity, there were two major centers of Jewish scholarship in the Mountain Arena, one in Galilee, the other in Babylonia. Each center produced its own Talmud: The Jerusalem Talmud was compiled in the fourth century and the Babylonian Talmud was compiled ca. 500, although the text did not reach its final form until 700, at the earliest.

Jewish communities living in Byzantium and Iran were incorporated into the legal systems of these two empires. Beginning in the third century, Jews living in the Palestine and the Levant became "citizens of Rome" who were subject to Roman civil law. Jews had their own courts, but they also had the right to bring lawsuits before imperial judges. Indeed, Justinian's Code prescribed that Jews must bring both civil and religious matters before imperial judges; and that certain disputes might be brought before a Jewish court only if both litigants agreed to do so. The Jewish community was led by a *nasi* (literally "prince") or patriarch who had the power to appoint and suspend communal leaders inside and outside of Palestine; and by *amoraim*, rabbinic sages who were active between ca. 200 and 425 and who served inter alia as legal specialists and judges.

There was a substantial Jewish community in Sasanian territories. A legal maxim that appears four times in the Babylonian Talmud – "The law of the land is the law" – acknowledges Jewish recognition of the legal authority of the Sasanian king of kings. The maxim was understood as signifying that Sasanian law was binding on Jews, and, in certain cases, preferable to Jewish law. The leaders of the Jewish community in Iran were the Exilarch or head of the exiles and the *amoraim* or rabbinic sages. Like their East-Syrian Christian counterparts, Persian Jews used Zoroastrian legal rules to settle disputes, transfer wealth and property, contract marriages, and make arrangements for inheritance.

Aramaic Common Law

Many of the legal traditions and institutions associated with the ancient Assyrian and Babylonian empires continued to be practiced in the Mountain Arena following the fall of those empires, albeit now as local provincial law. The inhabitants of Egypt, Syria, Mesopotamia, and Arabia shared a substantial body of legal practices and legal formulae. This shared legal tradition has been called Aramaic Common Law. Evidence for Aramaic Common Law has been found on tomb inscriptions produced between 100 and 300 in cities scattered across the Mountain Arena, including Elephantine, Petra, Palmyra, Hatra, and Edessa. These inscriptions were written in Middle Aramaic using the Nabataean cursive script.

I shall now present select examples of laws found in the Qurʾān that manifest a thematic and/or linguistic connection to laws found in the following texts, pronouncements, or inscriptions: The Hebrew Bible, Talmud, Syrian provincial law, an Iranian Church canon, Syriac *Didascalia Apostolorum*, Nabataean tomb inscriptions, and *Corpus Iuris Civilis*. The legal subjects to be addressed below include: the Ten Commandments, an ethical legal maxim, loan agreements, prohibited marriages, prohibited foods, sexual modesty, and inheritance practices.

Examples

The Hebrew Bible

The Qurʾān repeatedly asserts that it confirms the message of earlier Scriptures. Just as Jesus previously confirmed the Torah (Q 61:6), so too Muḥammad confirmed both the Torah and the New Testament. Several verses announce that the new Arabic revelation confirms "what was before it" (e.g. Q 2:97, 6:92, 10:37, 12:111, and 35:31), "the Book of Moses" (Q 46:12) or "all the Scriptures before it" (Q 5:48). Other verses specify that the new revelation confirms the Scriptures sent previously to the Jews and the Christians (Q 3:3), who are commanded to believe in the new revelation precisely because of the identity between it and the earlier Scriptures (Q 2:41, 3:81, 4:47). Conversely, members of the new community of believers are instructed to believe in the new revelation because it confirms the revelations sent previously to the Jews and Christians (Q 2:91). The Hebrew Bible, New Testament, and Qurʾān are successive links in a chain of divine revelations that all bear the same message.

It should come as no surprise that the Qurʾān contains echoes of, and references to, Mosaic Law. Consider, for example, the Ten Commandments or Decalogue, a set of biblical principles relating to ethics and worship, including positive instructions to worship only God, honor one's parents, and keep the Sabbath, as well as the prohibition of idolatry, blasphemy, murder, adultery, theft, dishonesty, and coveting. The Ten Commandments are listed twice in the Hebrew Bible, first at Ex 20:1–17, and again at Deut 5:6–21. Both versions state that God inscribed the commandments on two stone tablets, which he gave to Moses on Mount Sinai.

The Qurʾān introduces a list of moral and ethical injunctions that is similar to the Decalogue while differing in certain details. This list is found in Q 17:22–39 and in Q 6:152–54. The content, style, and form of the qurʾānic injunctions bear a clear resemblance to their counterparts in the Hebrew Bible. Both texts begin with mention of the oneness of God; both include a command to honor one's parents; and both prohibit murder, sexual misconduct, theft, bearing false witness, and coveting the property of others. Some Biblical injunctions, however, are not found in the Qurʾān, for example, the command to observe the Sabbath. Conversely, the Qurʾān includes several injunctions not found in the Hebrew Bible, for example, give a kinsman his due; do not kill your children as a consequence of poverty; practice fair trade; and do not follow others blindly. Clearly, Mosaic law and the biblical Decalogue were part of the Qurʾān's legal environment, even if the Qurʾān appears to have modified the Decalogue so as to make it more suitable for an Arabian environment.

The Talmud

1. A Legal Maxim

The Qurʾān also manifests familiarity with the Talmud. A famous maxim found in both the Jerusalem and Babylonian Talmuds (JT and BT, respectively) reads as follows: "Whoever destroys a soul, it is considered as if he destroyed an entire world. And whoever saves a life, it is considered as if he saved an entire world" (JT 4:9, BT Sanhedrin 37a). In Q 5:32, the authorial voice of the Qurʾān asserts that He had given this instruction to the Israelites, referring to the maxim without citing the exact Talmudic formulation: "From the time We prescribed for the Sons of Israel that whoever kills a person, except [in retaliation] for another, or [for] fomenting corruption on the earth, [it is] as if he had killed all the people. And whoever gives [a person] life, [it is] as if he had given all the people life." Note, first, that the order of the two clauses in the two texts is identical: whoever destroys/kills followed by whoever saves/gives life. However, the Qurʾān modifies the general rule that it is forbidden to take a human life by adding two exceptions: one may take the life of a murderer, in retaliation; and one may take the life of a person who foments corruption on the earth.

Like the Hebrew Bible, the Talmud was part of the Qurʾān's legal environment. Just as the Qurʾān modified the Decalogue to make it suitable for an Arabian environment, so too it modified a Talmudic maxim to make it suitable for an Arabian environment.

2. Writing Down Loan Agreements

A long verse in Sūrat al-Baqara (Q 2:182) regulates financial transactions, including loans. The verse reads as follows:

> You who believe! When you contract a debt with one another for a fixed term, write it down. Let a scribe write it down fairly between you, and let the scribe not refuse to write it down, seeing that God has taught him. So let him write, and let the one who owes the debt dictate, and let him guard [himself] against God his Lord, and not diminish anything from it. If the one who owes the debt is weak of mind or body, or unable to dictate himself, let his close associate dictate fairly. And call in two of your men as witnesses, or, if there are not two men, then one man and two women, from those present whom you approve of as witnesses, so that if one of the two women goes astray, the other will remind her. And let the witnesses not refuse when they are called on. Do not disdain to write it down, [however] small or large, with its due date. That is more upright in the sight of God, more reliable for witnessing [it], and [makes it] more likely that you will not be in doubt [afterwards] – unless it is an actual transaction you exchange among yourselves, and then [there is] no blame on you if you do not write it down. But take witnesses when you do business with each other. Only let the scribe or the witness not injure either party, or, if you do, that is wickedness on your part. So guard [yourselves] against God. God teaches you and God has knowledge of everything.

This verse instructs believers to record the terms of a loan agreement in writing. Curiously, this instruction is at variance with what would become classical Islamic legal doctrine, according to which written documents have no legal value and are merely aids to memory. Muslim jurists resolved the apparent tension between the qurʾānic prescription and classical legal doctrine by teaching that the linguistic command at the beginning of Q 2:282 ("write it down") should be understood merely as a recommendation.

It has recently been suggested that the original meaning of Q 2:282

comes into better focus when it is placed in the context of late antique law as practiced by Jews and others.[3] The argument runs as follows: Lev. 19:14 contains the following command: "You shall not ... place a stumbling block before the blind...." In their discussions of this biblical verse, the rabbis asked: Who are the blind? To this they responded that the word "blind" is a metaphor for a person who is not virtuous and law-abiding. In order to prevent such a person from committing a sin, they explained, it is necessary to place "a stumbling block" in front of him. But what sin did they have in mind? And what was the stumbling block?

The rabbis linked their discussion of Lev. 19:14 to loan transactions. In late antiquity, it was customary for a person who borrowed money or property to *unilaterally* declare his debt to the creditor and assume responsibility for the money borrowed. The only written record of the transaction took the form of a homology or handwritten note (Gr. *cheirographon*) in which the debtor acknowledged having received the money and agreed to return it at the appointed time. The note was written by the debtor himself or by a scribe. This legal form was widely used after the year 400. Note, however, that there were no witnesses to the transaction. Thus, the borrower subsequently might deny having received the loan and thus avoid repayment of the debt. According to the rabbis, this was the "sin" mentioned in Lev. 19:14. They were concerned that a debtor who was not virtuous and law-abiding (i.e. "blind") might deny having received the loan in order to avoid repayment of the debt (Baba Metzia 25b). To prevent this unscrupulous practice, the rabbis proposed putting a stumbling block in front of the blind. The stumbling block took the form of a two-witness rule: "A homology must be made in the presence of two persons, one of whom must say: 'Write'" (Baba Batra 40a). The two-witness rule was designed to deter or prevent a debtor from committing a sin. The two-witness homology was practiced in the Syrian provinces of Byzantium.

In Q 2:182, the Qurʾān arguably is referring to the rabbinic two-witness homology – or to a provincial variant thereof. The verse envisages a situation in which the creditor is not himself present at the recording of the debt obligation and therefore may not be able to verify the terms of the loan upon receiving the handwritten note. This is why two witnesses are required. Note, however, that the verse introduces a local modification of the two-witness rule by allowing for witnessing by one man and two women while at the same time transforming what was no doubt a conventional legal practice into a sacred injunction: it was God who taught the scribe the art of writing; the debtor should "guard himself against God his Lord" by specify-

3. Leicht 2011.

ing the full amount of the loan; the proper recording of the loan and its due date "is more upright in the sight of God"; and all of this is a matter of divine instruction and omniscience ("God teaches you and God has knowledge of everything"). In this manner, the two-witness homology of late antiquity became a divine commandment to put a loan agreement in writing. The thematic parallels between the Syrian provincial homology – as discussed by the rabbis – and Q 2:182 point clearly to a shared legal environment.

East Syrian Church Canons

In the sixth century, many elite Christians practiced certain Zoroastrian institutions and sought to have these practices authorized by Zoroastrian courts. The behavior of these elites was criticized by leaders of the Church of the East, who issued rules that were designed to deter members of the community from following Zoroastrian law and going to Zoroastrian courts. In 544, for example, the catholicos Mār Abā (r. 540–552) formulated a canon in which he attempted to prevent East Syrian elites from engaging in the practice of substitute successorship.[4] It is prohibited, Mār Abā declared, for a Christian man to marry the wife of his father or his uncle, his aunt, his sister, his daughter, or his granddaughter – as the "Magians do"; similarly, it is prohibited for a Christian man to marry the wife of his brother – as the Jews do. Mār Abā's efforts were unsuccessful, however, and elite Christians continued to engage in the Zoroastrian practice.[5]

One finds similar prohibitions in Q. 4:22: "Do not marry women whom your fathers have married, unless it is a thing of the past. Surely it is an immorality, an abhorrent thing, and an evil way." Q. 4:23 continues this line of thought by prohibiting marriage with "your mothers, your daughters, your sisters, your paternal aunts, [or] your maternal aunts…." The Qur'ānic prohibitions were introduced 50–75 years after Mār Abā's canon, and, like that canon, may have been a response to the widespread practice of substitute successorship.

4. One important goal of Zoroastrian aristocratic households was the transmission of wealth, status, and noble identity from one generation to the next. The successful achievement of this goal was facilitated by Sasanian jurists who created legal institutions that regulated marriage, inheritance, and adoption. See Payne 2015, 2016.

5. A generation later, in 585, the catholicos Ishoyahb I (582–596) issued two canons on civil matters, both of which treated the subject of inheritance. Another catholicos, 'Ishô'bokt (death date unknown), was the author of *Maktbânûtā d-'al Dinê* in which he attempted to create a unified corpus of ecclesiastical regulations – religious and civil – for the Church of the East. This text, which was composed only in the eighth century, nevertheless includes legal material from the years preceding the Arab conquest of Iran and is thus relevant to the legal environment of the Qur'ān.

The Didascalia Apostolorum

As noted, it has recently been argued that the Syriac *Didascalia Apostolorum* (DA) was circulating in or near Arabia prior to the emergence of Islam and is a "document of plausible relevance for the Qurʾān's original audience."[6] Let us consider two examples discussed by Zellentin.

1. Veiling Practices

The Syriac *Didascalia* makes the following statement about the veiling of women:

> If you want to become a believing woman (*mhymnt'*), be beautiful for your husband (*lb'lky*) only. And when you walk in the street, cover your head with your garment, that because of your veil your great beauty may be covered. And paint not the countenance of your eyes, but have downcast looks. And walk being veiled. (DA III, 26, 5–11).

The text is addressed directly to a believing woman (*mhymnt'*) whose beauty is reserved solely for her husband. Thus, when a believing woman ventures out in public, she should wear a veil, should not apply make-up to her eyes, and should cast her glance downwards. The purpose of this instruction is to channel sexual attraction into the approved realm of marriage.

In Q 24:30–31 God instructs His prophet to address believers - both men and women - as follows:

> Say to the believing men (*muʾminīn*) [that] they [should] lower their sight and guard their private parts. That is purer for them. Surely God is aware of what they do.
>
> And say to the believing women (*muʾmināt*) [that] they [should] lower their sight and guard their private parts, and not show their charms, except for what [normally] appears of them. And let them draw their head coverings over their breasts, and not show their charms, except to their husbands (*li-buʿūlatihinna*), or their fathers, or their husbands' fathers, or their sons, or their husbands' sons, or their brothers, or their brothers' sons, or their sisters' sons, or their women, or what their right [hands] own, or such men as attend [them who] have no [sexual] desire, or children [who are] not [yet] aware of women's nakedness. And let them not stamp their feet to make known what they hide of their charms. Turn to God--all [of you] - believers, so that you may prosper.

6. Zellentin 2013.

Whereas the Syriac *Didascalia* addresses only women (*mhymnt'*), the Qur'ān addresses both men (*mu'minīn*) and women (*mu'mināt*): Believing men are instructed to lower their glances (presumably not to look at women when they venture out into public) and to protect their private parts; believing women receive the same instruction, to which the Qur'ān adds that they must guard their charms and cover their heads and breasts. Whereas in the Syriac *Didascalia* the beauty of a believing woman is reserved exclusively for her husband, the Qur'ān makes exceptions for five groups: (1) close blood relatives; (2) relatives by marriage; (3) concubines owned by male relatives; (4) men who have no sexual desire; and (5) young children. Like the Syriac *Didascalia*, the Qur'ān seeks to channel sexual attraction into the realm of marriage. In addition to the clear thematic parallels between the two texts, there are also clear linguistic parallels, for example, *mhymnt'* v. *mu'mināt* and *lb'lky* v. *li-bu'ūlatihinna*. Again, these thematic and linguistic parallels are evidence of a shared legal environment and they suggest that the Qur'ān's immediate audience was familiar with the Syriac *Didascalia*. As it did with the Hebrew Bible and the Talmud, the Qur'ān modifies some of the rules found in the Syriac *Didascalia* to make them more suitable for an Arabian environment.

2. Prohibited Foods

In the first century, some members of the Jesus movement insisted that gentile believers were required to observe the law of Moses (Acts 15:5), while others, including Peter and Paul, argued that this burden should not be placed on the "necks" of the gentiles (Acts 15:10). The two opposing groups reached a compromise. The apostles and elders sent two representatives – Judas and Silas – to Antioch with a letter instructing gentile believers in Christ that they are required to abstain from only four practices. The letter is quoted in Acts 15:23–29. The relevant section reads as follows: "It seemed good to the Holy Spirit and to us not to burden you with anything beyond the following requirements: You are to abstain from food sacrificed to idols, from blood, from the meat of strangled animals and from sexual immorality. You will do well to avoid these things. Farewell."

In 683–84, the Decree of the Apostles in Acts 15 was quoted almost verbatim by Athanasius of Bālād, the Jacobite Patriarch of Antioch, in an encyclical letter, written in Syriac, in which, among other things, he invokes the words of the apostles who had instructed gentile believers to "distance themselves from fornication (*znywt'*)." To this instruction he adds that gentile believers also should distance themselves "from what is strangled (*ḥnyq'*) and from blood (*dm'*), and from the food of pagan slaughter (*dbḥ ḥnp'*), lest they be by this associates of the demons and of their unclean table."

Q 5:3–5 reads as follows:

> Forbidden to you [to eat] are: carrion, blood (*al-dam*), and the flesh of swine (*khinzīr*), and what has been dedicated to [a god] other than God. And the animal strangled (*wa 'l-munkhaniqat*[u]) or beaten to death, that which dies by falling or is gored to death, and that which is mangled by a beast of prey – except what you have slaughtered (*mā dhubiḥa*) and what is sacrificed on stone altars. [You are also forbidden] to divide (*tastaqsimū*) with divination arrows – all that is transgression.

Like Acts 15 and Athanasius, the Qurʾān prohibits believers from consuming the flesh of an animal that has been strangled (*ḥnyq'* v. *al-munkhaniqat*[u]), blood (*dm'* v. *al-dam*), and food slaughtered by pagans (*dbḥ ḥnp'* v. *mā dhubiḥa*) – although in the Qurʾān the order of presentation is different from that of the other two texts. Again, the thematic and linguistic parallels point to a shared legal environment.

Aramaic Common Law

Evidence for Aramaic Common Law is found, for example, on tomb inscriptions located in Madā'in Ṣāliḥ (Hegra), a large settlement at the southern end of the Nabataean kingdom, approximately 250 miles northwest of Yathrib. These inscriptions contain legal terms that are related linguistically to Arabic, for example, Aramaic *rhn*, "to give in pledge" (cf. Arabic *rahana*, with the same meaning). One inscription reads as follows: "This is the tomb that Ḥalafu son of Qôsnatan made for himself and for Suʿaydu, his son, and his brothers, for whatever male children may be born to this Ḥalafu, and for their sons and their descendants by hereditary title forever ...".[7] The inscription identifies the people who may be buried in the tomb and prohibits members of the family from selling the tomb or giving it away as a gift, warning that anyone who violates this instruction will be subject to a fine. Another inscription identifies the builder of the tomb and his heirs as the owners of the structure, levies a curse on anyone who might sell, purchase, or assign the tomb to someone as a pledge, and warns that a fine will be imposed on anyone who violates these instructions.[8]

7. Healey 1993, no. 36.

8. Tomb inscriptions also point to connections between South Arabian law and the Qurʾān. For example, in an inscription found in Haram, the authors ask the God Ḥalfān for forgiveness for having postponed (*nasha'aw*) the performance of an unspecified ritual by two months. The language of postponement here appears to anticipate that of Q 9:37, which criticizes unbelievers who attempt to align the calendar with the seasons and changes or modifies

Another source for Aramaic Common Law are legal texts written in Nabataean cursive script and recorded on papyri and other materials. A cache of such documents was discovered in a leather pouch in a cave in Nahal Hever on the western shore of the Dead Sea. These documents, which belonged to a Jewish woman named Babatha, had been drawn up and recorded in a Nabataean court. The documents were issued over a period of forty years, between 96 and 134, and they include contracts relating to marriage, property transfers, and guardianship. Some of the documents, for example, indicate that a surviving daughter does not automatically inherit from her father in competition with her male paternal uncles and cousins (as noted, the inheritance rights of daughters is a subject to which the Qur᾽ān pays close attention). The documents shed considerable light on the provincial legal system in this area at the turn of the second century. Clearly, Nabataean provincial law continued to be practiced in Judea after the annexation of this province by the Romans in 106. And there is reason to believe that the Arabic-speaking inhabitants of northern Arabia continued to practice this common law into the Byzantine and early Islamic periods. If so, then this material is part of the legal environment in which the Qur᾽ān was produced.

Corpus Iuris Civilis

Q 4:12 is a long verse that treats the subject of inheritance. It is composed of two distinct sections, the first dealing with a surviving husband or wife, the second with siblings. The first section – hereinafter Q 4:12a – reads as follows:

> And to you a half of what your wives leave, if they have no children. But if they have children, then to you the fourth of what they leave, after any bequest they may have made or any debt. And to them the fourth of what you leave, if you have no children. But if you have children, then to them the eighth of what you leave, after any bequest you may have made or debt.

Q. 4:12a awards a surviving husband one-half or one-fourth of his deceased wife's estate and it awards a surviving wife one-fourth or one-eighth of her deceased husband's estate; in both cases the difference in the size of the award depends on whether or not there are any children. In both instances, the surviving spouse receives the larger fractional share when the couple

---

the earlier practice: "The postponement (*al-nasī᾽u*) is an increase of disbelief by which those who disbelieve go astray..." See de Blois 2004.

has no children, the smaller when they have children. The share of the husband is awarded "after any bequest they (f. pl.) may have made or debt"; and the share of the wife is awarded "after any bequest you (m. pl.) may have made or debt"; in both instances, this phrase appears to refer to the order in which claims against an estate are to be settled: (1) bequests, (2) debts, followed by (3) the inheritance shares.

The Qurʾān treats a widow as an heir who has the same status as the deceased's children, parents, and siblings – even if her share is smaller than that of blood relatives. This is unusual. In ancient Babylonia, a wife did not inherit unless her husband expressly designated her as an heir in a last will and testament. In Jewish law, a husband is heir to his wife, but a wife is not a legal heir to her husband, although she does enjoy a number of rights that afford her a share in her husband's estate and that ensure provision for her sustenance and essential needs until her remarriage or death. In Egypt, a husband and wife inherited from their respective families, but not from each other. The same was true in Roman law and, no doubt, in Syrian provincial law as well. Compared to other Near Eastern legal systems in antiquity and late antiquity, the Qurʾān's treatment of wives as heirs is anomalous.

In late antiquity, it was customary for a husband to specify a sum of money for his wife's support and maintenance in the event that he divorced her or predeceased her. This provision might be made either prior to the marriage, as part of a pre-nuptial agreement, or at the time of the marriage, as part of a dower agreement; alternatively, a husband might leave a bequest for his spouse in a last will and testament. If, however, a man made no provision for his wife in the form of a pre-nuptial agreement, dower, or bequest, then the widow would have no claim whatsoever against the estate of her deceased husband. Byzantine law recognizes two forms of marriage, a normal form in which the husband pays a dower and acquires marital power over his wife, and an exceptional form in which no dower is paid. In a marriage of the exceptional type, the surviving spouse has no legal claim against the deceased's estate and her (or his) economic position may be precarious.

On October 1, 537 CE, approximately thirty years before the birth of Muḥammad, the Emperor Justinian enacted a *novella* or new law that was designed to alleviate the predicament of wives whose husbands had not specified a dower for them. This law, *Novella* 53.6, is entitled "Concerning a Poor Woman Who is Unendowed." The first section of the law treats the case in which there was no pre-nuptial agreement or dower provision:

> As every law enacted by Us is based upon clemency, and We see that when men married to women who have brought no dowry die, the children alone are legally called to the succession of their fathers'

> estates, while their widows, even though they may remain in the condition of lawful wives, for the reason that they have not brought any dowry, and no ante-nuptial donation has been given them, can obtain nothing from the estates of their deceased husbands, and are compelled to live in the greatest poverty, We wish to provide for their maintenance by enabling them to succeed to them, and be called to share their estates conjointly with the children. But as We have already enacted a law which provides that when a husband divorces his wife, whom he married without any dowry, she shall receive the fourth of his estate, just as in the present instance, whether there are few or many children, the wife shall be entitled to the fourth of the property of the deceased.

At this point, the law specifies a widow's entitlement in the case in which she does receive a legacy from her husband:

> If, however, a husband has left a legacy to his wife and this amounts to less than a fourth of his estate, this amount shall be made up out of the same. Hence, as We come to the relief of women who have not been endowed, or divorced by their husbands, so We assist them where they have constantly lived with them, and We grant them the same privilege.

The statute ends with a clause indicating that the new rule applies not only to poor wives but also to poor husbands:

> Again, everything that We have stated in the present law with reference to the fourth to which a woman is entitled shall equally apply to a husband, for like the former, We make this law applicable to both.[9]

Let us compare Q 4:12a and *Novella* 53.6: Q. 4:12a is formulated as a continuation of a divine instruction in 4:11 ("God commands you"), while *Novella* 53.6 is formulated as an imperial decree ("We" and "Us"). Both texts award a fractional share of the estate to a surviving husband or wife: In Q 4:12a, a widow is awarded an indefeasible share of the estate, irrespective of her economic circumstances and without any reference to a pre-nuptial agreement or dower. *Novella* 53.6, by contrast, deals with an exceptional case – that of a poor and unendowed spouse. The entitlement of a husband compared to that of a wife also differs in the two texts: in Q 4:12a, the share of a surviving husband is twice that of a wife; in *Novella* 53.6, a surviving husband or wife receives an equal share of the estate (one-fourth). Both texts draw a connec-

9. *Corpus Iuris Civilis*, edited by R. Schoell 3:304–305.

tion between the award and the existence of children: Q 4:12a reduces the share of a surviving spouse by half if the couple has children; *Novella* 53.6 awards a surviving spouse a fractional award of the estate "whether there are few or many children." Finally, both texts mention bequests or legacies: Q. 4:12a states that the award to a surviving husband or wife should be made after any bequest – or debt; *Novella* 53.6 specifies that if one spouse has left a legacy for the other, the survivor is entitled to the difference between the legacy and one-fourth of the estate.

The provisions of Q 4:12a and *Novella* 53.6 are clearly different. But the proximity in both time (less than seventy years) and space (Beirut v. the Hijaz) suggests that the Byzantine legislation was circulating in the legal environment in which the Qurʾān emerged. This assumption finds support in the second half of Q 4:12 – hereinafter Q 4:12b – which awards a small fractional share of the estate to siblings, and may be translated as follows:

> If a man is inherited by relatives other than a parent or child (*yūrathu kalālat*^an) – or a woman [is inherited by relatives other than a parent or child], and he [or she] has a brother or sister, each one of them is entitled to one-sixth. If they are more than that, they are partners with respect to one-third, after any bequest that is bequeathed or debt, without injury. A commandment from God. God is all-knowing, forbearing. (My translation)

Q 4:12b deals with a situation in which a man or woman dies without leaving either a parent or a child and his or her closest surviving relative is one or more siblings. A brother and sister inherit an equal share of the estate – one-sixth; three or more siblings share one-third of the estate, presumably on a per capita basis ("they are partners with respect to one-third"). Like the award to the surviving spouse in Q 4:12a, the award to siblings in Q 4:12b is made "after any bequest that is bequeathed or debt" – to which the phrase "without injury" is added. The Qurʾān characterizes the award as a "commandment from God," who is "all-knowing, forbearing," thus transforming a civil matter into a sacred injunction.

Muslim scholars have devoted considerable time and energy to the opening clause of Q 4:12b, with special attention to the word *kalāla*, which occurs only twice in the Qurʾān, here, and again in Q 4:176, another verse that deals with inheritance. In the last quarter of the first century AH (ca. 694–717 CE), the Kufan jurist Ibrāhīm al-Nakhaʿī circulated a short tradition in which ʿUmar b. al-Khaṭṭāb acknowledged that he did not know the meaning of *kalāla*. Over the course of the second century AH, additional reports focusing on ʿUmar were put into circulation. In some, he does not know the meaning of the word. In others, he claims to know its meaning but either withholds this information from the community or suppresses it. In others, ʿUmar defines *kalāla* as a person who dies without a parent or child. In addition to the meaning of the word, Muslim scholars also discussed its grammatical function (it occurs in the accusative case). And they wondered why the phrase *yūrathu kalālat^an^* is inserted between the two elements of the compound subject ("a man *yūrathu kalālat^an^* or a woman"). There are other problems, as well.

Elsewhere I have argued that the current understanding of Q 4:12b is not identical to what may have been the original text. I base this argument on the evidence of an early Qurʾān manuscript, among other things: Bibliothèque Nationale de France Arabe 328. On folio 10b of this manuscript, there are clear signs of textual manipulation – erasures and rewriting – in the immediate vicinity of the word *kalāla*. This evidence suggests that the original consonantal skeleton of this word was not *kalāla* – with two *lāms*, but rather a hypothetical **kalla* – with one *lām*. In other Semitic languages, nouns derived from the root *k-l-l* (e.g. Akk. *kallatu*, Heb. *kallāh*. Syr. *kalltā*) all signify a "daughter-in-law." If one reads **kalla* in *4:12b, the meaning of the opening clause changes dramatically, as follows:

> If a man designates a daughter-in-law or wife as heir (*yūrithu kallat^an^ aw imra't^an^*), and he has a brother or sister, each one of them is entitled to one-sixth ...

The opening clause now treats the case of a man whose closest surviving blood relatives are a brother and/or sister, but who, in a last will and testament, designates either his daughter-in-law or his wife as the testamentary heir. In the absence of the will, the siblings, as the deceased's closest surviving blood relatives, would have inherited the entire estate. The purpose of the new rule formulated in *Q 4:12b arguably was to prevent a testator from totally disinheriting his closest surviving blood relatives. Presumably, the will remained valid, but the siblings had a legal claim against the estate for up to one-third of its value. The rule strikes a balance between the personal wishes of the deceased, on the one hand, and the rights of his closest surviving blood relatives, on the other.

Note that my rereading of the opening clause of Q 4:12b has no connection whatsoever to what would become the so-called "science of the shares" or Islamic law of inheritance. In that system of law, a person contemplating death does not have the capacity to designate an heir in a last will and testament. In addition, a bequest may not exceed one-third of the estate and may not be made in favor of any person who receives a fractional share of the estate according to the Qurʾān. However, my rereading of Q 4:12b does bear a striking resemblance to a reform of the Roman law of testamentary succession introduced by Justinian. In my view, our understanding of the original meaning of Q 4:12b comes into better focus when we situate the Qurʾān in the legal environment of late antiquity.

In Roman law, a testator was free to dispose of his estate as he wished and could even disinherit close blood relatives, for cause. As a consequence of the many abuses that resulted from this exercise of freedom, during the late Republic a special remedy was introduced to protect the rights of the testator's immediate family. This remedy was known as the *querela inofficiosi testamenti* (objection against an unduteous will). The principle was that a testator who favored strangers over his close blood relatives was acting unfairly and failing in his natural duty to provide for his family. Such a will could be challenged in a special court; if the challenge was accepted, the will was declared invalid and the estate passed to the deceased's heirs in accordance with the rules of intestacy.

Originally, the *querela inofficiosi testamenti* could be brought only by descendants of the testator, or, in the absence of descendants, by ascendants. Late classical law opened the remedy to siblings of the deceased who had been disinherited by base persons or persons of ill repute. Subsequently, siblings were allowed to use this remedy if they received less than one-fourth of the amount they would have received if the deceased had died intestate. This one-quarter was known as the *pars legitima* or *portio legitima*. In post-classical law, an alternative to the *querela* was introduced according to which a testamentary heir was compelled to pay the statutory share in full (*actio ad supplendam legitimam*), thereby reducing their inheritance – without, however, invalidating the will. In the sixth century, Justinian raised the *portio legitima* to one-third of the intestate portion in those cases in which the testator left one to four children; and to one-half of the intestate portion in those cases in which the testator left five or more children.

Justinian's reform of the *querela inofficiosi testamenti* bears a striking resemblance to my rereading of a hypothetical *Q 4:12b. Both laws refer to an action taken by the siblings of a testator who had disinherited them; both leave the last will and testament valid and intact while awarding the disinherited siblings the same fractional share of the estate – one-third; and both strike a balance between the wishes of the testator, on the one hand, and his obligation to close blood relatives, on the other. Whereas there is no basis for a comparison between Q 4:12b, as traditionally understood, and Byzantine law, our hypothetical *Q 4:12b makes excellent sense when viewed in the context of Justinian's reform – just as Q 4:12a makes excellent sense when viewed in the context of Novella 53.6. Is it a coincidence that two Byzantine legal reforms formulated by jurists associated with the law school of Beirut approximately twenty years before the birth of Muḥammad – one dealing with the inheritance rights of a surviving spouse, the other with the inheritance rights of siblings – should find their way, albeit modified or in disguised form, into a single verse of the Qurʾān? If not, then two possible explanations come to mind: Either the resemblance between the qurʾānic instructions and Byzantine law is yet another example of divine providence or what the Qurʾān calls *sunnat allāh*. Or the thematic parallels in this case – as in the cases discussed elsewhere in this essay – are yet another indication that the Qurʾān's initial audience inhabited a legal environment that was closely connected to the legal environment of the Mountain Arena at large.

Bibliography

Brinner, W. M. 1986. "An Islamic Decalogue." In *Studies in Islamic and Judaic Traditions: Papers Presented at the Institute for Islamic-Judaic Studies*, edited by William M. Brinner and Stephen D. Ricks, 67–84. Atlanta.

Schoell. R., ed. 1954. *Corpus Iuris Civilis*, vol. 3. *Novellae*. Berolini.

Crone, P. 1987. *Roman, Provincial, and Islamic Law: The Origins of the Islamic Patronate*. Cambridge.

De Blois, F. 2004. "Qurʾān 9:37 and CIH 547." *Proceedings of the Seminar for Arabian Studies* 34:101–104.

Gibson, M. D., ed. 1903. The *Didascalia Apostolorum in Syriac*. Cambridge [Digitally reprinted 2011].

Günther, S. 2008. "O People of the Scripture! Come to a Word Common to You and Us (Q. 3:64): The Ten Commandments and the Qurʾān." *Journal of Qurʾānic Studies* 9.1:28–58.

Healey, J. 1993. *The Nabataean Tomb Inscriptions of Mada'in Salih*. Oxford.

Leicht, R. 2011. "The Qur'anic Commandment of Writing Down Loan Agreements (Q 2:282) – Perspectives of a Comparison with Rabbinical Law." In *The Qurʾān in Context: Historical and Literary Investigations into the Qur'anic Milieu*, edited by Angelika Neuwirth, Nicolai Sinai, Michael Marx, 593–614. Leiden and Boston.

Payne, R. E. 2016. "Sex, Death, and Aristocratic Empire: Iranian Jurisprudence in Late Antiquity." *Comparative Studies in Society and History* 58.2:519–549.

———. 2015. *A State of Mixture: Christians, Zoroastrians, and Iranian Political Culture in Late Antiquity*. Berkeley.

Powers, D. S. 1986. *Studies in Qurʾān and Ḥadīth: The Formation of the Islamic Law of Inheritance*. Berkeley.

——. 2009. *Muḥammad is Not the Father of Any of Your Men: The Making of the Last Prophet*. Philadelphia.

Simonsohn, U. I. 2011. *A Common Justice: The Legal Allegiances of Christians and Jews under Early Islam*. Philadelphia.

Zellentin, H. M. 2013. *The Qurʾān's Legal Culture: The Didascalia Apostolorum as a Point of Departure*. Heidelberg.

2

Ḥadīth between Traditional Muslim Scholarship and Academic Approaches

Andreas Görke

Introduction

THE *ḥadīth* is the record of reports of what the Prophet Muḥammad said, did, or tacitly approved. It constitutes the second most important source – after the Qurʾān – for Islamic law and Islamic theology, and it plays an important role in other fields of Islamic learning as well, such as Sūfism or qurʾānic exegesis. The term *ḥadīth* is sometimes also applied more widely to include reports about other early Muslims apart from the Prophet, but the following investigation will focus on *ḥadīth* in the narrower sense, that is Prophetic *ḥadīth*. It will also be mostly restricted to the core areas of *ḥadīth* scholarship, namely the study of the reports themselves and the criteria established to assess them as well as their relationship to and application within Islamic law.

Muslims and non-Muslims have used and studied *ḥadīth* for various reasons over the course of time. This led to very different, often opposing positions between internal (Muslim) and external (non-Muslim) approaches, but also within these approaches. In both the internal and the external approaches, it is possible to distinguish scholarly strands and non-scholarly strands. In the following, the focus will primarily be on the relationship of traditional Muslim *ḥadīth* scholarship and the modern academic study of *ḥadīth* from a non-religious perspective, but some thoughts will also be given to the use of *ḥadīth* outside the scholarly realm.

Traditional Muslim *ḥadīth* scholarship, which can be traced back to the first centuries of Islam, was instrumental in defining and shaping the corpus of traditions that became the basis for any study of *ḥadīth*. It emerged in connection with and in response to an initially uncritical handling of reports of what the Prophet Muḥammad allegedly had done or said. Such reports were transmitted and collected but also invented and recast for various reasons.

Most importantly, they served to support different legal and theological claims. While it may be assumed that at least some of the early believers regarded the behavior of the Prophet as a model to emulate and would thus refer to his sayings and deeds, there is also evidence that from an early time onwards people would likewise invent Prophetic traditions to promote certain political, legal, or theological views or for reasons of self-interest. Examples include alleged Prophetic statements on the virtues and merits of ʿAlī b. Abī Ṭālib (d. 40/661) or his political counterpart Muʿāwiya b. Abī Sufyān (d. 60/680), who fought for the caliphate, as well as opposing traditions disparaging them.[1] Other alleged Prophetic statements have him comment on groups that did not exist during his lifetime, such as the Zaydiyya (named after Zayd b. ʿAlī, who died in 122/740)[2] or praise cities such as Baghdad, Basra, and Kufa, which were only founded after his death.[3] An example for very brazen forgery is a tradition attributed to a certain Muḥammad b. al-Ḥajjāj al-Lakhmī (d. ca. 181/797), a Baghdadi food merchant who sold *harīsa*, a dish made of meat and bulgur. He spread a *ḥadīth* in which the Prophet claimed that he was given *harīsa* in paradise, and that this gave him the sexual energy of forty men.[4]

In response to this polemical use and invention of Prophetic traditions, *ḥadīth* scholars developed methods to assess the authenticity and reliability of traditions and to identify and discard forged ones. Over the course of time, reports of Muḥammad's statements or deeds concerning legal or theological matters that were deemed authentic came to be regarded as normative for the behavior of the believer and were transmitted and eventually fixed in writing in various collections. As the community split into several factions, each of these groups regarded different collections as particularly important, which resulted in the establishment of different *ḥadīth* corpora. Of these, the Sunnī and the Twelver-Shīʿī corpora are the two largest and most important, but there are also Ibāḍī, Zaydī, and Ismāʿīlī collections of *ḥadīth*.

Ḥadīth scholarship did not, however, end with the establishment of these corpora of authoritative *ḥadīth*s. *Ḥadīth*s form only one, albeit substantial, part of the legal framework, and there have always been different assessments of the reliability of individual *ḥadīth*s vis-à-vis each other and their relation to other relevant sources, such as the Qurʾān. The traditional Muslim approach to the *ḥadīth* therefore always encompassed two major aspects. It differentiated between scholars who were experts in the transmission, pres-

1. Mullā ʿAlī al-Qārī (d. 1014/1606), *Encyclopedia of Hadith Forgeries*, 571–572.
2. al-Qārī *Encyclopedia*, 517.
3. al-Qārī, *Encyclopedia*, 572.
4. al-Qārī, *Encyclopedia*, 342.

ervation, and assessment of the *ḥadīths* – the *muḥaddithūn* – and those who were experts in the application of these *ḥadīths*, such as legal and religious scholars. After the establishment of more or less fixed corpora of authentic traditions, the expertise of the latter group became more relevant, but the critical assessment of *ḥadīths* continued to be an important aspect and remains so until today. Scholars such as the Syrian Muḥammad Nāṣir al-Dīn al-Albānī (d. 1999), who devoted his life to studying *ḥadīth*, give evidence of the continuous relevance of *ḥadīth* scholarship.

Not all engagement with the *ḥadīth* has been scholarly, though; ordinary believers also engaged with *ḥadīths*, but their practice relied on the assessment of the *ḥadīths* by relevant authorities – those versed in *ḥadīth* proper or legal authorities. The vast majority of Muslims were never able to assess the context of a specific *ḥadīth*, its authenticity, or its implications in light of other relevant sources, und they therefore had to rely on the assessment and evaluation of experts in the field. But *ḥadīth* was not only relevant for its practical implementations, and the participation in public recitations of *ḥadīth*, for example, has been seen as a pious act.

Non-scholarly approaches can also be found in the polemical or apologetical engagement with other Muslims or non-Muslims. As indicated, the polemical use of *ḥadīth* began already at an early time and was one of the practices that gave rise to the development of the Muslim scholarly approach with its critical assessment of *ḥadīths*. But this scholarly approach was not able to eliminate the exploitation of *ḥadīths*, and throughout history they have been used in theological or sectarian disputes. Today they are, for example, employed by Islamist groups to support their view of society, or they are used to confirm the miraculous character of the Qurʾān, the humanity of the Prophet, or the imminence of the Day of Judgement. Thus one tradition has been used by the so-called Islamic State to justify the enslavement of Yazidi families,[5] and some people interpreted various apocalyptic traditions as referring to Saddam Hussein or the Taliban.[6] Common to these approaches is that they usually rely on a very limited number of *ḥadīths* that seem to support a specific view, while disregarding their contexts, their relationship to other *ḥadīths*, or the critical assessment of these *ḥadīths* by previous scholars.

This last approach is not very different from a non-Muslim, non-scholarly approach, which may best be termed polemical or hostile. Similar to both Muslim scholarly and non-scholarly approaches, it treats the *ḥadīth* corpus at least to some degree as authentic, but it uses *ḥadīth* mainly to discredit

5. Damir Geilsdorf and Franke 2015, 431.
6. Introduction to Nuʿaym b. Ḥammād (d. ca. 228/843), *The Book of Tribulations*, xxxiv.

the Prophet Muḥammad or the religion of Islam altogether. This approach has a long history, which already began with the initial encounters between Muslims and non-Muslims during the expansion of Islam, and it continues until today. Like the Muslim non-scholarly approach, it is not interested in the critical assessment of the traditions it employs, but instead relies on the apparent literal sense of a tradition. In more recent times, an apologetic approach can also be found amongst non-Muslims who try to defend Islam against specific accusations, in particular relating to violence and equality. Like the polemical approaches, this apologetic approach also usually disregards the contexts or scholarly assessment of the traditions.

The last approach to be discussed can be termed the academic approach, which has been the main approach of European scholarship on Islam from roughly the nineteenth century onwards. The term "academic scholarship" is preferred here over "Western scholarship" or "non-Muslim scholarship," as it increasingly also includes Muslim scholars. It is contrasted with "traditional Muslim scholarship," which does not need to be less scholarly, but relies on different premises as will be seen below. "Traditional" in this regard also does not mean backward or antiquated but implies that the basic assumptions and methods that are used follow those of classical Muslim *ḥadīth* scholarship. Academic scholarship of *ḥadīth* arose from a critical engagement with the Muslim scholarly tradition under the influence of Enlightenment ideas and in particular the use of historical-critical methods derived from the fields of history and biblical studies and their application to the Muslim sources. From the beginning of academic engagement with the sources of Islam, scholars have been cautious with regard to the reliability of the information contained in the *ḥadīth*. Contradicting *ḥadīth*s and their partly obviously miraculous, embellishing or tendentious character were reason enough not to accept traditions uncritically. Nevertheless, it was generally thought to be possible to discern tendentious shaping and sift out a considerable amount of historically reliable material from the *ḥadīth*.[7] This assessment changed, however, from the end of the nineteenth and beginning of the twentieth century. Two studies have been particularly influential in shattering the trust in the authenticity of the *ḥadīth* corpus, namely the second volume of Ignác Goldziher's *Muhammedanische Studien*, published in 1890,[8] and Joseph Schacht's *The Origins of Islamic Jurisprudence*, published in 1950.[9] Goldziher argued that the fact that several allegedly pro-

7. See for instance William Muir 1858, xxviii-lxxxvii, for a critical assessment of the traditions on the life of Muḥammad.

8. Goldziher 1890.

9. Schacht 1950.

phetic *ḥadīths* in fact reflected later political and theological debates and thus could not be regarded as statements from Muḥammad implies that the mechanisms of Muslim *ḥadīth* criticism had obviously not been successful in identifying forgeries.[10] Schacht held that legal *ḥadīths* traced back to the Prophet only became the rule after al-Shāfiʿī (d. 204/820) successfully had argued for the supreme authority of Prophetic *ḥadīths* over statements from later generations.[11] This, according to Schacht, led to the invention of traditions and to an ascription of statements by later figures to the Prophet.[12] While not all scholars followed Goldziher and Schacht in their assessment, their publications, amongst others, led to a generally much more cautious to skeptical view of the authenticity of the *ḥadīth* corpus in academic scholarship. This cautious to skeptical approach to the sources and the resulting debates about their reliability and the methods used to assess their significance has very much shaped academic scholarship on the *ḥadīth* ever since.

In the following, it will be explored to what extent classical Muslim *ḥadīth* scholarship has structured academic scholarship on the topic. To this end, different aspects will be taken into consideration, namely the form and scope of the *ḥadīth* as defined by classical Muslim scholarship, the different approaches to and interests in the *ḥadīth*, the methods developed in both traditions, the terminology used, and the boundaries between *ḥadīth* and other fields of learning.

The Framework of Early Muslim *Ḥadīth* Scholarship

The different scholarly and non-scholarly approaches discussed above have very different aims, but they are all to a large extent bound by the framework of early Muslim *ḥadīth* scholarship. This is first and foremost the case through the establishment of the *ḥadīth* format and the *ḥadīth* corpora.

The *ḥadīth* format describes the way the information is preserved in the sources, namely in usually very short and isolated reports about specific deeds and sayings of the Prophet (or in Shīʿī *ḥadīth* also of the Imams), which are provided with an *isnād*, a line of purported transmitters of the report from the original reporter to the collector and author of the source in which it is found. Both features find their explanation in the context in which the *ḥadīth* emerged. The atomistic nature of the *ḥadīth* is owed to its main purposes as well as its initially oral transmission. As indicated, the reports were mainly transmitted and collected to provide guidance in moral

10. Goldziher 1890, 147–152.
11. Schacht 1950, 2–3, 138; Schacht 1949, 150–151.
12. Schacht 1950, 165.

and legal questions. For this aim, providing a context for the statement or report was not essential, although the reports often contain some form of narrative framework. Short and concise reports were particularly suitable for an oral transmission as they were easy to memorize. The *isnād*, on the other hand, is the means of authentication of the report. It is often seen as a result of the split of the community into different groups, which made it necessary to establish a line of transmitters intended to document the reliability of the transmission.

This *ḥadīth* format implies that individual traditions are not in any obvious temporal or causal relation. It also facilitates the arrangement of these traditions in any order and putting them in almost any context, which may also affect their meaning and implications. Although the format was mainly suitable for normative traditions, it also affected other fields, such as historical traditions, despite being less suitable for these purposes.[13]

But it was not only the format of the *ḥadīth*s that was shaped by the interests and methods of Muslim *ḥadīth* scholarship, but likewise its scope, which defines the *ḥadīth* corpora that have come down to us. Since *ḥadīth*s were primarily, though not exclusively, transmitted and collected because of their normative value, *ḥadīth* scholars as well as legal or religious scholars mostly recorded those sayings and deeds that had practical implications. For the *ḥadīth*s to have normative value, it was important to ascertain that they were indeed authentic or could at least be considered to be so with a reasonable probability. By contrast, *ḥadīth*s that were identified as forgeries were as a rule discarded and ceased to be transmitted. This was justified by alleged sayings of the Prophet that condemned those who knowingly transmitted or recorded forged traditions. Later scholars nevertheless recorded a number of forged *ḥadīth*s, such as the ones mentioned in the beginning, in order to illustrate different kinds of forgeries and to prevent people from mistakenly relying on these forgeries. In fields outside *ḥadīth* and law, there are also numerous dubious traditions that survived although the *ḥadīth* scholars did not deem them authentic, as their standards were not applied as rigorously in other fields. Despite these exceptions, the scope of existing *ḥadīth*s is to a large part confined to what Muslim scholarship regarded to be reliable. This is particularly true for *ḥadīth* in the narrower sense of the word. The question of what was reliable was, however, controversial, and the split of the community ultimately led to the development of independent corpora of *ḥadīth*s that were considered authentic by different groups, and consequently to different and mutually exclusive scholarly traditions, despite considerable similarities in content.

13. Görke 2011, 174–177, 184–185.

These features of the development of the *ḥadīth* literature in the first four or five centuries of Islam necessarily influenced any subsequent scholarship as well as the use of *ḥadīth* outside the scholarly sphere. Any engagement with the *ḥadīth* was reliant on the material that had emerged from this process. This material consisted of fragmented, atomistic reports with purported lines of transmitters; recorded in writing only two hundred years or more after Muḥammad's death; recorded in different collections with several variants; confined mostly to what the respective collectors regarded as authentic reports; and assembled in what became separate corpora of *ḥadīths* in mutually exclusive scholarly traditions.

Ḥadīths As Normative and Historical Sources: Different Approaches to the *Ḥadīth*

This *ḥadīth* material did not suit all subsequent approaches to it equally well. Initially, it was obviously well suited for the needs of Muslim scholarly approaches that had shaped it. Later Muslim scholarship followed basically the same framework and showed the same interest in the material as their predecessors – namely to derive normative and spiritual guidance and legal rulings – interests that were mostly accommodated and satisfied by the existing corpora. Difficulties emerged, however, over the course of time. The material, once codified, could not necessarily address questions that arose through the spread of Islam into areas with very different climatic conditions and cultural backgrounds or through technological or scientific developments. And as the material not only relates to the behavior of the individual believer, but also provides general legal rules that are based on the assumption that these rules can and should be enforced by the state or the community, the question of the role and significance of *ḥadīth* in pluralistic societies and secular states has been highly controversial.

The *ḥadīth* material is also well suited for polemical and apologetical approaches. The very nature of the *ḥadīth* – isolated statements without a context – allows for the construction of a large variety of positions that appear to be supported by statements and deeds of the Prophet.

For the academic approach, by contrast, the scope and nature of the corpora do not conform well to some of the major research interests. It is true that the material is suitable for several aspects of the study of *ḥadīth*, such as the use of *ḥadīth* in various fields of learning from the third/ninth or fourth/tenth centuries onwards, the literary features of the *ḥadīth*, the emergence and characteristics of specific collections, or popular practices connected to the *ḥadīth*, such as public performances. These questions, however, have been marginal in academic scholarship. The major academic research interest in *ḥadīth* lay in the early period, in the question of what the *ḥadīth* can tell us about the first two centuries of Islam and in particular about the life and the teachings of the Prophet Muḥammad. In this regard, the existing corpora of *ḥadīth* are not particularly helpful. The lack of a historical context for most of the traditions, the lack of a chronology, the late date of the written *ḥadīth* collections as well as the confinement to traditions that Muslim scholarship regarded as genuine make it difficult to draw direct conclusions about the history of events or the development of ideas.

It has been a common perception that the main difference between traditional Muslim and academic approaches to the *ḥadīth* is the question of authenticity, with Muslims scholarship by and large accepting the authenticity of their respective *ḥadīth* corpora as reflecting the deeds and sayings of the Prophet Muḥammad, and academic scholarship rejecting a considerable part if not all of it as later inventions traced back to earlier authorities and ultimately the Prophet. This difference, however, is only a side aspect of the different approaches and research interests. For traditional Muslim scholarship, the *ḥadīth*s constitute first and foremost normative sources. *Ḥadīth*s were transmitted, collected, and studied to provide answers to questions related to the legal and moral code, the *sharīʿa*, as well as to some other fields such as theology. They are used to provide proof and legitimation for specific legal or otherwise normative positions. Academic scholarship, on the other hand, treats the *ḥadīth*s as historical sources. Its purpose in studying *ḥadīth*s is to gain information about the history of early Islam or the history of Islamic law or theology.

These different interests in *ḥadīth* necessarily lead to different foci and approaches. For traditional Muslim scholarship, the question of authority is essential. For a *ḥadīth* to be considered a valid normative source, it had to be established that it was authoritative, and it received its authority by establishing that it was, with a high degree of probability, authentic and indeed originated with the Prophet, or at least that it did not contradict reliable *ḥadīth*s.[14] To this end, Muslim *ḥadīth* criticism developed a sophisticated system of verifying the authenticity and reliability of a *ḥadīth*, mainly by its *isnād*, but to some degree also by its content.

For academic scholarship, on the other hand, the question of authenticity is relevant only for part of its research interests. A historical source

14. The normative value or authority of a *ḥadīth* would not necessarily have to be linked to its historical accuracy. A *ḥadīth* could be accepted to be true in normative terms without being historically exact, and this has in fact been practice in traditional Muslim scholarship to some degree. (Brown 2009, in particular 276–285; Brown 2011, in particular 4–15, 47–51). But at least in theory, the requirement for authority was authenticity.

can provide a lot of information even if it is a later forgery. In such a case, however, the information that can be derived from a source relates to the time in which it originated rather than to the time of which it speaks. The question of the authenticity or reliability of a Prophetic *ḥadīth* is obviously important if it is used as a source for the life and teachings of Muḥammad. It is not important, however, to get a deeper insight into the development of specific ideas, the development of Islamic law and theology, or into the historical context in which a *ḥadīth* was invented or circulated. To use a *ḥadīth* as a source for these aspects, it is instead necessary to establish when it originated and ideally also who was responsible for its circulation and for what reason. The focus thus has to be on the question of dating. The methods developed in academic scholarship for dating a *ḥadīth* mostly focused on its content rather than on its *isnād*, although the latter became more important in recent times.[15]

The different interests in the *ḥadīth* meant that the methods and criteria that traditional Muslim *ḥadīth* criticism had developed were not necessarily useful and applicable in academic scholarship. To establish whether they nevertheless affected the academic study of *ḥadīth*, it is necessary to have a closer look at the methods and criteria used in both traditions. The following analysis will focus on Sunnī *ḥadīth* criticism, as academic scholarship predominantly engaged with the Sunnī tradition. The methods and criteria developed in the Shīʿī and Ibāḍī traditions differ to some extent, but they nevertheless follow the same basic assumptions and approaches to the material.

Traditional Muslim Methods and Criteria for the Assessment of *Ḥadīth*s

It is difficult to say anything certain about Muslim *ḥadīth* criticism in the first two centuries of Islam, as there is no contemporary evidence of the practices of *ḥadīth* scholars and transmitters for this period. It is very likely that some rudimentary form of assessing *ḥadīth*s was practiced by some transmitters from a very early time onwards, such as looking for corroborating evidence for information, personal judgement of an informant's trustworthiness, or the probability of the veracity of a piece of information. However, works discussing formal criteria to distinguish forged *ḥadīth*s from reliable ones only begin to emerge in the fifth/eleventh century, the first such work being *al-Kifāya fī ʿilm al-riwāya* by al-Khaṭīb al-Baghdādī (d. 463/1071).[16] And

15. See Motzki 2005 for a survey of different methods of dating.
16. Brown 2008, 150.

while the authors of the *ḥadīth* collections of the third/ninth and fourth/tenth centuries sometimes provide their assessment of specific *ḥadīths*, and some of them also outline a basic methodology or criteria to be applied, it is mostly unclear how the compilers arrived at their conclusions with regard to the reliability of individual *ḥadīth* transmitters or the authenticity of specific *ḥadīths*. There is, however, evidence that some of the formal criteria discussed in the later theoretical literature were indeed practiced by *ḥadīth* scholars of the third/ninth century.[17]

While it is thus not possible to say much about *ḥadīth* criticism and how it shaped the *ḥadīth* corpus in the first two centuries, it is likely that at least from the third/ninth century, systematic *ḥadīth* criticism emerged and then developed into the complex system that can be found in the theoretical works of the fifth/eleventh century and later. A basic distinction can be made between criteria for assessing *ḥadīths* that relate to the *matn*, the actual content of the tradition, and others that relate to the *isnād*, the line of transmitters, and the reliability of individual transmitters within these *isnāds*. In both areas, the criteria should not be regarded as fixed and unanimously accepted and applied. They should rather be understood as considerations to assess the reliability of *ḥadīths* and as a repertoire of tools that could be employed in different ways.

With regard to the *matn*, criteria that were applied to identify forged *ḥadīths* include amongst others: the contradiction of a *ḥadīth* to qurʾānic statements; its contradiction to reason (*ʿaql*); its contradiction to well-established traditions; apparent anachronisms in the text; logical inconsistencies; and its incompatibility to established dogma or legal practice.[18] As indicated above, these criteria were not employed universally, and in particular the use of reason to evaluate the authenticity of *ḥadīths* was highly controversial. To avoid being arbitrary in their assessment, *ḥadīth* scholars came to focus more on the *isnād* and developed criteria to assess the quality of the *isnād*, the result of which was then applied to the whole tradition – the better the *isnād*, the more reliable the tradition to which it is connected.

The quality of the *isnād* could be assessed on different levels: it could be assessed on the level of the individual transmitters included in an *isnād*; it could also be assessed on the level of the *isnād* as a whole, taking into account amongst others the number of transmitters in an *isnād*, their relation to each other, and the modes of transmission used; finally, it could also be assessed on the level of the overall *isnād* situation, that is on the number of parallel versions that corroborate it.

17. Brown 2008, 154–160.
18. Brown 2008, 150–164.

On the level of the individual transmitters, the *ḥadīth* critics assessed their reliability, their integrity, and their capacity of memory,[19] but we know very little about how these criteria were actually applied by individual critics. We can, however, observe an apparent consensus over the reliability of a large number of transmitters.[20]

On the level of the single *isnād*, the *ḥadīth* critics determined whether the individual transmitters had actually met[21] and how they related material to each other, with some modes of transmission being regarded as more reliable than others.[22] They also looked at the number of transmitters present in a given *isnād*. An *isnād* with fewer transmitters was in general considered better than an *isnād* with many transmitters as it gave fewer opportunities for mistakes,[23] but some transmitters were said to have forgotten things when they grew old and were thus no longer regarded as reliable.[24]

Both aspects – the study of the reliability of the individual transmitters as well as of the nature of the transmission between different transmitters contributed to the emergence and development of the immense and rich biographical literature in Islam. A large part of this literature is concerned with transmitters, their biographical details – to identify when and where they lived – their teachers and students, and assessments of their reliability.

The third major aspect in the assessment of an *isnād* was the corroboration of one transmission through other *isnāds*. The more widespread a *ḥadīth* was, the more reliable it was considered to be. The most widespread ones, according to a common opinion with at least seven different transmitters in each generation, were called *mutawātir* and were considered to be as securely transmitted and thus authentic as the Qurʾān.

While the criteria according to which *ḥadīths* were assessed were based on the above framework, the results from applying these varied to some degree. Different scholars regarded different traditions and different transmitters as more reliable, and not all scholars agreed whether a specific transmitter had actually transmitted from another or not.

What can be observed, however, is a focus on the assessment of the lines of transmission and the transmitters rather than on the content itself. The advantage of focusing on the *isnād* was twofold. On the one hand, at least

19. See Ibn al-Ṣalāḥ al-Shahrazūrī (d. ca. 643/1245), *An Introduction to the Science of the Ḥadīth*, 81–94, for a detailed discussion of the different criteria that should be applied in determining the reliability of a transmitter.

20. Lucas 2004, 325–326.

21. Ibn al-Ṣalāḥ, *Introduction*, 299–302.

22. Ibn al-Ṣalāḥ, *Introduction*, 95–127.

23. Ibn al-Ṣalāḥ, *Introduction*, 183–188.

24. Ibn al-Ṣalāḥ, *Introduction*, 305–308.

at first sight this eliminated the danger of disregarding the practice of the Prophet in favor of human reason: if a *ḥadīth* was shown to go back to the Prophet, then it established what constituted Prophetic practice (independently of whether this appeared to be logical or opportune in the respective circumstances).[25] On the other hand, it was easier to agree on the specific criteria and framework for assessing the *isnād* than finding criteria to assess the *matn*. In many theological questions, for example, it would have been impossible to rely on human reason or experience.

Methods and Criteria for the Assessment of *Ḥadīth*s in Academic Research

For academic research, the *ḥadīth* has been important in different respects. It is, apart from the Qurʾān, the most important corpus of material that provides information about the time of Muḥammad and the early history of Islam. To use a *ḥadīth* for this purpose, however, it has to be established that the information it contains is indeed historically accurate, which is notoriously difficult.

The *ḥadīth* is also fundamental in understanding the development of Islamic law and, on a broader scale, Islamic intellectual history. It reflects controversies between different schools of thought, the development of specific dogmas, as well as the emerging consensus on which interpretations fall within the scope of orthodoxy and which ones do not. To understand these developments, it is irrelevant to what extent the traditions used to support the different positions reflect historical facts; they can be studied with regard to their use in the various debates. In this case, however, the question of dating is crucial.

For both goals, academic scholarship almost unanimously disregarded the methods of Muslim *ḥadīth* criticism. These had been deemed incapable of eliminating forgeries, and the existence of contradictions and anachronisms was seen to give ample evidence of this. Moreover, most of the early *ḥadīth* scholars had not made their criteria for assessment explicit or explained how they arrived at a particular judgement. Academic scholarship thus focused almost exclusively on the *ḥadīth*s themselves.

The methods that academic scholarship applied – initially mostly adopted from the fields of history or biblical studies – varied according to the research interests. To gain insights into the life and teachings of Muḥammad or into the earliest history of Islam, it was important to establish the historical reliability of the sources. More often than not, however, it was rather the unreliability that could be shown or argued for. Initially, many scholars

25. See also Brown 2008, 169–171.

held it to be sufficient to eliminate traditions that showed obvious anachronisms, embellishments, miraculous elements, or obvious tendencies that favored particular groups or individuals, while regarding other traditions as reliable unless there were specific reasons to distrust them.[26] The skeptical approaches of Schacht and later revisionist approaches such as those of John Wansbrough and others led some scholars to reverse the burden of proof and regard all traditions as forgeries unless proven authentic.[27] Overall, very few criteria remained that found more or less unanimous acceptance. The main guiding principle for these is to establish that a later forgery is highly unlikely. Following this argument, traditions that presented Muḥammad or the early community in a negative view were seen as likely authentic,[28] as were ones that seemed to contradict statements from the Qurʾān or later dogmatic positions.[29] This as a rule meant that traditions that were more likely to be regarded as authentic would more often be found outside the canonical collections, as the latter comprised mostly *ḥadīth*s that were within the accepted dogmatic and legal positions.

With regard to the second main research interest of academic scholarship, namely the emergence and development in particular of Islamic law and Islamic dogma, but also of specific political positions or debates, the focus of the methods was on dating traditions rather than on the question of their historical reliability or authenticity. In fact, most methods presumed, explicitly or implicitly, that the *ḥadīth*s did not reflect what the Prophet had said or done, but were later inventions or at least were fundamentally reshaped by later figures.

As very few *ḥadīth*s can be dated securely by their *matn* – with some exceptions, such as those containing obvious anachronisms, or, possibly, some eschatological traditions[30] – the methods usually tried to establish a relative chronology of different *ḥadīth*s. Similar to the methods that were employed to argue for or against the authenticity of *ḥadīth*s, few if any of the methods used to establish a relative chronology gained unanimous approval. Amongst the criteria suggested are that more complex or elaborate traditions emerged later than simpler ones on the same topic,[31] or that traditions that explicitly name a topic are later than ones that only contain it implicitly.[32] Some scholars argued that if a *ḥadīth* was not explicitly men-

26. See e.g. Muir 1858, xxviii–lxxxvii.

27. Schacht 1950, 149; Crone 1987, 32–34.

28. See e.g. Nöldeke 1914, 168; Forward 1997, 85.

29. See e.g. Kister 1970, 275.

30. See e.g. Madelung 1981, 291–297; Juynboll 1983, 207–213; Cook 1992a, 12–16. Cf. Cook 1992b, 26–38; Görke 2003, 196–207.

31. Speight 1973, 250, 265–267; cf. Motzki 2005, 212–214.

32. Schacht 1965, 393.

tioned in a debate where it would have supported an argument, it could only have emerged after that point.[33]

Criteria were also developed to establish a relative chronology based on the *isnād*. These include that variants of a *ḥadīth* where the *isnād* reaches back to the Prophet are later than those that are only traced back to a companion or successor,[34] or that *ḥadīth* variants featuring patchy and deficient *isnād*s are older than those with perfect *isnād*s.[35]

Attempts to not only establish a relative chronology, but to date individual *ḥadīth*s to a specific time and connect them with specific figures focus on the common link. More often than not, variants of a *ḥadīth* have part of their *isnād* in common – usually the two, three, or four transmitters after the Prophet. The last of these figures, the one in which the *isnād*s merge (or from whom they then spread out through different ways of transmission), has been dubbed the common link.[36] He is mostly regarded as the person with whom the *ḥadīth* originated or at least gained its characteristic form,[37] although different interpretations of the phenomenon exist.[38] The so called *isnād-cum-matn* analysis is based on the common link theory, but seeks to establish that the *isnād*s after the common link are independent of each other and constitute actual lines of transmission. To this end it examines to what extent differences in the actual text of a tradition (the *matn*) correspond to differences in the *isnād*s.[39] The method thereby tries to eliminate the possibility of the invention of a *ḥadīth* later than the common link as well as to identify later additions or changes to the *ḥadīth* and the figures responsible for these changes.[40]

While none of the criteria or methods are unanimously accepted in scholarship, most scholars would agree that by combining several criteria it may be possible in some cases to establish a relative chronology of variants of a *ḥadīth*. A majority would also hold that in certain cases it may be possible to link a *ḥadīth* to one key figure (the common link) and to identify figures who are responsible for specific changes to the tradition after that. And there seems to be some agreement that it is almost impossible to make secure statements about the existence or form of a specific *ḥadīth* before the time of the common link, and that all respective considerations are to some degree hypothetical.

33. Schacht 1950, 140; Juynboll 1983, 125; cf. Motzki 2005, 214–219.
34. Schacht 1950, 156–157.
35. Schacht 1950, 163–165.
36. Schacht 1950, 171–175.
37. Juynboll 1989, 353.
38. Cook 1981, 107-111; Motzki 2005, 227–228; Görke 2003, 188.
39. Motzki 2005, 251–252; Görke 2003, 188–194.
40. Görke, Motzki, and Schoeler 2012, 41.

It is obvious from this overview that the different approaches to assessing *ḥadīths* developed in classical Muslim *ḥadīth* scholarship and in the academic study of *ḥadīth* are virtually impossible to reconcile. The different interests and approaches of traditional Muslim and academic scholarship led to the development of very different – and often mutually exclusive – criteria with which to assess the individual *ḥadīths*. What traditional Muslim scholarship regards as criteria that support the authenticity of a *ḥadīth* – a perfect *isnād*, conformity with the Qurʾān and established legal or theological positions – in academic scholarship are rather indications of a late date of the respective report. And what academic scholars would regard as indications for an early date – such as an incomplete *isnād* or disagreement with the Qurʾān or later positions – would be signs of forgery or unreliability for Muslim scholars.

While traditional Muslim scholarship assumed that the *ḥadīth* critics by and large had been able to identify those *ḥadīths* that indeed constituted authentic reports of statements and deeds of the Prophet, scholars following the academic approach more or less agree that it is virtually impossible to securely date specific traditions to the time of the Prophet or the first generation of believers. Most studies so far have only been able to date traditions to roughly the turn of the first century of Islam (beginning of the eighth century CE) and to link them to specific figures of the second generation. This does not necessarily imply that there are no authentic Prophetic traditions, but the criteria and methods employed by academic scholarship are in general more suitable to identify and date forgeries than to identify authentic traditions going back to the Prophet. Moreover, if they are used to argue for the authenticity of specific *ḥadīths*, these *ḥadīths* are exactly those that are rejected by Muslim scholarship, such as those presenting Muḥammad in a negative light or disagreeing with the Qurʾān or later dogma.

Summarizing, it can be said that while academic scholarship on *ḥadīth* relies to a large degree on the material that was shaped by classical Muslim scholarship, it almost completely disregards the methods and criteria of assessment developed within this scholarship. Instead, it developed its own methods – often borrowing from other scholarly disciplines – that were more suitable for its research interests.

Terminology and Categorization

The terminology relating to *ḥadīth* that classical Muslim scholarship developed is mostly concerned with the different levels of soundness of a *ḥadīth*, with regard to the reliability of the transmitters, the modes of transmission, the characteristics of an *isnād* in particular concerning possible gaps, the number of parallel versions of the *ḥadīth* and thus its corroboration, and the assessment of the *ḥadīth* as a whole.[41]

As academic scholarship disregarded Muslim *ḥadīth* criticism because of its perceived unsuitability for distinguishing authentic *ḥadīth*s from forgeries, neither the terminology nor the categorization of *ḥadīth*s in Muslim scholarship have impacted on academic scholarship. The only terms that have been generally adopted are *ḥadīth* itself, as well as its main constituents, the *isnād* and the *matn*, sometimes used interchangeably with English translations (tradition or report, line of transmitters, text or content).

In contrast, academic scholarship has developed its own terminology, in particular with regard to the *isnād*. In addition to the common link, several other terms have been coined, such as the partial common link (a student of the common link, who himself has two or more students),[42] the dive (a single line of transmitters that reaches back to an authority earlier than the common link of a tradition),[43] the spider (a constellation which consists of only single strands to the common link and no partial common links),[44] the phenomenon of *isnād*s "spreading" (a deliberate omission of transmitters that leads to the creation of false common links and obscures the view to the originators of a tradition),[45] and several others are all particular to academic scholarship of *ḥadīth*, although some have parallels in Muslim scholarship.[46] There have also been attempts to categorize the people involved in the transmission and collection of the material, not according to their reliability or position in the *isnād*, but with regard to their role.[47] While some of these terms and the underlying concepts have not found universal recognition in academic scholarship, several are widely used and understood.

Scope and Boundaries of *Ḥadīth* Scholarship

As indicated above, academic studies of *ḥadīth* had to rely on the material shaped by classical Muslim scholarship. However, the boundaries between the different disciplines and the respective texts are not necessarily the same in academic and Muslim scholarship. In traditional Muslim scholarship, the boundaries between *ḥadīth*, traditions about the biography of the Prophet (*sīra* or *maghāzī*), historical traditions (*akhbār*), or exegetical tradi-

41. Robson 1971, 24–27, and Pavlovitch 2018 provide overviews of the terminology with regard to these aspects.

42. Juynboll 2007, xx.

43. Juynboll 2007, xxii–xxiii.

44. Juynboll 2007, xxii–xxiii.

45. Schacht 1950, 166–171; Cook 1981, 107–111.

46. See e.g. Ozkan 2004.

47. Günther 2005.

tions of the Qurʾān (*tafsīr*) seem to have been established rather early with the different fields exhibiting different criteria and a different amount of scrutiny to assess the reliability.[48] In academic scholarship, by contrast, the boundaries between these genres do not necessarily exist, and some scholars regarded the traditions in all these fields as consisting of essentially the same material.[49] Academic scholarship, in line with its disregard of the results of Muslim *ḥadīth*, also had no incentive in limiting its research to those collections that were deemed the most reliable in Muslim scholarship. However, the availability of sources effectively reduced the possible expansion of the scope, as the major collections were also the ones most easily accessible.

One boundary that has remained in academic scholarship is that between the different *ḥadīth* corpora. Most scholars confined their research to Sunnī *ḥadīth*, far less focused on Twelver Shīʿī *ḥadīth*, and only very few studied *ḥadīth*s from different corpora, such as Ibāḍī, Zaydī, or Ismāʿīlī sources. Scholars would generally focus on one of these corpora only and not take into account similar *ḥadīth*s from other traditions, although there are some notable exceptions.[50] So far, no attempt has been made to systematically compare the different corpora and to establish and critically assess the overlaps and differences between them.

Conclusion

As was shown, classical Muslim *ḥadīth* scholarship has to a large degree defined the form and the corpora of *ḥadīth* and structured them according to their main interest, namely to serve as a means for providing legal and moral guidance. This has provided the framework for the study of *ḥadīth* and shapes all engagement with the *ḥadīth* to a certain degree. But Muslim *ḥadīth* scholarship was never able to retain control over the engagement with the *ḥadīth*. While it managed to some extent to rein in Muslim non-academic approaches because of its quasi-monopoly on the ability to assess the soundness of a *ḥadīth* and its context, the influence on academic engagement with the *ḥadīth* was limited to a few aspects.

Thus the criteria academic scholarship used to date traditions are generally at odds with Muslim scholarly ones and in many cases result in exactly opposite conclusions. This is also one of the reasons why there has been little mutual influence between contemporary Muslim and academic approaches to the study of *ḥadīth*.

One important influence classical Muslim scholarship had on the study

48. See, for example, Görke 2011 and Tottoli 2014.
49. Becker 1913, 263–264; Horovitz 1918, 39–40; cf. Görke 2011, 185.
50. See e.g. Kister 1970.

of *ḥadīth* is the split into different sectarian traditions. This split is mirrored in academic scholarship on *ḥadīth*, which has mostly been organized along the sectarian lines. This is to some degree justified if studies are interested in the development of specific aspects within the individual scholarly traditions – Sunnī, Twelver-Shīʿī, etc. – but studies aiming at a broader view of developments within the Islamic world would benefit from overcoming these boundaries.

The academic study of *ḥadīth* – be it with regard to the development of the genre of itself, the development of Islamic law or other fields of learning, or its value as a historical source for the life of Muḥammad – has usually been confined to the discipline of Islamic studies or related disciplines. While methods, theories and findings from other fields were occasionally applied to the academic study of *ḥadīth*, such as oral tradition/oral history, narratology, literary studies and others, studies of *ḥadīth* had little impact on other fields. This, however, is less due to a lack of results or scholarly findings that could be relevant for other fields such as history, literary studies, or religious studies, but largely due to the small size of the discipline and its marginal role vis-à-vis these larger fields to which it could contribute.

Bibliography

Becker, C. H. 1913. "Prinzipielles zu Lammens' Sīrastudien." *Der Islam* 4:263–269.

Brown, J. A. C. 2008. "How We Know Early Ḥadīth Critics Did *Matn* Criticism and Why It's So Hard to Find." *Islamic Law and Society* 15:143–184.

——. 2009. "Did the Prophet Say it or Not? The Literal, Historical and Effective Truth of Ḥadīths in Early Sunnism." *Journal of the American Oriental Society* 129:259–285.

——. 2011. "Even If It's Not True, It's True: Using Unreliable Ḥadīths in Sunni Islam." *Islamic Law and Society* 18:1–52.

Cook, M. 1981. *Early Muslim Dogma: A Source-Critical Study*. Cambridge.

——. 1992a. "The Heraclian dynasty in Muslim eschatology." *Al-Qantara* 13:3–23.

——. 1992b. "Eschatology and the dating of traditions." *Princeton Papers in Near Eastern Studies* 1:23–47.

Crone, P. 1987. *Roman, Provincial and Islamic Law: The Origins of the Islamic Patronate*. Cambridge.

Damir-Geilsdorf, S., and L. M. Franke. 2015. "Narrative Reconfigurations of Islamic Eschatological Signs: The Portents of the 'Hour' in Grey Literature and on the Internet." *Archiv Orientální* 83:411–437.

Forward, M. 1997. *Muhammad: A Short Biography*. Oxford.

Goldziher, I. 1890. *Muhammedanische Studien*, vol. 2. Halle.
Görke, A.. 2003. "Eschatology, History, and the Common Link: A Study in Methodology." In *Method and Theory in the Study of Islamic Origins*, edited by Herbert Berg, 179–208. Leiden.
——. 2011. "The relationship between *maghāzī* and *ḥadīth* in early Islamic scholarship." *Bulletin of the School of Oriental and Asian Studies* 74:171–185.
——, H. Motzki, and G. Schoeler. 2012. "First-Century Sources for the Life of Muḥammad? A Debate." *Der Islam* 89:2–59.
Günther, S. 2005. "Assessing the Sources of Classical Arabic Compilations: The Issue of Categories and Methodologies." *British Journal of Middle Eastern Studies* 32:75–98.
Horovitz, J. 1918. "Alter und Ursprung des Isnād". *Der Islam* 8: 39–47.
Ibn al-Ṣalāḥ al-Shahrazūrī. 2005. *An Introduction to the Science of Ḥadīth: Kitāb Maʿrifat anwāʿ ʿilm al-ḥadīth*, translated by Eerik Dickinson. Reading.
Juynboll, G. H. A. 1983. *Muslim Tradition: Studies in Chronology, Provenance and Authorship of early Hadith*. Cambridge.
——. 1989. "Some *isnād*-analytical Methods Illustrated on the Basis of Several Women-demeaning Sayings from *Ḥadīth* Literature." *Al-Qantara* 10:343–384.
——. 2007. *Encyclopedia of Canonical Ḥadīth*. Leiden.
Kister, M. J. 1970. "'A Bag of Meat': A Study of an Early *Ḥadīth*." *Bulletin of the School of Oriental and African Studies* 33:267–275.
Lucas, S. C. 2004. *Constructive Critics, Ḥadīth Literature, and the Articulation of Sunnī Islam: The Legacy of the Generation of Ibn Saʿd, Ibn Maʿīn, and Ibn Ḥanbal*. Leiden.
Madelung, W. 1981. "ʿAbd Allāh b. al-Zubayr and the Mahdi." *Journal of Near Eastern Studies* 40:291–305.
Motzki, Harald. 2005. "Dating Muslim Traditions: A Survey." *Arabica* 52:204–253.
Muir, W. 1858. *The Life of Mahomet*, vol. 1. London.
Nöldeke, Th. 1914. "Die Tradition über das Leben Muhammeds." *Der Islam* 5:160–170.
Nuʿaym b. Ḥammād al-Marwazī. 2017. *"The Book of Tribulations": The Syrian Muslim Apocalyptic Tradition*. Edited and translated by David Cook. Edinburgh.
Ozkan, H. 2004. "The *Common Link* and its Relation to the *Madār*." *Islamic Law and Society* 11:42–77.
Pavlovitch, P. 2018. "Ḥadīth." In *The Encyclopaedia of Islam Three.* Leiden.
al-Qārī, M. ʿA. 2014. *Encyclopedia of Hadith Forgeries*. Introduction, Translation and Notes by Gibril Fouad Haddad. London.

Robson, J. 1971. "Ḥadīth." In *The Encyclopaedia of Islam. New Edition*, vol. III: 23–28. Leiden.
Schacht, J. 1949. "A Revaluation of Islamic Traditions." *Journal of the Royal Asiatic Society of Great Britain and Ireland* 2:143–154.
——. 1950. *The Origins of Muhammadan Jurisprudence*. Oxford.
——. 1965. "Modernism and Traditionalism in a History of Islamic Law." *Middle Eastern Studies* 1:388–400.
Speight, R. M. 1973. "The Will of Saʿd b. a. Waqqāṣ: The Growth of a Tradition." *Der Islam* 50:249–267.
Tottoli, R. 2014. "Interrelations and Boundaries between *Tafsīr* and Hadith Literature: The Exegesis of Mālik b. Anas's *Muwaṭṭa*ʾ and Classical Qurʾānic Commentaries." In *Tafsīr and Islamic Intellectual History: Exploring the Boundaries of a Genre*, edited by A. Görke and J. Pink, 147–171. Oxford.

3

Tafsīr as Discourse: Institutions, Norms, and Authority

Johanna Pink

THE STUDY OF QUR'ĀNIC EXEGESIS, whether performed by Muslims or non-Muslims, inside or outside the Islamicate world, is to a large extent governed by the label *tafsīr*. This term denotes both the general activity of interpreting, or more precisely, "explaining" the Qur'ān and a specific genre of scholarly literature, that of the qur'ānic commentary. The ambiguity entailed by this dual meaning of *tafsīr* is today most commonly resolved by focusing on the second meaning of the term, that is, on qur'ānic commentaries – at least with respect to the premodern period,[1] which is the main subject of this chapter. This implicit decision to favor a specific exegetical genre over other ways to interpret the Qur'ān comes with its own drawbacks. It excludes by definition, and not always consciously, other types of qur'ānic interpretation. It also equates qur'ānic interpretation with a specific genre to such a degree that the contours, mechanisms, and social function of that genre become obscured. If no other type of exegesis is taken into consideration, there is no frame of reference against which to compare the qur'ānic commentary and to recognize its limitations.

Tafsīr, in the sense of the qur'ānic commentary, is thus typically taken for granted, both from an insider and an outsider perspective, as the privileged or even only way in which premodern Muslims interpreted the Qur'ān, and as a genre whose main function was to offer access to the "true meaning" of the Qur'ān. Maybe this is one reason for which, according to Bruce Fudge, many Western scholars, in the study of qur'ānic interpretation, "tended merely to copy their medieval sources, and thus conveyed uncritically the methodologies, assumptions, and prejudices of the medieval authors."[2]

1. This refers to the period until, roughly, the last third of the nineteenth century when new modes of interpreting the Qur'ān started to emerge, besides the older ones that continued to be practiced by *ʿulamāʾ*.

2. Fudge 2006, 116.

Of course, the attempt to distinguish insider and outsider perspectives, in this field as in any other, is fraught with difficulties. Scholarship conducted by Muslims is not necessarily governed by religious considerations, nor is scholarship conducted by non-Muslims by definition objective, neutral, and free of normative assumptions. Nor is there a single, homogeneous, and exclusively non-Muslim "Western academe" that stands in sharp contrast to a monolithic, pious "Muslim scholarship." Yet, it is possible to identify in *tafsīr* studies different discourses shaped by a set of authorities and shared assumptions that have been influential in either Western or Islamicate academic spaces for a long period of time. In the twenty-first century, the boundaries between these discourses, which have never been rigid, have blurred and overlapped even more, as is evident from an ample amount of promising directions in current scholarship.[3] It is the tension between these discursive positions, as well as productive venues of research beyond it, that this chapter aims to describe. These discursive positions do not represent essentialized, monolithic "Western" or "Muslim" approaches. They have only ever constituted trends that individual scholars have followed to a greater or lesser extent; but they have nevertheless brought forth their own authorities.

The tension between them is not so much based in epistemology or in the choice of categories; it mostly results from a divergent assessment of these categories. In much of the Muslim religious literature produced by *ʿulamāʾ*, the *tafsīr* tradition is treated as authoritative. This is not necessarily true for every individual premodern work of *tafsīr* but it is true for an imagined consensus, or *ijmāʿ*, of legitimate, mainstream exegesis, often embodied in the works of exegetes who are seen as the pinnacle of that tradition. For example, Ṭabarī[4] and Ibn Kathīr[5] are today often attributed that role in Sunnī circles. There is a counter trend, represented by modernist Muslim scholars and intellectuals, that vehemently questions the authority of these exegetes, pointing, for example, to their misogyny or their lack of historical contextualization. In either case, there is little interest in examining power dynamics and historical circumstances that brought forth such notions of authority.

For Western scholarship of Islam, when it emerged, the question was not so much whether the *tafsīr* tradition was authoritative but whether it did what exegesis was supposed to do, according to Islamicists: to provide access to what the Qurʾān meant to its original audience by the use of his-

3. Fudge 2006, 127n25.
4. Abū Jaʿfar Muḥammad Ibn Jarīr al-Ṭabarī, d. ca. 310/923.
5. Abū l-Fidāʾ Ismāʿīl b. ʿUmar Ibn Kathīr, d. ca. 774/1373.

torical-critical methods; or to construct a coherent and systematic qurʾānic worldview; or at least to offer new and original ideas about the Qurʾān's message to Muslims. Since large parts of the *tafsīr* genre failed to fulfil these expectations, the interest of Western Islamicists in *tafsīr*, by and large, and with a few exceptions, was not very high up until the 2000s. There seemed to be little relevance to the study of a genre that mainly consists of the seemingly haphazard citation of traditions about earlier authorities whose authenticity seemed doubtful. Few exegetes were credited with expressing original ideas, beyond the endless repetition of the same material. The reasons for the seemingly repetitive nature of qurʾānic commentaries, rooted in the historical development of a scholarly discipline and its social and pedagogical function, were not taken into consideration, let alone seen as a valid subject of research. Many Islamicists, when trying to find a point of reference in the *tafsīr* tradition, which is too be vast to be manageable, took recourse to mainstream Sunnī works of *tafsīr* at the expense of works whose authors were associated with the Shīʿah, Ṣūfism or the Muʿtazila. Such an uncritical adoption of faith-based epistemologies raised at least two problems: the inherently polemical and apologetic aspects of mainstream Sunnī works of *tafsīr* were not recognized, and potentially central and influential works by Muʿtazilī, Ṣūfī, or Shīʿī authors were marginalized.

The scholarly treatment of *tafsīr* is thus fraught with problems of categorization and framing. This chapter will outline these problems, as well as successful attempts to resolve them. I argue that it is imperative to analytically distinguish between *textual genres* and *textual practices* and to situate both in their social context. The modern genre of the Qurʾān translation will serve as a case in point. First, though, the basic assumption that the qurʾānic commentary is the main locus of qurʾānic interpretation needs to be discussed.

Tafsīr Inside and Outside *Tafsīr*

The widespread conflation of *tafsīr* as an activity and *tafsīr* as a genre is based on the assumption that the act of interpreting the Qurʾān, at least as far as premodern Muslim scholarship is concerned, mostly or exclusively takes place in works belonging to the genre of the qurʾānic commentary. This assumption is not entirely unfounded. Qurʾānic commentaries contain the most voluminous and exhaustive collections of interpretive traditions and opinions that we possess and they were probably the most important point of reference for a Muslim scholar looking for solutions to a particular exegetical problem.

However, as Jane McAuliffe remarks:

> *Tafsīr* as a genre and *tafsīr* as an intellectual exercise of the Muslim religious imagination are not necessarily coterminous categories. Despite the countless shelves of published commentaries and the many collections of *tafsīr* manuscripts that await editing, medieval exegesis of the Qurʾān cannot be caught or contained within these boundaries.[6]

Studying qurʾānic interpretation that takes place outside qurʾānic commentaries – *tafsīr* outside *tafsīr*, as it were – allows us to gain a perspective on how Muslim scholars interpreted the Qurʾān when they were free of the restrictions that are inherent in the genre of *tafsīr*. One of those restrictions is rooted in the invariable strategy to comment on the Qurʾān verse by verse. While exegetes could include cross-references and in fact did so, they still tended to focus on the problems raised by a particular verse and not so much on the function of a term or concept across the entire Qurʾān. Furthermore, there was a pool of exegetical resources, traditions, and debates that exegetes were expected to demonstrate knowledge of, even if they had some leeway in their decision on how to present them, how much space to give to them, and whether to evaluate them. As a result, qurʾānic commentaries typically cite certain agreed-upon "occasions of revelation" (*asbāb al-nuzūl*) or *ḥadīth*s even when those have no apparent function for the interpretation of a verse and no argument is derived from them. This is because the authors of those commentaries needed to cite them in order to demonstrate their mastery of the exegetical tradition.[7] Once they were writing outside this particular genre, however, they were free to combine only those qurʾānic verses that matched their topic and to cite only those exegetical resources that served their argument.

Karen Bauer has underlined the importance of genre and the restrictions inherent in qurʾānic commentaries by conducting interviews with *ʿulamāʾ* on their interpretation of qurʾānic verses pertaining to gender hierarchies. These interviews yielded substantially different, more extensive and coherent arguments from the ones found in works of *tafsīr*.[8] The absence of genre restriction allows for the kind of fundamental and systematic discussion of a topic that is impossible within the sequential, verse-by-verse structure of qurʾānic commentaries. How exactly scholars made use of the Qurʾān outside qurʾānic commentaries depends on the context, form, and purpose of their statements. For example, Kristian Petersen has shown that in the Sino-Muslim tradition, writings on Islamic law tended to include ver-

6. McAuliffe 2003, 454.
7. Bauer 2015, 15–18.
8. Bauer 2015.

batim translations of the Qurʾān as evidence (*dalīl*) for a specific legal norm while treatises on faith often preferred to loosely allude to qurʾānic concepts and terminology.[9]

It might be argued that the above-mentioned cases do not represent "exegesis proper" but rather the use of the Qurʾān to serve an outside purpose, for example, to bolster a particular legal doctrine. Even when this is true, however, the discussion of the Qurʾān in works that are not qurʾānic commentaries may be based on coherent hermeneutical principles. They might even be more coherent than those applied in many qurʾānic commentaries, which are notorious for failing to execute what they promise to do in their introductions.[10] For example, the Mamluk scholar Ibn Taymiyya,[11] while not having written a qurʾānic commentary that we know of, heavily drew on the Qurʾān in some of his other works and composed a number of explicitly exegetical treatises. He did not content himself with subjecting the qurʾānic material he quoted there to the *ḥadīth*-based methodology that he had developed in his "Introduction to the Principles of Exegesis" (*Muqaddima fī uṣūl al-tafsīr*).[12] Rather, he deliberately developed and applied additional hermeneutical principles that he found lacking in qurʾānic commentaries. Among those was a type of historical criticism pertaining to the biographies of prophets mentioned in the Qurʾān as well as the use of the Bible, which Ibn Taymiyya considered to largely represent God's speech, in order to interpret God's speech in the Qurʾān.[13]

Even if the interpretation of the Qurʾān outside *tafsīr* is sometimes subordinate to a non-exegetical purpose, it has to be understood that the authors of qurʾānic commentaries do not always limit themselves to performing exegesis for exegesis' sake either. They typically have stakes in theological, rhetorical, legal, philosophical, or mystical discourses and use *tafsīr* as a respectable arena for polemicizing against their opponents.[14] Often, this is hard to discern unless a reader is intimately familiar with the particular and often highly intricate scholarly debates that took place in the exegete's milieu. For example, Shuruq Naguib has shown to what extent the seemingly detached qurʾānic commentary by the sixteenth-century Ottoman scholar Abū l-Suʿūd Efendi was embedded in polemical academic debates on language and rhetoric.[15] It is all too easy to overlook this con-

9. Petersen 2018, 123–156.
10. Forster 2001; Bauer 2013a.
11. Taqī al-Dīn Aḥmad Ibn Taymiyya (d. 728/1328).
12. Saleh 2010a.
13. Mirza 2017; Pink forthcoming.
14. Fudge 2006, 146.
15. Naguib 2013.

text, thereby failing to understand what motivated an exegete, when one reduces qurʾānic exegesis to qurʾānic commentaries and is insufficiently familiar with their intellectual milieu. Since we often lack detailed information about that milieu and qurʾānic commentaries do not readily provide explanations of what really interested their authors, the study of qurʾānic exegesis outside the confines of that genre can be highly illuminating. Topical works of all kinds often contain the type of explicit statements of their authors' concerns that qurʾānic commentaries are lacking.

One unfortunate result of the reductionist tendency, particularly in the Western study of Islam, which equates qurʾānic exegesis with *tafsīr* is the lack of interest in *ʿulūm al-Qurʾān*: the broader academic discipline concerned with the Qurʾān, its occasions of revelation, chronology, or variant readings. Exploring this discipline might be a way to understand premodern exegetical approaches beyond the qurʾānic commentaries' often highly idealized introductions[16] or the methods they apply to specific qurʾānic material. It opens a window into the resources they had at their disposal, which is an oft-overlooked factor in the analysis of exegetical works.

Taking into consideration exegetical material outside *tafsīr* also allows us to better understand the development and boundaries of *tafsīr*, in the sense of qurʾānic commentaries, and their relation to other fields of knowledge. For example, Roberto Tottoli has shown that Sunnī *ḥadīth* collections may contain exegetical *ḥadīth*s in sections that are specifically labeled *tafsīr*, but that the same traditions do not appear in qurʾānic commentaries,[17] at least not until Suyūṭī's[18] encyclopedic attempt to rectify that problem in his *al-Durr al-manthūr*. This can only be explained if we understand the emergence of the qurʾānic commentary not only as an intellectual exercise, but as a distinct genre and scholarly discipline, separate from *ḥadīth* scholarship. Similarly, Pieter Coppens has shown that the reception of theological ideas formulated outside *tafsīr*, while not absent, has its limits even within the relatively less formalized genre of Ṣūfī *tafsīr*;[19] and Rebecca Sauer has outlined a similar semi-detachment of legal discourses from *tafsīr*.[20]

Precisely because the framing of *tafsīr* as a genre and scholarly discipline is so important, it is imperative to look beyond it. Only this will allow us to grasp its rules and limitations, as one particular locus of exegetical activity among others. Understanding *tafsīr* not as an essential category of

16. See Bauer 2013a.
17. Tottoli 2013; 2014.
18. Jalāl al-Dīn al-Suyūṭī (849/1145–911/1505).
19. Coppens 2018a.
20. Sauer 2014.

knowledge, but as a highly specific and partly contingent system of scholarly production helps to gain a perspective on the indispensable but also limited role it plays in Muslim efforts to make sense of the Qurʾān.

Tafsīr As a Genre and Its Elusive Center

In a seminal essay in 1993, Norman Calder characterized the qurʾānic commentary as a literary genre with clearly defined characteristics.[21] Where previous historians of *tafsīr*, the most prominent of whom were the Hungarian Islamicist Ignác Goldziher (1850–1921) and the Egyptian scholar Muḥammad al-Dhahabī (1915–1977), had mostly focused on the exegetes' theological leanings and sectarian identity,[22] Calder examined the structure and methods of their works. In doing so, he was remarkably resilient to a tendency, apparent in many academic studies of *tafsīr*, to place works that were considered authoritative in the nineteenth or twentieth centuries at the center of the *tafsīr* tradition, treating them as prototypical works that define the characteristics and hermeneutics of mainstream *tafsīr*, regardless of how important and authoritative they had been in earlier periods. Goldziher and Dhahabī, for example, implicitly set up Ṭabarī's Sunnī, tradition-based commentary as the norm against which other works are measured.

This bias towards Sunnī, tradition-based exegesis was to a large extent shaped by the politics of print in the Muslim world.[23] For Orientalists in European universities, the perception of what was authoritative and important was additionally skewed by their focus on those regions of the Muslim world that they predominantly engaged with, especially the Ottoman Empire, Egypt, and India. Works that were printed early there were more accessible to Islamicists than those of which only a small number of manuscripts were available or which were published in regions that received less attention. Ṭabarī's qurʾānic commentary benefited from this fact; published in Cairo in 1903, it was a favorite resource of Orientalists. Goldziher's subsequent decision to situate Ṭabarī at the center of the *tafsīr* tradition carried right into the first edition of the *Encyclopaedia of Islam*, which also reveals a distinctly Ottoman bias, for example by singling out the eighteenth-century Ottoman exegete Ismāʿīl Ḥaqqī Bursāwī among the few authors of qurʾānic commentaries who are mentioned by name or by emphasizing the importance of the qurʾānic commentary of Bayḍāwī[24] which was the central resource for

21. Calder 1993.
22. Goldziher 1920; al-Dhahabī 1961.
23. Saleh 2010b.
24. ʿAbdallāh b. ʿUmar al-Bayḍawī (d. ca. 685/1286).

teaching *tafsīr* in Ottoman *madrasas*.[25] A part of Bayḍāwī's qurʾānic commentary was translated into English in 1894 already, based on the assumption that it was representative of the genre of *tafsīr* and therefore particularly useful to students of Orientalism.

Of course, Muslim historians of *tafsīr* such as Dhahabī were influenced by the emergence of print capitalism just as much as Orientalists, although Ottoman scholarship might have been of lesser interest to the Arabs among them. By placing Ṭabarī at the center of the *tafsīr* tradition, they shaped a normative ideal of qurʾānic hermeneutics that was not coincidental. Since the production of printed editions of *tafsīr* works was time-consuming and costly and rarely promised huge commercial success, it was often motivated by an agenda. Many of the persons and institutions involved in funding or producing such publications were interested in spreading precisely the type of Sunnī, tradition-based hermeneutics that Ṭabarī stood for, and to an even greater extent Ibn Kathīr. Ibn Kathīr's qurʾānic commentary was the first to be published in a modern, easily usable layout. In contrast to the nineteenth-century *madrasa* prints directed at aspiring religious scholars, it could be consulted by readers who were not religious scholars and did not know the Qurʾān by heart. The ascension of Ibn Taymiyya's hermeneutics and Ibn Kathīr's qurʾānic commentary to a position of authority in the Sunnī field is a result of political and ideological developments in modern Sunnī thought that motivated Salafi actors in Damascus, Cairo, India, and Saudi Arabia to print their works. The preference for their approach reflects the conviction that "authentic" *ḥadīth*s are the preferred sources of exegesis whereas philosophy, "unauthentic" traditions of non-Muslim origin (*isrāʾīliyyāt*), overly narrative material, speculation, differences of opinion, Ṣūfism, and philosophy are to be treated with suspicion despite the fact that they characterized much of the premodern *tafsīr* tradition. Walid Saleh has termed this approach to qurʾānic exegesis "radical hermeneutics" and has shown to what extent twentieth-century print politics contributed to its rise to hegemony.[26]

Disregarding the modern ideological background of print politics and the narrative of *tafsīr* that results from it may become a problem when contemporary researchers evaluate the history of qurʾānic exegesis based on Salafi paradigms, assuming that these were just as authoritative and normative centuries ago as they are today.[27] Defining the center and margins

25. Carra de Vaux 1934.

26. Saleh 2010a; 2010b.

27. See, for example, the otherwise excellent work by Riddell (2017), which seems to assume that narrative exegetical genres would have been considered suspect by a "Salafi" trend

of *tafsīr* from a modern perspective is anachronistic. For example, writing the career of *isrāʾīliyyāt* traditions as a history of failure would disregard the enormous longevity of myriad narrative traditions of Jewish or Christian origin, which is until now insufficiently understood.

Not all researchers have subscribed to the hegemony of the Salafi approach, of course. There have always been counter-currents, such as the Azhar's attempt to popularize Rāzī's[28] qurʾānic commentary, which was deeply rooted in the tradition of scholastic theology (*kalām*).[29] Some Muslim scholars – especially, but not exclusively the non-Sunnī ones – are directly opposed to Salafi hermeneutics; others scholars, such as Calder, are simply unimpressed with what they perceive as Ibn Kathīr's single-minded dogmatism.

Still, many modern researchers seem to have bought into the claim to orthodoxy that radical hermeneutics raise. This probably has reasons besides the reliance on the print politics of earlier generations, which are continued in today's digitalization politics.[30] It might be grounded in the ability of this approach to meet contemporary expectations of what exegesis should be or do. Rather than engage in mythological narration, multivocal debates or discussions that might seem inconsequential to the exegetical problems posed by the text, many modern readers of *tafsīr*, scholars included, expect it to aim at identifying the "true meaning" of the Qurʾān.

That expectation is a distinctly modern phenomenon. The idea of treating the Qurʾān as the central and unifying source of guidance for Muslims and of teaching all Muslims its meaning, as opposed to merely its recitation, was proposed by Muslim modernists in the late nineteenth century and proved hugely influential. It altered the role of *tafsīr* from a scholarly discipline to that of a guidebook that contains the ethical values of the Qurʾān.[31] Hierarchies and positions of authority within the *tafsīr* tradition shifted accordingly, favoring modernist as well as Salafi approaches. This needs to be critically reflected in academic studies of *tafsīr*, whether from insider or outsider positions. More fundamentally, implicit normative conceptions of

in seventeenth-century Aceh. For further discussion of this, see my review of the book (Pink 2018b).

28. Abū ʿAbdallāh Muḥammad b. ʿUmar Fakhr al-Dīn al-Rāzī (d. ca. 606/1209).

29. Saleh 2010b.

30. Ibn Kathīr's qurʾānic commentary, in various editions and translations, is pervasive on the internet. Nevertheless, the digitalization of *tafsīr* works is certainly not an exclusively Salafi domain. The leading *tafsīr* website, altafsir.com, for example, is run by a Jordanian foundation connected to the country's royal family which makes a great effort to promote "moderate Islam." The website offers access to an enormous number of *tafsīr* works, including Ṣūfī, Shīʿī, and Ibāḍī works; but it does conspicuously not include Islamist qurʾānic commentaries.

31. Pink 2018a, 14–29.

orthodoxy and their underlying sectarian and ideological biases need to be uncovered and questioned.

The Inner Workings and Taxonomies of *Tafsīr*: Constructions of Orthodoxy

The emergence of *tafsīr* as a genre of scholarship was a process that took several centuries and was isolated neither from the emergence of other disciplines of learning nor from larger discourses about religious legitimacy and authority. As such, exegetes have always been involved in the process of drawing boundaries not only of the discipline itself, but also of legitimate and illegitimate forms of exegesis. This resulted in the construction of various types of seemingly neutral methodological dichotomies that are, in actual fact, highly polemical.

One such notion is the distinction between exegesis based on sound tradition (*tafsīr bi l-maʾthūr* or *al-tafsīr bi l-riwāya*) and exegesis based on unfounded speculation (*tafsīr bi l-raʾy*). This distinction is fundamental to the above-mentioned project of radical hermeneutics. The problem with it is not only that it rejects any type of discussion that is not based on *ḥadīth* or "the clear meaning of the Qurʾān" as unfounded speculation; it is also that there is no hope of ever identifying a universally accepted dividing line between the two categories. One scholar's *tafsīr bi l-raʾy* is the other scholar's outstanding masterpiece. When is it ever possible to unequivocally determine whether any given interpretation is based on an irrefutably authentic *ḥadīth* or on the "clear meaning of the text"? Despite these difficulties, the distinction between *al-tafsīr bi l-raʾy* and *al-tafsīr bi l-maʾthūr* has become pervasive in academic works on qurʾānic exegesis.[32] It owes much of its prominence to Dhahabī's work on the history of exegesis, which follows a Salafi paradigm of what qurʾānic exegesis should look like.[33] However, the analytical value of this dichotomy is marginal and applying it to the history of *tafsīr* results in gross misrepresentations. As Walid Saleh puts it, "[c]lassification of a commentary as belonging to *tafsīr bi-al-maʾthūr* means only that it was acceptable to the Sunnī camp. It sheds little light on what it is actually about."[34]

The same can be said for the terms *tafsīr* and *taʾwīl*, initially largely synonymous, which came to be used to distinguish the legitimate explanation of the "external" (*ẓāhir*), that is, literal meaning of the text (*tafsīr*) from the allegedly illegitimate allegorical interpretation that seeks for an "inner"

32. For a particularly striking example of the adoption of this paradigm, see Abdul-Raof 2013.

33. Saleh 2010b.

34. Saleh 2004, 17.

(*bāṭin*) meaning (*taʾwīl*).[35] Methodologically, such a distinction is defensible. There is certainly a difference between explaining the semantics of a term such as "tree" and reading it as an allegorical reference to a caliph, imam, or mystical station.[36] The dichotomy of *tafsīr* and *taʾwīl* is, however, rarely used neutrally. It is often invoked to delegitimize one of those two approaches, most commonly by proponents of a "literal" approach who polemicize against *taʾwīl*. In the reverse case, many proponents of allegorical interpretation argue for the superiority of *taʾwīl* in gaining access to the Qurʾān's meaning but hardly claim that a literal reading is not permissible.[37]

Such polemics that took place inside the field of *tafsīr* have informed scholarship on qurʾānic exegesis to a remarkable degree. They have contributed to engendering an implicit, probably often unconscious, bias towards a particular type of Sunnī normativity. As mentioned above, for Goldziher, not only was the norm represented by Ṭabarī's tradition-based *tafsīr* but he also classified many other premodern works as deviations devoted to the defence of particular sectarian tendencies such as Ṣūfism, Shīʿism, or the theological school of the Muʿtazila. In a similar vein, but drawing slightly different boundaries, Helmut Gätje's 1971 classic reader *Koran und Koranexegese* (translated into English as *The Qur'án and its Exegesis*) comprises nine thematic chapters that present excerpts of non-allegorical works, including Sunnī exegetes as well as the Muʿtazilī al-Zamakhsharī,[38] as constituting the mainstream, followed by chapters on "mystical and philosophical," Shīʿī, and modern exegesis.[39]

The resulting impression is that of exoteric Sunnism as the invisible norm; a neutral position among a variety of "sects." This is a rather distorted picture. As recent research has underlined, Ṭabarī does not, in fact, neutrally present the entirety of the material that was at his disposal.[40] Like all Sunnī exegetes, he too belonged to a denomination and had a theological agenda. Sunnī exegetes were involved in all kinds of polemics and some of them were highly invested in the defense of their norms and view of early Islamic history. Just as some Shīʿī exegetes, such as al-Qummī (d. after 307/919) and al-Kāshī (d. ca. 1505), were prone to reading qurʾānic utterances as allegorical references to ʿAlī, Fāṭima and their descendants, the *ahl al-bayt*, there are Sunnī exegetical traditions that read qurʾānic statements as allegori-

35. Poonawala 2000.

36. See, for example, the Shīʿī allegorical interpretation of Q 14:24–26 or the Ṣūfī interpretation of Q 20:17–22 translated by Gätje; Gätje 1971, 308–311, 317–318.

37. For an example, see Pink 2018a, 206.

38. Abū l-Qāsim Maḥmūd b. ʿUmar al-Zamakhsharī (d. ca. 538/1144).

39. Gätje 1971.

40. Saleh 2016.

cal references to the excellence of Abū Bakr, the first caliph, or to the four "rightly-guided caliphs" in an obvious attempt to support the Sunnī view of the prophet's succession. For example, on Q 103:3 – "those who believe, do good deeds, urge one another to the truth, and urge one another to steadfastness" – there is a tradition on the authority of Ubayy b. Kaʿb (d. between 19/640 and 35/656) according to which the prophet Muḥammad said:

> "Those who believe," that is Abū Bakr, "do good deeds," that is ʿUmar, "urge one another to the truth," that is ʿUthmān, "and urge one another to steadfastness," that is ʿAlī.[41]

Reading the four attributes mentioned in the plural form in the verse as a reference to four individuals who were to become Sunnī Islam's "rightly-guided caliphs" is a highly allegorical and apologetic interpretation, which is nevertheless cited by a number of Sunnī exegetes.[42]

Not every Sunnī exegete subscribes to this approach, but nor does every Shīʿī or Ṣūfī exegete. Many Shīʿī exegetes use the same methods and interpretations as Sunnī exegetes do; in both cases, the exegete's sectarian identity is occasionally discernible whenever the Qurʾān touches upon concrete differences between Sunnī and Shīʿī Islam but it does not shape their entire *tafsīr*. It is one thing to establish an exegete's religious affiliation and another thing to understand his approach in his qurʾānic commentary. For example, Zamakhsharī was doubtlessly affiliated with Muʿtazila theology but that alone is not sufficient to explain his commentary's enormous popularity. It was popular for reasons that had nothing to do with his occasional attempts to argue in favor of the freedom of will and other Muʿtazilī doctrines. If Zamakhsharī's Muʿtazilī leanings had dominated the reception of his *tafsīr*, it might have been excluded from the mainstream, as Dhahabī's or Goldziher's narratives suggest; but in fact, it was central to the *madrasa* curriculum for centuries.[43]

Dividing the field of *tafsīr* into neat sectarian categories is thus problematic not only because these divisions often neglect the sectarian nature of Sunnī Islam. They also ignore commonalities between *tafsīr* work from different denominations, and they often pay insufficient attention to the shared structures that characterize them as works of *tafsīr*.[44] That is not to say that one should ignore an exegete's affiliations, allegiances, and potential biases.

41. Al-Qurṭubī (d. ca. 671/1272), *al-Jāmiʿ*, 22:466–467.

42. The tradition is probably taken from Thaʿlabī's (d. ca. 427/1035) commentary and was also cited by Qushayrī (d. ca. 465/1072), Wāḥidī (d. ca. 468/1076) in his *al-Wajīz*, and Baghawī (d. ca. 510/1117 or 516/1122), according to a search on https://altafsir.com.

43. Saleh 2013.

44. Bauer 2013b; Pink and Görke 2014.

One should, however, not expect such affiliations to be all-encompassing and all-explaining, and one should be careful not to mix an insider with an outsider perspective by privileging particular types of allegiance over others, guided by a notion of orthodoxy that can only ever by normative. The concept of orthodoxy only makes sense with respect to a specific historical context and, importantly, a specific power constellation, because orthodoxy can only exist when there is someone to defend and enforce it. Notions of orthodoxy should thus not be used as an analytical category in the academic study of *tafsīr*. Rather, it might be fruitful to ask what types of *tafsīr* were considered orthodox in a specific time and place, and for what reason; and which powers acted in its defence.[45]

Tying the study of the history of *tafsīr* more closely to political history will be helpful for understanding the precise nature of apologetics and polemics that took place within qurʾānic exegesis, rather than simply buying into them. At times, these polemics might have been largely limited to the realm of scholarship, such as the rhetorical debates that influenced Abū l-Suʿūd's[46] *tafsīr*.[47] At other times, they were tied to macro-political structures such as the ascendancy of the Fatimid caliphate and the political and, at times, terrorist activity of other branches of Ismāʿīlī Shīʿism between the tenth and thirteenth centuries. These factors might have influenced the acerbic polemical attacks by Sunnī scholars against the so-called *bāṭiniyya*, a derogatory term meant to denote branches of Islam that allegedly sought for an inner meaning of the religious sources, rather than applying its literal meaning. In this context, the defamation of *taʾwīl* as a heterodox, baseless type of allegorical exegesis that was allegedly meant to invalidate the literal meaning of the Qurʾān was an obvious strategy.[48] However, despite all criticism uttered by Ibn Taymiyya and like-minded scholars, Ṣūfism and Ṣūfism-inspired modes of qurʾānic interpretation remained embedded in the mainstream of the exegetical tradition, a fact that is fortunately increasingly recognized in Islamic Studies.[49]

Tafsīr as Discourse: Power and Social Spaces

Just like the boundaries between legitimate and illegitimate exegesis, the very nature of *tafsīr* as a genre is based on concrete social relations and power dynamics. A genre is defined by rules, the compliance with which

45. Wilson 2009; van Ess 2011, 2:1298–1308.
46. Muḥammad Abū l-Suʿūd al-ʿImādī or Ebū l-Suʿūd Efendi (d. ca. 892/1574).
47. Naguib 2013.
48. Hodgson 1960.
49. Keeler et al. 2016; Coppens 2018b.

determines whether a work is recognized as belonging to the genre or not.[50] It is thus a discourse in the Foucauldian sense: a set of norms shaped by power structures and by people who enact them or, occasionally, choose to defy them. In the case of premodern *tafsīr*, the people in question are predominantly male[51] religious scholars (*ʿulamāʾ*) who established *tafsīr* as both a textual genre and a discipline of scholarship, not necessarily in a conscious act of creation but rather through proposing and perpetuating models of interpretation that then shaped expectations of what a qurʾānic commentary should look like.

For a long time, a historical perspective on these social spaces in which *tafsīr* was produced was almost completely absent from research. Some recent studies have aimed at changing this, trying to shed light on the social function of *tafsīr* and the rules shaping it. Norman Calder's attempt to describe *tafsīr* as a genre was a starting point since he examined the rules that were at work in qurʾānic commentaries. But only much later did researchers make inquiries into the production of those rules. This production was closely tied to the status group of *ʿulamāʾ*. Karen Bauer has shed light on the crucial role of the genre rules for members of the *ʿulamāʾ* class who write a qurʾānic commentary. Adherence to those rules demonstrated a scholar's mastery of the tradition and thereby situated him at the center of an established field of knowledge.[52] Breaking the rules therefore created risks for a scholar, either of outright rejection or, more likely, of not receiving recognition for his work as a contribution to the *tafsīr* discourse. Only scholars who were either unconcerned with such recognition or who derived their authority from a different source, as might have been the case in the realm of esoteric interpretation, could afford to ignore the rules. In the modern period, when the nature of scholarship and the target group of literature on the Qurʾān shifted, the situation allowed for a conscious dismissal of the rules of *tafsīr* and the creation of entirely new forms of qurʾānic interpretation. Still, the genre of *tafsīr* persisted because of its continuing potential for enhancing a scholar's status.

Within the discursive field in which scholars produced qurʾānic commentaries, there were different social spheres and target groups that were connected to different sub-genres. Walid Saleh has proposed to distinguish between, on the one hand, encyclopedic commentaries that strove to provide an exhaustive discussion of existing exegetical opinions, or at least those considered relevant by the exegete, and, on the other hand, *madrasa*-

50. Kecia Ali has described this for the field of Islamic law. Ali 2010, 25.

51. For a discussion of the roles ascribed and permitted to women in qurʾānic exegesis, see Geissinger 2015.

52. Bauer 2015, 15.

style commentaries that succinctly summarized from among the wide array of interpretations the ones that the exegete considered the most important. The former category built and expanded upon existing scholarship and was meant to demonstrate the exegete's mastery of the tradition to other scholars; the latter category contained an exegete's briefer description of the state of the field for student audiences. This was not necessarily an inferior form of *tafsīr*; it requires a special degree of authority, after all, to present a defining summary of the most important insights of a field of scholarship, targeted at emerging scholars.

The importance of the field of education for the establishment and continuation of *tafsīr* can hardly be overestimated and yet it has barely been explored. Scholarship in Islamic Studies in the Western academe was, for a long time, preoccupied with texts rather than their place in society, whereas traditional Islamic religious scholarship was preoccupied with the degree of authority that could be attributed to any given work of *tafsīr*. Of course, when assessing that degree of authority, scholars and biographers were, and still are, highly aware of the central role of teaching: the location of a particular exegete within a chain or genealogy of teachers and students is a central component in much of the Islamic literature on the history of *tafsīr*. However, this interest is rarely connected to the question how these social circumstances shaped the production of qur'ānic commentaries and the discursive structure that was *tafsīr*.

It might be productive to frame this question in the categories of the modern social sciences: What role did the habitus of *ʿulamāʾ* play for the production of *tafsīr*? Which modes of knowledge production and what kind of power relations shaped the genre and its discursive structures? How did the rules of the genre develop to an extent where scholars were able to recognize a "normal" work of *tafsīr* as well as deviations from the standard? What were the benefits of producing a typical or deviant work of *tafsīr*, of bending the rules, breaking them, or playing with them? What examples do we have of this, and what might their reception tell us? Finding answers to those questions is largely dependent on our reading of texts, which continues to make philological expertise tremendously important. At the same time, the social sciences can inspire different ways to think about these texts.

An anthropological perspective, for example, calls into question the commonplace dichotomy of religious doctrine and religious practice. If we treat text production not as a purely intellectual or doctrinal affair but as a religious practice, the creation of doctrine itself ceases to be an abstract intellectual endeavor but rather becomes a social activity.[53] Applying such an approach to the history of *tafsīr* does have its limits, simply due to lack

53. Schielke and Debevec 2012.

of sources. Also, the field of Islamic studies lacks the amount of manpower that would enable us to make effective use of the enormous amount of material contained in manuscript collections. Nevertheless, in the past years, thinking about the social circumstances and functions of *tafsīr* has proven extremely fruitful. It has enabled Islamicists to increasingly understand *tafsīr* on its own terms, rather than compulsively searching, among the seemingly repetitive, for "original ideas" – or for the "origins of ideas."

The Quest for Origins and the Quest for Originality

Until around the turn of the millennium, the study of *tafsīr* conformed to a general, and fortunately receding, tendency in Islamic studies to focus on origins; to see "genuine Islam" represented by its foundational texts and the intellectual production of the formative period; and to show little interest in anything that happened after the "golden age" of the ʿAbbasid caliphate, let alone outside Sunnī realms.[54] Thus, the Qurʾān was considered more important than later Muslim readings of it, and if those readings occurred later than the thirteenth century CE or so, they were mostly ignored. If *tafsīr* is mainly seen as an, albeit imperfect, tool to understanding the Qurʾān, this naturally results in the assumption that those works that are historically closer to the emergence of the Qurʾān are more useful. In that regard, the general tendency in Western Islamic studies was a curious echo of the Salafi paradigm. It is no coincidence that Ṭabarī is so popular with modern Muslim scholars as well as Islamicists. His qurʾānic commentary gives the impression of providing access to the entirety of the earliest strata of Muslim qurʾānic interpretation although it has been shown that Ṭabarī was, in fact, selective and had his own biases with regard to the material he cited.[55]

As far as later works of *tafsīr* were studied, this was often with a focus on what was unique about them, on the author's theological positions and "original" ideas, with little to no interest devoted to the citation of earlier authorities or *ḥadīths*. Gätje's reader of qurʾānic exegesis, which mainly highlights theological arguments delivered by Zamakhsharī, Bayḍāwī and Rāzī, is a prime example. It was one of the merits of Norman Calder's article that he pointed out the importance both of the post-formative period and of citation practices to the entire genre, discarding the usual focus on early and "original" material.

Andrew Rippin's entry on *tafsīr* in the *Encyclopaedia of Islam*, second edition, published in 2000, likewise shows that it is possible to treat the *tafsīr* tradition as it was established and taught in *madrasas* after the tenth century

54. On periodization, see Bauer 2011, 20–24.
55. Saleh 2016.

CE as something more than a repetitive and even "sclerotic" discipline.[56] Rippin labelled the period starting in the eleventh century CE, after a curiously short "classical" period that mainly consists of Ṭabarī and his contemporaries, the "mature" period, thereby indicating that it was a natural stage in the development of a genre of scholarship that reached its culmination during that period, rather than going through a process of decline.[57]

And indeed, it is imperative to think about *tafsīr* as a genre of scholarship that underwent an evolution. During that process, it brought forth authorities, and later scholars build upon the insights of earlier scholars, rather than continuing to reinvent the wheel century after century. This type of evolution is neither unique to *tafsīr* nor to Muslim religious scholarship. Would it make sense to criticize a contemporary work of, for example, sociology for "reiterating" dozens of earlier theories, extensively explaining the state of the art, and applying a theory that was not invented by the author herself? Or should we assume that this is what a "mature" discipline looks like, with a solid body of scholarship that subsequent generations of scholars may expand upon, and the expectation that new writers in the field demonstrate their expertise by acknowledging existing scholarship? Entirely unconventional approaches that disregard the rules of the field might occasionally be refreshing; often, they come from outsiders to the field. It would hardly do justice to a discipline of learning to treat them as the only desirable type of writing, however.

A discipline of learning, whether it be twenty-first-century sociology or fifteenth-century *tafsīr*, is a discourse that has its own norms and authorities. Participants in the discourse will need to signal their knowledge and acceptance of that frame of reference in order to be accepted as such. Some participants might dare, or be able to afford to, be more independent and original than others. At times, the result of this might be that their work receives no recognition; at other times, it might be treated as a successful innovation that contributes to the development of the discipline, which is more often of the evolutionary rather than revolutionary type. There will also be participants in the discourse who take care to make their texts appear neutral, downplaying their own voice, because those texts are meant to be reference works or resources for teaching, claiming to give an unbiased overview of the field. Such works, if successful, may grant their authors high status, not *despite* their lack of innovation and creativity, but *because* of it. They provide access to the state of an entire field at a given time, from an individual scholar's perspective.

56. Fudge 2006, 125, esp. n. 19.
57. Rippin 2000.

This is true for the shorter works of *tafsīr* that Walid Saleh has dubbed "*madrasa*-style."[58] It is telling that this subgenre has largely been neglected in academic research, which has tended to focus on the more extensive encyclopedic commentaries. These certainly contain more material for analysis but it was probably the *madrasa*-style genre, the authoritative summary of the field, that most shaped and fortified the contours of the exegetical discourse. While the *madrasa*-style commentary by Zamakhsharī has been the subject of a number of studies,[59] largely due to its Muʿtazilī leanings, no in-depth study of either al-Bayḍāwī's *tafsīr* or the *Tafsīr al-Jalālayn* has been written despite the fact that they appear to have been the most widely-used qurʾānic commentaries from West Africa to Southeast Asia until at least the twentieth century, and in the case of *Tafsīr al-Jalālayn* possibly until today.[60]

Another blind spot of *tafsīr* studies becomes visible when one thinks about the fact that *tafsīr* works were not merely written by individual scholars to establish their status within their discipline but took shape in the concrete social space of the *madrasa*. When Rippin writes that "[w]ithin the mature phase of *tafsīr* there is an abundant number of works, the full dimensions of which have not been fully catalogued,"[61] this is particularly true for the *ḥāshiya*, that is, the gloss or meta-commentary, a genre of enormous importance that defies modern notions of authorship and is therefore all but ignored in most Arabic as well as practically all Western historiographies of *tafsīr*, including Rippin's.[62] Its place in premodern Muslim exegesis is attested by large numbers of manuscripts and early prints, yet, since it is usually considered derivative and unoriginal, it barely receives attention. Thus, we are far from understanding the ways in which exegetical discourses played out by way of glosses. The synchronicity between modern scholarship in the Islamicate and Western world, with respect to the lack of interest in the *ḥāshiya*, suggests that there are close parallels between religious notions of authenticity and modern academic notions of original authorship, both of which distort our view of the *tafsīr* tradition.

Tarjama and *Tafsīr*: Language and Genre

There is another conspicuous gap in many historiographies of *tafsīr*: the entire post-Mamluk tradition between the sixteenth and late nineteenth centuries is a near-complete void. One reason for this, besides a general

58. Saleh 2004, 16.
59. Lane 2006; Ullah 2017.
60. See, for example, Brigaglia 2014; Hussin 2016; van Bruinessen 1990.
61. Rippin 2000.
62. Saleh 2010b.

"golden age" bias, might be that the genre of *tafsīr* is predominantly treated as an Arabic affair: qurʾānic commentaries are perceived as authentic and authoritative when they are written in Arabic. This, again, is true for both insider and outsider perspectives, and it reflects a more general bias in Islamic studies. There is a marked tendency in Islamicate as well as Western scholarship of privileging Arabic, and to a smaller extent Persian, writings as more authentic and authoritative expressions of the normative doctrines of Islam and of relegating the study of Muslims in China, Southeast Asia or sub-Saharan Africa to the realm of ethnography.[63] Even from a religious insider perspective, it is debatable if this can be justified, and it is, indeed, debated in many places, such as in the Indonesian discussions over the role of *Islam nusantara* ("archipelago Islam") versus *Islam arab*. From an outsider perspective, there is no justification at all for privileging any particular regional tradition or language over others, beyond taking note of what relative prestige believers ascribe to these languages.

Nevertheless, we know very little about the non-Arabic exegetical field, including the centuries of Ottoman *tafsīr* production. This is slowly starting to change,[64] but we are still far from having a sound understanding of how non-Arabic exegetical traditions developed and interacted with Arabic ones.

Muslim engagement with the Qurʾān in languages other than Arabic has increased enormously in the twentieth century for a number of reasons, including the rise of nation states and national languages, the advent of mass literacy, the fact that much of that literacy is obtained in non-religious schools in which Arabic is not taught, the advent of print and other mass media, and the influence of reform movements who call for a return to the foundational sources of Islam. All this has led to the emergence and proliferation of a new exegetical genre that is commonly distinguished from *tafsīr*. In English, it is called "translation."[65] In some languages predominantly spoken by Muslims, other terms are preferred for dogmatic reasons. The idea behind this is that it is impossible to render the divine words of God in human terms with any degree of accuracy, let alone produce a faithful "equivalent." Such a faithful equivalent, however, is what translation theorists have often considered to be the aim of translation. Therefore, in Turkish, a Qurʾān translation is called *meâl* (meaning) and not *çeviri* or *tercüme* (translation). At the same time, it is semantically distinguished from a qurʾānic commentary, which is called *tefsîr*. Thus, even in languages – such

63. Petersen 2018, 3–5.
64. See e.g. Zadeh 2012; Riddell 2017.
65. Pink 2018a, 17–28.

as Turkish – that do not acknowledge the existence of Qurʾān translations, they are, in fact, perceived as a distinct genre of exegetical text, different from a qurʾānic commentary, by Muslim audiences as well as academic researchers. That genre is characterized by conciseness and coherence. It is constituted by texts that can be read separately from the Arabic Qurʾān and capture the gist of its meaning, without extensive explanations.

This is an example of an entire genre, complete with rules and boundaries, that was introduced into Muslim exegetical discourses from the outside, and highly successfully so; yet it is rarely examined as part of the field of qurʾānic exegesis despite the fact that it clearly belongs there. Qurʾān translations include any number of interpretive moves on the translators' part that are very often based on the *tafsīr* tradition, much as the *Tafsīr al-Jalālayn* and similar works tried to summarize the mainstream of the *tafsīr* tradition in a brief, accessible form.[66] However, these premodern works differed from modern Qurʾān translations in that they inextricably interwove the Arabic text with their interpretation, quoting short segments of the Qurʾān and then glossing them. This was but one of many premodern Muslim exegetical practices that we might call "translation"; but we do not usually do that, at least not without a qualifier such as "interlinear translation" or "paraphrastic translation," because we have a contemporary understanding of what a translation looks like, and it is not like the works that premodern Muslim scholars produced in vernacular languages, however concise those might have been.

This brings us back to the outset of this chapter, because what applies to *tafsīr* applies to Qurʾān translation as well. Just as it is important, for analytical purposes, to distinguish *tafsīr* as a genre from *tafsīr* as an activity, it is helpful to distinguish translation as a genre, in a modern sense, from translation as an activity. The latter might take many forms and is indeed until today practiced in many ways that differ from European models of translation. Privileging one particular form that was influenced by these European models, particularly that of Bible translation, makes perfect sense for some purposes but is misleading in other ways.

Further clarity would be gained if the dependence of many translations – including those produced by non-Muslim academics – on the *tafsīr* tradition was recognized and studied. We need to situate Qurʾān translation, as well as other types of non-Arabic exegesis, within the study of *tafsīr*. The universe of qurʾānic exegesis is large, varied, and expanding and should

66. For example, many Indonesian Qurʾān translations translate God's throne as "God's knowledge" or "God's power," which is based on an exegetical discourse that draws on theological arguments about God's attributes and anthropomorphism. See Pink 2015, 110.

not be essentialized by focusing on one particular genre, disregarding its branches, subsidiaries, and rivals, new and old.

Conclusion

In the twenty-first century, *tafsīr* studies are gaining ground. Many advances have been made towards a historically accurate understanding of what the study of *tafsīr* can and cannot tell us. This is, however, still largely confined to *tafsīr* as a genre, namely, the qurʾānic commentary. There is as yet very little research on the types of qurʾānic interpretation that were carried out outside the commentary tradition and on their hermeneutical underpinnings, despite some recent forays into that field.[67] It is not only the hermeneutical underpinnings that might vary; it is also the social function of this type of exegetical activity and its benefits for the *ʿulamāʾ* who are conducting it.

Studying *tafsīr* as a genre, within and without its boundaries, needs to be connected to a study of the environment in which it was carried out and the audiences it targeted. Such a socio-historical reading of *tafsīr* needs to be mindful of normative dimensions, not in order to disprove or dismiss them, but to understand the nature and the limits of their claim to orthodoxy as part of the discursive structure of the genre. Orthodoxy is always a relational phenomenon and, like any norm that shapes a discourse, it needs to be constantly reinstated and defended. *Tafsīr*, besides many other genres of scholarship, is a locus of such practices and needs to be read as such, whether it is Sunnī, Shīʿī or Ṣūfī.

Of course, *tafsīr*, or qurʾānic exegesis, is by no means exceptional in this regard. Any scholarly discipline is a discourse with its own boundaries, functions, implicit rules and power structures. Some fields, such as Islamic law or *ḥadīth* studies, have been studied far more consistently in that framework than qurʾānic exegesis, though. Applying the discursive lens to *tafsīr* will further our understanding of the mechanisms by which disciplines emerge and systems of knowledge are produced. It will furthermore show how these are translated into specific literary structures and hermeneutical strategies. This will allow the field of *tafsīr* studies to move beyond normative biases, whether these are explicitly expressed and framed in religious terms or implicitly taken for granted.

67. Görke and Pink 2014; Bauer 2015; Mirza 2017.

Bibliography

Abdul-Raof, H. 2013. *Schools of Qur'anic Exegesis: Genesis and Development*. London.

Ali, K. 2010. *Marriage and Slavery in Early Islam*. Cambridge, Mass.

Bauer, K. 2013a. "Justifying the Genre: A Study of Introductions to Classical Works of *Tafsīr*." In *Aims, Methods and Contexts of Qur'anic Exegesis (2nd/8th–9th/15th c.)*, edited by K. Bauer, 39–65. Oxford.

———. 2013b. "Introduction." In *Aims, Methods and Contexts of Qur'anic Exegesis (2nd/8th–9th/15th c.)*, edited by K. Bauer, 1–16. Oxford.

———. 2015. *Gender Hierarchy in the Qur'ān: Medieval Interpretations, Modern Responses*. New York.

Bauer, Th. 2011. *Die Kultur der Ambiguität. Eine andere Geschichte des Islams*. Berlin.

Brigaglia, A. 2014. "*Tafsīr* and the Intellectual History of Islam in West Africa: The Nigerian Case." In Tafsīr *and Islamic Intellectual History: Exploring the Boundaries of a Genre*, edited by A. Görke and J. Pink, 379–415. Oxford.

van Bruinessen, M. "Kitab kuning: Books in Arabic Script Used in the Pesantren Milieu." *Bijdragen tot de Taal-, Land- en Volkenkunde* 146:226–269.

Calder, N. 1993. "Tafsīr from Ṭabarī to Ibn Kathīr. Problems in the Description of a Genre, Illustrated with Reference to the Story of Abraham." In *Approaches to the Qur'ān*, edited by A. Shareef and G. R. Hawting, 101–140. London.

Carra de Vaux, B. 1934. "Tafsīr." *Encyclopaedia of Islam*. 1st ed. 1913–1936.

Coppens, P. 2018a. "Sufi Qurʾān Commentaries, Genealogy and Originality." *Journal of Sufi Studies* 7:102–124.

———. 2018b. *Seeing God in Sufi Qur'an Commentaries: Crossings between this World and the Otherworld*. Edinburgh.

al-Dhahabī, M. 1961. *Al-Tafsīr wa-l-mufassirūn*. Cairo.

Ess, J. van. 2011. *Der Eine und das Andere: Beobachtungen an islamischen häresiographischen Texten*. Berlin.

Forster, R. 2001. *Methoden mittelalterlicher arabischer Qur'ānexegese am Beispiel von Q 53, 1–18*. Berlin.

Fudge, B. 2006. "Qurʾānic Exegesis in Medieval Islam and Modern Orientalism." *Welt des Islams* 46:115–147.

Gätje, H. 1971. *Koran und Koranexegese*. Zurich.

Geissinger, A. 2015. *Gender and Muslim Constructions of Exegetical Authority: A Rereading of the Classical Genre of Qur'ān Commentary*. Leiden.

Goldziher, I. 1920. *Die Richtungen der islamischen Koranauslegung*. Leiden.

Görke, A., and J. Pink. 2014. *Tafsīr and Islamic Intellectual History: Exploring the Boundaries of a Genre*. Oxford.

Hodgson, M. G. S. 1960. "Bāṭiniyya." *Encyclopaedia of Islam*. 2nd ed. 1960–2004.

Hussin, H. 2016. "The Emergence of Qurʾanic Exegesis in Malaysia." In *The Qurʾān in the Malay-Indonesian World*, edited by M. Daneshgar, P. G. Riddell, and A. Rippin, 137–174. London and New York.

Keeler, A., and S. Rizvi, eds. 2016. *The Spirit and the Letter: Approaches to the Esoteric Interpretation of the Qur'an*. Oxford.

Lane, A. J. 2006. *A Traditional Mu'tazilite Qurʾān Commentary: The* Kashshāf *of Jār Allāh al-Zamakhsharī*. Leiden: Brill.

McAuliffe, J. D. 2003. "The Genre Boundaries of Qur'ānic Commentary." In *With Reverence for the Word. Medieval Scriptural Exegesis in Judaism, Christianity, and Islam*, edited by J. Dammen McAuliffe, B. D. Walfish, and J. W. Goering, 445–461. Oxford.

Mirza, Y. Y. 2017. "Ibn Taymiyya as Exegete: Moses' Father-in-law and the Messengers in *Sūrat Yā Sīn*." *Journal of Qur'anic Studies* 19:39–71.

Naguib, S. 2013. "Guiding the Sound Mind: Ebu's-su'ūd's *Tafsir* and Rhetorical Interpretation of the Qur'an in the Post-Classical Period." *Journal of Ottoman Studies* 27:1–52.

Petersen, K. 2018. *Interpreting Islam in China: Pilgrimage, Scripture, and Language in the Han Kitab*. Oxford.

Pink, J. Forthcoming. "Ibn Taymiyya, the Bible and the Qurʾān: From Polemics to Scriptural Hermeneutics."

———. 2018a. *Muslim Qur'ānic Interpretation Today: Media, Genealogies and Interpretive Communities*. Sheffield.

———. 2018b. "Riddell, Peter G. Malay Court Religion, Culture and Language." *Orientalistische Literaturzeitung* 113:482–484.

———. 2015. "'Literal Meaning' or 'Correct ʿ*aqīda*'? The Reflection of Theological Controversy in Indonesian Qur'an Translations." *Journal of Qur'anic Studies* 17:100–120.

Pink, J., and A. Görke. 2014. "Introduction." In *Tafsīr and Islamic Intellectual History: Exploring the Boundaries of a Genre*, edited by A. Görke and J. Pink, 1–23. Oxford.

Poonawala, I. 2000. "Taʾwīl." *Encyclopaedia of Islam*. 2nd ed. 1960–2004.

al-Qurṭubī, Abū ʿAbdallāh Muḥammad b. Aḥmad b. Abī Bakr. 2006. *Al-Jāmiʿ li-aḥkām al-Qurʾān*. Beirut.

Riddell, P. G. 2017. *Malay Court Religion, Culture and Language: Interpreting the Qur'an in 17th-century Aceh*. Leiden.

Rippin, A. 2000. "Tafsīr." *Encyclopaedia of Islam*. 2nd ed. 1960–2004.

Saleh, W. A. 2004. *The Formation of the Classical* Tafsīr *Tradition: The Qurʾān Commentary of al-Thaʿlabī (d. 427/1035)*. Leiden.

——. 2010a. “Ibn Taymiyya and the Rise of Radical Hermeneutics: An Analysis of *An Introduction to the Foundations of Qur'ānic Exegesis*.” In *Ibn Taymiyya and His Times*, edited by Y. Rapoport and S. Ahmed, 123–162. Oxford.

——. 2010b. “Preliminary Remarks on the Historiography of *tafsīr* in Arabic: A History of the Book Approach.” *Journal of Qur'anic Studies* 12:6–40.

——. 2013. “The Gloss as Intellectual History: The *ḥāshiyahs* on *al-Kashshāf*.” *Oriens* 41:217–259.

——. 2016. “Rereading al-Ṭabarī through al-Māturīdī: New Light on the Third Century Hijrī.” *Journal of Qur'anic Studies* 18:180–209.

Schielke, S., and L. Debevec. 2012. “Introduction.” In *Ordinary Lives and Grand Schemes: an Anthropology of Everyday Religion*, edited by S. Schielke and L. Debevec, 1–16. New York.

Tottoli, R. 2013. “Methods and Contexts in the Use of Hadiths in Classical *tafsīr* Literature: The Exegesis of Q. 21:85 and Q. 17:1.” In *Aims, Methods and Contexts of Qur'anic Exegesis (2nd/8th–9th/15th c.)*, edited by K. Bauer, 199–215. Oxford.

——. 2014. “Interrelations and Boundaries between *tafsīr* and Hadith Literature: The Exegesis of Mālik b. Anas' *Muwaṭṭaʾ* and Classical Qur'anic Commentaries.” In *Tafsīr and Islamic Intellectual History: Exploring the Boundaries of a Genre*, edited by A. Görke and J. Pink, 147–186. Oxford.

Ullah, K. 2017. *Al-Kashshāf: Al-Zamakhsharī's Mu'tazilite Exegesis of the Qur'an*. Berlin.

Wilson, M. B. 2009. “The Failure of Nomenclature: The Concept of ‘Orthodoxy’ in the Study of Islam.” *Comparative Islamic Studies* 3:169–194.

Zadeh, T. 2012. *The Vernacular Qur'an: Translation and the Rise of Persian Exegesis*. Oxford.

4

Overlooked Modern Persian-Shīʿī *Tafsīr* Schools: The Maktab-e Tafkīk in Contemporary Iran

S. M. Hadi Gerami

As an Iranian teenager, I was impressed with Tehran's traditional educational system. In particular, I was introduced to a new religious-intellectual school of thought, called "Circles (*jalasāt*) of Tafkīkī Teachings," where I passed various courses pertaining to Shīʿī Islam. The Tafkīkīs belonged to a new-born Shīʿī trend impressed with pre-revolutionary intellectual and religious works. It aims to reform Shīʿī Islamic tradition significantly in light of the Qurʾān and Sunna.

Despite being acquainted with their intellectual principles during the last twenty years, neither I nor any of my former colleagues paid attention to the way Tafkīkīs viewed and interpreted the Qurʾān. Soon, it became very clear to me that this is an under-researched issue not examined by either Western or Muslim scholars of Islam in general and of *tafsīr* in particular.

Studying in both Islamic and Western academic contexts has thus led me to combine the so-called western-oriented critical approach to shed light on the Tafkīkī *tafsīr*, which is an unexamined side of the Iranian exegetical intellectual tradition.

Introduction[1]

It is a commonplace belief that Ignác Goldziher (d. 1921) added "*tafsīr* studies" into western Islamic studies literature for the first time in 1920. His "Die Richtungen der islamischen Koranauslegung" (Schools of Qurʾānic Commentators) is still considered one of our main sources linking classical and modern Islamic exegetical thought. Many Islamicists have followed his approach, which primarily views *tafsīr* through the lens of Arabo-centric sources. The result is that *tafsīr* studies now suffers from a lack of reference

1. I thank Majid Daneshgar, Ali Imran, and Sajjad Rizvi for their feedback and comments on the earlier draft of this paper. I should also thank Mohammad Ghandehari and Hossein Mofid for their information on some sources of this paper.

to Shīʿī and Ṣūfī commentaries produced and circulated in non-Arabic contexts.

The post-9/11 period has witnessed scholars begin to (re-)examine different aspects of Islam, including its literary sources. Though many have begun to unpack the history of *tafsīr*, many still follow Goldziher and largely focus on commentaries in the Arabic language.

Thanks to a *small* number of historians and Islamicists, non-Arabic commentaries are now taken into account. Peter G. Riddell, Travis Zadeh, M. Brett Wilson, and Susan Gunasti have shown, for example, that *tafsīr al-Qurʾān* is a complex of interconnected Arabic and non-Arabic sources produced over the course of history. Riddell, who began his research on Malay-Indonesian exegetical literature in the 1980s, published a new monograph in which he shows how Malay commentaries on the Qurʾān produced in the seventeenth century are linked to classical Arabic sources such as *Tafsīr al-Baghawī*, *Tafsīr al-Jalālayn*, *Tafsīr al-Khāzin*, *Tafsīr al-Bayḍāwī*, *Saḥīḥ al-Bukhārī*, among others.[2] Moreover, Zadeh as well as Wilson and Gunasti have depicted the rise and development of Persian and [Ottoman] Turkish exegetical literature, respectively.[3]

Apart from these significant works, however, a huge research gap remains observable. What do we really know about Persian Shīʿī exegetical movements since the early sixteenth century, when the Safavid rulers chose Shīʿism as the state religion of Persia and promoted it across their territory? The majority of Safavid studies in European languages dealt with Safavid court, commerce, culture, philosophy, and literature with very few touching on the notion and development of *tafsīr*.[4] One may wonder how and under what circumstances *tafsīr*, as an independent Islamic discipline, was systematically produced during the Safavid period and onwards. This is despite the fact that Persian scholars of Islam inclined to produce more indigenized commentaries on the Qurʾān on the basis of Shīʿī teachings as well as Persian literary sources. In what follows I refer to this as "Persian Shīʿī Tafsīr Literature."

Scholars' interest in [Persian-] Shīʿism studies peaked in the late 1970s in general and more specifically after the Iranian revolution of 1979. We should admit the tremendous impact of the revolution on different subsets of Middle Eastern and Islamic studies. As such, post-revolutionary Iran has been the center of recent scholarly attention.

To examine the content and evolution of post-revolutionary Shīʿī *tafāsīr*, the majority of studies, both inside and outside of Iran, largely dealt with

2. See Riddell 2001; 2017.
3. Zadeh 2012; Wilson 2014; and Gunasti 2019.
4. For instance, see Lawson 2012.

prominent Iranian clerics, such as Muḥammad Ḥusayn Ṭabāṭabāʾī (d. 1981) and Ruh Allah Khomeini (d. 1989), among others. The result is that commentaries on the Qurʾān by other Persian-Shīʿī scholars have not been thoroughly examined yet.

Furthermore, many Western scholars who work on *tafsīr* are largely ignorant of local primary and secondary sources produced in Iran. Due to the lack of philological expertise, their study of Muslim *tafsīr* literature is not accurate and remains inspired by a "Goldziherian" approach. Often overlooked is whether new schools of *tafsīr* have been established and promoted in contemporary Iran.

This chapter tries not only to introduce a new exegetical school in Iran, but also displays the way a pre-revolutionary school of *tafsīr*, namely, the *Maktab-e Tafkīk*, has treated the Qurʾān differently.

Since the early twentieth century, much of the Muslim world has been wrestling with the notion of intellect (*al-ʿaql*) and its application to daily life. Arab commentators and activists based in Egypt, including Muḥammad ʿAbduh (d. 1905), Rashīd Riḍā (d. 1935), Ṭanṭāwī Jawharī (d. 1940), among many others, raised serious questions regarding how, for example, a Muslim should treat Islamic-qurʾānic teachings in the modern world by means of *ʿaql*. Subsequently, other Muslim communities became interested in finding answers for such questions. Nonetheless, they were rejected by local traditionalists, fundamentalists, and various groups of religious thinkers whose main reference to interpret the Qurʾān was the Qurʾān itself, the Sunna, or both.[5]

In this context, the *Maktab-e Tafkīk* emerged in Iran, which was not only scripture-centric, but was also a deductive-based school of thought. In the early twentieth century, Mīrzā Mahdī Iṣfahānī (d. 1365/1945) founded a Shīʿī theological school, called *Maktab-e Tafkīk* (The School of Separation), in Mashhad, Iran.[6] Contrary to many Shīʿī clerics, he believed that the Islamic creed ought to be independent of philosophy (*falsafa*) and mysticism (*taṣawwuf*). He considered the Qurʾān and *ḥadīth* as the only reliable sources according to which the Islamic thought and theological system should be justified.[7] He wished to encourage Muslims to reread Islamic concepts merely on the basis of the Qurʾān and *ḥadīth*.[8]

5. We may also name Tawfīq Ṣidqī and Amīn al-Khūlī, who raised different issues about reading the Qurʾān.

6. Some scholars have discussed the three Tafkīkī pioneers, namely Mīrzā Mahdī Iṣfahānī, Sheikh Mojtabā Qazvīnī (d. 1386/1966), and Seyed Mūsā Zarābādī (d. 1353/1932), in respect to their roles in the school's founding (see Gleave 2010, 72–73; Rizvi 2012, 492).

7. To get a general impression of their critical approach, see Rizvi 2012, 501–502, where he discusses the Tafkīkī attitude to the Sadrian notion of bodily resurrection.

8. To get the most extended discussion on his life, see Mofīd 1387/2008, 22–38; Ḥakīmī

According to Iṣfahānī, the Shīʿī approach to the "intellect" is different from that of other Muslim philosophers, who have been largely and deeply influenced by translations of Greek philosophical works. By contrast, he contends that Shīʿī *aḥādīth* clearly introduce the human intellect as *ʿaql-e fiṭrī* or "innate intellect."[9] In terms of *ijtihād*, as will be seen, Tafkīkīs strictly deny any affiliation to the Akhbārī School and insist on their adherence to the *mujtahid* (jurist).[10]

The "Maktab-e Tafkīk" is meant for refining contemporary religious thought according to the so-called genuine and purified revealed knowledge. It emphasizes the thorough independence of Islam from all other human sciences, and criticizes the incorporation of philosophy and mysticism into religious knowledge.[11]

This new trend was also referred to as *Maktab-e Maʿārif-e Ahl al-Bayt* (the school of the teachings of *Ahl al-Bayt*)[12] or *Maktab-e ḥawza* (Islamic Shīʿī seminary) of Khorasan,[13] because it emerged in the *ḥawza* of Mashhad, where the tomb of the eighth Shīʿī Imam, ʿAlī b. Mūsā, is located. Upon the death of Iṣfahānī, a number of his disciples, including Mīrzā Javād Āqā Tehrānī (d. 1410/1989), Sheikh Ḥasan ʿAlī Morvārīd (d. 1425/2004), Sheikh Maḥmūd Ḥalabī (d. 1419/1998), Sheikh Mojtabā Qazvīnī (d. 1386/1966) and Sheikh Muḥammad Bāqer Malekī Mīyānajī (d. 1419/1998), promoted his teachings.[14] Nonetheless, the title of the school, "Maktab-e Tafkīk," was coined by Moḥammad Riḍā Ḥakīmī (b. 1353/1935), who not only was a religious expert but also a close friend of the Iranian religious social activist, ʿAlī Shariʿatī (d. 1977). Apart from the school's social agenda, which was in contrast to a set of social and political policy decided by the Pahlavi rulers, the school's reading of Islam was controversial, too. According to Ḥakīmī:

1382/2003(a), 211–235; Gleave 2010, 72. This attitude might have been derived from what Shīʿī jurists had already pointed out (on this attitude among imāmī scholars and their works in this regard, see Anzali, and Gerami 2017; Naṣīrī 1386/2007, 383–406; Makārem 1378/1999; Makārem 1380/2001).

9. For further information on *ʿaql-e fiṭrī* according to Iṣfahānī and Ḥakīmī, see Dānesh Shahrakī 1396/2017.

10. See the following pages.

11. Ḥakīmī 1382/2003(a), 46–47. R. Gleave describes this position more smoothly as such: "The principal doctrine of the school is that there is a category distinction between human concepts and ideas on the one hand, and the pure divine knowledge on the other. By this, they mean that ideas derived from the former category cannot be used to inform or explicate notions contained within the latter. In the former category one finds philosophical truths and inner, mystical truth (*falsafa* and *ʿirfān*) and in the latter, one finds revelation (*waḥy*)." See Gleave 2010, 74.

12. See a very wide usage of this entitling in Seyedān 1378/1999.

13. Ḥakīmī 1384/2005, 47.

14. On his impact on Shīʿī Iranian discourse, see Ḥakīmī 1382/2003(b), 47–55; Ḥakīmī 1382/2003(a), 221–225; Rizvi 2012, 493; Gleave 2010, 73.

> The School stands for an approach distinguishing three methods of perception: of the Qurʾān, of mysticism and of philosophy, derived from three epistemic schools rooted in the history of human knowledge and thought.[15]

The next generation of Tafkīkīs dedicated their time to *tafsīr* production, that which enabled them to refine religious knowledge and separate it from that of human sciences.[16] Contrary to Robert Gleave's suggestion that this *Maktab* is generally a "reformed" version of earlier Shīʿī schools,[17] some Tafkīkīs' commentaries on the Qurʾān, are replete with new exegetical ideas and approaches, which have yet to receive the attention they deserve.[18] It seems that the Maktab-e Tafkīk can be considered as also having an independent school of *tafsīr*, namely, "*Maktab-e tafsīr ḥawza-yi Khorasan.*"[19]

One of the most significant commentaries produced by Tafkīkīs is *Manāhij al-Bayān* by Muḥammad Bāqer Malekī Mīyānajī. Although a few studies in Iranian academia have addressed this commentary, they have tended to examine it only in terms of its methodology and failed to study how Mīyānajī elaborated his project to introduce and establish a new *tafsīrī* school in contemporary Iran.[20]

Earlier studies in Persian languages have gone through Iṣfahānī's school from a polemical perspective by criticizing his independent approach to the Qurʾān. All of them, however, are in agreement that the Maktab-e Tafkīk, due to its exegetical features, may be regarded as a new school in comparison to other schools of *tafsīr*. Despite this, many of these studies have failed to provide an objective and systematic analysis of Tafkīkīs' hermeneutical perspectives.[21]

Meanwhile in the western academia the tendency has been to focus on how this school approaches *ʿaql*, *naql*, *falsafa*, including its relationship with Akhbārism and its position in contemporary Shīʿī discourse. For some

15. Ḥakīmī 1382/2003(a), 46–47; for more on this appellation and what tafkīk means, see Gleave 2010, 74; Rizvi 2012, 493–495.

16. As it will be seen later in the paper.

17. Gleave 2010, 71.

18. Recently, in Iranian academia, a researcher has tried to address the issue in a comprehensive fashion, though he seems to have not produced an unbiased academic investigation in this regard. See ʿAlī-Akbar-zādeh 1392.

19. For the first time, Gerami suggested this epithet. See Gerami 1388/2009, 134.

20. The most extended academic work in the field is ʿAlī-naqī Khodāyārī's MA thesis, in which he addresses this commentary to investigate its approach to *tafsīr*. Later, he published an essay out of his thesis (Khodāyārī 1379/2000; Khodāyārī 1381/2002). Besides, S. M. ʿAlī Ayāzī has produced a lengthy work on this commentary (Ayāzī 1377/1998).

21. For example, see Masʿūdī 1387/2008, 39; Hemāmī 1390/2011; Hemāmī, 1391/2012(a); Hemāmī, 1391/2012(b).

scholars, the epistemological point of view of the school represents a strong anti-intellectual trend in modern Shīʿī thought. Ali Paya, in his "*normative*," "*philosophical*" as well as "*polemical*" essay claims that Tafkīkīs' epistemological model will not bring about the emergence of "healthy knowledge." He argues that the epistemic claims of the school are unreliable since they fail to distinguish between the actual content of the message, viz., the Qurʾān and the genuine *ḥadīth* on the one hand, and believers' perceptions of it on the other. Paya even imagines that if the Prophet and Imams were alive today and could speak to us directly, each one of us could only understand them by means of our reconstructions of their utterances, and the degree of representativeness of such reconstructions would differ from individual to individual as a result of differences in the individual's knowledge and interpretive abilities.[22]

Sajjad Rizvi has also examined the legitimacy of philosophy between the philosophical school of Ṣadr al-Dīn Muḥammad Shīrāzī, also known as Mullā Ṣadrā (d. ca. 1 045/1635), dominant in the present Shīʿī seminary in Iran, and its detractors in the Maktab-e Tafkīk circle. He deems that this school and its objections to the hegemony of Sadrian philosophy in the *ḥawza* cannot just be dismissed as unsophisticated obscurantism. As in the earlier epistemological conflict located primarily in jurisprudence between the Uṣūlīs and the Akhbārīs, the struggle between the Sadrians and Tafkīkīs, is really about the true nature of Shīʿī intellectual life. The most important point highlighted by Rizvi is that the Tafkīk is not an anti-rational movement; rather, it emphasizes that our assumptions about the nature of the intellect and the epistemic faculties need to be challenged and investigated in the light of scripture.[23]

Recently, Saeid Jazari Mamoei published a monograph on the Tafkīk school. He considers the growing influence of the Maktab-e Tafkīk on Shīʿī *ḥawza* as an important phenomenon deserving of special attention. He argues that it is a movement according to which faith and intellect are quite distinct without being hostile to one another. He considers that the Tafkīk school separates the language and multiple discourses of Scripture as well as philosophy and mysticism. He points out that the school also distinguishes between a legitimate form of intellectual inquiry that is rooted in revelation, and two artificial forms of inquiry that represent the "deviations" of philosophy and mysticism.[24]

Also R. Gleave, in addition to his discussions on how much Tafkīk is

22. See Paya 2016, 411–412.
23. See Rizvi 2012, 502–503.
24. See Jazari Mamoei 2016.

relevant to Akhbārism, has also addressed the school's approach to the interpretation of Islamic scriptural texts.[25]

Throughout history, the dilemma of identity as the main base of social recognition has been an important challenge with which new schools have grappled. Intellectual ideas hardly suffice to establish new schools, discourses, or networks if the community fails to recognize them. History reveals that putting forward a critical discourse has always been the best tool through which new identities have been established and recognized. For it is the ground upon which a new school can distinguish itself from other traditional attitudes. Suggesting innovative ideas, in addition to critical approach, can also be considered as another factor making newborn schools more able to highlight their intellectual identity.

This chapter sheds more light on how one particular commentator, Malekī Mīyānajī, established a particular *tafsīrī* school that belongs to the Maktab-e Tafkīk. What I will try to elaborate on is something beyond the usual conception of studying *tafsīrī* approaches. The aim of study is not Mīyānajī's hermeneutics per se. Rather, I take a fresh look, using a sociological lens, at his "project" to establish a new hermeneutical identity in contemporary Iranian *tafsīrī* discourse. That is, I show how he has introduced and presented himself and the school, with an aim to stabilize the Tafkīkī hermeneutical identity.

To that end, in addition to usual discussions on his hermeneutics and *tafsīr*, I will argue that the way he elaborated his "exegetical project" shows that his aim was not just to put forward some new *tafsīrī* ideas. On the contrary, he also introduced and established an independent *tafsīrī* school for Tafkīkīs to complete the Tafkīkī schema also in the Qur'ān interpretation. We see this in his substantial critical attitude toward famous contemporary commentators, philosophers, and mystics in addition to his efforts to suggest new and independent *tafsīrī* ideas.

Maktab-e Tafkīk: Akhbārī or Uṣūlī?

Akhbārism refers to a school of thought founded by earlier Shīʿī scholars, one which systematically and thoroughly relies on Shīʿī traditions. The conflict between the Akhbārīs and Uṣūlīs dates back to Mawlā Muḥammad Amīn Astarābādī (d. ca. 1 033/1624). More than merely possessing a theological or

25. See Gleave 2010, 87–91. Also, as far as I know, Hamid Reza Maghsoodi wrote his PhD dissertation under the supervision of R. Gleave on the Tafkīk. However, I was not able to view his dissertation.

doctrinal nature, Astarābādī's school had a legal nature. Astarābādī was trying to confront the rise of Uṣūlī approaches to law adopted by Shīʿī scholars.[26] Having encountered numerous contradictions in the traditional Islamic legal methodology, or *uṣūl al-fiqh*, he spent a significant period of time in Medina to revise and study prophetic traditions. This ultimately led him to compile his famous book, *al-Fawāʾid al-Madanīyya.*[27] Nevertheless, Astarābādī did not consider himself the founder of the Akhbārī school. Instead, he has stated that the methods used by the early Imāmīs to arrive at the *aḥkām* (legal rulings) differed from those used by the later Uṣūlīs.[28] It seems that he referred to the early *Imāmī* traditionalists by the term "Akhbārīs" just to show that their approach was based on the usage of *aḥādīth*. He considered himself the only adherent to this early school. This is probably why Astarābādī has often been introduced as the founder of the Akhbārī school.[29]

Since the Tafkīk has been accused of being the new Akhbārism,[30] it is necessary to investigate the relationship between the Tafkīk and Akhbārism. Both insiders and outsiders have discussed whether this is an Akhbārī or anti-rational movement. There are a few scholars who have deemed that Tafkīk is not an anti-rational movement. For instance, even though Rizvi acknowledges the school attacks on the legitimacy of *falsafa*, he argues that the school insists that our assumptions about the nature of the intellect and the epistemic faculties (*qovāy-e maʿrefatī*) need to be challenged and investigated in the light of scripture.[31]

However, the *Tafkīk* is largely known as a pro-Akhbārism school of thought, which does not take rationality into account seriously. Other scholars who believe that Tafkīkīs' religious concerns are in line with those of Akhbārīs.[32] Ḥakīmī, the pioneer leader of the school, argues that it is im-

26. There is an entire body of Western studies on the Akhbārī-Uṣūlī conflict. One of the most recent scholarly studies of Astarābādī's school is what Rula Jurdi Abisaab has written at length on the epistemology and legal methodology of Astarābādī. Rula Jurdi Abisaab argued that Akhbārism maintained discursive ties to earlier trends within the Shīʿī and Sunnī traditions but she rejected the view that Astarābādī's traditionalism was a mere resumption of past leanings in legal, *ḥadīth*, and *rijāl* scholarship. According to her, it went further in attacking ijtihād, which had developed only in the thirteenth century. More importantly, she noted that, "the meanings of Akhbārī and Ūṣūlī changed over time and across genres and scholarly contexts," but they carried a specific meaning in the late sixteenth century under the Safavids (Abisaab 2015, 18; for more information on this conflict, see Newman 1992; Newman 1986; Cole 1985, 1722–1780; Gleave 2000; Gleave 2007; Kohlberg 1987; Kohlberg 2011; Algar 1995; Algar 2011; Madelung 2012).

27. Astarābādī (d. 1033/1624), al-Fawāʾid al-Madanīyyah, 27.

28. Astarābādī, al-Fawāʾid al-Madanīyyah, 91–92, 97, 104, 111, 136.

29. Astarābādī, al-Fawāʾid al-Madanīyyah, 104.

30. Mūsavī 1382/2003, 6; Dīnānī 1384/2005, 293.

31. See Rizvi 2012, 503.

32. For instance, see Sorūsh 1395/2016, 64; Sājedī 1397/2018.

possible to apply the term "Akhbārī" to the Maktab-e Tafkīk as Akhbārī is restricted to a movement concerned primarily with jurisprudence, while the Maktab-e Tafkīk addressed the matters of belief.[33] According to him, the Tafkīkīs' claim that their approach is not identical with the Akhbārī approach in that the Tafkīkī scholars use the tool of *uṣūl al-fiqh* whereas the Akhbārīs are against the use of the intellect and the practice of *fuqahā* (jurists) who act as sources of emulations (*marjaʿ-e taqlīd*) for the faithful.[34] Ḥossein Mofīd, one of the Iranian editors of Tafkīkī books, has written a paper on *ḥojjiyyat-e ẓavāher* (probative validity of the text of the Qurʾān) from the stand point of Iṣfahānī. He argues that even though we cannot recognize Iṣfahānī's approaches to be in complete agreement with Uṣūlīs, he cannot also be counted amongst the Akhbārīs due to his belief in *ḥojjiyyat-e ẓavāher*, which has never been upheld by the Akhbārīs. Seemingly, Iṣfahānī's belief in *ḥojjiyyat-e ẓavāher* is the main argument for his adherents to prove his affiliation with the Uṣūlī school.[35]

Gleave, on the contrary, states that the school could most likely be considered as following Akhbārism. In this regard, he argues that Iṣfahānī's statements are not fraught with the usual anti-Akhbārī polemic, one which is usually expected from an Uṣūlī.[36] According to him,

> With respect to the problematic relationship between Akhbārīsm and the Maktab-e Tafkīk, the above (emphatically preliminary) observations indicate that the Tafkīkī method of argumentation can, in certain areas, be seen as a continuation of previous Akhbārī explorations.... The two movements represent the most successful explorations of the scripturalist impetus within post-classical/modern Shīʿī Islam. That the scripturalist label is apt for both movements implies that it is in this minimal sense that the *Maktab-e Tafkīk* might be considered a continuation of certain elements within Akhbārīsm. Such an assessment, however, should not lead to the inevitable conclusions either that there is a lack of originality within the "Maktab", or that there is a clear line of influence between the two.[37]

Even though Gleave has presented some similarities between the two schools' conceptions of *ʿaql* and their use of qurʾānic language, his argument

33. Ḥakīmī 1382/2003, 366–367; Gleave 2010, 82.

34. Ḥakīmī 1382/2003, 41; Paya 2016, 395.

35. See Mofīd 1389/2010, 21–27; also, see Mofīd 1395/2016. At the same time some other Tafkīkīs would like to insist on and show that Iṣfahānī has a Uṣūlī approach and is affiliated with that school (see Ṭāromī 1391/2012; Shāhrūdī 1397/2018).

36. Gleave 2010, 82.

37. Gleave 2010, 92.

is inadequate, primarily because he fails to distinguish clearly between "continuity" and "similarity." It is undeniable that several similarities may exist between the two schools, or any other two schools for that matter. However, this does not suffice to infer the continuity.

Relatedly, it is also very important to see which characteristics have been adduced to discuss the question of continuity. Obviously, the argument needs to be based on those characteristics belonging exclusively to Akhbārism. From an insider perspective, Ḥakīmī's emphasis on the anti-*uṣūlī* nature of Akhbārism does not mean that the movement is restricted to such legal characteristics; rather, an insider investigator knows that the anti-*uṣūlī* characteristic is the only unchallengeable feature that one can clearly attribute to Akhbārism; for being exclusively in the Akhbārī movement and not in others.[38] As such, epithets like "rational" or "anti-rational," which are used in some studies, are not appropriate jargon for such analysis. For instance, Ali Paya in his "normative polemical dialogue" with the Tafkīkīs was successful to a great extent in showing that the Tafkīk had an epistemological defeat, since the Tafkīk fails to make the basic distinction between the actual content of a message, in this case the Qurʾān and the genuine *aḥadīth*, and believers' understanding of the message in question.[39] However, one may raise the objection that he has put some completely "abstract concepts" like rationality, anti-rationality, or non-rationality at the core of his argumentation. To me, as a *contextualist historian of ideas*, not an *analytic philosopher*, such abstract concepts have no capacity to be at the core of such argumentation. Such conceptions have no concrete meaning and would differ from individual to individual according to their intellectual and social backgrounds. Accordingly, one should add some more objective factors to analyze and compare schools of thoughts. In our case, if we want to use epithets such as "Akhbārism," "anti-*uṣūlism*," "rationalism" and so on, we can utilize them in the context of who used such terminologies and also when and how, not in an abstract fashion. According to this epistemological notion, studying the continuity between the Tafkīk and Akhbārism, without putting the anti-*uṣūlī* epithet of Akhbārism at the core of argumentation, as the most objective and concrete factor of Akhbārism, will remain challengeable.

38. In addition to what Ḥakīmī has mentioned in this regard, a Tafkīkī can also argue that his colleagues have authored an entire body of *uṣūl al-fiqh* works, and have also admitted the Ijāzeh Ijtihād (the permission to practice Ijtihād), which are not usual in Akhbārism. Furthermore, the Tafkīkīs have accused Akhbārīs of refusing the Intellect authenticity (see Morvārīd 1418/1997, 13). It has even been reported that Malekī Mīyānajī himself had some disputes with an Akhbārī jurist in Ardabil, a city in northwestern Iran (see Malekī 1372/1993, 70).

39. Paya 2016, 411–412.

Thus it can be said that Gleave's argument on the basis of the two schools' conceptions from *ʿaql* and qurʾānic language needs further argumentation. Gleave fails to show how Tafkīk has an anti-*uṣūlī* nature, one which throughout the history of Shīʿism has always been the main factor, from an insider perspective, for the accusation of being Akhbārī.

It also seems that the Maktab-e Tafkīk, contrary to that of Akhbārism, enjoys an intellectual creativity that is marginalized in Gleave's discussion. This creativity is highlighted in that the school clearly tries to emphasize its new intellectual ideas within the sphere of the current Shīʿī discourse. The school, as well as being in hostility with incorporation of *falsafa* and Ṣūfism into the revelatory sciences, attempts to construct an innovative and apocalyptic system of epistemology. What is being taught in *jalasāt-e maʿāref* (private courses on *Ahl al-Bayt*'s teachings) in Tehran and other Iranian cities like Qum and Mashhad, engages extensively with concepts like *lā-fikrī* (abandonment of opinions), *shohūd* (intuition), and *vejdān* (conscience). Therefore, it is hardly possible to catch on to the current Tafkīkīs' epistemology, unless one investigates much more the aforementioned concepts.[40] It comes as no surprise that these lesser-known new teachings have led the Maktab-e Tafkīk to be accused of representing a new Ṣūfī thought by those who have in common with them the hostility toward the philosophy and Ṣūfism. This fact is extensively related to the aforementioned Tafkīkīs' new epistemological system, which is similar to the Ṣūfī tradition. This kind of conflict, between the opponents of *falsafa*, indicates the extent of splits in contemporary Iranian anti-philosophical discourse.[41]

As an ex-insider and on the basis of external evidences, it is clear to me that the school relies on traditions and transmitted materials more than other Shīʿī circles do. Despite this, however, the Maktab-e Tafkīk can hardly be considered as the continuation of Akhbārism. This idea has even been upheld by some of the school's opponents and famous Iranian philosophers.[42]

The School's Literature on Qurʾānic Studies

Commonly there are two types of literature related to the Qurʾān in the traditional classification of Islamic sciences. The first type is *tafāsīr*, produced by Muslim scholars to interpret the Qurʾān. The second type is a combination of different literature and themes under a well-known Islamic field entitled *ʿulūm al-Qurʾān* (the sciences of the Qurʾān). Qurʾānic attitudes of the

40. To get a better impression from such circles, see Ansari 1392/2013, no.5.

41. More information on these recent debates, see Mīlānī 1389/2010(b), 155–180; Mīlānī 1389/2010(a); Maghṣūdī 1389/2010.

42. Dīnānī 1384/2005, 293.

school can be studied through two types of works. The first type deals with qur'ānic thematic issues and/or its interpretation. The second type just utilizes qur'ānic topics and verses in order to support foundational notions and principles of the Tafkīk, like *Abwāb al-Hudā* by Iṣfahānī. Given the nature of this chapter, only the works in the genres of *tafāsīr* or *ʿulūm al-Qur'ān* should be examined here. Accordingly, the works in the second group cannot be classified in the qur'ānic literature, though they are some polemical works in the field of *ʿaqāyed* (dogmas).

Malekī Mīyānajī's *Manāhij al-Bayān* is largely known as the most significant commentary of the school, besides which there is *Miṣbāḥ al-Hudā* by Mīrzā Javād Āqā Tehrānī (d. 1410/1989), which is a selective commentary on the Qur'ān covering Q1 and Q2 (up to verse 253).[43] In line with some recent commentaries on the Qur'ān across the Muslim world which are transcribed by students of *mufassir*,[44] this commentary has been compiled by Muḥammad Bāqer ʿAbdollāhiyān on the basis of Tehrānī's *tafsīrī* courses, later published in two volumes in Qum in 1388/2009.[45]

In addition to *Manāhij al-Bayān*, Malekī Mīyānajī has authored an independent legal Qur'ān commentary entitled *Badā'iʿ al-Kalām fī Tafsīr-i Āyāt al-Aḥkām*, discussing legal issues in light of just legal verses.[46] Also his sessions on interpretation of *Sūrat al-Fātiḥah* was later compiled and published by Muḥammad Biyābānī in Qum in 1413/1992.[47]

The Tafkīkīs have also authored some works in relation to qur'ānic knowledge and wisdom. In addition to the *Maʿārif al-Qur'ān*, written by Sheikh ʿAbd Allāh Vāʿiẓ Yazdī (d. 1412/1991),[48] another treatise has been attributed to the founder of the school with the same name. The latter is one of those important works of Iṣfahānī, treating some dilemmas such as the nature of Qur'ān's knowledge and the divine speech.[49]

The Tafkīkīs are also very interested in the *iʿjāz* (inimitability) of the Qur'ān. The founder of the school as well as his disciples have produced a couple of works in this regard. Iṣfahānī authored four treatises; some of which have been edited by Mofīd and published in *Rasā'el-e Shenākht-e*

43. Needless to say that the claim considered Miṣbāḥ al-Hudā, derived from Mīrzā Javād Āqā Tehrānī's courses, the first and pivotal qur'ānic commentary of the school is inappropriate, see [Anonymous] 1389/2003, 66.

44. Like *Tafsīr Namūna*, by Makārem Shīrazī.

45. More information on this commentary and its author, see [anonymous] 1389/2003, 66–68; Salīm-gandomī 1389/2010(a); ʿAbdollahiyān 1387/2008.

46. See Qahremānī 1382/2003, 89.

47. Qahremānī 1382/2003, 90; more on his qur'ānic works, see Khodāyārī 1379/2000, 30.

48. Ḥojjatī-niā 1378/1999, 214.

49. For more information, see Mofīd 1387/2008, 63–67.

Qur'ān.[50] Sheikh Muḥammad ʿAlī Ḥaqqī Sarābī (d. 1419/1999) also authored a treatise regarding the inimitability of the Qur'ān,[51] in addition to Sheikh Maḥmūd Ḥalabī's treatise, entitled *Ḥujjīyat al-Qur'ān*, within which the notion of inimitability has also been discussed.[52]

Mīyānajī's Exegetical Approach

Mīyānajī's commentary remains the most organized and outstanding commentary of the Qur'ān in the school. The commentary is collected according to the author's *tafsīr* courses in Qum in 1378/1958. The first volume of the *Tafsīr*, *Tafsīr Fātiḥat al-Kitāb*, was published in 1413/1992. Subsequently, other volumes, covering six *juz* (the four starting and two ending *juz*) of the Qur'ān, were published by the Iran's Ministry of Culture.

At the beginning of each qur'ānic chapter, Mīyānajī provided some generalities to pave the way for interpretation. He then divided each *sūrah* into several paragraphs. In addition to examining qur'ānic expressions, words and phrases, Mīyānajī links related *aḥādīth* to his commentaries. He provides the reader with the ideas of both Sunnī and Shīʿī commentators, and adopts a critical approach toward them in some cases. He benefited from a wide variety of exegetical literature, including, but not limited to, *Majmaʿ al-Bayān fī Tafsīr al-Qur'ān*, *Tafsīr Mafātīḥ al-Ghayb*, *al-Kashshāf ʿan Ḥaqā'iq al-Tanzīl wa ʿUyūn al-Aqāwīl fī Wujūh al-Ta'wīl*, *al-Tibyān fī Tafsīr al-Qur'ān*, *Tafsīr al-Manār*, and *al-Mīzān fī Tafsīr al-Qur'ān*.[53]

Given the controversy surrounding the exegetical application of *ʿaql* (intellect) across the Muslim world in the early twentieth century, Iranian scholars have ambivalent views towards his exegetical approach: some assume that Mīyānajī has a vigorous inclination toward *kalām* (Islamic systematic theology), inasmuch as one may classify it within important theological commentaries in contemporary Shīʿism such as *Alā' al-Raḥmān fī Tafsīr al-Qur'ān*, written by Sheikh Moḥammad Javād Balāghī (d. 1352/1933).[54] Others consider *Manāhij* as a combination of legal and theological features; this may be why Mīyānajī criticizes, over his legal discussions regarding the *Ḥajj*, the mosque, divorce and the inheritance, some famous jurists such as

50. Iṣfahānī 1388/2009, 115–223; For further information on these treatises, see Mofīd 1387/2008, 45–63.

51. Ḥojjatī-niā 1378/2008, 203.

52. Ḥojjatī-niā 1378/2008, 204; currently, the manuscript is available at the Library of Āstān-e Qods in Mashhad, by no.1239.

53. To get more generalities regarding his *Tafsīr*, see Ayāzī 1377/2008, 40–42.

54. Maʿāref 1382/2003, 102.

Fāḍil Miqdād (d. ca. 826/1422), al-Bayḍāwī (d. ca. 682/1286), and Muḥaqqiq Ardabīlī (d. ca. 993/1585).[55]

Manāhij al-Bayān's introduction describes the author's exegetical approach in a different way. Briefly speaking, he tries to present himself in such a way that his approach was already applied by previous Shīʿī jurists.[56] He contends that the Ijtihādī approach is more authentic, since all interpretive factors are utilized in the *right* direction, leading to releasing God's intention. He discusses how the practice should be adopted according to reliable and authentic methods like *uṣūl al-fiqh*. He believes the sources for this *ijtihād* are confined to the *al-adillah al-arbaʿah* (the four reasons), including the intellect, in addition to *al-qarāʾin al-muttaṣilah wa al-munfaṣilah* (the joint and detached evidences) derived from the Qurʾān and the Sunna.[57] He has thus collected and analyzed the related traditions in his discussions. Then, in order to reconcile them and interpret meanings that conflict with each other, he has applied the so-called *jamʿ-e uṣūlī*, which treats the conflict between traditions according to *uṣūl al-fiqh*.[58]

One can also delve much deeper to catch the core of his hermeneutical theory. He has, for example, revealed his actual and real attitude toward the Qurʾān while dealing with the verses in practice. Mīyānājī says of this,

> I do not believe that understanding the prophets' knowledge requires studying what has been obtained by others; this is a pointless idea. The prophets' knowledge is higher and clearer than can be perceived by seeking external help and tools, including human sciences, philosophical ideas, and mystical ways.[59]

This view was also upheld by Ḥakīmī. He elaborated this opinion to the extent that he compared it with Ṭabāṭabāʾī's idea of *tafsīr al-qurʾān b-i al-qurʾān* (interpreting the Qurʾān by the Qurʾān itself). Ḥakīmī mentions that the Tafkīkīs' ideas are very similar to that of Ṭabāṭabāʾī which recognizes an independent discursive system for *waḥy* (divine revelation). Accordingly, to understand Islamic scriptural texts, one has no need of anything, including *falsafa* and *ʿirfān*, out of this discursive system.[60] In addition to his belief in this independent discursive system, Ḥakīmī sees that Ṭabāṭabāʾī also believed that it is hardly possible to reconcile between *falsafa*, Qurʾān, and *taṣawwuf*.

55. Qorbānī Zarrīn 1382/2003, 100.
56. In this regard, see Khodāyārī 1379/2000, 57.
57. Malekī Mīyānajī 1377/1998, 88.
58. For some examples, see Malekī Mīyānajī 1414–1418/1994–1998, 2:225–226; Malekī Mīyānajī 1414–1418/1994–1998, 30:247–248.
59. Malekī Mīyānajī 1373/1994, 13.
60. Ḥakīmī 1382/2003(a), 39; Ḥakīmī 1384/2005, 47; also, see ʿĪsā-nejād, 1383/2004.

Relying on a quotation from Ṭabāṭabāʾī, he concludes that Ṭabāṭabāʾī is in the same camp with the Tafkīkīs who consider that there are three different epistemological systems, namely *falsafa*, Qurʾān, and *taṣawwuf*.[61] Ḥakīmī's idea was extreme to the extent that it encouraged several writers to produce some essays against him and prove that there is a huge gap between what the *Tafkīk* believe in and what Ṭabāṭabāʾī has upheld.

It would seem that even though Mīyānajī has tried to put himself on the safe side by representing himself as an *ijtihādī mufassir* in the introduction,[62] he has taken the aforementioned general Tafkīkī position of "qurʾānic underk standing," in which *wahy* produces for itself a discourse which is not subject to the structures arrived at through *falsafa* and *ʿirfān*.[63] That is, as will be seen, while he tries to present his *tafsīr* as an *ijtihādī* one, in practice, he has not treated verses in a way that an utter *mujtahid*, like Abū al-Qāsim al-Khūʾī (d. 1413/1992) in *al-Bayān fī Tafsīr al-Qurʾān*, dealt with them. Simultaneously, according to the previous discussions on the relationship between the *Tafkīk* and Akhbārism, and what also he has taken on in practice, Mīyānajī cannot be considered as an Akhbārī *mufassir*.

Advancing Tafkīkī's Hermeneutical Identity: Criticism and Construction

As mentioned, Mīyānajī's *Tafsīr* reveals that he was on the path of establishing a Tafkīkī hermeneutical identity. The most important evidence in this regard, which should be considered here, is to study how Mīyānajī dealt with the Tafkīk intellectual rivals, and how he raised the significance of Tafkīkī's hermeneutical project. As will be seen, he has followed his exegetical project by his extensive efforts in three arenas. First of all, Mīyānajī refuses philosophical and mystical ideas and principles in a wide range. In the second arena, his *Tafsīr* pushes his bitter criticism toward his famous contemporary *mufassirūn* from both Sunnī and Shīʿī discourses. The third arena is his new and innovative opinions in terms of *ʿulūm al-qurʾān*, through which he has also addressed critically the ideas of *mufassirūn*.[64]

In the first arena, as a Tafkīkī, he has certainly criticized philosophir cal and mystical points of view. His theological approach, indicative of the school's general theological trend, is the refinement of traditional Shīʿī

61. See Ḥakīmī 1382/2003(a), 176; Ṭabāṭabāʾī 1390/2011, 5:382–383.

62. About the *ijtihādī* approach in Imāmī Shīʿī *tafsīr*, see Rād 1389/2010.

63. Gleave 2010, 90; Gerami 1388/2009, 155–156.

64. One might raise this objection that putting forward new ideas is usual in commentaries; however, the most contemporary of Shīʿī commentators, apart from Tafkīkīs, have not utilized the criticism toward Ṭabāṭabāʾī.

theology. While classical Shīʿī theology, as manifested in the works of Naṣīr al-Dīn al-Ṭūsī (d. ca. 673/1274),[65] engaged in protecting the exterior borders of Shīʿī creed against Sunnīs and atheists, the Maktab-e Tafkīk undertakes to refine and improve the inner contents of the Shīʿī theology in what relates to the topics of *al-mabdaʾ wa l-maʿād* (the Origin and the End). At the same time, in what concerns the doctrine of *Imāmah*, the *Tafkīk* is not far from the aforementioned *Imāmī* classical theology.[66]

He has also audaciously critiqued famous Islamic philosophers and mystics, including Ibn ʿArabī (d. ca. 638/1240), Mīr Dāmād (d. 1040/1631), Mullā Hādī Sabzevārī (d. 1289/1873), and Mullā Ṣadrā (d. ca. 1050/1640).[67] The main topics of wide criticism by him are *ṣifāt al-dhāt* (God's attributes of essence), *maʿād-e jesmānī* (bodily resurrection), and characteristics of the world of the afterlife.[68] The author, in some important theological problems like monotheism, God's names and attributes, the pre-eternal world, the human nature, resurrection in the human body,[69] and embodiment of deeds (*tajassom-e aʿmāl*), has put forward some Tafkīkī ideas and solutions.[70] Time and again in *Manāhij al-Bayān*, he discusses philosophers and their hermeneutical approach to the Qurʾān. Coming to Q 76:12, Miyānajī has challenged the philosophers, who believe that the system of Reward and Punishment (*niẓām al-thawāb wa l-ʿiqāb*) is based on the embodiment of deeds (*tajassom-e aʿmāl*). He has upheld that as far as Heaven and Hell exist currently, the syss tem of *tajassom-e aʿmāl* cannot replace them, though it may be implemented in some cases.[71] Slightly ahead, he has taken Q 76:20 as a clear testimoney to his discussion to the effect that otherworldly graces and retributions are made from *jesm-e laṭīf* (soft material), leading to the fact that otherworldly graces and retributions will not be some immaterial (*mujarrad*) phenomena derived from human actions.[72]

In the second arena, *Manāhij al-Bayān* endeavors to adopt a critical approach to its rivals from both Shīʿī and Sunnī discourses. In this, it needs to be classified within the most critical contemporary Shīʿī and Sunnī com-

65. On his works, see Panzeca 2010, 826–828.

66. For more studies on the Imāmī classical doctrine of Imāmah with special reference to al-Ṭūsī, see Yūnus 1976, 27–38.

67. Salīm-gandomī 1389/2010(b), 139; for more information on how he has dealt with Mullā Ṣadrā as a pivotal figure in current Shīʿī philosophy, see Gleave 2010, 76–78; Rizvi 2012, 498.

68. Ayāzī 1377/1998, 53.

69. Ayāzī 1377/1998, 53.

70. For more information, see Khodāyārī 1379/2000, 132.

71. Malekī Mīyānajī 1414–1418/1994–1998, 29:321–322.

72. Malekī Mīyānajī 1414–1418/1994–1998, 29:327–328; Malekī Mīyānajī 1414–1418/1994–1998, 30:25, 126, 135, 137, 347.

mentaries. Mīyānājī has mostly analyzed and criticized the two famous commentators, namely Ṭabāṭabāʾī and Muḥammad Rashīd Riḍā (d. 1935), the two highly critical exegetes in contemporary Islamic discourse.

Ṭabāṭabāʾī's approach to the Qurʾān, usually called "*tafsīr al-qurʾān bi l-qurʾān*," is known as the most innovative and popular approach of Qurʾān interpretation in the contemporary Shīʿī world. He believed that the source of Qurʾān interpretation ought to be the Qurʾān itself.[73] In accordance with some verses of the Qurʾān, Ṭabāṭabāʾī upheld that the Qurʾān does not need anything outside of itself, even *aḥādīth,* to be interpreted. In his interpretative school, the main principle is that the Qurʾān clarifies everything, even itself.[74]

Maktab-e Tafkīk, indeed, is the only school in contemporary Shīʿism which has severely criticized Ṭabāṭabāʾī's approach to the *tafsīr*, whose commentary is highly respected in professional and ordinary spheres. An overview of *Manāhij al-Bayān* reveals that the author has criticized Ṭabāṭabāʾī's overall approach to Qurʾān interpretation, in addition to his critical comments within the explanation of verses. According to Mīyānājī, the Qurʾān has addressed people on two levels, the public and the private one. He has seen that the public address is the low layer of the qurʾānic indication, which is achievable by coming directly to the Qurʾān.[75] He has considered the private address dedicated to specific people; that is, the Qurʾān has some superficial and high-level meanings for those specific people and the Qurʾān is not confined to the public layer. According to him, the private level has basically addressed the Prophet Muḥammad, then, his rightful successors and, then, those who possess the entire knowledge of the Qurʾān, including *ẓahr* (apparent meaning), *baṭn* (hidden meaning), *tanzīl* (revelation), and *taʾwīl* (analogical interpretation).[76]

Miyānajī's conception of *ʿaql* also has no affinity with Ṭabāṭabāʾī. Under the explanation of Q 2:164, Ṭabāṭabāʾī has upheld that the intellect is an instrument by which one can distinguish the right from the wrong, and depravity from happiness, and truth from falsehood. Mīyānajī, on the contrary, has considered *ʿaql* as a divine light emanating from the human soul and heart, which distinguishes goodness from foulness, and the good act from the shameful one.[77] As a Tafkīkī scholar, Mīyānajī has distinguished the *ʿaql-e fiṭrī* (innate intellect) from what has usually been called the intellect

73. Ṭabāṭabāʾī 1360/1981, 69–70.
74. Ṭabāṭabāʾī 1390/2001, 1:11
75. Malekī Mīyānajī 1377/1998, 28.
76. Malekī Mīyānajī 1377/1998, 33.
77. Malekī Miyānajī 1373/1994, 21; Ṭabāṭabāʾī 1390/2001, 1:412.

(ʿ*aql*).[78] This seems to be due to the Tafkīkī's epistemology, which is based upon *fiṭra* (God-given nature). While under Q 2:213, Ṭabāṭabāʾī has considered religion as a means by which the people's daily problems could be fixed,[79] Mīyānajī has seen that the prophets' mission was to stir, arouse and recall the *fiṭra* within whoever forgot it.[80] Regarding the concept of *tadhakkur* (reminding), while Ṭabāṭabāʾī has suggested a philosophical meaning to the effect that *tadhakkur* is to come to the result from the premise and vice versa, Mīyānajī has mentioned that *tadhakkur* is something contrary to *nisyān* (forgetfulness) and *ghaflah* (heedlessness). He has considered Ṭabāṭabāʾī's notion inappropriate, being in contradiction with the qurʾānic standpoint to the effect that seeking the truth needs only to stir *fiṭra* through *tadhakkur*, not to apply philosophical demonstrations and to move from the premises to the result.[81] It is highly significant to also know how he reconciles the intellect and the Sunna. He has put forward the claim that no conflict exists between innate intellect and the Sunna, being that both are derived from the same source. He has admitted, on the other hand, that the Sunna and the common intellect may contradict each other, mostly in areas relating to the Lord's commandments, the divine teachings, and the metaphysical matters. The author, then, has discussed how such controversial issues in these three areas could be explained and resolved.[82]

Regarding Arab commentators, although it is a common view that, for example, Rashīd Riḍā sees the Qurʾān neither as a book of science nor of philology,[83] Jafar has shown how Rashīd Riḍā, in practice, attempts to justify the scientific theory with qurʾānic verses.[84] In contrary, Mīyānajī has disagreed with Rashīd Riḍā and some modernists in many cases, and has believed that the Qurʾān is in conflict with modern achievements and scientific facts.[85] The author of *al-Manār* has also taken some positions in favor of the Sunnī dogma, in what concerns the *imāmah* (leadership), *shafāʿah* (intercession), etc., in some verses. In such polemical cases, Malekī Mīyānajī, taking the position of a Shīʿī jurist and theologian, and relying on teachings of *Imāmī* Shīʿism, has challenged Riḍā's hermeneutical perception to defend

78. Meyānajī says: "ʿ*aql*, in both the Book and the Sunna is an explicit light (*al-nūr al-ṣarīḥ*) which God pours out onto the spirits of humankind. It is manifest by its essence and the illuminator of things other than it. It is a divine proof (ḥujjat elāhīyya), immune from sin essentially and prevented from any error" (see Miyānajī 1373/1994, 21; trans. by Gleave 2010, 86).

79. Ṭabāṭabāʾī 1390/2001, 2:115.

80. Malekī Miyānajī 1414–1418/1994–1998, 2:173–175.

81. See Ṭabāṭabāʾī 1390, 2:396; Malekī Miyānajī 1414–1418/1994–1998, 3:67–68.

82. For further information, see Malekī Mīyānajī 1373/1994:39–41.

83. See Pink 2016, 3.

84. To see how he uses scientific discoveries in his *Tafsīr* in practice, see Jafar 1998, 104–109.

85. For more discussions and some cases, see Khodāyārī 1379/2000, 71.

the Shīʿī faith. In addition to discussing the main Shīʿī *imāmah* principles under Q 2:124,[86] Mīyānajī has addressed the *shafāʿah* to challenge Riḍā's reading concerning the *shafāʿah* verses as *mutashābihāt* (ambiguous).[87] He has pointed out that those verses denying the *shafāʿah* seek to remind that the absolute possession is just dedicated to God, that is, no one possesses *shafāʿah* independently and without God's permission.[88]

In the third arena, Mīyānajī has also taken up a revisionist approach to the qurʾānic sciences (*ʿulūm al-qurʾān).* The author, relying on teachings of his mentor at the Khorasan seminary, has endeavored to reconstruct classical qurʾānic sciences in various issues such as *muḥkam* (the explicit verse), *mutashābih* (the ambiguous verse), the inimitability of the Qurʾān (*iʿjāz*), *naskh* (abrogation), and *taʾwīl* (allegorical interpretation).[89] He has proposed one of his significant ideas on the quiddity of the *muḥkam* and *mutashābih* in the Qurʾān. According to him, to interpret *mutashābih*, it is not sufficient to refer it to *muḥkam*, and to explain the former by the latter, which is the most usual suggestion in classical qurʾānic sciences. In his reading, the reference to *muḥkam* only makes the literal meaning of *mutashābih* invalid without any indication of what has been meant by *mutashābih*. Mīyānajī has upheld that qualities like *iḥkām* (clearness) and *tashābuh* (ambiguity) do not relate to the meaning and signified; rather, they relate to the word and signifier. He has also offered that the *muḥkam* and *mutashābih* divide not only the qurʾānic verses, but also the people into *al-rāsikhūn fī al-ʿilm* (those firmly grounded in knowledge) and *al-munḥarifūn* (those who are deviators).[90] In addition, he has considered that the knowledge of *taʾwīl al-Qurʾān* is not available for common people, even for scholars, since it has been dedicated to the infallible *Imams*.[91] *Manāhij al-Bayān* also has a specific standpoint regarding the Qurʾān's inimitability, one of the most controversial issues in qurʾānic studies. Malekī Miyānajī, in addition to his discussion regarding this topic within the introduction, has delved much deeper into the issue when he has come to Q 2:23. He has put forward that the Qurʾān, itself, is the proof of its au-

86. See Malekī Mīyānajī 1414–1418/1994–1998, 1:338–339, 333–334; Rashīd Riḍā, 1:455.

87. Rashīd Riḍā, 1:307.

88. Malekī Mīyānajī 1414–1418/1994–1998, 1:225; He has delved much deeper into some Shīʿī issues such as *ʿilm al-ghayb* (knowledge of the unseen), *tawallī* (friendship) and *tabarrī* (disassociation) and infallibility of Imams (see Malekī Mīyānajī 1414–1418/1994–1998, 29:121–123; Malekī Mīyānajī 1414–1418/1994–1998, 4:187–191, 139, 200; Malekī Mīyānajī 1414–1418/1994–1998, 3:197; Malekī Mīyānajī 1414–1418/1994–1998, 1:338–360).

89. To get an entire impression from his attitude to the qurʾānic sciences, see Malekī Mīyānajī 1377/1998.

90. See : Salīm-gandomī 1389/2010(b), 131–133 ; Malekī Mīyānajī 1414–1418/1994–1998, 1:19–28.

91. Salīm-gandomī 1389/2010(b), 139.

thenticity. In other words, the miracle ascribed to the Prophet Muḥammad is his revealed Book. That is, it is not possible to differentiate between the Qurʾān and Muḥammad's miracle, which means that the Qurʾān has acquired its authenticity from itself.[92]

Conclusion

This chapter argues that pre-revolutionary Iranian exegetical schools have been largely overlooked by both Iranian and Western scholars of *tafsīr*. Indeed, Iran has been the focus of politicians, historians, and anthropologists interested in Middle Eastern issues. No one, to my knowledge, has discussed the development of Persian Shīʿī *tafsīrs* in contemporary Iran in European languages.

Along with the early twentieth-century exegetical movement that emerged in the Muslim world, the exegetical school of Maktab-e Tafkīk played a role in pre-revolutionary Iran. While various groups of influential religious figures and clerics in Qum and Mashhad were engaged with mystical and philosophical reading of the Qurʾān, *Manāhij al-Bayān* manifested as a fresh voice, deconstructing the overwhelming philosophical and mystical discourses of *tafsīr*.

Although Mīyanājī introduced his *tafsīr* under the genre of *Ijtihādī tafāsīr*, in practice he has taken a Tafkīkī position of "qurʾānic understanding." In this context, revelation produces for itself a discourse which is not subject to the structures arrived at through *falsafa* and *ʿirfān*. Moreover, although the school relies on traditions and transmitted materials more than other Shīʿī currents do, the Maktab-e Tafkīk could hardly be considered as the continuation of Akhbārism.

I have here argued that the way through which he has elaborated his "exegetical project" reveals that his aim was not just to put forward new *tafsīrī* ideas; rather, he has also introduced and established an independent *tafsīrī* school for Tafkīkīs to complete the Tafkīkī schema using qurʾānic interpretation. He has thus elaborated his exegetical project by his extensive efforts in three arenas.

First, Miyānajī rejects philosophical and mystical ideas and principles. He has audaciously attacked the ideas of famous Islamic philosophers and mystics, including, but not limited to, Ibn ʿArabī, Mīr Dāmād, Mullā Hādī Sabzevārī, and Mullā Ṣadrā. The main topics of wide criticism by him are God's attributes of essence, bodily resurrection, and characteristics of the world of the afterlife.

92. See Salīm-gandomī 1389/2010(b), 143–144; Malekī Mīyānajī 1414–1418/1994–1998, 1:184–185.

Secondly, his *Tafsīr* reveals bitter criticism toward famous contemporary *mufassirūn* from both Sunnī and Shīʿī discourses. In particular, Mīyānājī has analyzed and criticized the work of the two famous commentators Ṭabāṭabāʾī and Rashīd Riḍā. In this regard, Maktab-e Tafkīk is the only school in contemporary Shīʿism that has severely criticized Ṭabāṭabāʾī's approach to the *tafsīr*.

Thirdly, we witness his new and innovative opinions of *ʿulūm al-qurʾān*. In this, Mīyānajī and the Tafkīkī school provide a distinguished system of thought. Mīyānajī has thus taken up a revisionist approach to issues like *muḥkam*, *mutashābih*, Qurʾān's inimitability, etcetera.

In sum, I trust that this chapter has opened the way to investigate Tafkīkī hermeneutics as a new interpretive identity in contemporary Iran. The state of the field surely welcomes more such studies in the future.

Bibliography

Primary Sources

Dhahabī, M. Ḥ. n. d. *al-Tafsīr wa al-Mufassirūn*. Beirut, Dār Iḥyāʾ al-Turāth al-ʿArabī.

Iṣfahānī, M. M. 1387/2008. *Abwāb al-Hudā*. Edited by Ḥossein Mofīd. Tehran.

——. 1388/2009. *Rasāʾil Shenākht Qurʾān*. Edited by Ḥossein Mofīd. Tehran.

Malekī Mīyānajī, M. B. 1414–1418/1994–1998. *Manāhij al-Bayān*. Edited by M. Bīyābānī and ʿA. Malekī Mīyānajī. Tehran.

——. 1373/1994. *Tawḥīd al-Imāmīyyah*. Edited by M. Bīyābānī and ʿA. Malekī Mīyānajī. Tehran.

Morvārīd, Ḥ. 1418/1998. *Tanbīhāt Ḥawl al-Mabdaʾ wa al-Maʿād*. Mashhad.

Rashīd Riḍā, M. n. d. *al-Manār*. Cairo.

Ṭabāṭabāʾī, M. Ḥ. 1360/1981. *Qurʾān dar Islām*. Qum.

——. 1390/1970. *al-Mīzān fī Tafsīr al-Qurʾān*. Tehran.

Secondary Sources (English and French)

Abisaab, R. J. 2015. "Shīʿī Jurisprudence, Sunnism, and the Traditionist Thought (*Akhbārī*) of Muhammad Amin Astarābādī (d. 1626–27)." *International Journal of Middle East Studies* 47(1):5–23.

Algar, H., and Najam Haider. 1995. "Akhbārīyah." In: *Encyclopedia of the Modern Islamic World*. Oxford.

——. 2011. "AḴBĀRĪ, MĪRZĀ MOḤAMMAD." *Encyclopedia Iranica*. 29 July. www.iranicaonline.org/articles/akbari-mirza-mohammad.

Anzali, A., and S. H. Gerami, eds. 2017. *Opposition to Philosophy in Safavid Iran: Mulla Muḥammad-Ṭāhir Qummi's Ḥikmat al-ʿĀrifīn*. Leiden.

Cole, J. 1985. "Shi'i Clerics in Iraq and Iran, 1722–1780: The Akhbari-Usuli conflict reconsidered." *Iranian Studies* 18(1):3–34.
Gleave, R. 2010. "Continuity and Originality in Shīʿī Thought: The Relationship between the Akhbāriyya and the Maktab-i Tafkīk." In *Shi'i Trends and Dynamics in Modern Times (XVIIIth–XXth Centuries)*, edited by D. Hermann and S. Mervin. Beirut/Frankfurt.
——. 2000. "Inevitable Doubt: Two Theories of Shī'ī Jurisprudence." In *Studies in Islamic Law and Society*. Vol. 12. Leiden.
——. 2007. *Scripturalist Islam: The History and Doctrines of the Akhbārī Shīʿī School*. Vol. 72. Leiden.
Gunasti, S. 2019. *The Qurʾān between the Ottoman Empire and the Turkish Republic: An Exegetical Tradition*. London and New York.
Jafar, I. 1998. *Modern Qurʾānic Exegesis: A Comparative Study of the Methods of Muḥammad Abduh and Muḥammad Rashīd Riḍā*. MA Thesis, McGill University. Montreal.
Jazari Mamoei, S. 2016. *Le chiisme, quête de la fidélité aux imams: l'école théologique du Tafkîk en Iran contemporain*. Paris.
Kohlberg, E. 2011. "AḴBĀRĪYA." *Encyclopedia Iranica*. 29 July. http://iranicaonline.org/articles/akbariya.
——. 1987. "Aspects of Akhbari thought in the Seventeenth and Eighteenth Centuries." *Eighteenth Centuries Renewal and Reform in Islam*:133–153.
Lawson, T. 2012. "EXEGESIS vi. In Aḵbārī and Post-Safavid Esoteric Shiʿism." *Encyclopedia Iranica*. January 20. http://www.iranicaonline.org/articles/exegesis-iv.
Madelung, W. 2012. "Akhbāriyya." *Encyclopedia of Islam*, 2nd edition. 10.1163/1573-3912_islam_SIM_8312.
Newman, A. J. 1986. *The Development and Political Significance of the Rationalist (Uṣūlī) and Traditionist (Akhbārī) Schools in Imāmī Shīʿī History from the Third/Ninth to the Tenth/Sixteenth Century*. PhD Thesis, University of California. Los Angeles.
——. 1992. "The nature of the Akhbārī/Uṣūlī Dispute in Late Ṣafawid Iran. Part 1: ʿAbdallāh al-Samāhijī's Munyat al-Mumārisīn." *Bulletin of the School of Oriental and African Studies* 55(1):22–51.
Paya, A. 2016. "The Disenchantment of Reason: An Anti-rational Trend in Modern Shiʿi Thought – The *Tafkikis*." *Journal of Shiʿa Islamic Studies* 9(4):385–414.
Panzeca, I. 2010. "Naṣīr al-Dīn al-Ṭūsī." In *Encyclopedia of Medieval Philosophy: Philosophy Between 500 and 1500*. Edited by Henrik Lagerlund, vol. 1. Springer Science & Business Media.

Pink, J. 2016. "Riḍā, Rashīd." *Encyclopedia of the Qur'ān*. Edited by Jane Dammen McAuliffe. http://dx.doi.org/10.1163/1875-3922_q3_EQCOM_050503.
Riddell, P. G. 2001. *Islam in the Malay-Indonesian World: Transmission and Responses*. Honolulu.
——. 2017. *Malay Court Religion, Culture and Language: Interpreting the Qur'ān in 17th Century Aceh*. Leiden and Boston.
Rizvi, S. H. 2012. "Only the Imam Knows Best: The Maktab-e Tafkīk's Attack on the Legitimacy of Philosophy in Iran." *Journal of the Royal Asiatic Society* 22(3–4):487–503.
Wilson, M. B. 2014. *Translating the Qur'an in an Age of Nationalism: Print Culture and Modern Islam in Turkey*. Oxford.
Yunus, M. R. 1976. *The Necessity of Imāmah According to Twelver-Shi'ism with Special Reference to Tajrīd al-Iʿtiqād of Naṣīr al-Dīn al-Ṭūsī*. MA thesis, McGill University. Montreal.
Zadeh. T. 2012. *The Vernacular Qur'an: Translation and the Rise of Persian Exegesis*. Oxford.

Secondary Sources (Persian)

ʿAbdollāhiyān, M. 1387/2008. "ravesh-e tafsīrī āyatollāh Mīrzā Javād Aqā Tehrānī va vījegīhāy-e tafsīr-e Miṣbāḥ al-Hudā." In: *Āfāq-e Nūr*, no.7: n.p.
ʿAlī-akbar-zadeh, Ḥ. 1392/2013. *Tafsīr va Ta'vīl dar Maktab-e Tafkīk*. Qum.
[Anonymous]. 1389/2010. "Tafsīr-e Miṣbāḥ al-Hudā: nakhustīn athar-e tafsīrī dar maktab-e tafkīk." In *Kitāb-e Māh-e Dīn* 154:66–68.
Ansari, H. 1392/2013. "maktab-e tafkīk: taḥlīlī goftemānī." http://ansari.kateban.com/post/1999.
Ayāzī, S. M. ʿA. 1377/1998. "nigāhī be tafsīr-e Manāhij al-Bayān va mo'allef-e gerān-qadr-e ān." In *Bayyenāt* 18: n.p.
Dānesh Shahrakī, Ḥ. and Ḥ. Yaʿqūbī. 1396/2017. "ʿaql az dīdgāh-e Mīrzā Mahdī Iṣfahānī va Moḥammad Riḍā Ḥakīmī." *Do-faṣl-nameh-ye ʿAql va Dīn* 16:55–76.
Dīnānī, Gh. H. 1384/2005. "ru'yāy-e khulūṣ." In: *Negāhī be Maktab-e Tafkīk*. Edited by B. Mīr-ʿAbdollāhī and ʿA. Pūr-Muḥammadī. Tehran.
Gerami, S. M. Hadi. 1388/2009. "Manāhij al-Abayān: talāshī barāy-e pāyegozārī maktab-e tafsīrī ḥavzeh khurāsān." In *Pazhūhesh-nāmeh Qur'ān va Ḥadith* 6:133–160.
Ḥakīmī, M. R. 1382/2003(a). *Maktab-e Tafkīk*. Qum.

——. 1382/2003(b). "Bā fajr-e qurʾān." In *Motaʾalleh-e Qurʾānī*. By M. ʿA. Raḥīmīān Ferdusī. Qum.

——. 1384/2005. "ʿaql-e khod-bonyād-e dīnī." In *Negāhī bi Maktab-e Tafkīk*. Edited by B. Mīr-ʿAbdollāhī and ʿA. Pūr-Muḥammadī. Tehran.

Hemāmī, A., and Ḥ. ʿAlī-Akbar-zādeh. 1390/2011. "taʾvīl-e qurʾān dar maktab-e tafkīk." *Pazhūhesh-nāmeh Qurʾān va Hadīth* 9.

——.1391/2012(a). "ʿaql va naqsh-e ān dar tafsīr az negāh-e maktab-e tafkīk." *Pazhūhesh-e Dīnī* 24: n.p.

——. 1391/2012(b). "maktab-e tafkīk va tafsīr-e atharī." *Hadīth Pazhūhī* 8: n.p.

Ḥojjatī-niā, G. 1378/1999. "kitāb-shenāsī maktab-e tafkīk." *Andīsheh Ḥavzeh* 3: n.p.

ʿĪsā-nejād, S. M. 1383/2004. "taqāron va taghāyor-e naẓarīyyeh tafsīrī ʿAllāmeh Ṭabāṭabāʾī va maktab-e tafkīk." *Golestān-e Qurʾān* 192:18–21.

Khodāyārī, ʿA. 1379/2001. *Naqd va barrasī Mabānī va ravesh-e tafsīrī Manāhij al-Bayān*. MA Thesis, University of Qum.

——. 1381/2002. "Qurʾān-shenāsī va Qurʾān-shenāsān: morūrī bar zendegī va ravesh-e tafsīrī Āyatullāh Malekī Mīyānājī." *Golestān-e Qurʾān*:127.

Maʿārif, M. 1382/2003. "Rūykard-e kalāmī dar tafsīr-e Manāhij al-Bayān." *Safīneh* 1: n.p.

Maghṣūdī, H. R. 1389/2010. "Molāḥeẓe-ʾī bar mulāḥeẓāt pīrāmūn-e Maktab-e tafkīk." *Samāt* 4:148–157.

Makārem, H. 1378/1999. "khordeh-gīrān bar ḥekmat-e mutaʿālīyeh va muntaqedān Ṣadr al-mutaʾallehīn." *Ḥawzah* 93: n.p.

——. 1380/2001. "khordeh-gīrān bar ḥikmat-e mutʿālīyeh (2)." *Ḥawzah* 103–104.

Malekī, ʿA. 1372/1993. "naqd-e ʿayār" *Keyhān-e Andīsheh* 49: n.p.

Malekī Mīyānajī, M. B. 1377/1998. *Negāhī be ʿUlūm-e Qurʾānī*. Edited by ʿA. Khodāyārī and ʿA. Malekī Mīyānajī. Qum.

Masʿūdī, M. M. 1387/2008. "naqd-e gūneʾī bar Maktab-e Tafkīk dar zamīne-ye tafsīr-e Qurʾān." *Mishkāt* 98:52–74.

Mīlānī, Ḥ. 1389/2010(a). "pāsukhī be defāʿīyyāt tafkīkīan." *Samāt* 4:158–177.

——. 1389/2010(b). "mulāḥeẓātī pīrāmūn-e Maktab-e Tafkīk." *Samāt* 2:148–188.

Mofīd, Ḥ. 1387/2008. "moqaddameh." in: Iṣfahānī. Tehran.

——. 1389/2010. "ḥojjīyat-e ẓavāher az manẓar-e Mīrzā Mahdī Iṣfahānī." *Meshkāt* 106:19–41.

——. 1395/2016. "āyā mīrzāy-e Iṣfahāni Akhbārī ast?." In *Mashʿal-e Maʿrefat*, 1:587–638. Qum.

Mūsavī, S. M. 1382/2003. *Āʾīn va Andīsheh*. Tehran.

Naṣīrī, Mahdī. 1386/2007. *Falsafeh az Manẓar-e Qurʾān va ʿEtrat*. Tehran.

Qahremānī, A. 1382/2003. "zedegī-nāmeh Āyatullāh Malekī Mīyānajī." *Safīneh* 1.
Qorbānī Zarrīn, B. 1382/2003. "negāhī kullī be tafsīr-e Manāhij al-Bayān." *Safīneh* 1.
Rād, ʿA., and. K. Qāḍī-zādeh. 1389/2010. "shākheṣe-hā-ye naẓarīye-hā-ye tafsīrī ijtihādī mofassirān-e Imāmīyyah." *ʿUlūm-e Qurʾān va Ḥadīth* 85:175–202.
Sājedī, A., and Ḥ. J. Nobāri. 1397/2018. "īmān-gerāyī ʿashʿarī akhbārī va Maktab-e Tafkīk." *Māh-nāmeh Afāq-e ʿUlūm-e Ensānī* 19:95–112.
Salīm-gandomī, Ḥ. 1389/2010(a). "tafsīr-e miṣbāḥ al-hudā" *Safīneh* 27: n.p.
——. 1382/2010(b). "ʿulūm-e qurʾānī dar tafsīr-e Manāhij al-Bayān." *Safīneh* 1.
Seyedān, S. J. 1378/1999. "Maktab-e Tafkīk ya ravesh-e fuqahā-ye Imāmīyyeh." In *Pazhūhesh-hāy-e Ejtimāʿī Islāmī* 19:67–105.
Shāhrūdī, M., M. A. Tafaḍḍulī, and M. Pahlavān. 1397/2018. "jāygāh-e ḥadīth dar fahm-e Qurʾān: muqāreneh va taṭbīq-e ārāʾ-ye mīrzā Mahdī Iṣfahāni va Akhbāriān." *Pazhūheshhāy-e Qurʾān va Ḥadīth.* 51(1):89–110.
Sorūsh, J. 1395/2016. *ʿAql dar Ḥekmat-e Mutaʿāliyeh va Maktab-e Tafkīk*. Qum.
Ṭāromī, Ḥ. 1391/2012. "justārī dar bāb-e akhbārī-garī va nesbat ān bā rahyaft va manẓūmeh-e fekrī mīrzā Mahdī Gharavī Iṣfahānī." *Safīneh* 34:145–169.

5

On Secularization of *Fiqh* in Contemporary Iran

Mahmoud Pargoo

Introduction

IN THE WAKE of Islamic encounter with Europe, *sharīʿa* has undergone a revolutionary transformation. Initially it was redefined (metamorphosed and constructed) as positive law of newly formed nation-states (*étatisation*) and its jurisdiction shrank and was limited mainly to personal status. This was in tandem with the European invention of the modern concept of religion[1] and the process of *scripturalism*, which made *sharīʿa* central to the social imaginary in many Muslim societies. Subsequently, a general reaction of revival of *sharīʿa* began, which took different shapes depending on varying local circumstances and sociocultural milieux. Simultaneous with these processes, the Muslim world has undergone a deep process of secularization, which has undermined the pillars upon which a firm belief in *sharīʿa* rested. This paper focuses on how *sharīʿa* was secularized during its modern transformation; in so doing, it argues that the contemporary concept of *sharīʿa* has metamorphosed into a secular one, thereby creating new secular *sharīʿa* that is removed from its past moral, cosmological and ontological grounds. The first part of my chapter covers the wider Islamicate world while the second part pays particular attention to the Iranian Shīʿī experience, in which I explain the contemporary drivers of secularization of *fiqh* as a disengaged enquiry.

What Is Secularization?

"Secularization" in its most broad sense signifies the displacement of religion from the center of the human life[2] or the decline in social significance of religion.[3] Secularization may address different realms of human life. It may denote a decline in individual religious belief or practice, including

1. Smith 1964; Asad 2009, 27–54; Nongbri 2013.
2. Bruce 2011, 1.
3. Wilson 1983, 149.

dwindling membership in churches. A weakening of the observance of religious duties and rituals such as rites of passage (baptism, marriage, death) is also associated with this meaning of secularity. It may also denote a decline in religious beliefs and practices not only in extension (represented by the decline in statistics of participation) but also in intensity and meaning – that is, in how seriously people take their religion. Is it the driving force and the orienting vector of life around which all other parts derive meaning, or is it only a spice, a color on the hard bedrock of so-called "material life," which gets its fundamental orientation from other sources? Thus, secularization, does not denote exclusively a decline in religious belief or practice but also a change in the meaning of those beliefs or the interpretations of those practices.

Another definition of secularization focuses on functional differentiation: that gradually, the previously unitary society is disintegrating into separate functional units, each almost autonomous.. Thus, the sub-system of economics has its own framework of value and is not governed by the religious values. Taylor also proposes a third sense of the secular: that while belief in God in the past was unchallenged, and indeed axiomatic, in our secular age it is only "one option among others."[4] This option becomes available because of the "possibility of exclusivist humanism,"[5] the idea, not available in the premodern world, that human flourishing is possible without any reference to transcendence. A secular age in this sense, Taylor points out, is "one in which the eclipse of all goals beyond human flourishing becomes conceivable; or better, it falls within the range of an imaginable life for masses of people."[6] In this third meaning, he argues, most of the modern history of the US has been secular. This is the opposite of most Muslim countries, where (dis)belief in God still may not be an option. I will provide an understanding of secularity close to the third Taylorian sense but within an Islamic context.

Substantive Secularity in the Islamic World

The "shift of orientation from the hereafter to this world" better explains secularity in Islamic contexts.[7] If secularity is a change of orientation to the

4. Taylor 2007, 3.

5. Taylor 2007, 3.

6. Taylor 2007, 3. In a similar vein, Geertz refers to religious societies as those in which "believing is, so to speak, easy, almost as easy as speaking." See Geertz 1971, 101.

7. It is still an open question if and when the immanent has been distinguished from the transcendent in the Islamic history. Taylor traces this distinction in Christianity to the beginning of the seventeenth century. See Taylor 2011, 32–33.

earth, then most Islamic societies have already been in the process of substantive secularization since the nineteenth century, when they adopted the fundamental modern European visions of the universe and history. Muslim thinkers used to measure everything by heavenly and metaphysical meters; however, upon interacting with the modern West, they tried to view things through the prism of earthly criteria.[8] Indeed, as Reinhard Schulze has pointed out, Muslim modernists "had provided a major impulse to the development of secular Islamic modernism."[9] This Islamic secular turn required a revolutionary paradigm shift in the web of Islamic beliefs, which displaced its most vital nodes with new ones that were previously trivial. The shift in attention to the earth did not immediately translate into an entirely new religious doctrine; it was more an evolution in the most fundamental background assumptions, the interpretive bedrock of Muslim imaginaries that gives meaning to all other ingredients of the system. The issue was not that people stopped believing in God, the Qurʾān or the Day of Judgement, but that the weight they conferred to these concepts in their overall understanding of the universe was reversed. The same theological propositions were valid, but meanings and assumptions were changed.

In contrast to Said's views[10] in which Muslims are usually portrayed as inferior and powerless people, recent scholarly works agree that Muslims had previously thought of themselves as the epicenter of the world and they viewed Europe as only a terra incognita.[11] During colonialism, Muslims increasingly thought of themselves as participants in a competition with their Western peers over worldly domination. To win, or at least not lose this competition, they needed to learn how to play: get acquainted with rules, goals, and values of the game. At the outset, they accepted the framework of earthly competition and began to compensate for their *decadence* in that competition by internalizing their rival's master narrative of the universe and its purposes. Later developments were only different strategies for winning this game – Western strategies to win the race of material superiority and worldly domination versus Islamic ones. Essentially, differences were in strategies rather than in the basic framework.

Legal Reform and the Secularization of *Fiqh*

In the eighteenth and nineteenth centuries, Europe's domination in the Muslim world was felt in three dimensions: (a) military expansion and colonization; (b) missionary activities, and (c) modern empirical science and

8. See Massad 2008.
9. Schulze 2002, 89.
10. For example, see Said 1979.
11. Matthee 1998.

technologies.[12] Muslim rulers accordingly reacted to this breakdown by implementing reforms in the areas of the military, industry, education, and law.

The *sharīʿa* before modernity was only one constituent of the faith and a whole range of other elements would shape the public imaginary of a moral life. In many Muslim societies including the Persianate, *adab*, often dominated by Ṣūfī teachings, would be much more of an influence than *sharīʿa* or *fiqh*. Often folk rituals of martyrdom, shrine pilgrimage, and saint worship were at the center of religiosity. The *sharīʿa* was a matter more for adjudications in urban settings and among the religious virtuosi.[13] In terms of its contents, *sharīʿa* was not a body of laws but, more generally, a comprehensive guideline of practice including worship, ethics, and other areas.[14]

For instance, while *sharīʿa* and administrative laws had different functions in the Ottoman Empire, reforms of the *Tanẓīmāt* in the nineteenth century shrank the jurisdiction of the *sharīʿa*. Different phases of legislation in the Ottoman Empire (for example, the 1839 Edict of Gülhane [*the Gülhane Hatt-ı Şerif*], the 1856 Hatt-ı Hümayun Edict, the Commercial Code of 1856, and the Penal Code of 1858) also all marginalized *sharīʿa*.[15] Mecelle, a collection of sixteen legal books, presented a unified version of Ḥanafī legal precepts in areas of commercial and civil law and was valid in much of the Ottoman territories.[16] The unification of laws in Mecelle meant that jurists no longer needed to refer to the classical *sharīʿa* compendia to interpret them and choose a view among the often-incompatible legal opinions of previous jurists. Codification of the *sharīʿa*, Zubaida argues, "cut the Shari'a off from its traditional locus" and its "sacred ancestry."[17] Furthermore, forms of practice of law became much different from what was the norm in the traditional context:

12. Hefner 2010.

13. The long-held dichotomy between Ṣūfism and *sharīʿa*, the former prevalent in villages and the latter in urban centers, though problematic in many ways, sheds some light on what has been the case in some societies. For some articulation of this: Geertz 1971; Gellner 1970. For Talal Asad's critic of this view see Asad 2003, 205–256.

14. Asad insists that though we may have such a distinction between law and ethics in *sharīʿa* it does not match the same terms in their modern meanings. He writes: "in brief, I submit that although *sharīʿa* does distinguish between "law" and "ethics," neither term should be understood in its modern, secular sense." Asad 2003, 248.

15. For a comparative study of the modernization of the *sharīʾa* in Iran and Turkey see Pfaff 1963, and Zubaida 2005, 129–132.

16. The books of the Mecelle covered these areas: Sale, Hire, Guarantee, Transfer of Debt, Pledges, Trust and Trusteeship, Gift, Wrongful Appropriation and Destruction, Interdiction, Constraint and Pre-emption, Joint Ownership, Agency, Settlement and Release, Admissions, Actions, Evidence and Administration of an Oath, Administration of Justice by the Courts.

17. Zubaida 2005, 134.

> The Islamic nature of the Shari'a is surely closely related to the forms of practice of the legal craft, and the location and personnel of this practice: al-Azhar and other madrasas, the books, the forms of argument and disputation, the institutions and procedures of judgement, the location of qadi courts, often in mosques, and above all the designation and qualification of the practitioner. All these institutional props and their relation to the sacred and to worship are what make the law religious. Codification as civil law practised in civil courts denudes the Shari'a of all its institutional religious garb, it is "dis-embedded" and de-ritualized. The content in the new form is a different and entirely profane creature.[18]

Talal Asad also explains how modernizers' overemphasis on the distinction between *ʿibādāt* and *muʿmalāt* has eliminated the element of the righteousness of the judge.[19]

Unlike the Ottoman Empire, nineteenth-century Persia lacked a powerful state, a standing and permanent army, and a systematized judicial apparatus. A large number of legal needs were addressed by informal local customs, family, village, or clan mediations. Other than these, there were two formal judiciary courts: *ʿurfī* courts under the administration of the government, which dealt with order and security as well as major crimes (*aḥdāthi arbaʿi*: murder, rape, assault, and theft), and *sharīʿa* courts run by local *mujtahids*, which dealt with personal status, marriage, divorce, property, and inheritance issues. The latter were also doing the tasks of today's notaries. Practically, they did not have executive power, and enforcement of their verdicts was referred to the government.[20]

Though there were some minor legal reforms before the twentieth century in Iran, the 1906 Constitutional Revolution addressed deeper areas of public sovereignty, equality, and rule of law and was more progressive than its Ottoman counterpart Tanzimat. The primary and key slogan of Constitutionalism remained "the rule of law" (*qānūn*). *Qānūn*, which was in use in the Ottoman Empire from the time of Tanzimat, found its way to Iranian pro-constitution literature in the late nineteenth century. It was not, however, conceived simply as a positive law of state; different parties had different definitions of it. Some understood it as the *sharīʿa* exacto senso; others saw principles of parliamentarianism in it; still others saw in it prospects for annihilation of the *sharīʿa*. Indeed, the demands of Constitutionalists evolved from the establishment of houses of justice (*ʿidālat-khāneh*) to a council or

18. Zubaida 2005, 134.
19. Asad 2001, 13.
20. Enayat 2013.

assembly of justice (*majlis-e ʿadliye*) and later to "a full-blown constitution" in which "the Shah and the beggar will be equal within the confines of the law."[21] Interestingly enough, the general public mistook the parliament for the judiciary and brought their numerous petitions to the House.[22]

The main phase of modernization of the legal system came with ʿAlī Akbar Dāvar (1885–1973), the minister of justice during Reza Shah. Dāvar dissolved the whole judiciary for seven months to give it a complete overhaul. His reforms resulted in recruiting new judges, writing new laws and regulations, and establishing a new administrative order for the judiciary. The most important law written in this period was the three-volume Iran Civil Code 1928–35, a scrupulous codification of Shīʿī jurisprudence into European (mainly French) legal forms. Despite his setting of a series of modern criteria for the employment of judges, the clergy reserved their weighty presence in the system by retaining almost exclusive dominion over notaries' licenses and offices of registration of marriage and divorce.[23]

This reduction of *fiqh* or the *sharīʿa* in other Muslim territories (Egypt, British India, Dutch Indonesian Archipelago)[24] to – and indeed construction as – a system of positive *laws* resulted in the relegation of major parts of *fiqh* (including worship) to the status of "the cult and ritual and other purely religious duties."[25] Thus *fiqh* (or the *sharīʿa*) became *Islamic law*. This contraction of the jurisdiction of the *sharīʿa* led to later calls to revive its previous grandeur and comprehensiveness.

The Elements of Secularization of the *Sharīʿa*

Codification and immutability

Apart from scripturalism and its consequences, probably the most fundamental impact of modernity on the *sharīʿa* was the reconstruction of the normative *ideal* fiction of immutability of law, rule-boundedness, objectivity, and literality into a legal *reality* and practice.[26] Thus, what was a sacred *ideal*

21. Enayat 2013. It is also revealing how conceptions of justice have been associated with and invoked by democracy and freedom in Iranian politics from the Constitutional Revolution up until Khatami's reformist campaign in 1997.

22. Bayat 1991.

23. Enayat 2013, 129.

24. For Egypt, see Hussin 2016, 100; also, Wood 2016. For British India and the Dutch Indonesian Archipelago, see Hallaq 2009, 86.

25. Schacht 1964, 76.

26. Anderson has rightly noticed that "in simplifying indigenous legal arrangements to a form that could be administered by colonial courts, Anglo-Muhammadan scholarship reduced living norms to immutable concepts of purely divine inspiration." Anderson 1993, 19.

and, in retrospect, a *salvation history* was (mis)taken as a *reality* and a fact-based *legal history*.

In this misconception, Western scholarship on *fiqh* and its basic assumptions, taxonomies, and background knowledge was informed by the classical writings of *uṣūl al-fiqh*, which depicted a very neat, rule-governed, objective account of the processes of law-making (*istinbāṭ*) where the Qur'ān and Sunna are the scriptural sources determining the final law (*al-ḥukm al-sharʿī*). Europeans (and, for that matter, later Muslim scholars of *fiqh* as well) who learnt the idea of immutability from this literature made the same mistake which had deluded early positivist historians of science, that of mistaking scientists' retrospective accounts of their work as factual accounts of science-in-making.[27] Similar to science, we may imagine two accounts of *istinbāṭ*: "one uttered when it is finished, the other while it is being attempted."[28] Modern scholarship has cleaved to the former idealistic retrospective account, not bothering to try the latter factual one until very recently.[29] The modern transformation of the *sharīʿa* into something canonical and subject to print technology have left it bereft of practical means of adaptation and change by eliminating the very grounds for variation, toleration, malleability, and case-by-case treatment. So, modernity provided a means to turn the *ideal* of immutability into *reality*.

Scripturalism eliminated non-textual accommodative means such as local customs and made any kind of conflict resolution a matter of the judiciary. *Centralizing* the legal system annihilated the theoretically endless diversity of law and brought to the fore a limited number of religious persuasions. Within this context, only a few texts were selected for the canon, similar to Roman Law. The codification of laws made them rigid and fixed and conferred upon them categorical and precise meanings, which in turn resulted in the eradication of the negotiating space that had been possible given the interpretational multiplicity of classical *fiqh*. One can imagine that such a clear-cut *sharīʿa* code can easily be interpreted as having been derived *logically* and inevitably from its scriptural sources.[30]

While on the surface this codification and legalization has led to the

27. Latour 1987.

28. Latour 1987.

29. For scholarship on *fiqh*-in-making see Sadeghi 2013; Hallaq 1984; Hallaq 1994; Hallaq 2001; Hallaq 2005.

30. Probably it was because of the realization of this arbitrary relationship between scriptural sources and laws that the British did not allow such deductions from scripture: "New rules of law are not to be introduced because they seem to lawyers of the present day to follow logically from ancient texts, however authoritative, when the ancient doctors of the law have not themselves drawn those conclusions." Mulla 1905, 17.

centralization of Islamic law compared to its previously indeterminate, pluralistic, and casuistic nature, a more fundamental transformation was going on at the same time. The *sharīʿa* now became detached from the cosmology and ontology that had carried its whole moral weight and justified and facilitated its enforceability: it was substantively secularized.

Substantive secularization

In its pre-secular settings, belief in the *sharīʿa* and its moral justifiability and enforceability was based on the idea of the enchanted world and the ultimately otherworldly goal of life. When those elements began to collapse one by one, the relationship between these elements changed, with the result that the same belief in the *sharīʿa* was not possible anymore. Society, universe, and the complex web of Islamic beliefs no longer testified to the *sharīʿa*. Thus, there was a need to find other bases for the preservation of belief in the *sharīʿa* while trying to reconcile it with modernity. Muslim reformers (*iṣlāḥ* or *nihḍa*) tried to provide this new ground for keeping the *sharīʿa* by invoking it as an appropriate Islamic way to achieve *civilization* and *progress,* and thus superior to what the Europeans offered. So, the Muslim reformists' approach was not so much a fundamental *return* to the *sharīʿa* as it was a *reconstruction* of it. Secularization of the Muslim social imaginary is best manifested in the following two phenomena in relation to the *sharīʿa.*

A. Utilitarian rationalization of the *sharīʿa*

In the secular Muslim imaginary, the acceptability of any dictum of the *sharīʿa* should be justifiable by the criteria of that field. For example, in economics, the *sharīʿa*'s plausibility is measured by it capacity to deliver what is required from the economy: prosperity, economic equality, fairness, or whatever is believed to be the primary value there.[31] One can see such a utilitarian approach in justifications of the prohibition of usury (*ribā*) by showing that usury allegedly does not lead to sustainable and fair economic growth. Similarly, the modern understanding of the *fiqhī* rule of "prohibition of anything harmful to the human body" (which justifies the loosening of many previously difficult *sharīʿa* injunctions) is based on an overarching utilitarian background.[32] To make these profane considerations compatible with the traditional body of *fiqhī* literature, jurists have used a myriad of

31. See for example al-Afghānī's "Risāliy-e naychiriya." (2000).

32. One may invoke a more recent example that stirred controversy in Iran. Makārem Shīrāzī, one of Qom's ultraconservative *marājiʿ*, issued a fatwa that if wearing *hijab* results in social disadvantage such that non-*hijabis* become superior to Muslims, its removal is allowed in non-Islamic countries.

hermeneutical tools, including the ubiquitous and often unprincipled invocation of, for example, *maṣlaḥa* and *ḍarūra*.[33]

B. Pluralization and diversity

Pre-secular Muslims were triumphalist in terms of themselves and their religion. They felt pride in their conviction that their beliefs and ways of life constituted the exclusive way sanctioned by God, and that distinguishing them from the plurality and inferiority of false religions (*ḍālla*). Islam was the normative center of the universe to which all of humanity ultimately had to *re*-turn. A quick look at how proudly and confidently they described their ways of life attests to this mindset. Pre-secular Islamic triumphalism was much like the way Western culture today boasts of itself as being the vanguard and pioneer of the values of the Enlightenment. It bluntly proclaims its alleged break with its *dark* past, and emphasizes its intellectual achievements it sees as unprecedented in human history. In the same way, the early classical Islamic intelligentsia would see themselves as the culmination of all virtues and would emphasize their rupture with their imagined ignorant past (*jāhilliyya*).

Faced with the modern superiority of Europeans and their assaults on the Muslim world, the modern mentality of Muslims not only lost such narcissistic worldviews but also fell into a passive defensive posture. Muslim intellectuals' primary concern changed from that of proving Islam's superiority to that of showing that it is, at least, not exceptionally backward. This, in turn, inadvertently gave way to Islamic pluralism, the conviction that Islamic beliefs and practices enjoy the same standing as other belief systems do. Muslim intellectuals excavated other cultures' literature to substantiate their claims. Thus, for example, in one of the earliest treatises written to defend the hijab in Iran, Muḥammad Ṣādiq Urūmī Fakhru l-Islām (d. 1951) dedicated almost a third of his writing to demonstrating that the *hijab* has existed not only in Christianity and Judaism but also in paganism – "and thus we saw that hijab and niqab have been widespread among women, even among idolaters."[34] More recently, justifications for observing the *sharīʿa* are being expressed in a postmodern, multiculturalist rhetoric. For example, advocates of mandatory *hijab* speak of cultural difference and defend it by attesting to the allegedly similar case of the burqa ban in France. Cultural preferences are different, in one case it leads to banning burqa and in another case to the mandatory *hijab*.[35] Thus, de-

33. Layish 1978.
34. Jaʿfarian 2001, 1, 70.
35. See for example: https://tinyurl.com/zs8b6ac.

fenders of the *hijab* investigate dress codes in other countries to prove its neutral non-exceptionalism. The *hijab* falls from a mysterious ordinance of the divine that should have been submissively accepted and observed to a profane everyday rational norm common also to other cultures and to whose truth every reasonable human would admit. To adapt the hijab to modern Western convictions, some even tried to show that it is compatible with the exhibition of feminine beauty by showcasing sexy *hijabi* models. If the utilitarian rationalization of the *hijab* served as a motivation for believers to prove that they do not sacrifice any this-worldly advantage by observing the *hijab* but also benefit from it, pluralization furthered it by providing more evidence from other *advanced* cultures and showing its *normality*. Thus, gradually an exclusivist understanding of *sharīʿa* as an absolute truth fades away and it is increasingly being justified by a utilitarian rationality and a cultural pluralism. Bruce has persuasively explained a similar trajectory in Christianity:

> Diversity also had consequences for consciousness. It called into question the certainty that believers could accord their religion. Ideas are most convincing when they are universally shared. If everyone shares the same beliefs, they are not beliefs; they are just how the world is. Any world view is most powerful, not when it is supported by aggressive propaganda but when it is so much taken for granted that it does not require such promotion. The elaboration of alternatives provides a profound challenge. Believers need not fall on their swords when they find that others disagree with them. Where clashes of ideologies occur in the context of social conflict or when alternatives are promoted by people who need not be seriously entertained, the cognitive challenge can be dismissed. [36]

Secularization of *Fiqh* in Contemporary Iran

The confluence of two factors has recently contributed to the further secularization of *fiqh* in Iran. The first was the preexisting but expanding familiarity with the modern field of Islamic studies in the West, which has triggered the formation of projects to present a more "modern-scientific"-looking rebranding of fiqh. Whereas past theologians – in the words of Anselm of Canterbury – *believed* so that they could *understand* religion (*credo ut intelligam*), modern scholars of "religious studies" studied religion with a

36. Bruce 2011, 37. For correlation between secularity and pluralism also see Berger and Luckmann 1981; Berger and Luckmann 1966.

third-person disengaged perspective.[37] This *scientific* method of the study of religion (*fiqh* included) lured many Muslim intellectuals and caught them in a dilemma: while they admired the robustness of the methodology of modern Islamic studies they rejected the substantive views reached by its methodologies. Thus, Muslims' reaction to such modern studies addressed mainly the *content* while accommodating the methodology as a rigorous, impartial, and academically valid approach. The result was to adopt certain elements of modern methodologies of religious studies and then apply them in their research for the purpose of defending their long-held dogmas about the history of Islam in general and *fiqh* in particular. Though the methods of the scientific study of religion were not fully accommodated into the new researches, even partial implementation of those methods had long-term effects in changing the conceptions of the scholars of *fiqh*.

The other factor was the desperate need of the new religious elite (especially after the Islamic Revolution of Iran) for more effective ways to expand the reach and the jurisdiction of *sharīʿa*. This need for more efficiency led them to the adoption of secular religious institutions and genres of religious education. In other words, the need to expand the audience and jurisdiction of *fiqh* resulted – ironically and self-destructively – in its secularization.

The Role of Institutional Change

During the middle and later decades of the twentieth century, the Shīʿī centers of *fiqhī* production in seminaries – whether in Qom or Najaf – underwent a structural and organizational transformation which had far-reaching and deep consequences on *fiqh* and *sharīʿa*. In Iran, concurrent with the introduction of a modern central state by Reza Shah, the Qom Seminary also became structurally centralized under the auspices of Abdul-Karīm Hāʾerī Yazdī (1859–1937). Later, with Seyyed Ḥosain Borūjerdī (1875–1961) becoming the uncontested grand *marjaʿ taqlīd*, this centralization even was intensified.

During this period of organizational change in the seminary, the modernist clerics including Morteza Motahhari (1919–1979), Sayyed Mohammad Beheshti (1928–1981), Mohammad-Javad Bahonar (1933–1981), Akbar Hashemi Rafsanjani (1934–2017), Mohammad Mofatteh (1928–1979), Sayyed Mahmoud Taleghani (1911–1979) critiqued the traditional education of *fiqh* because it did not pay attention to real problems of the Islamic world and was instead preoccupied with imaginary, unrealistic, and abstract jurisprudential issues. They also argued that the traditional *fiqh* is ossified and became obsolete and irrelevant because it does not take into account the

37. Giurlanda 1987, 192.

changing requirements of time (*muqtaḍiyāt-e zamān*). They furthermore claimed that religious education is mainly limited to the *fiqh* and does not allocate enough space to the Qurʾān, and is too individualistic and pays too much attention to ritual acts (*ʿibādāt*) at the expense of the immediate needs of the Muslim community.[38]

These modernist clerics pushed for the modernization of religious seminaries through the reform of the traditional curriculum and the introduction of modern structural changes to the madrasa. This was resisted by most of the seminarians who saw in the old structure a sacred heritage shaped by generations of pious *ʿulamāʾ*. Any change in those structures and their contents was deemed anathema to the spirit of authenticity and popular credibility of that institution. It is famous that when Borūjerdī accepted the initiative to include European languages in the seminary curriculum, a group of bazaar merchants objected to the initiative and threatened Borūjerdī with cutting their religious endowments (*wujūhāt*) and jeopardizing the financial flow of the Qom Seminary.[39] Similar concerns applied about teaching non-*fiqhī* subjects such as philosophy, *kalām*, and *tafsīr*. In the *waqf* documents (*waqf-nāmeh*) of some religious madrasas the condition was stipulated to limit the usage of the property in question to the study of *fiqh* and exclude education in philosophy and "other illusionary sciences" (*ʿulūm-e wahmiyy-e*).[40] Despite all resistances shown by traditional segments of the *fuqahāʾ*, the modernists embarked upon reform of seminary with several initiatives. One of these was the establishment of schools and universities which offered simultaneously traditional seminary subjects and modern humanities and social sciences. Haqqani school, among the first of this kind, was established by the politically active clerics such as Ali Qoddusi (1927–1981), Mohammad-Taqi Mesbah-Yazdi (b. 1935), Ahmad Jannati (b. 1927), Beheshti, Ali Meshkini (1921–2007), and Taleghani.[41] It was followed by dozens of other schools and institutes such as Muʾassesse-ye Dar Rāhe Haqq by Misbah-Yazdi (later evolved into Imam Khomeini Institute), Dār al-Tablīgh of Sayyed Mohammad Kazem Shariat-madari (1906–1986), and others. In Najaf, Muḥammad Bāqer al-Ṣadr (1935–1980), Muḥmamd Jawād Mughniyya, and Muḥammad Riḍā al-Muẓaffar (1904–1964) started the movement of reform of *ḥawza* by establishing new schools similar to the modern European universities and writing professional textbooks for education of Islamic sciences.

38. Motahhari 1982; Abulḥuseynī 2006; Ranjbar 2004. It is also interesting that during this time there was a surge in the Qurʾān-only approach as is evident in the surge of *tafāsīr* written in this period.

39. Ranjbar 2004.

40. See Aḥmad 2014, 21:488–489.

41. Nome and Vogt 2008; Arjmand 2017.

After the revolution, the initiative continued with the establishment of the Imam Sadiq University, Mofid University, and Baqer al-Ulum University, among others. Structurally and organizationally, these hybrid institutes were a copycat of modern universities, but in terms of contents, they offered a plethora of subjects in Islamic studies and modern humanities and social sciences. The mentality behind these institutes was that there is no meaningful link between the modern *structure* of the production of knowledge and their *contents*. The form of the modern university is a universal and neutral instrument, which can accommodate any content and can be used for any purpose. Those who believed in this misconception have unintendedly contributed to secularization of Islamic studies and *fiqh* in particular.

By the victory of the revolution, the Islamist-modernists took the control of the seminary and marginalized the traditional groups. Khomeini established the Higher Council of Seminary (*Shorā-ye ʿālī-ye ḥawzeh*) in 1979 to centralize the administration of religious education. The change in the seminary was accelerated after the death of Khomeini in 1988 when Khamenei assumed the leadership. Khamenei established the Center for the Management of the Seminary Schools in 1991 and concentrated all administration in it.[42] This organization controls all seminary schools in the county except for seminary schools in Mashhad and Isfahan, which have their independent councils. The foreign seminarians are also all concentrated under a new organization named The Center for Islamic Sciences (later renamed Al-Mustafa International University). These organizations made the conferral of any state benefit to the seminarians conditioned on being enrolled under these new schemes. Those state benefits include: exemption from military service; payment of Khamenei's monthly stipend (*shahriye*), which had the lions' share of the monthly stipends; housing loans; superannuation and health cover insurance; visa sponsorship for foreign students; and many other concessions.[43] The new structure incorporated most of the elements of the university system: semester credit system; unified and centrally organized exams; university degrees (Bachelor, Master of Arts, and Doctorate) among others. Thus, when a seminarian accomplished his initial introductory subjects (*saṭḥ* level) he is granted the bachelor degree. Upon taking more advanced units in *fiqh* and other subjects and writing an academic thesis he is granted a Masters degree and finally if he is talented enough he may proceed to the PhD level with a panel of advanced professors. The proceeding are copycat of modern universities.

The study (*taʿallum*) of religious sciences in traditional settings was

42. https://tinyurl.com/y6bnegud.

43. For a list of services offered by the government to the seminaries see the website of Hawzeh Services Center on: http://csis.ir/.

closely associated with a range of sacred spaces, objects, and jargon. The old madrasas were generally a part of the mosque and together formed unitary spaces in which the worship of God was the first and foremost objective. This essentially other-worldly orientation was manifested even in their architecture and vibe. The modernization of religious seminaries has largely removed this heritage and has cut off this sacred historical imaginary, making it an institute on a par with other educational institutions though with somehow different subject matters.

Another more recent development is the admission of thousands of university graduates into the body of traditional seminaries, which might undermine the traditional pursuit of knowledge and make deeper rifts between the older jurisprudential methods and the modern ones. Their mentality is mainly shaped by the modern scientific imaginary, is evidence-based, and values impartial disengaged observation, unlike the pristine mind of those seminarians who start their religious education when fifteen years old. The university graduates are also more intelligent and efficient than the traditional clergies, and thus exert more influence in the power structure of the seminaries.

The Role of Modern Genres of *Fiqh* Production

Modernist clerics believed that the traditional *fiqhī* genres are incapable of effective defense of faith and spreading its mission to a wider population. Apart from writing more accessible, less complex, and simple treatises and books with larger readership for the Farsi readers, and modern textbooks,[44] three modern European genres of scholarly writing were crucial in this change towards more efficiency, which in turn contributed to more secularization: history, encyclopedia, and research papers.

Noel James Coulson, the famous historian of Islamic law, has rightly singled out Islamic law as an "extreme example of a legal science divorced from historical considerations."[45] The immutable law of Islam is based on the will of God (at least in the perception of the Muslims if not fully in legal practice) and thus there can "be no notion of the law in itself evolving as an historical phenomenon closely tied with the progress of society."[46] Writing a history of law showing its relevance to the vicissitudes of time rather than a *salvation*

44. Such as al-Muḍaffar's book "ʿUṣūl al-fiqh" and al-Ṣadr's famous *al-Dorūs fī al-uṣūl* (also known as *al-Ḥalaqāt*). Al-Ṣadr in his other *fiqhī* writings, especially in his categorization of topics of *fiqh* was clearly influenced by European jurisprudence. He believed that textbooks should always change based on the modern innovations in "scientific methods." See: https://hawzah.net/fa/Magazine/View/4518/5455/51318.

45. Coulson 2011, 1.

46. Coulson 2011, 1.

story and the very idea that the *sharīʿa* injunctions are a result of historical evolution, contingent, and not necessarily a result of sacred design did not fit well into a perception of an immutable law as ordained by God. Historicity implied profanity and worldly and casual links rather than a sacred plan and design. Writing history requires distance from the devotional and emic perspective to, at least temporarily, an outsider and etic perspective – one which was intrinsically in tension with the very idea of a sacred God-given law.[47] That is why it was the *fuqahāʾ* in academia who wrote histories of *fiqh* as opposed to seminary jurists to whom transcending the first-person, devotional, and polemical context of the *ḥawza* proved to be a difficult task. Abu l-Qāsim Gorjī in Tehran University clearly stated in his "*Tārīkh-e fiqh va fuqahā*" that upon detailed examination of the Shīʿī jurisprudential compendia he could not find any books on the history of Shīʿī *fiqh*.[48]

Despite these internal tensions in writing a history of *fiqh* (which was the reason behind the lack of such a genre in the first place) the necessity of defending the faith against the historical criticism of Western Islamicists such as Ignác Goldziher and Joseph Schacht provided a good reason to embark upon such a project. Since the historical approach was not a flagrant breach of any religious dogma, it was very difficult to defy and stigmatize it from a religious point of view. Rather, for the clerics, it was merely a matter of methodology and *form* rather than substantive issue of the content, and thus very difficult to formulate a comprehensive opposition. The creeping infusion of neutrality and dispassionate impartiality as a scholarly value and criterion of excellence was an unintended consequence of the adoption of those genres which were not seen correlated with the substantive views about *fiqh* or Islam in general.

The second more important genre is the encyclopedia, which became more prevalent after the revolution and had a deep but difficult-to-spot effect on the secularization of *fiqh*-discourse. The genre presumes all existing stances on a given dispute as of an equal standing, describes its subject from a third-person and disengaged perspective, and avoids devotional and value-laden language and commits to an objective language. More important, this requires the researcher to suspend his belief in all supernatural forces and think in an entirely naturalistic causal terms – what Peter Berger called it "methodological atheism" and now is taken for granted in many branches

47. Temporarily "giving up faith" was advised to students of Islamic philosophy when they were engaged in philosophy discussions.

48. Gorjī 2012, 1. Universities had a subject about the history of *fiqh* and *fuqaha* while seminaries did not include it in their curriculum. The curriculum of *fiqh* at the University of Tehran: https://ftis.ut.ac.ir/.

of religious studies.[49] Thus, instead of assuming narcissistically that one's stance is self-evident and God-given and is the only moral and *normal* view in town and thus, all other views are morally wrong, banal and stupid, the new method required stripping off all personal and vernacular biases and subjecting one's reason to a universal, cosmopolitan, independent, and disengaged rationality. Perhaps the best phrase articulating this "dispassionate impartiality" – as Tylor calls it – is the second sentence of the Manual of Style of *Dāneshnāme-ye Jahān-e Islām*: "in writing [encyclopedia] articles, judgements without references and reasons, and biased views should be avoided and in addition, prejudiced predilections of resources should be moderated [corrected] and their one-sided judgements and impressions should be criticized and disclosed. Panegyrism and the use of cliché eulogistic expressions is not allowed."[50]

As I have mentioned earlier, the perceptions and exposure to diversity and pluralism also played an important role in the acceptance of this trend among new generations, in particular those who were pursuing *fiqhī* education in academic or semi-academic settings. The implicit belief that rival *fiqhī* approaches or schools have somehow a similar status, made it acceptable to write an encyclopedia from a third-person perspective and compare those schools.[51] It is ironic that the modern encyclopedias on Islam written in Iran were predominantly driven by polemic religious motivations to introduce Islam in an academic way. Among the most important encyclopedias written in Iran about Islam are the followings: *Great Islamic Encyclopedia*, by Mousavi Bojnurdi;[52] *Dāneshnāme Jahān-e Islām*, edited by Haddad Adel; *The Shīʿa Encyclopedia, The Encyclopedia of Qurʾān-e Karīm, The Encyclopedia of Ḥajj, Dāiʾra al-Maʿāref-e Fiqh-e Ahl-e Beyt*. These are considered rivals to and are written in response to the influential *Encyclopaedia of Islam* published by Brill of the Netherlands, *The Encyclopaedia of Qurʾān*, and others with the intention of correcting their errors and anti-Islamic biases.

The third genre that contributes to this trend of the secularization of *fiqh* in the long run is the mushrooming of research journals modeled after modern Western journals. These publications, like their Western counterparts, use blind peer-review, and include articles with different sections

49. See Berger 1969, 100. Also see Porpora 2006.

50. http://rch.ac.ir/ContentP/shivenameKolliDetail.

51. Writing encyclopedias in the traditional meaning has a long history in the Persian language (including *Iḥṣāʾ al-ʿulūm* of al-Fārābī, Treatises of Purity Brethren (*Rasāʾil Ikhwān al-Ṣafāʾ*), and *mafātiḥ al-ʿulūm* of al-Khwārazmī) but these are not in any sense similar to the specifications I have mentioned about the modern genre of encyclopedia. For a list of traditional encyclopedias see: Rūdgar 2015, vol. 17.

52. Twenty-four volumes of which is published.

such as introduction, literature review and background, methodology, results, and discussion.[53] The rules of scientific research similar to the encyclopedia genre apply here also: objective and unbiased analysis; disengaged language; and so on. Again, however, these rules are not strictly observed in the dozens of specialized journals of *fiqh*, but instead only function as *guiding principles* and *criteria of excellence* meant to guarantee *good* research. There is also a career-related motivation to this surge. Since any promotion in the universities as well as many seminary-affiliated centers is conditioned on authoring a certain number of papers in the journals certified as "Research Journal" by the Ministry of Science, Research, and Technology, in the long run, more scholars have to adopt these genres if they want to benefit from the advantages associated with publishing in scholarly journals.

These genres result in secularizing the language of the *fiqhī* production in the long-term. What I mean by secularizing the language is changing it from a language steeped in background assumptions of an exclusivist belief in one's faith, devotional, value-laden, and panegyrist to a neutral, value-free, third-person, disengaged one. There is a deep shift from *"haẓrat-e imām Ḥusain farmūd"* (His Excellency Imam Husain said) to "*dar ḥadīthī muntasab be imām-e sevvum-e Shīʿayān āmadeh ast*" (a *ḥadīth* attributed to the third Shīʿa Imam says). The first conveys the sacredness of Husain, that the interlocutor believes in his being an imam, and his/her paying respect for Husain. The second is linguistically agnostic if not atheist: the author distances him/herself from being attached to a belief in the imamate of Husain by ascribing it to the Shīʿa rather than to him/herself. It also casts doubt on the historical accuracy of the *ḥadīth* since it only "attributes" the saying to Husain. The language either is silent on the author's personal beliefs and devotional character or it presumes that religious convictions do not represent the reality. In either case the linguistic expressions in this so-called neutral tone fall short of endorsing religious dogmas. Another example might be the change from *aʾimmi-ye maʿṣūmīn* to *imāmān-e Shīʿa* or from *ḥaram-e aʾimme* to *amāken-e moqaddas-e Shīʿa.*[54] Thus, in a majority of cases there is a clear shift from a *restricted code* to an *elaborated code*, in Basil Bernstein's[55] words – or for that matter, from a high-context cultural setting to a low-context one.[56] In the restricted code, the speaker shares a deep understanding,

53. Thirty-seven journals on *fiqh* and *uṣūl* are listed in the Noor Specialized Magazine Website, which is a Qom-based online database and indexing service. See https://www.noormags.ir/view/en.

54. Or from *Sālār-e Shahīdān* to *Imām-e sevvum-e Shīʿayān.*

55. Bernstein 2004.

56. Hall 1989, 68–69.

background knowledge, and assumptions with the listeners; thus, it skips many of them. With more acknowledgement of the diversity among people, restricted codes lose their ground as a proper way of communication and people tend to transcend and find ways to include those also who might not share their highly devotional version of faith. Thus, in this change there is a tacit acknowledgement of the existence of a legitimately different Other who is now respected by the speaker by changing the language in a way to include his possible views also into account. By using the elaborated code, the speaker acknowledges that the audience might not belong to our group – in itself great difference.

This change also shows itself in translatability, that is, how much information is lost or preserved in the translation of a specific phrase to another language and how much of extra explanations needs to be added so that the phrase could be understood easily in the target language. For example, a phrase of the entry of *Ahl-e Kitāb* in the *Great Islamic Encyclopedia* reads: "In a verse of Quran, their [i.e. the People of the Book] food is known to be halal for Muslims (Q 5:5) ... but in juristic investigations, interpretations of jurists have been varied about this verse."[57] This is easily translatable to other languages and could be read and understood without the reader sharing any religious convictions with the writer. In other words, the text does not reveal any information about the author or what his/her religious preferences are. It could be anyone writing that phrase, for example, a Japanese researcher on Islam, an atheist expert, or a Muslim one. Another phrase reads "Sunni jurists and some Imamite jurists have allowed eating the food of the People of the Book including meat and other foodstuff, and marrying women of the People of the Book absolutely, though with variations on the details of the [interpretation] of the verse."[58] Here, the author equates Sunnī and Shīʿī jurists. He has a disengaged language and a flat universal perspective which is not affiliated with any party in the discussion, and he only *reports* their views. There is a clear distinction between the traditional vernacular and participant perspective and the new universal non-participant one. The secular language is a language without perspective.

However, this does not mean that scholarly works in these genres in Iran are not polemical, or that their writers do not intend to defend the faith against presumed offenders. Quite the contrary, these genres were principally adopted to shield the faith against intruders and expand its reach. Almost all encyclopedias after the revolution have been established by passionate believers who felt threatened by the increasing reception of

57. Pakatchi 1989, l:10, 475.
58. Pakatchi 1989, l:10, 475.

the modern European scholarship in Iran, whose content was not endorsing their traditional dogmas.

Conclusion

Joseph Schacht once opined that perhaps "the concept of law did not exist in Islam."[59] He was correct in that, as Wood has also confirmed, in the modern era "the very conception of *sharīʿa* changed."[60] This fundamental transformation of the concept of the *sharīʿa*, together with its marginalization into personal status, led to the emergence of Islamic legal revivalism in the 1930s and onward. While the *sharīʿa* co-existed unproblematically with secular laws before modernity, it was "identified and advertised as a singularly complete and valid source for the development of a comprehensive system of positive laws that was created, managed, and enforced by the state."[61]

In exploring the genealogy of the *sharīʿa*, one must be vigilant about anachronism; the *sharīʿa*, its meaning and connotations, as well as the constellation of relevant concepts and practices, have all been transformed fundamentally in their encounter with modernity. As Asad[62] has argued, the whole category of religion is constructed in modern times, and the modern conception of the *sharīʿa* is one of these constructs.

I have tried to show in this chapter that, in the wake of the Islamic encounter with Europe, *sharīʿa* has undergone a revolutionary transformation. Initially it was redefined (metamorphosed and constructed) as positive law of newly formed nation-states (*étatisation*), and its jurisdiction increasingly shrank and was relegated to mainly the personal status. This was in tandem with the European invention of the modern concept of religion and the process of scripturalism that made the *sharīʿa* central to the social imaginary in many Muslim societies. The process of selection of some classical schools and books as the main source of codification (which in any case was inevitable) contributed to the formation of a mainstream Islamic legal mentality at the expense of the marginalization or elimination of others. A combination of an upsurge in the use of print technology with the subsequent dissemination of a codified *sharīʿa*, made those fixed codes part of a self-evident Islamic imaginary that is very hard to alter. Indeed, these processes helped the *sharīʿa* to become rigid, unchangeable, rule-bound, and, thus, immutable. These features provided the means to make the imaginative and normative *ideal* of immutability (which has never been invented

59. Schacht 1964, 200.
60. Wood 2016, 4.
61. Wood 2016, 4.
62. Asad 2009.

as an immediate practical instrument to be applied homogeneously to all environments) a *reality*. Islamic law became immutable precisely because the now-homogenized, unified, and rigidified dicta were disseminated to the whole population. It was not that the *sharīʿa* was immutable in nature, but that modern transformations built unchangeability into its fabric. Subsequently a general movement of revival of the *sharīʿa* began, which took different shapes depending on diverse local circumstances and sociocultural milieux. Simultaneous with these processes, the Muslim world has undergone a deep process of secularization which has undermined the pillars upon which a firm belief in the *sharīʿa* had rested. I have explained that the modern concept of the *sharīʿa* has been transformed into a secular one, and thus a new, secular *sharīʿa* is constructed whose roots are cut off from its past cosmology.

Fast-forward to the more recent transformations of the institutions of *fiqhī* education and the genres of *fiqhī* production, I have shown how the modern Western institutions, methodologies, and knowledge production further contribute to the birth of a new secular and impartial approach vis-à-vis a devotional, value-laden, and engaged rhetoric. I believe the triumph of the first approach will have deep secularizing effects in the long "run in the content of those writings as well.

Bibliography

Abulḥoseynī, S. 2006. Pīshgāmān-e aqrīb: Shaikh Muḥammad-Riḍā Muẓaffar iṣlāḥgar-e ḥawze-hā." *Andīshe-ye taqrīb* 4.

al-Afghānī, S. J. 2000. "Risāliy-e naychiriya." In *Majmūʿiyi rasāʾil wa maqālāt Sayyid Jamāl al-Dīn Ḥusiynī*, edited by Sayyid Hādī Khosroshāhī, 11–63. Qom.

Aḥmad, P. 2014. "Ḥawzey-e ʿilmiyy-e." *Great Islamic Encyclopedia*. Tehran.

Anderson, M. R. 1993. "Islamic Law and the Colonial Encounter in British India." In *Institutions and Ideologies: A SOAS South Asia Reader*, edited by D. Arnold and P. Robb. Surrey.

Arjmand, R. 2017. "Islamic Education in Iran." In *Handbook of Islamic Education*, edited by H. Daun, H. and R. Arjmand. Berlin.

Asad, T. 2001. "Thinking about Secularism and Law in Egypt." *ISIM paper 2*. Leiden.

———. 2003. *Formations of the Secular: Christianity, Islam, Modernity*. Stanford.

———. 2009. *Genealogies of Religion: Discipline and Reasons of Power in Christianity and Islam*. Baltimore.

Bayat, M. 1991. *Iran's First Revolution: Shiʾism and the Constitutional Revolution of 1905–1909*. Oxford and New York.

Berger, P. 1969. *The Sacred Canopy: Elements of a Sociological Theory of Religion.* New York.
Berger, P. L., and T. Luckmann. 1966. "Secularization and Pluralism." *International Yearbook for the Sociology of Religion* 2:73–84.
——. 1981. "The Heretical Imperative: Contemporary Possibilities of Religious Affirmation." *Religious Studies* 17:109–120.
Bernstein, B. 2004. *Applied Studies towards a Sociology of Language.* New York.
Bruce, S. 2011. *Secularization: In Defence of an Unfashionable Theory,* Oxford.
Coulson, N. J. 2011. *A History of Islamic Law.* Piscataway.
Enayat, H. 2013. "Law, State, and Society in Nineteenth-Century Iran." In *Law, State, and Society in Modern Iran,* edited by H. Enayat. Basingstoke.
Geertz, C. 1971. *Islam Observed: Religious Development in Morocco and Indonesia.* Chicago.
Gellner, E. 1970. "A Pendulum Swing Theory of Islam." In *Sociology of Religion: Selected Readings,* edited by R. Robertson. Middlesex.
Giurlanda, P. 1987. *Faith and Knowledge: A Critical Inquiry.* Lanham.
Gorjī, A. Q. 2012. *Tārīkh-e fiqh wa fuqahā.* Tehran.
Hall, E. T. 1989. *Beyond Culture.* New York.
Hallaq, W. B. 1984. "Was the Gate of ijtihad Closed?" *International Journal of Middle East Studies* 16:3–41.
——. "From Fatwās to Furū: Growth and Change in Islamic Substantive Law. *Islamic Law and Society* 1:29–65.
——. 2001. *Authority, Continuity and Change in Islamic Law.* Cambridge.
——. 2005. *The Origins and Evolution of Islamic Law.* Cambridge.
——. 2009. *An Introduction to Islamic Law.* Cambridge.
Hefner, R. W. 2010. "Introduction: Muslims and Modernity: Culture and Society in an Age of Contest and Plurality." In *The New Cambridge History of Islam: Volume 6, Muslims and Modernity: Culture and Society since 1800,* edited by R. W. Hefner. Cambridge.
Hussin, I. R. 2016. *The Politics of Islamic Law: Local Elites, Colonial Authority, and the Making of the Muslim State.* Chicago.
Jaʿfarian, R. 2001. *Risāʾil-e ḥijābiyy-e.* Qom.
Latour, B. 1987. *Science in Action: How to Follow Scientists and Engineers through Society.* Cambridge.
Layish, A. 1978. "The Contribution of the Modernists to the Secularization of Islamic Law. *Middle Eastern Studies* 14.3:263–277.
Massad, J. 2008. Civilized or Decadent? Time and the Culture of the Arabs. In *Islam and the Orientalist World-System,* edited by K. Samman, and M. Al-Zo'by, M. New York.
Matthee, R. 1998. Between Aloofness and Fascination: Safavid Views of the West. *Iranian Studies* 31:219–246.

Motahhari, M. 1982. "Mushkel-e aṣlī dar sāzmān-e ruwḥāniyat." *Dah goftār.* Tehran.
Mulla, D. F. S. 1905. *Principles of Mohammedan Law.* Bombay.
Nome, F. A. and K. Vogt. 2008. "Islamic Education in Qom: Contemporary Developments." *Acta Orientalia* 69:35–75.
Nongbri, B. 2013. *Before Religion.* New Haven.
Pakatchi, A. 1989. "Ahl-e Kitāb." *Great Islamic Encyclopedia.*Tehran.
Pfaff, R. H. 1963. "Disengagement from Traditionalism in Turkey and Iran." *Western Political Quarterly* 16:79–98.
Porpora, D. 2006. "Methodological Atheism, Methodological Agnosticism and Religious Experience. *Journal for the Theory of Social Behaviour* 36:57–75.
Ranjbar, M. 2004. "Faḍāy-e tanaffus-e Shīʿa : goftimān-e iṣlāḥ dar ḥawze-ye ʿilmiy-ye Qom dar dahe-ye 1340 Shamsī." *Zamāneh* 16:22–30.
Rūdgar, G. 2015. "Dānishnāmeh negārī." *Dāneshnāmeye Jahān Islām.* Tehran.
Sadeghi, B. 2013. *The Logic of Law Making in Islam: Women and Prayer in the Legal Tradition.* Cambridge.
Said, E. W. 1978. *Orientalism.* New York.
Schacht, J. 1964. *An Introduction to Islamic Law.* Oxford.
Schulze, R. 2002. *A Modern History of the Islamic World.* New York.
Smith, W. C. 1964. *The Meaning and End of Religion.* Minneapolis.
Taylor, C. 2007. *A Secular Age.* Cambridge.
———. 2011. "Western Secularity." In *Rethinking Secularism*, edited by C. Calhoun, Mark Juergensmeyer, and Jonathan VanAntwerpen. Oxford.
Wilson, B. 1983. *Religion in Sociological Perspective.* Oxford.
Wood, L. 2016. *Islamic Legal Revival: Reception of European Law and Transformations in Islamic Legal Thought in Egypt, 1875–1952.* Oxford.
Zubaida, S. 2005. *Law and Power in the Islamic World.* London.

6

Kalām: Constructing Divinity

Aaron W. Hughes

THEOLOGY IS OSTENSIBLY about the articulation of truth-claims on behalf of a faith community that imagines itself as divinely chosen. It is the name given to the discipline, often constructed as "divine," that is ultimately responsible for the elucidation of correct belief and the subsequent differentiation of such belief from that which is imagined as either misinformed or incorrect. In order to undertake such articulation and differentiation, theologians develop certain agreed-upon or consensual techniques with which to mine their sacred scriptures in order to clarify proper or normative belief for their own community of believers while simultaneously defending the tradition from various despisers. The latter can be either different religious traditions or different sects within the same religion. On account of their exegetical work, theologians tend to envisage themselves less as social actors responding to historically contingent events and more as timeless agents engaged in the articulation of correct belief from sources (e.g. scripture) imagined as eternal and sacred.

The modern Western and largely secular academy, however, tends to eschew such claims of timelessness and the concomitant pursuit of that which is imagined as some capital-T truth. In its stead, this academy is predicated on showing, especially in the aftermath of Michel Foucault's work, how such "truth-claims" are less about actual truths than they are about much larger and more complex issues of politics and ideology, and how these two principles are often heavily invested in the construction of so-called orthodoxy. The emphasis, in other words, is on the construction or the manufacture as opposed to the eternal or the divine.

This tension is palpable in the ways in which theology is studied. In religious seminaries and conservative departments, for example, God's existence, the sacrality of religious texts, and the hermeneutical principles used to interpret both are often simply assumed and taken for granted. Move such principles into the secular academy, including departments of religious studies, however, and a much different set of issues – and questions – begin to emerge. The theologian stands aghast at the prevailing god-less discourses of the academician, just as the latter is disquieted by the perceived gullibility of the former.

If we transfer this general schema, and the inherent tensions it engenders, onto the register of Islam, we certainly see a similar situation. *Kalām* – often translated as "Islamic theology," though not unproblematically, as we shall see below – is about ascertaining, and subsequently defending, proper belief as if it existed in some sort of timeless vacuum. The majority of contemporary Western Islamic studies, however, tends to focus on the requisite historical and intellectual contexts of, including non-Muslim influences on, Islamic theology's development and florescence. There also exists a fairly significant expenditure in contemporary Western Islamic studies to engage in a quasi-*kalāmic* enterprise, albeit under the guise of secular scholarship, that seeks to define an "authentic" Islam that coincides with liberal values.[1] This latter enterprise, I shall suggest in the final section of this chapter, is structurally similar to that of classical *kalām*.

The present chapter, however, wishes to go a step further and argue that the study of what practitioners and believers imagine to be a divinely-constructed *kalām* can and ought to be situated, at least academically, much more profitably within the more critical wing associated with the contemporary and largely secular discipline of religious studies. The latter, in particular, avoids the thorny issue of truth-claims and instead situates theology within the larger context of orthodoxy as something imagined, articulated, and subsequently disseminated. *Kalām*, on this reading, is not a divine activity, but an activity that is constructed as divine in order to protect certain interests.

In order to do this, I organize the present chapter into the following parts. First, I provide a brief overview of *kalām* by both defining it and subsequently charting its origins and some of its major historical permutations. Following this descriptive section, I move towards an examination of some of the various ways Islamic theology has been integrated into the Western academy, primarily through the study of Orientalism. The latter has tended to emphasize the rationalist and rationalizing tendencies of medieval Islam, constructing *kalām* as the precursor of the subsequent Islamic philosophical tradition, and the emergence of the "great men" of that tradition, such as al-Fārābī (d. ca. 331/950), Ibn Sīnā (d. ca. 428/1037), and Ibn Rushd (d. 595/1198). Finally, in the third part, I endeavor to make a bolder statement that shows the broader significance of the secular study of *kalām* for the hu-

1. E.g. Safi 2003; Kugle 2010; Chaudhry 2014. I have been critical of such approaches. See, for example Hughes 2015.

manities by situating the topic, as just mentioned, firmly within the field of religious studies. I do this by demonstrating how works of *kalām* – and those who produce them – become the prime matter for the active manufacture of Islam. This, I trust, will help to nudge or reorient the academic study of *kalām* by showing how the topic is integral to the social construction of identity.

Kalām: A Historical Overview (of sorts)

Since the goal of the present chapter is to deconstruct the very category of *kalām*, it makes little sense to give an extensive overview of the history of theological speculation in Islam, a topic about which much has already been competently written.[2] My aim instead is to show how the category has played a key role in the shaping of Islamic identities since the earliest – and, by extension, most formative – period of Islam. From this earliest period, as the section will show in greater detail, *kalām* has been invested in the construction of "proper" or "authentic" Muslim belief. Of course, the main way to articulate such belief is to show how others (whether non-Muslims or other, "heterodox," Muslims) are defined by their own set of improper beliefs. This most often takes the form of theological summae, heresiographies, and commentaries, in addition to other related genres.

Despite this, however, allow me to highlight certain aspects of the tradition – to show something of its depth and breadth – with an eye toward establishing how exactly it manufactured normative belief and praxis. In early Islam, theological speculation seems largely to have arisen on account of the perceived need to define correct belief in the light of a series of political controversies that included, among other things, the debate over the status of the "grave sinner" (*murtakib al-kabīra*) that broke out between two rival groups, the Kharijites and the Murjiʾites.[3] This was a particularly acute issue on account of the fact that fellow Muslims assassinated three of the first four successors to Muhammad. Did the assassins, for example, remain Muslims? Or, did their acts somehow separate them from the community of believers, both in this life and the next one? The Kharijites held the grave sinner to be an infidel (*kāfir*) and, thus, beyond the pale of the community in both this life and beyond; the Murjiʾites, by contrast, argued that such individuals remained Muslims and that only God had the power to decide their

2. Indeed there exist many such fine studies that do this. Those I have found influential include: Goldziher 1981; MacDonald 1903; Watt 1973; Wolfson 1976; Winter 2008; and Schmidtke 2016.

3. For requite overview, consult Rippin 2012, 72–87.

fate. Other debates involved predestination (*qadar*) between the Qadarīya and the Jabrīya, not to mention the problem of how to interpret anthropomorphic and other problematic language in the Qur'ān.[4]

Although it is important not to reduce theological speculation in early Islam to outside influence,[5] many western commentators, such as Goldziher and Fakhry, as we shall see shortly, seem content to claim that the most important reason behind the rise of rationalist theology was contact with Greek sources, often through Syriac Christian mediation. Such claims, however, are either denied or ignored among Islamic scholars, where the emphasis is less on the anxiety of influence and more on the actual contents – including creedal formulations – found in works of *kalām*. Western scholars, however, stress the importance of logic and the concomitant need to try to reconcile the terminology and categories of Greek-inflected rationalism with those of monotheism. Abū Ḥayyān al-Tawḥīdī (d. ca. 414/1023) provides an early account of the tensions between these two types of epistemologies –"Greek" and "indigenous" – in his record of the debate between the grammarian Abū Saʿīd al-Sīrāfī (d. ca. 368/979) and the philosopher Abū Bishr Mattā b. Yūnus (d. ca. 328/940).[6] Mattā b. Yūnus, one of the teachers of al-Fārābī, argues that logic is a universal science and thus is central to clear thinking; al-Sīrāfī, who by all accounts wins the debate, counters that logic is not universal, but a Greek linguistic habit and consequently unnecessary for Arab speakers, who have all they need in the rules of Arabic grammar.

Regardless of who actually won this argument, the terms of the debate and the subsequent attempt at reconciliation between these two types of epistemologies return us to the heart of *kalām*, whose practitioners are referred to as *mutakallimūn* (sg. *mutakallim*). The *mutakallim*, literally a "speaker" is, in the words of Goldziher, "one who made a dogma or controversial theological problem into a topic for dialectical discussion and argument, offering speculative proofs for the position he urged."[7]

One such very early example comes by way of Jahm b. Ṣafwān (d. ca. 128/745–746), among the first Muslim scholars do deal with matters of nature, ontology, and epistemology.[8] Though no extant writings of his survive, and what we do possess come from later doxographical, and often polemi-

4. Treiger 2016, 27–43.

5. This influence is usually imagined as either Greek or Syriac. On the latter see Cook 1980, 32–43.

6. al-Tawḥīdī 1939, 108–128. An English translation may be found in Margoliouth 1905, 111–129. See, also, Mahdi 1970, 102–113.

7. Goldziher 198, 85.

8. Schöck 2016, 55–80.

cal, accounts attributed to him, we do at least get a rather clear sense of a number of issues that were behind some of the earliest theological speculation. According to al-Ashʿarī's *Maqālāt*,

> Jahm said: "God's knowledge is temporally originated [*muḥdath*]. He has brought it into temporal existence [*aḥdathahu*] with the result that He knew by it. It is something other than God [*ghayru allāh*]." According to him it is possible that God knows all [particular] things [*ashyā'*] prior to their existence by a knowledge that he brings into existence prior to them.[9]

From this passage we can see how at issue for Jahm b. Ṣafwān is what he imagines to be the nature of God, His "true" or "authentic" relationship to the world, and, in particular, how He is imagined to have knowledge of all the particulars – including humans – that exist within the world. If God reasons and subsequently knows in the same manner that humans do, for example, then His knowledge – and, by extension, God Himself – risks being reduced to human epistemological categories. This would mean, by Jahm's reasoning, that God, the Creator of the world, would become little more than a "superman" and would differ little, for example, from a Greek god. Jahm also sought to resist such a reduction and, in the process, he is often recounted to be among the first to argue that the Qurʾān was created. This would become such an important issue because, at least for those who denied an eternal Qurʾān, such a principle would posit something coeval with God, and thus set up two divine principles, à la Zoroastrianism. The existence of a created Qurʾān would subsequently become, as we shall witness shortly, an important and central feature of Muʿtazila *kalām*.

Jahm b. Ṣafwān was subsequently associated, at least in the later Islamic theological tradition, with a school that was eponymously attributed to him, known as the Jahmites. According to al-Malaṭī (d. 377/987), the Jahmites

> are a people who deny God all attributes [*ṣinf min al-muʿaṭṭila*]. They say, God is not a thing" [*lā min shayʾin*], nor is he "of" a thing [*mā min shayʾin*], nor is he "in" a thing [*mā fī min shayʾin*]. Nor does the attribute [*ṣinf*] of a thing apply to Him, nor the knowledge [*maʿrifa*] of a thing, nor the estimation [*tawahhum*] of a thing. They further argue that they know God only by intuition [*bi-l-takhmīn*]. They apply to Him the name "godhead" [*ism al-ulūhiyya*], but do not describe Him by an attribute [*ṣifa*] that pertains to the godhead.[10]

9. al-Ashʿarī 1963, 494.10.
10. al-Malaṭī 1968, 96.2–5.

Again, at least according to al-Malaṭī, the Jahmites claim that we are unable to know anything of or about God because if we imagine Him as in possession of attributes we then ascribe to him a set of characteristics that humans possess, thereby again reducing and limiting Him to human categories and emotions. Since God cannot be an object of knowledge, we can only have recourse to him through the spontaneous act of intuition (*al-huds*).

Despite the importance of such early debates in Islam, the earliest full-blown "school" of *kalām* was known as the Muʿtazila, also referred to as *ahl al-ʿadl waʾl-tawḥīd* (the people of [divine] justice and unity) on account of their main principles of emphasis. In addition to stressing God's unity and justice – by which they meant that He could not do that which would contravene justice – they emphasized the importance of reason (*ʿaql*) in religious speculation. One of the most important synthetic works describing the doctrine of the Muʿtazila may be found in ʿAbd al-Jabbār's (d. 416/1025) *Al-mughnī* ("Summa"), which emphasizes the importance of four sources for ascertaining truth: the Qurʾān, agreed upon *ḥadīths* (sayings of Muḥammad), rational argument, and *ijmāʾ* (i.e. consensus). To reinforce the point that theologians are simultaneously involved in the establishment of religious doctrine *and* criticism of the doctrines of other religions and/or sectarian movements, ʿAbd al-Jabbār also wrote *Tathbīt dalāʾil al-nubuwwa* ("Confirmation of the Proofs of Prophecy"), which, among other things, offers a critique of other religions, in this case providing an attempt to undermine Christian origins, doctrine, and history.[11]

The Muʿtazila subsequently developed a comprehensive theological framework that revolved around a number of key features: God's unity, God's justice, the intermediate state of the grave sinner (i.e. as neither an infidel nor pious Muslim), reward and punishment in the afterlife, the ethical notion that one must avoid sin and practice virtue, and an emphasis on the created nature of the Qurʾān (so as, as just witnessed, to prevent the existence of something coeval with God).[12] During the ninth and tenth centuries, the Muʿtazila enjoyed tremendous success, using their rationalist principles to develop an important and influential body of scientific and exegetical literature, indeed going so far as to impose a litmus test that all intellectuals had to swear that they believed in the created nature of the Qurʾān.[13]

Most works of *kalām*, regardless of the particular school, share a similar style and structure. This usually involves taking the form of theological *sum-*

11. al-Jabbār 2010.
12. See the exhaustive study in Cook 2010, 32–45.
13. The following paragraphs are based on Hughes 2016, 77–94.

mae to define correct belief and practice.[14] Such treatises, for example, tend to begin by establishing universal principles (e.g. creation of the universe, epistemology) and, from there, they move on to more specific concerns (e.g. prophecy, the afterlife). The texts are usually polemical, providing the believer with a convenient set of responses to perceived criticisms of his or her religion (e.g. "if an unbeliever should say 'x,' one should subsequently respond to him with the claim that....").

On account of its bold claims regarding the unaided human intellect another school, the Ashʿarīya, subsequently challenged the Muʿtazila's general framework in the early eleventh century. Much more traditional than their predecessors, though certainly not "anti-rational," this school stressed the importance of traditional Muslim sources at the expense of the unaided human intellect. According to one sixth/twelfth-century theologian, associated with the Shāfiʿī *madhhab*,

> The people of the truth make the Qurʾān and the Sunna their model (*imam*) and they search for religion through both of them. What they have attained through their intellect and mind, they subject to the examination of the Book and the Sunna. If they find it compatible with both of them, they accept it, and they thank God for showing them this and for His guidance. If they find it opposing the Qurʾān and the Sunna, they leave what they have attained and turn to both of them and blame themselves. This is because the book and the Sunna guide the people only to the truth, while man's opinion may be true or false.[15]

The Ashʿarīya claimed, as may be witnessed in this passage, that unaided human reason was incapable of establishing truth claims with absolute certainty or confidence because God transcended the narrow parameters of human reason, including human conceptions of justice. The founder of the school, Abū al-Ḥasan al-Ashʿarī (d. 324/936) had begun his theological career belonging to the Muʿtazila school, but gradually criticized it for the belief that the Qurʾān was created, that humans have freedom of choice, and the denial that God lacks attributes such as sight and speech, attributes that the Muʿtazila had sought to explain away through allegorical exegesis. Instead, al-Ashʿarī followed ibn Ḥanbal and argued that if the Qurʾān ascribes attributes to God, we must accept them "without asking how" (*bi-lā kayf*). In al-Ashʿarī's creedal statement, for example, we read, "God has a face,

14. On the form of the theological summa in medieval Islam and Judaism, see Hegedus 2019.

15. al-Taymī 1990, 2:224.

without asking how, as it says 'the face of your Lord endures, full of majesty and honor.'"[16] Or, again, believers "affirm hearing and sight of God, and do not deny that as do the Muʿtazila."[17] Such theological pronouncements subsequently became enshrined in various creedal statements and were responsible for the articulation of theological orthodoxy within Sunnī Islam.

It would, however, be a mistake to conceive of al-Ashʿarī or the school that subsequently bore his name simply as steadfastly opposed to the principles of reason. In this regard, they developed a highly technical and atomistic occasionalist framework, wherein God constantly engages in the act of creation, meaning that God could, should He so desire, create a different world at any moment from the one we know.[18] Such a position, needless to say, protects the absolute omnipotence of God, whereas the Muʿtazila – at least according to this position – sought to harness God's power by subsuming it under human rationalism. The Ashʿarīya also developed a technical description of human will that tried to combine human freedom (so people are responsible for their actions) with determinism (to maintain God's omniscience and omnipotence). According to al-Ashʿarī, the faithful "hold that a [person] has no acting-power to do anything before he [actually] does it, and that he is not able to escape God's knowledge or do a thing that God knows he will not do."[19]

Before examining the ways in which *kalām* came to be vectored in the Western academy, it might also be worthwhile to examine the place of theology in thought associated with the Shīʿa. Not unlike their Sunnī colleagues, Shīʿī *mutakallimūn* used theological principles to defend Shīʿī concepts, such as the Imamate.[20] Many theologians associated with this sectarian movement tended, as Madelung notes, to be influenced by the Muʿtazilites.[21] These thinkers articulated Shīʿī principles of both God and human action emphasizing the primacy of reason over prophetic tradition. This enabled Shīʿī *mutakallimūn*, in the words of Ansari and Schmidtke, "to combine the notions of God who creates and controls everything and of Him being a just judge who rewards and punishes human beings on the basis of their actions."[22]

Allow me to conclude this section by restating a feature that will become key to my analysis in the final section below: *Kalām* provided elite

16. Quoted in Watt 1994, 41.
17. Quoted in Watt 1994, 42.
18. See, for example, Fakhry 2004, 43–55.
19. Quoted in Watt 1994, 42.
20. For an overview, see Ansari and Schmidtke 2016, 196–214.
21. Madelung 2014, 468.
22. Ansari and Schmidtke 2016, 198.

thinkers with a vocabulary and a hermeneutic to articulate Islam, be it in Sunnī or Shīʿī iterations. It was the *mutakallimūn*, in other words, who helped to fashion Islam as a philosophical, theological, and legal tradition because they were the ones self-styled as Islam's custodians. They did this in the name of religion and imagined themselves as the only ones able to articulate proper belief from its opposite. This, as we shall see subsequently, is the way that these activities are presented in the secondary literature, though, of course, once removed. That is, while modern Western scholarship is more skeptical of theology and truth-claims, it nonetheless has largely continued to describe such activities in the same manner that the actual *mutakallimūn* do, that is, as engaged in some sort of divine activity. Rarely, in other words, are the motives or the ends of their theological endeavors discussed. On the contrary, I want to suggest, the *mutakallimūn* instead ought to be imagined, and redescribed, as actively engaged in the construction of Islamic belief and ritual activity. They are, in other words, the ones responsible for the very creation of Islam. In the following section, therefore, I begin to turn from the insider or emic approach to one that begins to emphasize an outsider or etic one.

Oriental Studies

If we take the aforementioned approach – label it as the insider or etic one – and then examine the way the exact same material is contextualized and analyzed in the non-Islamic world, be it traditional Orientalism or the modern academy, we begin to see a number of tensions quickly emerge. Despite the Western academy's self-conscious appeals to secularism and objectivity, when it comes to dealing with the religious traditions of others, it is surprisingly dependent upon traditional epistemologies that govern how the past is preserved, displayed, and disseminated. This often equates to simple *descriptions* of classical texts and approaches to them, as opposed to using different and non-indigenous analytical frames of reference. The pasts of other religions, in other words, though historicized and contextualized according to Western academic custom, nevertheless remain dependent upon the same, or at the very least similar, categories of analysis as those indigenous voices responsible for their production. For some reason – or, indeed, perhaps set of reasons – it becomes difficult to untangle the two approaches from one another.

The default position used to study *kalām* in the Western academy, I now suggest, differs little from how it is presented in the Islamic world. The main difference is that whereas the former tends to refer to the tradition by its indigenous name, "*kalām*," the latter employs a term more familiar to Western readers, and with all the concomitant baggage that it carries, to wit, "theology," "systematic theology," or "dogmatic theology." Another difference is that whereas the Islamic tradition tends to be more interested in the conclusions reached and their importance for various Islamic creedal formulations, the tendency in the Orientalist tradition emphasizes *kalām*'s social and intellectual contexts, its casuistry, and the subsequent theological debates between various schools. Despite such discrepancies between the two narratives, however, they seem to roughly coincide with one another. Rarely, for example, does the Western academic tradition *redescribe* the arguments and debates using other categories, such as those that involve political and ideological concerns. Moreover, there is a tendency in the latter tradition to eschew the ways in which theology can be cynically evoked by certain elite classes to construct identities of both self and other. While social theory informs us that identities are always imagined, constructed, and patrolled, such theory rarely makes inroads into secondary studies of *kalāmic* literature in the Western academy.

What we witness instead is a Western emphasis on often the exact same texts of Islamic theology, but with the caveat that minor treatises are frequently added to the list of canonical texts. The only difference is that such texts are now historicized as opposed to simply existing as statements of, among other things, timeless formulations or articulations of what is imagined to be an "eternal creed" (*ʿaqīda*). We can list, for example, the six "articles of faith" (*arkān al-īmān*): belief in God and monotheism, angels, holy scriptures, prophets and angels, the last judgement, and predestination – but we rarely bring in other materials, be it comparative or analytical, to begin the process of moving beyond descriptive and largely historical analyses. It is unclear why this is the case. It may stem from the unfamiliarity on the part of Western scholars of Islam with social theory or other literature produced by those in the academic study of religion. Or it may well stem from an unwillingness on the part of Western scholars to use categories of analysis that are foreign to those responsible for the production of such texts in the first place.

While this unwillingness might strike us as more on display in more recent apologetic and non-Orientalist studies produced by the Western academy,[23] we nevertheless still encounter *description* as the default methodology in Orientalism.[24] The major stumbling block to a new approach to

23. I have been very critical of these apologetic approaches over the years. See, for example Hughes 2012a, 2012b; and, most recently, 2015.

24. Perhaps I should be clear that by "Orientalism" I do not refer to the exaggerated and polemical treatises analyzed by Said in his classic 1978 work of the same name. Rather, I refer primarily to the tradition of Western writing about Islam.

kalām, like other categories discussed in this volume, is the sheer weight that "Islamic sciences" (*ulūm al-dīn*) plays not only in Muslim history, but also in the consciousness of Western scholars of Islam. *Kalām*, as witnessed in the previous section, is about the articulation of non-historical and non-contingent truth claims. Theologians, in other words, perceive themselves and are perceived by others to be engaged in a divine activity, namely, articulating proper belief for the community of believers. In many ways, this becomes difficult to square with the modern Western academy, where such truths are not only historicized, but imagined as contingent and dependent upon distinct times and places. There is no capital-T truth, in other words, that awaits simple articulation. There are, however, regimes of truth that make appeals to that which is imagined as divine or metaphysical. In the words of the historian of religions, Bruce Lincoln,

> When one permits those whom one studies to define the terms in which they will be understood, suspends one's interest in the temporal and contingent, or fails to distinguish between "truths," "truth-claims," and "regimes of truth," one has ceased to function as historian or scholar. In that moment, a variety of roles are available: some perfectly respectable (amanuensis, collector, friend and advocate), and some less appealing (cheerleader, voyeur, retailer of import goods). None, however, should be confused with scholarship.[25]

Lincoln here shows what is at stake in the emic/etic debate. If we simply describe, as so much modern scholarship on Islam does, what the *mutakallimūn* were doing, we fail to make this material translatable to larger audiences inside the academy. We instead rehearse the quasi-philosophical arguments of *mutakallimūn* with an eye towards how they understood God, the world, and the nature of the relationship between the two. Rarely, however, do we transform these believers into historical actors and connect their ideas to the realm of politics or ideology. God, for example, is simply assumed to exist, just as the ability to ascertain His motives (or not) is.

One way to avoid such difficult questions is to focus, as much scholarship does, on possible external influences for the rise of *kalām*. Greek, Syriac, Sasanian, Jewish, and Manichean influences are all alternatively posited to explain the origins of theological thinking in the early centuries of Islam.[26] Implicit in this question of origins is the notion that Arabs were unable to engage in ratiocination on their own, and that they needed external nudges in order to engage in such activity. Not surprisingly,

25. Lincoln 1996, 227.
26. See, for example, Cook 1980.

the most important impetus for the rise of such rationalist theology was contact with Greek sources often on the part of Arab Christians. Such contact, especially with "foreign" treatises devoted to logic subsequently lead, it is frequently assumed, to the need to try to reconcile the terminology and categories of rationalism with those of monotheism. Again, we witness the Orientalist *imaginary* at work: just as Christian and Jewish theologians had to mediate these same tensions earlier, their acts at mediation influenced Muslims. Once again, Islam is imagined as derivative of these other, older monotheistic traditions.

There exist numerous debates about the rise of theological thinking in Islam, none of which need concern us in the present context.[27] It is perhaps worth pointing out, however, that Josef van Ess, one of the most important scholars working on the rise of *kalām* eschews such an external influence and instead posits a set of internal reasons for the rise of theological speculation in the Islamic tradition. In this regard, *kalām* is largely an internal production to ascertain who a "real" Muslim was upon the death of Muḥammad.[28] According to van Ess,

> Theology in Islam did not start as polemics against unbelievers. Even the *kalām* style was not developed or taken over in order to refute non-Muslims, especially the Manicheans, as one tended to believe when one saw the origin of *kalām* in the missionary activity of the Muʿtazila. Theology started as an inner-Islamic discussion when, mainly through political development, the self-confident naïvité of the early days gradually ended.[29]

This is interesting because it shows that regardless of whether or not theology entered Islam from without or was an elaboration of some prototype of indigenous thinking, there nevertheless remains an overarching interest (or even obsession) about where, how, why, and when such speculation arose in the first place. Even if it is impossible to ascertain the origins of *kalām*, Western approaches that seek to historicize the beginnings of Islamic theology ultimately work on the assumption that if we understand where Islamic theology originated we can somehow better understand it. Such approaches, as I shall argue in the following section, largely ignore the role that all those schools, and their debates, associated with *kalām* played in the manufacture of what was – and, indeed, still is – perceived to be "good" or "authentic" Islam.

27. Requisite bibliography may be found in note 2 above.
28. I owe this point to my colleague Majid Daneshgar.
29. van Ess 1975, 101.

It might be worth, briefly, to examine how the early Orientalist tradition dealt with the rise of Islamic theology. According to the Hungarian scholar, Ignác Goldziher (1850–1921), also one of the pioneering figures of German Orientalism, *kalām* was intimately connected to the rise of religious law, and the need to derive from the Qurʾān a set of systematized beliefs and practices.[30] Immediately, then, we see how Goldziher transforms an emic problem – how do we ascertain the true nature of God, His relationship to the world, and his plan for us – into an etic one, namely, how did the rapid political expansion of Islam create the need for developing new institutions in light of religious demands. Here we see clearly, in other words, the tensions between the two approaches, a set of tensions that reverberates throughout the academic study of Islam in both the Islamic world and the secular Western academy.

Regardless, Goldziher continues that the rise of theological speculation was largely dependent upon the Islamic world's increasing familiarity with Aristotelian philosophy.[31] On account of the fractures and ambiguities of this intersection, Goldziher writes, "A new speculative system was needed to maintain Islam and Islamic tradition among rational thinkers. In the history of philosophy, this system is known as *kalām*."[32] *Kalām*, on this largely familiar and today largely orthodox reading, becomes but the initial stage that paved the way for the great Islamic philosophical tradition that found its zenith in the likes of al-Fārābī, Ibn Sīnā, and Ibn Rushd before, it was imagined, anti-rationalism's defeat of philosophy. Indeed, we witness this in almost any introductory book on Islamic philosophy, wherein the first chapter is always that of the story of the rise of *kalām* before proceeding to the subsequent philosophical tradition.

Goldziher, as is customary in so many Western treatments of *kalām*, subsequently subdivides the tradition into the familiar one (the one presented in section one above). *Kalām* is thus historicized and its debates discussed within the history of Islamic rationalism. Unlike the approach witnessed in the previous section, these theological debates are largely stripped of their actual vitriol and the seminal role they played in the shaping of orthodoxy.

In keeping with the schema, Goldziher situates the Muʿtazila as philosophically transforming a more primitive notion of God:

> The Muʿtazilis waged the first religious campaign when, to assure the purity and dignity of the Islamic concept of God, they gave metaphorical interpretation and spiritual sense to every

30. Goldziher 1981, 68.
31. Goldziher 1981, 71.
32. Goldziher 1981, 85.

> anthropomorphic expression in the sacred writings. Out of such endeavors a new method of Qurʾānic exegesis arose, which was called by the old terms *taʾwīl* (in the sense of figurative interpretation), and against which, in all periods of Islamic history, the Ḥanbalites protested.[33]

It is however worth noting that Goldziher was the first in the Orientalist tradition to resist the tendency to imagine the Muʿtazila as "free-thinkers," that is, as the harbingers of subsequent medieval rationalism.[34] According to him and many others who followed in his wake, nonetheless, *kalām* is always associated in some way with rationalism, representing the imposition of Greek thought into the heart of Islam.

The question we must now ask ourselves is: do external/objective/scholarly approaches differ from internal/committed/indigenous approaches? If so, how and why? To answer this question, we must acknowledge that we, as scholars, can never access the primary dispositions of those we study. This is another way of saying that the internal lives of individuals – their moods and motivations – remain impervious to us as scholars, who are only able to work with the "secondary" products, if we can even call them this, such as texts and other forms of material culture. This does not mean, however, that we simply describe and empathize with these so-called secondary manifestations and historical products.[35] Often avoided in such descriptions is the notion that religion – of which we must certainly include theology – can be explained using numerous cultural and historical processes.

Whereas an emic or insider approach will always emphasize the internal aspects of theology, often reducing it to religious or other transcendent values and feelings, an etic approach, in theory if not always in practice, ought to avoid such language. Rarely, however, do such etic approaches do this. In the editorial introduction to her impressive *Oxford Handbook of Islamic Theology*, Sabine Schmidtke writes,

> In their attempts to systemize doctrinal thinking, the various theological schools in Islam have provided an abundance of often contradictory answers to the questions. Moreover, in terms of methodology, Muslim theologians championed two different, contradictory approaches – while rationally minded theologians employed the methods and techniques of speculative theology, "*kalām*" or "*ʿilm al-kalām*," as it is typically called, traditionists

33. Goldziher 1981, 93
34. Goldziher 1981, 101.
35. See, for example, the comments in McCutcheon 2001, 1–10.

> categorically rejected the use of reason and instead restricted themselves to collecting the relevant doctrinal statements found in the Qur'ān and prophetic tradition.[36]

The theological tradition in Islam, in other words, is here reduced to a set of historical dialectic forces, for example, those of reason vis-à-vis those of tradition, or, alternatively, to that of various anti-rationalist approaches to such rationalist forces. Regardless, the traditional Western academy reduces *kalām* to a set of historical responses as opposed to treating it as a sacred activity, as envisaged by the Islamic tradition. Whereas the latter imagines theology as an "eternal science" (*ʿilm*), the former transforms it into a set of arguments and debates contingent upon various political and historical forces.

Redescription

Muslims have traditionally approached their own tradition, and by extension all human knowledge, through a set of categories imagined, as any set of indigenous categories (including, of course, Western academic ones) inevitably are, as God-given and as simply mirroring the natural world. Many of these categories within the Islamic tradition, despite appeals to the contrary, subsequently helped to shape – and indeed continue to shape – the Euro-American field of Islamic studies. It is within this latter context that we often encounter indigenous terms that are simply translated directly into Western academic ones, and often without due concern for the manifold ways in which such translation occurred (and indeed continues to occur) in the first place, and the semantic slippage engendered therefrom.

Among such categories we must certainly include that of *kalām*, which is often simply translated as "theology." The two terms are not necessarily congruous, nor do they even necessarily mean the same thing.[37] Theology, for example, refers to a particular type of thinking about God and Christology in Christian universities and seminaries where it is derived from the Greek *theologia* (θεολογία), which derives from *theos* (θεός) or "god," and *logia* (λογία), referring to utterances or sayings. The sense the word has in English depends in large part on the sense the Latin and Greek equivalents had acquired in patristic and medieval Christian usage. *Kalām*, in contrast, refers to a particular and *different* set of discourses developed in the Islamic world at the end of late antiquity to address the problem of correct belief that

36. Schmidtke 2016, 2.

37. In the Muslim academy, the term theology is sometimes used interchangeably with "Ilāhiyyāt" which is similar to "Divinity" in the Western academy. And in some Turkish and Iranian institutions, departments of Islamic studies are called "Ilāhiyyāt."

wracked the burgeoning caliphate. *Kalām*'s stating point is thus different, both conceptually and historically, than that found in the largely Christian tradition of theology. *Kalām*'s methods of argumentation, its concerns, its conclusions, and its debates are all different from its Christian predecessor.

From this semantic slippage we begin to witness a number of other repercussions that further reveal just how potentially difficult it is to translate *kalām* as "theology." Or, perhaps this is a better way of saying that even though the literal translation may be easy, the analytic payoff of such an act is a largely superficial endeavor. Within this context, it is important to remember that *kalām* offers not so much a particular iteration of some universal or Platonic notion of theology so much as it affords us access into a particular Islamic way of perceiving or thinking about God and His relationship to the world and, by extension, to humans.

The question for us today in the modern academy, then, should be less about how Islamic theology is like (Christian) theology, and more about how *kalām* – indeed, like theology more generally – can be of significance to contemporary humanities, which tends to eschew theology as a divine science and that seeks to avoid investiture in the elaboration of creed or capital-t Truth. To this end, the rest of this chapter will be devoted to showing how *kalām* is less about the construction of Islamic truth claims and more about the active construction of Islamic identity. In this, I suggest, *kalām*, like theology more generally, is intimately wedded to the social construction of realities, in this case Muslim ones.

Immediately, then, we must, resist the reification of terms like "Muslim" or "Islam," terms that the theological tradition has no problem both creating and subsequently reifying and essentializing. Appeals of *mutakallimūn* to the contrary, there is no "good" Islam, but instead what we witness are competing Islams brought into existence through the very act of theologizing. *Kalām*, in other words, is that which enables various social groups to imagine themselves, to stake out truth claims for themselves, and, in the process, to differentiate themselves from other social groups, whether constructed as Muslim or non-Muslim. Such terms would certainly not have emerged fully formed from the Bible or the Qur'ān.

Allow me to use some of the examples encountered in the first section of this chapter to elucidate what I mean. Jahm b. Ṣafwān, for example, proclaimed that God's knowledge is "temporally originated" (*muḥdath*), and that God brings this knowledge "into temporal existence" (*aḥdathahu*). With such a locution, then, Jahm seeks to protect God's unity even if this means not ascribing knowledge, a human category, to Him. All those Muslims who read verses of the Qur'ān that make such ascriptions, according to Jahm, do so incorrectly and are thereby guilty of incorrect belief. Only those who believe what Jahm says, in other words, are imagined as "normative" or "good" Muslims.

In like manner, Ismāʿīl b. Muḥammad al-Taymī, also discussed above, engages in a similar move by arguing that those who find that their human intellects contradict the Qurʾān and/or the Sunna, must ignore the former since only the latter sources provide the "true guide" to proper belief. In so doing, he constructs a "normative" Islam that eschews human knowledge that exists independently of what is revealed in authoritative Muslims sources. Though, of course, he does not bother to mention that those authoritative sources must also be interpreted according to human reason. But the result is the same as witnessed in Jahm b. Ṣafwān: Islam is constructed through the theological endeavor.

Allow me to discuss briefly how this act of construction continues today. I want to do so not so much in the context of the Islamic world, but rather in its use in the contemporary Western academy. This will highlight why it is so difficult to differentiate between emic and etic approaches to the subject, and I trust will also reveal why such a differentiation is surely a scholarly desideratum. As with classical *kalām*, there is also a tendency in certain sectors of the Western academy to reify Islam with the aim of creating a normative tradition, and subsequently to show how this creation fits effortlessly with the values of those doing the interpreting, or perhaps better, "theologizing." These acts of interpretation, however, do not represent a set of objective historical facts that simply exist in the past and that await uncovering in the present. Rather they represent a set of constructions imagined in the present and then made to perform intellectual work for those who back-project them onto the past.

In terms of the insider/outsider debate that has meandered slowly through the previous pages, it is worth noting that it is frequently a debate that is invoked as a way to establish or signal authority.[38] By placing themselves inside the tradition of *kalām*, for example, those who engage in constructing "good" Islam in the context of the modern Western academy still perceive themselves as having some sort of unique access, through the use of proper hermeneutics if not actual genetic predisposition, to the eternal truths of Islam; whereas, those who exist outside of the Islamic tradition, such as Orientalists, use their own knowledge of intellectual history and system of influences/anticipations, to show how *kalām* developed historically and sociologically. If one styles oneself an insider, in other words, an outsider will necessarily lack some sort of metaphysical or intangible connection

38. See, for example, the sources cited in note 1 above.

to the tradition in question. Framed across the hermeneutical divide, a self-styled outsider sees the insider as someone who is hopelessly incompetent when it comes to understanding the latter's own religion objectively.

It might be worth noting in the present context that a lot of what currently passes for "critical" Islamic studies in the Western academy resembles this *kalāmic* construction of truth claims. When, for example, we read an academic monograph showing that, when understood properly, Islam is about social justice or when another study argues that those who are misogynist or engage in acts of violence are not really Muslim, we again witness the active construction of Muslim identity. The hermeneutic, the casuistry, the conclusions, and so on differ little from the constructions of earlier centuries. Yet, as I have argued here, it is our job in the secular Western academy neither to take such pronouncements as the articulation of some divine truth or to read them as "primary" as opposed to "secondary" sources. Rather, they represent the active construction on the part of human actors in particular social contexts to create what they consider to be "good," "true," or "authentic" Islamic teaching, and to differentiate it from its opposite.

To give but one example: In her recent *Domestic Violence and the Islamic Tradition*, Ayesha Chaudhry, seeks to locate the Qurʾān in a non-historical or non-political space, not unlike what *mutakallimūn* have done and indeed continue to do, where it is imagined to exist purely and pristinely, uncontaminated by either culture or gender. Since the Qurʾān was revealed in a patriarchal society, she reasons, there was only one way to interpret problematic verses *at that time*. This does not rule out the notion, though, that the Qurʾān (or, presumably its divine author) did not know that things might be different at some point in the future where it could be interpreted in a more egalitarian manner.[39]

I do not wish to argue with her interpretation here because it is, after all, her interpretation. Rather, I want to point out in the present context that her approach to the qurʾānic narrative differs little from that which we witnessed in the classical traditions associated with *kalām*. The main difference is that this is now done by a female trained in the secular Western academy and the results are published by Oxford University Press. The key issue for the future of an academic study of Islamic theology within the context of the modern, and *secular*, study of religion is that we need to move beyond such a hermeneutic and instead imagine *kalām* as an activity that establishes truth claims for believers, as opposed to a divine activity to bring creed and belief to earth from some cosmic text.

39. Chaudhry 2014, 6–7.

Conclusions

In this chapter, I have tried to do three things. First, I provided a brief overview of *kalām*, which is usually translated into English as "theology," the latter being a term with a distinct genealogy in the Euro-Christian intellectual tradition. While such a translation is not necessarily incorrect, it nevertheless risks subsuming *kalām* into a larger (Christological) tradition wherein it does not necessarily belong. Moreover, such a translation also implies that the concerns, methods, and conclusions of *kalām* and the Christian theological tradition are identical to one another. This, as I tried to demonstrate, is most certainly not the case. I then sought to show some of the major issues and schools of classical *kalām* with an eye towards an examination of some of its major features.

While practitioners of *kalām*, *mutakallimūn*, imagine themselves as engaging in a timeless and contextless activity, those who study the tradition in the Western academy beg to differ. In the second section I thus emphasized some of the ways in which this study has preoccupied the traditions associated with Orientalism. Now the tendency becomes decidedly historical, something that is perhaps on clear display in the Orientalist search for origins and influences. The assumption, in other words, is that Arabs could not have developed such traditions on their own and instead had to learn them from the Greeks by way of the Syriac Christian tradition. Since Orientalists construct rationalism as a Greco-European activity, Arabs had to have teachers. Moreover, in light of the Orientalist concern with anticipations and influences, the Orientalist tradition subsequently constructed *kalām* as the first iteration of the Islamic philosophical tradition, which was imagined to culminate in the likes of Ibn Sīnā and Ibn Rushd. In so doing, the emphasis tends to be on the often poor quality of the *mutakallimūn*'s methods when compared to the subsequent towering Islamic thinkers of the Western philosophical tradition.

Finally, in the third part of the chapter, I moved beyond the Orientalist paradigm and sought to find new ways to study *kalām*, especially ways that might better fit with contemporary trends in the secular humanities, which tends to eschew the language of capital-t Truth and the mistaking of truth claims for regimes of truth. The natural place for such study, I further argued, was in the field of religious studies. The latter, though, also concerned with history and origins, is less dismissive of Muslim voices. However, rather than take such voices at face-value, it tends to show how they are part and parcel of the social construction of reality, in particular that of identity formation. On this reading, *kalām* becomes less about the quality of its argumentation, the idiosyncracies of those doing the arguing, and the subsequent development of various creedal statements that are paraded before the reader in chronological fashion, and more about how such activities actively construct Islam and notions of who is inside the largely social community of believers, and who is outside.

Bibliography

Ansari, H., and S. Schmidtke. 2016. "The Shīʿī Reception of Muʿtazilism (II): Twelver Shīʿīs." In *The Oxford Handbook of Islamic Theology*, edited by S. Schmidtke, 196–214. Oxford.

al-Ashʿarī, A. Ḥ. ʿA. 1963. *Maqālāt al-islāmiyyīn: Die dogmatischen Lehren der Anhänger des Islam*. Edited by H. Ritter. Wiesbaden.

Chaudhry, A. 2014. *Domestic Violence and the Islamic Tradition*. Oxford.

Cook, M. 1980. "The Origins of the *Kalām*." *Bulletin of the School of Oriental and African Studies* 43:32–43.

———. 2010. *Commanding Right and Forbidding Wrong in Islamic Thought*. Cambridge.

van Ess, J. 1975. "The Beginning of Islamic Theology." In *The Cultural Context of Medieval Learning*, edited by J. E. Murdoch and E.D. Sylla, 87–111. Dordrecht and Boston.

Fakhry, M. 2004. *A History of Islamic Philosophy*. 3rd ed. New York.

Goldziher, I. 1981. *Introduction to Islamic Theology and Law*. Translated by A. and R. Hamori. Princeton.

Hegedus, G. 2019. "Does Judaism Make Sense? Early Medieval *Kalām* as Literature." In *Medieval Jewish Philosophy and Its Literary Forms*, edited by A. W. Hughes and J. T. Robinson,161–184 . Bloomington.

Hughes, A. W. 2012a. *Theorizing Islam: Disciplinary Deconstruction and Reconstruction*. Sheffield.

———. 2012b. "The Study of Islam Before and After September 11: A Provocation." *Method and Theory in the Study of Religion* 24.4–5:314–336;

———. 2015. *Islam and the Tyranny of Authenticity: An Inquiry into Disciplinary Apologetics and Self-Deception*. Sheffield.

———. 2016. "Theology: The Articulation of Orthodoxy." In *The Routledge Handbook of Jewish-Muslim Relations*. Edited by J. Meri, 77–94. London.

Abd al-Jabbār. 2010. *A Critique of Christian Origins*. Edited and translated by G. S. Reynolds and S. Kh. Samir. Provo, UT.

Kugle, S. S. al-H. 2010. *Homosexuality in Islam: Critical Reflection on Gay, Lesbian, and Transgender Muslims*. Oxford.

Lincoln, Bruce. 1996. "Theses on Method." *Method and Theory in the Study of Religion* 8:225–227.

MacDonald, D. B. 1903. *Development of Muslim Theology, Jurisprudence, and Constitutional Theory*. New York.
Madelung, W. 2014, "Early Imāmī Theology as Reflected in the *Kitāb al-Kāfī al-Kulaynī*'." In *The Study of Shi'i Islam*, edited by F. Daftary and G. Miskinzoda, 465–474. London.
Mahdi, M. 1970. "Language and Logic in Classical Islam." In *Logic in Classical Islamic Culture*, edited by G. E. von Grunebaum, 102–113. Wiesbaden.
al-Malaṭī, A. Ḥ. M. 1968. *Al-tanbiḥ wa l-radd ʿalā ahl al-ahwāʾ wa l-bidaʿ*. Baghdad and Beirut.
Margoliouth, D. S. 1905. "The Merits of Logic and Grammar." *Journal of the Royal Asiatic Society*. January: 111–129.
McCutcheon, R. T. 2001. *Critics, Not Caretakers*. Albany, NY.
Rippin, A. 2012. *Muslims: Their Religious Beliefs and Practices*, 4th ed. London.
Safi, O., ed. 2003. *Progressive Muslims: On Justice, Gender, and Politics*. Oxford.
Schmidtke, S., ed. 2016. *The Oxford Handbook of Islamic Theology*. Oxford.
——. 2016. "Introduction." In *The Oxford Handbook of Islamic Theology*, edited by S. Schmidtke, 1–23. Oxford.
Schöck, C. 2016. "Jahm b. Ṣafwān (d. 128/745 – 6) and 'Jahmiyya' and Ḍirār b.ʿAmr (d. 200/815)." In *The Oxford Handbook of Islamic Theology*, edited by S. Schmidtke, 55 –80. Oxford.
al-Tawḥīdī, A. Ḥ. 1939–1944. *Al-imtāʿ wa l-muʾānasa*. Vol. 1. Edited by A. Amīn and A. al-Zayn. Cairo.
al-Taymī, I. 1990. *Al-ḥujja fī bayān al-maḥajja wa sharḥ ʿaqīda ahl al-sunna*. Edited by M. b. Rabīʿ. Riyadh.
Treiger, A. 2016. "Origins of *Kalām*." In *The Oxford Handbook of Islamic Theology*, edited by S. Schmidtke, 27–43. Oxford.
Watt, W. M. 1973. *The Formative Period of Islamic Thought*. Edinburgh.
——. ed. 1994. *Islamic Creeds: A Selection*. Edinburgh.
Winter, T., ed. 2008. *The Cambridge Companion to Classical Islamic Theology*. Cambridge.
Wolfson, H. A. 1976. *The Philosophy of the Kalam*. Cambridge, MA.

7

ʿ*ilm* Is Islam: The Islamic Concept of Knowledge from Classical Traditions to Modern Interpretations

Christopher A. Furlow

"There is no god but He: That is the witness of Allah. His angels, and those endued with knowledge, standing firm on justice." (Q 3:18)[1]

"Seeking knowledge is obligatory upon every Muslim" (Saying of Muḥammad)

"ʿIlm is Islam"[2]

Introduction

LET ME BEGIN with a brief story. In 1998, I was in Malaysia doing fieldwork for my dissertation on contemporary debates about Islam and science. I spent most of my time at the International Islamic University, Malaysia (IIUM). There was an active Islamization of Knowledge (IOK) Circle comprised of students and faculty, which met about twice a month. At each meeting there were one or more speakers who presented either a short talk on topics related to the IOK or a commentary on a book at the heart of the IOK debate. For one meeting, I, along with the then Dean of the Research Centre Louay Safi, was invited to present a commentary on then IIUM Rector AbdulHamid AbuSulayman's book *Crisis in the Muslim Mind*[3] as a last-minute substitute for the Rector himself. I offered a fairly critical commentary on the book – not on the aim of the book, which is to revitalize Islamic civilization from within, but on the execution, which I argued failed to meet the standards for good scholarship that AbdulHamid AbuSulayman had himself outlined in the book.

A question-and-answer session followed the commentaries. The audience reaction was quite spirited and included some individuals defending

1. Yusuf ʿAli 1989.
2. Rosenthal 2007, 2.
3. AbuSulayman 1993.

AbuSulayman's book and others agreeing with some of the critiques Louay Safi and I had made. The interesting aspect of the question-and-answer session, for this chapter, was that some audience members questioned whether I could legitimately criticize AbuSulayman's book. How familiar was I with the Islamization of knowledge debates? Did I read the book in the original Arabic or the English translation? Left unspoken was the fact that I am not a Muslim. In other words, the underlying question is the question of authenticity and authority which also underlies this book project.[4]

The goal of this volume is to examine the way classical Islamic categories, like *ʿilm* in this chapter, are approached depending on whether a scholar approaches the concept from a classical/internal/committed/indigenous position or a modern/external/objective/scholarly position. Let me be clear, first and foremost, that even these labels are loaded and problematic. For example, if we accept the linkage of "objective" and "scholarly" to modern/external approaches alone, we are by default denying the possibility that classical/internal approaches could ever be objective or scholarly and implying that all modern/external approaches are objective and scholarly. I am not arguing that this volume is destined to fail based on presuming these particular distinctions and categories; rather I am highlighting the difficult task that the editors and authors have set for themselves that are inherent in any attempt to compare "classical" and "modern" approaches to Islamic concepts.

For myself, I will reflect on my own and others' research to examine the Islamic concept *ʿilm* to try to outline and interrogate the tensions in different approaches to Islamic concepts. I am a cultural anthropologist and I also have a MS degree in the interdisciplinary field of science and technology studies (STS) which includes the history, philosophy, and sociology of science and technology (and increasingly other disciplines like anthropology). My path to studying debates about Islam and science is not the "traditional" path of going through religious studies or Islamic studies departments and also helps illustrate many of the tensions among different approaches to studying Islam.

ʿIlm and Related Concepts: Boundaries of the Study

Since its beginnings, a small number of concepts have been at the heart of Islam. *ʿIlm* is one of these key concepts. Indeed, Franz Rosenthal, the well-known orientalist widely-known for his canonical translation of Ibn

4. For many fundamentalists, Arabic is the only main Islamic language and languages from non-Muslim majority areas are particularly problematic. For a different view see al-Faruqi 1995. For more detail on the Islamization of Knowledge Circle meeting see Furlow 2009.

Khaldūn's *Muqaddimah*, argued that "ᶜilm is Islam."[5] Furthermore, al- *ᶜAlīm*, The Knowing or All-knowing, is one of the names or attributes of God. But what is "*ᶜilm*"?

At the most basic level, *ᶜilm* is the Arabic word for "knowledge".[6] However, *ᶜilm* can also be translated as "religious knowledge," "learning," or "science(s)" (particularly in the plural, *ᶜulūm*) depending on the context.

In this chapter, I will critically examine the concept *ᶜilm*. I will begin with an overview of the development of the concept *ᶜilm* as its meaning expands from a narrower concept (religious knowledge) to a broader concept (knowledge) or (science), including non-Islamic sciences, before moving on to examine modern scholarship.

Rosenthal notes the widely repeated fact that there are approximately 750 occurrences in the Qurᵓān of the root *ᶜ-l-m* and its derivatives, which equates to about 1 percent of the 78,000 words in the Qurᵓān.[7] Indeed, the first revelation sent to the Prophet Muḥammad commanded him to read and declared Allah as the teacher of humanity: "Proclaim! (or Read!) In the name of thy Lord and Cherisher...He who taught (the use of) the Pen – taught man that which he knew not" (Q 96:1, 4–5).[8] From this initial revelation, learning and knowledge have been central to Islam.

According to the Qurᵓān, *ᶜilm* is hierarchical and controlled by God. *ᶜilm* is the term used in the Qurᵓān for God's knowledge. God knows more than humans and has knowledge of "secret matters" (Q 6:59; 11:31). All human knowledge comes from God (Q 2:140) and even angels know only what God has taught them (Q 2:32). And, divine knowledge is only knowable if God wills it to be so (Q 2:255–256).[9]

Beyond the Qurᵓān, *ᶜilm* (knowledge) is also ever-present in the traditional sayings (*aḥādīth*, singular *ḥadīth*) of the Prophet Muḥammad, which are considered the second most important source for religious law after the Qurᵓān . Of the six collections of *ḥadīth* considered authoritative, four have Books of Knowledge (*Kitāb al-ᶜilm*). Al-Bukhārī, the oldest of the six collections, placed his *Kitāb al-ᶜilm* near the beginning just after his introduction and a book on faith (*imān*). Abū Dāwūd, Muslim, and at-Tirmidhī also include Books of Knowledge. The two collections that do not have a separate Book of Knowledge, Ibn Mājah and an-Nasāᵓī, still include many references to *ᶜilm*.[10]

5. Rosenthal 2007, 2.
6. "Maᶜrifa" is another Arabic term often translated into English as "knowledge" or "cognizance."
7. Rosenthal 2007, 20.
8. Yusuf ᶜAli 1989, 1672–1673.
9. Rosenthal 2007, 28–29.
10. Rosenthal 2007.

Some of the well-known *aḥādīth* concerning *ʿilm* attributed to the Prophet Muḥammad include:

1. He who pursues the road of knowledge God will direct to the road of Paradise.
2. The brightness of a learned man compared to that of a mere worshipper is like that of the full moon compared to all the stars.
3. Obtain knowledge; its possessor can distinguish right from wrong; it shows the way to Heaven; it befriends us in the desert and in solitude, and when we are friendless; it is our guide to happiness; it gives us strength in misery; it is an ornament to friends, protection against enemies.
4. The scholar's ink is holier than the martyr's blood.
5. Seeking knowledge is required of every Muslim.[11]

These inspirational words in the qurʾānic revelation and the sayings of the Prophet Muḥammad moved the early Muslims to strive to learn about God and His creation. Thus, the religious sciences emerged, including sciences related to the Qurʾān (*ʿulūm al-Qurʾān*) like qurʾānic recitation *(ʿilm al-qirāʾa)*, qurʾānic exegesis (*ʿilm al-tafsīr*), and jurisprudence (*fiqh*) followed by sciences related to the sayings (*aḥādīth*) of the Prophet Muḥammad like the science of biographies (*ʿilm al-rijāl*), science of genealogy (*ʿilm al-ansāb*), and the science of history (*ʿilm al-taʾrīkh*). As Muzaffar Iqbal notes, studying the Qurʾān and Ḥadīth in the past was the intellectual context from which the study of other subjects emerged, and some methods and intellectual attitudes initially developed to study the Qurʾān and Ḥadīth were later adapted to study the natural world. Iqbal notes that these attitudes and methods included "an uncompromising adherence to truth and objectivity, a respect for corroborated empirical evidence, an eye for detail and a refined taste for proper categorization and classification of data".[12]

As the Muslim community expanded and transformed into an empire, Muslims encountered new peoples, knowledge, and sciences from the Atlantic Ocean to the Indian Ocean in Europe, Africa, and Asia. Major civilizations included Egypt, Mesopotamia, Persia, India, and Hellenized Greek areas around the Mediterranean Sea, all with impressive scientific traditions. The desire to collect and classify data and systems of knowledge was evident when it came to these scholarly legacies.

11. Cited in Turner 1995, 17.
12. Iqbal 2002, 2. Here we can see the clear tension the presumptive linking of "objective" and "scholarly" to modern/external approaches can have.

Muslims translated vast quantities of scientific treatises into Arabic, which became the lingua franca for science, religion, and government across an enormous stretch of the globe. Scholars from many disciplinary backgrounds began to create classifications of all the knowledge from the known world from al-Kindī (d. ca. 801–873 AD) in the third/ninth century until Shah Waliallāh (1703–1762 AD) in the twelfth/eighteenth century.[13] Some of the better-known classifications include: al-Fārābī (256/870–339/950 AH/AD), al-Ghazālī (1058–1111 AD), Ibn Sīnā, Ibn Rushd (520/1126–595/1198 AH/AD), al-Shīrāzī (1236–1311 AD), and Ibn Khaldūn (732/1332–808/1406 AH/AD).

Here I will focus on the classification of Ibn Khaldūn. In the pre-modern period, the classification of knowledge by Ibn Khaldūn in the *Muqaddima* is both comprehensive and authoritative. S. H. Nasr, the eminent scholar of Islamic science, stated that Ibn Khaldūn's classification should be considered the "final version" of the Islamic division of knowledge.[14]

Ibn Khaldūn first distinguishes between two broad categories of knowledge: (1) philosophical and intellectual sciences and (2) transmitted sciences. The philosophical and intellectual sciences can be learned by humans through reason and intelligence, while the transmitted sciences can be learned only through transmission going back to the founder of the science or to the origin of the revelation in the case of religious sciences.

Next Ibn Khaldūn outlines the traditional religious sciences or transmitted sciences (including auxiliary linguistic sciences, specifically sciences of Arabic, which he describes after the philosophical sciences), followed by the philosophical sciences:

Traditional Religious Sciences or Transmitted Sciences

1 Sciences of the Qurʾān

Tafsīr

Recitation

2 Sciences of the Traditions of the Prophet Muḥammad (*Ḥadīth*)

3 Science of Jurisprudence (sacred law) (*Fiqh*)

4 Science of Theology

5 Science of Ṣūfism

6 Science of Dream Interpretation

7 Sciences of Arabic/linguistics

13. Bakar 1998, 1.

14. Nasr 1968. What makes Ibn Khaldūn so interesting here, though, is the renaissance of interest in Ibn Khaldūn's scholarship: Abaza 2002, Alatas 2013, Alatas 2006.

Grammar

Lexicography

Syntax, Style, and Literary Criticism

Literature

Philosophical and Intellectual Sciences

1 Logic

2 Physics

Medicine

Agriculture

3 Metaphysics

Sorcery and Talismans

Science of Secrets of Letters

Science of Alchemy

4 Sciences of Measurement/Mathematics

Geometry

Arithmetic

Music

Astronomy (includes astrology)

A number of critical themes are present in Ibn Khaldūn's classification of *ʿilm*. First, *ʿilm* is divided into traditional religious sciences (*al-ʿulūm al-naqliyya*) that are transmitted (*naqlī*) from the original revelation or Prophet through a series of teachers and philosophical (*al-ʿulūm al-hikmiyya al-falsafiyya*) or rational sciences (*al-ʿulūm al-ʿaqliyya*) that humans have the capacity to learn on their own.

Second, the traditional religious sciences are given primacy over the philosophical sciences, which is in line with earlier classifications, like al-Ghazālī, but differs from previous classifications that elevated the philosophical sciences to equal status with or even higher status than the religious sciences, like al-Fārābī, Ibn Sīnā, and Ibn Rushd. Al-Fārābī in his Enumeration of the Sciences (*Ihsāʾ al-ʿulūm*) goes so far as to argue that true sciences are always rational.[15]

Third, Ibn Khaldūn supports the position that the traditional religious sciences had by his time already reached their ultimate limits and no more

15. El-Rayes 2016.

major advances could be made in these sciences. This idea, known as the closing of the door of *ijtihād* (effort or exertion), was increasingly common among Sunnī jurists since the fourth/tenth century and argued that in most cases jurists need only imitate (*taqlīd*) or follow previous decisions.

Fourth, Ibn Khaldūn, like al-Ghazālī and others before him, criticized many (physics, alchemy, astrology), if not all (he praises the science of logic for example), areas of the philosophical sciences seemingly despite his goal of creating a new rational science of civilization (*ʿilm al-ʿumrān*).

Ibn Khaldūn is an interesting figure because the *Muqaddima* has undergone a renaissance over the last century. On the one hand, his work seems very modern in certain respects, like the development of the science of civilization, and he has thus been identified as the "father of sociology." On the other hand, his work can also be seen as very anti-modern in the sense that the critique of the philosophical sciences in his work and the attitudes it represents (and also al-Ghazālī's) have been pointed to as responsible for the decline of science in the Muslim world, which some argue is ultimately responsible for the decline of Islamic civilization vis-à-vis other world powers, like Europe. Indeed, the decline of the power and influence of Islamic civilization and the perceived connection to the decline in science in the Muslim world are the taking off points for the contemporary discussion of *ʿilm* and the opening of many of the fault lines and tensions between classical/internal perspectives and modern/external ones.

Modern Interpretations: Debates about Islam and Science/Islamization of Knowledge

The contemporary Islamization of knowledge (IOK)/Islamic science debate emerged in the 1970s and 1980s in the context of decolonization and development and a perceived crisis in Islamic civilization, and I began studying these debates in 1992 as a Masters student in STS at Virginia Tech University.[16] I approached these IOK/Islamic science debates from the perspective of STS. I was interested in the historical development and legitimization of the various epistemological approaches within the debates and studied this primarily through textual sources (books and journal articles) that were widely available in academic libraries.[17]

16. Very few non-participants were studying these debates. Mazyar Lotfalian (2004) and Leif Stenberg (1996), both graduate students at the time, like myself, also began to study these debates in the 1990s.

17. I had hoped to conduct interviews with some of the founders and leaders of the International Institute of Islamic Thought (IIIT), located three hours away in Herndon, Virginia. Unfortunately, I had to cancel those plans.

I found that the contemporary participants in the IOK/Islamic science debate shared many similarities with earlier Muslim reformers in the late-nineteenth and early-twentieth centuries known as the Islamic modernists, like Syed Aḥmad Khān (1817–1898), Jamāl al-Dīn al-Afghānī (1838–1897), Muḥammad ʿAbduh (1849–1905), and Rashīd Riḍā (1865–1935).[18] Furthermore, I argued that Muslims engaged in the contemporary debate about science held three different epistemological positions on the appropriate relationship between Islam and modern science/knowledge and, thus, three different solutions to the perceived crisis of Islamic civilization with respect to *ʿilm*. I labeled these three approaches modernization, indigenization, and nativization, and summarize each below.

The Modernization Approach

Advocates of the modernization approach hold that science is value-free, neutral, objective, and universal. Any values that do surround science are primarily personal in nature and do not affect the content of science.

The modernists legitimize their position by constructing modern science as Islamically authentic and relevant to the problems of contemporary Islamic civilization.

Authenticity

1. The Qurʾān and the Prophet both advocate the search for knowledge.
2. Modern science is a part of the Islamic legacy.

Relevance

1. Modern science solves the problems of many different countries.
2. Modern science would solve the problems of Islamic civilization also if governments provided the necessary infrastructure and let them pursue their research free from the constraints of government and the ulama.

The Indigenization Approach

18. For example, the contemporary participants in the IOK debate and the Islamic modernist reformers of the late nineteenth and early twentieth centuries share a belief in: (1) the primacy of the original sources of Islam (the Qurʾān and Sunnah), (2) the importance of *ijtihād*, (3) the integration of Islam with science and technology, and (4) the self-sufficiency of Islam. Ṭanṭāwī Jawharī also worked on the relationship of Islam and science. While not directly impacting IOK, his work and approach certainly impacted the debates over the last fifty years.

Advocates of the indigenization approach hold that the crisis of Islamic civilization resulted from the division of knowledge into two separate spheres: the "rational" or "modern" sciences and the Islamic sciences *(uṣūl al-fiqh*/legal theory; *ʿilm al-kalām*/theology, *tafsīr*/qurʾānic sciences; *ḥadīth* sciences; *ʿilm al-tajwīd*/ qurʾānic recitation). This division of knowledge, which mirrors that of Ibn Khaldūn described earlier, is institutionalized in Middle Eastern educational systems, and educational reform is needed in order to re-unify knowledge. The reformed educational systems advocates of the indigenization approach propose will, they argue, produce individuals who have a unified knowledge that is relevant to Islamic civilization. Further, the indigenists argue that Euroamerican science must be integrated with Islamic values because Euroamerican science cannot work within the context of Islamic civilization if adopted wholly and uncritically.

Legitimacy is derived through the production of relevant knowledge. Relevant knowledge is produced through the synthesis of "modern" and Islamic knowledge. The centrality of Islamic values and sciences provide a de facto authenticity to this position.

The Nativization Approach

The advocates of the nativization approach hold that the modernist model of science is a product of the Western worldview. Therefore, the modernist model is not relevant to or compatible with the problems of Islamic civilization and therefore cannot solve them. Rather, an authentic Islamic science is needed to solve the problems of Islamic civilization. For the nativists, Islamic science is a new and different science built upon Islamic metaphysical and epistemological principles derived from the Qurʾrān and Sunna and not an adaptation of the modernist model of science.

For nativists, without authenticity, there can be no relevance.

An STSer's Perspective

As I said earlier, my Masters research was grounded in the core concerns of STS, and the labels I chose for the three epistemological positions were chosen based on their relevance for STS, not with respect to classical/internal conceptions of *ʿilm*, *maʿrifa*, or any other concept, or even to concepts from modern/external sister disciplines that would be more likely to study debates about Islam and science like Islamic studies. The terms "indigenization" and "nativization" came from the anthropology and sociology of knowledge. Interestingly I chose these labels based not on studies of "primitive" peoples but on modern academic scholars in places like Scandinavia and Canada who were arguing to indigenize or nativize their social science disciplines by supporting national journals publishing in the national language rather than privileging scholars who published in English, French, or German in journals in other countries.

"Modernization" actually was a term that replaced "traditional," which I had used in my Masters thesis, in the first journal article I published based on this research.[19] I chose "traditional" initially because in philosophy of science the dominant or "traditional" view of science was "positivism," which views science as value-free, neutral, and objective, and matched very well what I later labelled "modernization." I decided to change the name of the first epistemological position based on a comment from the eminent anthropologist Michael M. J. Fischer, who suggested "traditional" would be confusing for scholars of Islam, who used the term very differently, and that "modernization" better captured the meaning I intended.

An Anthropologist's Perspective

Following completion of my Masters degree in STS in 1993, I returned to the University of Florida, where I had received a BA in anthropology to pursue a PhD in anthropology. Cultural anthropologists are expected to engage in an extended period of field research, and I knew I wanted to continue my research on IOK/Islamic science through ethnographic fieldwork at institutions where IOK/Islamic science was being proposed and/or implemented. Ultimately, I chose to do fieldwork at four institutions: IIIT; what was then known as the School of Islamic and Social Sciences (SISS) in northern Virginia in the United States; the International Islamic University, Malaysia (IIUM); and International Institute of Islamic Thought and Civilization (ISTAC) near Kuala Lumpur, Malaysia.[20]

In 1981 in Washington, DC, the late Ismail R. al-Faruqi, a Palestinian, and a small group of colleagues including AbdulHamid AbuSulayman, a Saudi, and Taha Jabar al-Alwani, an Iraqi, established the International Institute of Islamic Thought (IIIT). Growing out of a 1977 conference on Islamic education held in Mecca and a conference held in Lugano, Switzerland that same year, the IIIT was founded upon the ideas that: (1) there is a malaise in Islamic civilization clearly evident in its political, economic, and cultural spheres; (2) the core of the crisis is a crisis of intellectual thought and methodology; (3) this crisis of thought is the result of the bifurcation of the education system into traditional Islamic and modern European-style educational institutions; and (4) the solution, therefore, is to reform education by rein-

19. See Furlow 1996.
20. The following account of SISS draws heavily upon Furlow 2011.

tegrating Islamic and modern knowledge, thus renewing the link between knowledge and values; and (5) the social sciences and humanities are the appropriate targets for this intervention because they are most susceptible to corrupting influences of ideology.[21]

Al-Faruqi and the IIIT called their project the "Islamization of knowledge" (*Islamiyya al-maʿrifa* in Arabic)[22] and conceived a twelve-step work plan. According to the work plan both the so-called modern disciplines and the Islamic legacy would be mastered and critically evaluated before being synthesized and disseminated in the form of textbooks. Later moving its headquarters to Herndon, Virginia, about a thirty-minute drive west of Washington, the IIIT quickly became a global organization, opening branch offices around the world including London, Cairo, Jordan, the Sudan, Morocco, Pakistan, Bangladesh, and Kuala Lumpur, Malaysia.[23] After al-Faruqi along with his family were murdered or possibly assassinated in 1986, Abu-Sulayman and then al-Alwani headed the IIIT. What I was interested in learning about through fieldwork was how the original ideas and work plan of the IIIT was transformed and reshaped as it traveled to the School of Islamic and Social Sciences (SISS)[24] and the International Islamic University, Malaysia (IIUM).

SISS

In the Fall of 1996, the School of Islamic and Social Sciences opened its doors for classes in half of an unassuming building at the back of an airport office park in Leesburg, Virginia, about an hour drive west of Washington, DC. Beginning with a core staff and faculty that moved from the IIIT and with Taha al-Alwani as President, the school offered programs leading to either a MA degree in Islamic studies or a MA degree in imamate studies.[25]

At the time I was doing fieldwork there in 1997, SISS was struggling to create an institutional identity. In a sense, SISS was a global space trying to

21. al-Faruqi 1982.

22. The use of "*maʿrifa*" rather than "*ʿilm*" is significant and controversial in the IOK/Islamic science debates, which I discuss further when I discuss my Malaysian fieldwork later in the chapter.

23. The offices varied in size and activities greatly. Some small offices consisted of no more than a room with a desk, a phone, and a fax machine while others, like Cairo and Kuala Lumpur, were large and very active in the intellectual life of their countries.

24. SISS began as School of Islamic and Social Sciences (SISS) but added "Graduate" to the name, thus becoming GSISS, as many people initially thought it was a school for children since no Islamic universities existed in the US. In Arabic the name was *Jāmiʿa al-ʿulūm al-Islāmiyya wa l-Ijtamīʿī*. In later years GSISS became known as Cordoba University.

25. The Imam program primarily trained Muslims to be chaplains in the US armed forces and state prison systems.

reach out to disparate audiences. In an interview with Dr. Taha, as fellow faculty and administrators call him, or Sheikh Taha as most of the students call him, he explained that his goal was for SISS to be a recognized American-style graduate school specializing in Islamic studies. Dr. Taha was very clear that he did not want SISS to be an "Islamic seminary." Dr. Taha was upset about local media coverage that portrayed the school exclusively as an Islamic seminary latching onto the imam program and ignoring what Dr. Taha saw as the school's core function, the MA degree in Islamic Studies. The playing down of the imam program, despite a full third of SISS students being in the imam program, was a conscious strategy resulting from the negative stereotype prominent in the Middle East and still held among many first generation immigrants to the United States of imams as ignorant prayer leaders.

This strategy clearly was evident in a comparison of English and Arabic versions of the catalog. In the English "official" catalog, the imam program is present and prominently discussed. In the Arabic "unofficial" catalog created for Arabic language audiences who might send students, sponsor scholarships, or provide other financial support, however, the imam program is buried in a long list of professional programs of which only the imam program actually existed. However, extensive sections on the SISS mission, its uniqueness, and a justification of its location in the United States are present that are not included or only briefly mentioned in the English language catalog. These sections construct SISS as a global space distinct from both its physical location in Leesburg, Virginia and free from the problems of the locations where the catalog is being read in the Middle East. SISS is presented as a utopian field where the best of East and West combine to create a whole greater than the sum of its parts that "goes beyond the contradictory dualism between science and values and negates the dualism between East and West."[26] To quote from the Arabic catalog:

> The location SISS has chosen is a virgin land, which has not experienced the complicated cultural legacy, or the contradictory ideological formulations [that the Middle East has]. It does not contain stale old civilizational inheritances. It is a land in which pluralism and freedom constitute its basic foundations.... [It] constitutes a unique location which has no equal in the modern world for such a project....The United States of America, with its academic environment, is the place where intellectual trends are formed on a worldwide level.... North America constitutes an unequaled place for

26. SISS 1997, 14.

> this university where SISS can be a fruitful fountain of knowledge in contact with all the peoples of the world. This university is not simply a normal academic institution that can be counted among the existing list of universities. It is not a university limited to a particular culture reflecting a nationalist, ethnic, religious, or sectarian mindset ... It contains an intellectual proposal reflecting a paradigm [which is one of only a half dozen words or so that appears in English in the Arabic catalog] which attempts to encompass and go beyond what is present in the modern social sciences (which are of European origin) and the Islamic sciences (which possess a traditional methodology) [*al-manhajia al-taqlidia*].[27]

This utopian vision contrasted markedly with SISS's modest circumstances in the far suburbs of Washington, DC. The location in the last building of a small airport office park and the physical structure of the building itself do not attract attention. The lettering above the entryway was nearly too small to see from the parking lot. The marginalization of Islam from the American mainstream is self-consciously duplicated in the materiality of the school.

The conflict between the contrasting representations of SISS's institutional identity in the Arabic catalog with its declaration of the negation of East and West in the English language catalog, where it is portrayed as an American-style graduate school, and in the media's description as an Islamic seminary was also apparent inside the school where individuals' own identities and backgrounds impacted their views of SISS identity.

Students raised in the United States and used to American categories concerning religion and education and religious and educational institutions viewed SISS, much like the American media, more as an Islamic seminary than as a graduate school. One second-generation American, for example, asked me how I liked being at SISS. When I replied I enjoyed being there and that everyone was very friendly and helpful, she got a surprised look on her face and said, "Really! I could never feel comfortable in a Christian seminary." Another American student with whom I was discussing my thoughts about the school's identity stated, "Well if it isn't an Islamic seminary, then what is it?" A third American student who dropped out of course work for the semester but was visiting asked me whether the school was "more academic now." I asked what she meant and she replied that she wondered whether there was more room for "analysis" and discussion of readings rather than just acceptance at face value of whatever the professors say.

27. SISS 1997, 14.

In contrast, two students raised and educated through the undergraduate level abroad told me how different SISS was from schools in the Middle East and that there was much more freedom to think for oneself rather than being told what to think. One of the students thought the increased intellectual freedom had to do with the school being in the United States, where there was generally more freedom in everything, while the other attributed it to the general condition of "modernity' which was increasing freedom everywhere. However, there were still limits to this freedom. A couple weeks later, when I asked one of the same students who had told me how much freedom there was at SISS why none of the students had challenged Dr. Taha when he said that women are naturally better at raising families than at intellectual studies, she replied, "He is our sheikh, what would you have us do"?

As an anthropologist, I tend to see concepts like "*ʿilm*," "*maʿrifa*," "science," and "knowledge" as embedded in and constructed by socio-cultural contexts and not in the abstract or at the level of pure thought. While the faculty were more discerning and had all been engaged in the theoretical/philosophical development of IOK or Islamic science and knew a lot about the internal differences, for example, between the IOK of the IIIT and the view of Islamic science proposed by S. H. Nasr, who also lectured at SISS, the vast majority of students only differentiated between "Islamic" and "non-Islamic" knowledge without concern for the Arabic source word being translated into English as "knowledge" even if the student in question was a native speaker of Arabic.

At the institutional level, American bureaucracies also did not know how to classify SISS and its programs for accreditation or to construct working relationships. Educational officials with the Commonwealth of Virginia ultimately refused to offer accreditation to SISS because they felt SISS fell into the seminary category rather than the college or university category and thus deferred to organizations that accredited seminaries. Those organizations were only familiar with Christian seminaries so they said they were not competent to judge SISS. SISS ultimately formed a new organization to accredit imam programs in the United States; however their dreams of being a peer university to other religiously affiliated universities in the United States like Georgetown, Harvard, and Duke never came to fruition.

My own positionality within SISS also impacted individuals' views of the knowledge I held and produced. For the semester I was at SISS, I was one of only two non-Muslims at the institution.[28] I sat-in on most of the core

28. The second non-Muslim while I was doing fieldwork was a former administrator at the University of Southern California hired to help with the accreditation process. When I revisited SISS a couple years later, another American, non-Muslim had been hired to help run the school and pursue accreditation.

curriculum classes each week, met with and interviewed faculty, staff, and students, and even shared an apartment with two students, and the dynamic was often interesting. Sometimes I was just like any of the other students in a class. At other times, I was seen as the one person who could explain the "American" view or even the "Western" perspective on a particular topic even though many of the other students had been born and raised in the United States, and I was occasionally introduced as the one "Christian" student at SISS. At still other times, I was asked to present my research to a class or to the entire SISS community as an expert on Islamization of knowledge and Islamic science, which of course SISS was partly founded to promote largely because I had American educational credentials, that is, a Masters degree and a published journal article.[29]

I traveled to Malaysia the following year to continue my research. In Malaysia I spent about 75 percent of my time at the International Islamic University, Malaysia (IIUM) with the remaining time spent primarily at ISTAC, at that time an autonomous research and teaching unit of IIUM led by Syed Muhammad Naquib al-Attas, and Universiti Malaya. I stayed in a hotel in Kuala Lumpur central to all the institutions after my initial plans to rent Dr. Munawar Anees' spare room fell through, and traveled by bike, bus, or light rail. Dr. Anees was the speechwriter for Deputy Prime Minister Anwar Ibrahim, who had been ousted from office when he was arrested three days before I was to travel to Malaysia and falsely accused of allowing himself to be sodomized by Anwar. Dr. Anees was also a prominent scholar within the Islamic science debates and we had been communicating via email for some time. I postponed my trip a month, and sadly Dr. Anees was in prison and on trial for my entire time in Malaysia. I did manage to meet with Dr. Anees' wife and brother-in-law shortly before my departure.

IIUM, Universiti Malaya, and ISTAC were all larger institutions than SISS and I spent most of my limited time interviewing faculty and attending seminars and events related to the Islamization of knowledge and Islamic science. IIUM offered an interesting contrast to SISS. SISS was small and founded directly by members of IIIT who espoused a particular approach to the Islamization of knowledge that was described briefly earlier. IIUM, in contrast, was quite large with multiple campuses, thousands of students, and an interest in also implementing IIIT's version of IOK. IIUM hosted IIIT's Malaysian office and there were many back and forth exchanges of ideas and person-

29. Perhaps the most fun duty I performed as an "expert" was at the American Anthropological Association meetings which were in Washington, DC the Fall I was at SISS, when a professor and two students met me at the book exhibit with a SISS credit card and asked me to take them through the entire exhibit and recommend all the important books available for them to purchase for the SISS library. Now that is a grad student's dream job!

nel among IIIT, IIUM, and SISS. The implementation of an IOK perspective on knowledge at IIUM was not entirely successful[30] due to the size of the institution and focus of students on training for jobs, among other factors. However, the Malaysian context was illuminating for our interests in *ʿilm*.

The contrast in perspectives between the advocates of IOK at IIUM and the Islamization of knowledge agenda of Syed Muhammad Naquib al-Attas and his faithful lieutenant Wan Mohd Nor Wan Daud at ISTAC was stark to say the least.[31] And it is here in these stark differences that we can examine the concepts of *ʿilm* and *maʿrifa* more closely.

In Arabic, the IIIT refers to its Islamization of knowledge project as "*Islamiyat al-maʿrifa*" and thus equates *maʿrifa* with the "knowledge" that needs to be Islamized. For al-Attas and his adherents, knowledge is truth and therefore cannot be Islamized. For this group, *maʿrifa* is a type of knowledge that is unique and personal. Professor Wan described *maʿrifa* as akin to something learned in a conversation or through casual observation. According to Professor Wan, *maʿrifa* cannot be Islamized because it is personal regardless of any method used. Similarly, Professor Wan argues that *ʿilm* cannot be Islamized because all knowledge must be true and all true knowledge must be Islamic.[32]

Louay Safi, who worked with IIIT in Malaysia and the United States, parsed the definitions differently. For Safi,

> [knowledge] is the outcome of the human intellect interacting with its environment [and science is] an attempt to look systematically in terms of examining the knowledge that you have.... [S]cience is more nomothetic, more systematic, more questioning, more logical in trying to decipher or classify the various bits of information you have.[33]

According to Safi, knowledge is *maʿrifa* and *ʿilm* is science. Every individual possesses *maʿrifa*, which is derived from "intuition" and "is the function of the human mind." Science or *ʿilm* occurs when someone begins to evaluate intuitive knowledge or *maʿrifa* according to certain standards using reasoning rather than intuition. Science/*ʿilm* is a collective activity while intuitive knowledge/*maʿrifa* is individual. And while *ʿilm* is not always superior to *maʿrifa* because one can arrive at false conclusions using reason,

30. See Furlow 2009.

31. See Professor Wan's book (Daud 1998) for the extent of the disagreement between the proponents of each position.

32. Personal communcation with Wan Mohd Nor Wan Daud at ISTAC on November 19, 1998.

33. Personal communication with Louay Safi at IIUM on December 9, 1998.

as a whole, *ᶜilm* "denotes a higher level of social development."[34] Thus, for Safi and the IIIT, the Islamization of knowledge is the evaluation of intuitive knowledge using reason derived from Islamic epistemological principles. However, this raised the question of whether a non-Muslim, like myself, can produce *ᶜilm*/science?

In a separate interview, Safi and I discussed this question and Safi related his answer back to the question of authenticity. Safi argued that all scholarship depends upon a particular worldview and is thus not value free: "there is no escape from metaphysical understanding ...you cannot say that people can do research without having any metaphysical commitments or any ontological understanding." Thus, religion is central to research because religion "gives answers to the most basic and profound questions about life – who we are, where we come from, where we are heading, what is the purpose of what we see around us." Therefore, those researchers who hold an Islamic understanding of the universe must relate their scholarship to their metaphysical beliefs "or otherwise something will be missing there. You can never be authentic if you ignore those fundamental things that influence your outlook in life." When I then suggested that this leads logically to the point that Westerners could not do Islamic social science, Safi agreed partly. According to Safi, the West can critique Islamic scholarship but not advance it. He stated, "You can critique something you don't believe in, something you don't agree with, but you can't bring it to heart. So, definitely, Western scholars can be authentic only if they were true to their own experiences and consciousness."[35]

The question of authenticity also applies to Muslims working in the Western tradition. According to Safi, the result of Muslim individuals working within the Western tradition is inauthentic scholarship that mimics others.

Tafsīr ᶜilmī

I now want to move on to discuss *tafsīr ᶜilmī*. A few years ago, Majid Daneshgar, a co-editor of this volume, approached me about writing a chapter examining the relationship between science and qurʾānic exegesis in the Malay-Indonesian world.[36]

Scientific qurʾānic exegesis, known as *tafsīr ᶜilmī* in Arabic, entails the exegesis of the Qurʾān to demonstrate that the way the world was described in the Qurʾān during the seventh century AD is the same, or strikingly simi-

34. Personal communication with Louay Safi at IIUM on December 9, 1998.

35. Personal communication with Louay Safi.

36. The following discussion draws heavily on my chapter in *The Qurʾān in the Malay-Indonesian World* (Furlow 2016).

lar to, the way modern science describes and explains the world.[37] Thus, the supporters of scientific qurʾānic exegesis argue that this correspondence of the Qurʾān with modern scientific theories demonstrates (1) the inimitability of the Qurʾān, and (2) the harmony between Islam and science. The approach in which proponents of scientific qurʾānic exegesis argue that the Qurʾān is inimitable or miraculous is often known as the scientific miracles school of exegesis or, occasionally, Bucaillism after Maurice Bucaille, a leading proponent of this approach.

Interestingly for our current chapter, Bucaille is a French medical doctor and non-Muslim whose books on the correspondence of the Qurʾān to modern science are best sellers in the Muslim world and have helped popularize *tafsīr ʿilmī* among Muslims far and wide. Additionally, Keith L. Moore, a Canadian embryologist, and many other non-Muslim scientists and medical doctors are also well known for their comments on the scientific accuracy of the Qurʾān and these comments are often collected and placed online to support the scientific superiority of the Qurʾān.[38]

Scholars studying qurʾānic exegesis have noted the growth of interpreting/explaining the Qurʾān in relation to modern science since at least the 1880s in the Muslim world and the 1960s in the West. For example, Baljon's *Modern Muslim Koran Interpretation (1880–1960)*, published in 1968, dedicates a third of the section on "Koran and Modern Time" to "Scientific Aspects."[39] While advocates for modern scientific exegesis of the Qurʾān can and sometimes do trace this approach to *tafsīr* back to well respected and prominent Muslim scholars, like Abū Ḥāmid Muḥammad al-Ghazālī (d. ca. 1111 AD), Fakhr al-Dīn al-Rāzī (d. ca. 1209 AD), and Niẓām al-Dīn Nīsābūrī (d. ca. 1330 AD), scientific qurʾānic exegesis has expanded and flourished primarily since the last quarter of the twentieth century.[40]

Scholars, both Muslim and non-Muslim, have critiqued scientific qurʾānic exegesis from a variety of perspectives. A few widely discussed

37. Baljon 1968, 89 also notes a strain of exegesis in which some scholars use science to elucidate or explain qurʾānic passages that are difficult to understand for modern readers or that may seem "antiquated."

38. See https://www.islamic-awareness.org/quran/science/scientists as just one example.

39. While currently out of print, Baljon's book (1968) is widely available on the internet. Eleven of thirty-three pages of the section "Koran and Modern Time" are dedicated to science.

40. See Ansari 2001 for an overview of scientific qurʾānic exegesis in the modern period. While a full review of the qurʾānic scholars who developed *tafsīr ʿilmī* in the early modern period is not possible here, al-Iskandarānī, Ṭanṭāwī Jawharī, al-Kawākibī, Muhammad Abdullah Draz, and Said Nursi (1877–1960) are among the more important contributors to this discourse. Ṭanṭāwī Jawharī has been particularly well studied of late in the Malay speaking world, see Daneshgar 2013 and 2017, and Rahman 2008.

criticisms include the following. First, Muslim scholars like al-Shāṭibī and al-Dhahabī have argued that the purpose of the Qurʾān is to provide general principles to live by rather than deliver a compendium of scientific explanations. Second, few classical Muslim scholars thought to link the Qurʾān and cosmological phenomena or natural wonders. Third, the contemporary writers of this genre often are not trained in the methods of *tafsīr* and rarely approach their work using standard methods. And fourth, what happens if the scientific theories that the Qurʾān is said to have revealed change or are shown to be incorrect?[41]

When I discuss Islam and science with Muslims, whether scholars, students, or individuals unconnected to my research, I am often asked what I think about Maurice Bucaille or some other proponent of scientific qurʾānic exegesis. As a non-Muslim, my first thought and typical response is to raise the fourth critique. What does it mean if, as often happens, the scientific theories change? Clearly, for a Muslim, the Qurʾān cannot be wrong; therefore, the author connecting the Qurʾān to a scientific theory that is no longer accepted must be wrong. Certainly, however, there is at least a small hidden danger here of increasing doubt in the veracity of the Qurʾān being a true revelation.

Conclusions and Final Thoughts

Now that you have suffered through this long and winding road[42] of a quarter century of my research on contemporary debates about Islam and science, what are the take-aways that we are left with?

First, I hope I have convinced you that *ʿilm* is an important and central concept in both Islam and Islamic studies, for Muslim scholars, non-Muslim scholars of Islam, and for the everyday Muslim. *ʿIlm* is one of the most common words in the Qurʾān and Muslims since the Prophet Muḥammad have been invoking the importance of *ʿilm* from the collectors of *ḥadīth* to lay Muslims today. A new generation of scholars and everyday Muslims are increasingly interested in *ʿilm* and are actively transforming the discourse surrounding *ʿilm* and related concepts like *maʿrifa*.

Second, I hope the complexity of drawing boundaries between say an external/objective/scholarly approach and an internal/committed/indigenous approach is apparent. My own shifting status from presumed

41. Baljon (1968) is one early critic of scientific qurʾānic exegesis. Many Muslim scholars have also offered extended critiques. For example, see Sardar 1989 and Guessoum 2008. For a nuanced perspective on Bucaille from a non-Muslim scholar see Bigliardi 2011 and 2012.

42. Those who have studied or participated in the Islam and science debates as long as I have may remember and appreciate the use of song titles from The Beatles by Ziauddin Sardar long ago.

ignorance to student to scholar to expert even within the same field site illustrates this as does the fact that within the contemporary debates about Islam and science Muslim scholars like S. H. Nasr, Ismail al-Faruqi, and Syed Naquib al-Attas are both internal/committed and external/scholarly with academic degrees from and appointments at some of the finest universities in the world as well as universal recognition as leading scholars in the academic field of Islamic studies. Insider/outsider dichotomies are difficult to sustain in a globalized world.

Disciplinary boundaries are as important as whether one is internal or external in shaping the ways that concepts like *ʿilm* are studied, classified, and labeled, as should be clear from my example of the shift in labels I used to classify the epistemological positions within the IOK/Islamic science debates. "Traditional/traditionalist" and "modernization/modernist" have significantly different meanings if one is writing from/for an STS audience or an Islamic studies audience.

Third, while these insider/outsider boundaries are often fluid, they are also very real. Authenticity and authority are connected to power. Local institutional and national contexts have a significant impact on the construction and interpretation of insider/outsider boundaries and on the construction of authenticity and authority, as was clear in the difficulties SISS had of being recognized as an American-style university, even by its own Muslim students, and with navigating an American bureaucratic system that was not capable of classifying and dealing with an institution like SISS.

Finally, I want to look to the future and suggest that perhaps the most interesting projects and research findings might result not from staunchly mapping out and defending internal/external boundaries or even disciplinary boundaries like religious studies/Islamic studies/STS/anthropology. Rather, I find the most interesting work is often done by individuals who are either consciously or unconsciously crossing boundaries to look at the world anew with fresh eyes and different ways of seeing and knowing. Huge innovations are rarely made by those that strictly adhere to the tried and true rules of a discipline. What might advocates of Islamic science gain by finding and engaging with other kindred spirits who study comparative epistemologies in the sciences or elsewhere, or critique "Western" science from various positionalities like feminism, Marxism, or the global south, among others? What might we all gain by increasing dialogues across all boundaries?

Bibliography

Abaza, M. 2002. *Debates on Islam and Knowledge in Malaysia and Egypt: Shifting Worlds.* New York.

AbuSulayman, A. 1993. *Crisis in the Muslim Mind.* Herndon.

Alatas, S. F. 2013. *Ibn Khaldun.* Oxford.

——. 2006. "Ibn Khaldun and Contemporary Sociology." *Inernational Sociology* 21.(6):782–795.

Ansari, Z. I. 2001. "Scientific Exegesis of the Qur'an." *Journal of Qur'anic Studies* 3(1):91–104.

Bakar, O. 1998. *Classification of Knowledge in Islam.* Cambridge, UK.

Baljon, J. M. S. 1968. *Modern Muslim Koran Interpretation (1880–1960).* Leiden.

Bigliardi, S. 2001. "Snakes from Staves? Science, Scriptures, and the Supernatural in Maurice Bucaille." *Zygon: Journal of Religion and Science* 46(4):793–805.

——. 2012. "The Strange Case of Dr. Bucaille: Notes for a Re-examination." *The Muslim World* 102(2):248–263.

Daneshgar, M. 2013. *An Analytical Study on Two Modern Approaches to Science in the Qur'an: Tantawi and Bucaille.* PhD Thesis, University of Malaya. Kuala Lumpur.

——. 2017. *Tantawi Jawhari and the Qur'an: Tafsir and Social Concerns in the Twentieth Century.* New York.

Daud, W. M. N. W. 1998. *Educational Philosophy and Practice of Syed Muhammad Naquib Al-Attas: An Exposition of the Original Concept of Islamization.* Kuala Lumpur.

El-Rayes, W. 2016. "ʿIlm." In *The Encyclopedia of Islam and the Modern World.* 2nd ed., Edited by Richard C. Martin.

al-Faruqi, I. R. 1995. *Toward Islamic English.* 4th ed. Herndon, VA.

Furlow, C. A. 2016. "Intersections of Qurʾān and Science in contemporary Malaysia." In *The Qurʾān in the Malay-Indonesian World: Context and Interpretation*, edited by Majid Daneshgar, Peter G. Riddell, and Andrew Rippin, 229–250. New York.

——. 2011. *Islam, Science, and Modernity: From Northern Virginia to Kuala Lumpur.* Saarbrucken.

——. 2009. "Malaysian Modernities: Cultural Politics and the Construction of Muslim Technoscientific Identities." *Anthropological Quarterly* 82 (1):197–228.

——. 1996. "The Islamization of Knowledge: Philosophy, Legitimation, and Politics." *Social Epistemology* 10 (3/4): 259–271.

Guessoum, N. 2008, "The Qur'an, Science, and the (Related) Contemporary Muslim Discourse." *Zygon* 43(2):411–431.
Iqbal, M. 2002. *Islam and Science.* Burlington, VT.
Lotfalian, M. 2004. *Islam, Technoscientific Identities, and the Culture of Curiosity.* Lanham, Maryland.
Nasr, S. H. 1968 *Science and Civilization in Islam.* Cambridge, MA.
Rahman, F. 2008. *Tafsir Saintifik Atas Surah Al-Fatihah.* Yogarta.
Rosenthal, F. 2007. *Knowledge Triumphant: The Concept of Knowledge In Medieval Islam.* Leiden.
Sardar, Z. 1989. *Explorations in Islamic Science.* London.
SISS. 1997. *SISS Daleel al-diraasaat al-`leeyaa 1997–1998.* Herndon, VA.
Stenberg, L. 1996. *The Islamization of Science: Four Muslim Positions Developing an Islamic Modernity.* Lund.
Turner, H. R. 1995. *Science in Medieval Islam: An Illustrated Introduction.* Austin, TX.
Yusuf ʿAli, ʿA. 1989. *The Meaning of the Holy Qur'an.* Beltsville, MD.

8

Reconstructing *Adab* in Islamic Studies

Nuha Alshaar

ADAB IS A COMPLEX AND SOMEWHAT ELUSIVE CONCEPT. Thus, it can be one of the least useful genre designations when used vaguely to refer to an immensely diverse corpus of pre-modern writings and vast subjects in Arabic literary traditions. This vagueness has occurred since there is not much agreement as to what *adab* is and what it is not in terms of scope and content. *Adab* on the one hand is described as a genre of literature,[1] and on the other hand as an approach to writing or a repertoire of literary anecdotes.[2] Defining *adab* also involves the relationship between history and narrative, as well as the complexity of the various meanings of the term *adab*, as rightly highlighted by Hilary Kilpatrick, due to new semantic nuances that evolved over time without completely shedding previous ones.[3]

This chapter aims to engage with the term *adab* by exploring the system of *adab* and its development as discussed by its early practitioners. The chapter will survey how the term has been used in both theological, religious and non-religious contexts, and will highlight the differences inherent to these contexts. The second part of the chapter will examine modern approaches toward the term *adab* in order to show that many of these studies have been influenced by a set of methods and theories concerning literary texts that neglected these early contexts. By doing so, the chapter will offer a revision of the concept of *adab*, and suggest that the best way to understand it is to contextualize it in its literary, historical, and intellectual contexts rather the impose on it ideas that do not exist in the sources.

1. Among the meanings that Wolfhart Heinrichs identifies for the word *adab* in the fourth/tenth century is its signification of "a genre of anecdotal and anthological literature which serves as a quarry of quotable materials (*muḥāḍarāt*) for the bel-esprit"; see Heinrichs 1995, 120. For other meanings of *adab* identified by Heinrichs see the discussion below in this section. For the concept of *adab* as a genre, see Lichtenstädter 1943, 33; see also further discussion below in this section.

2. On *adab* as an approach, see von Grunebaum 1946, 255; see also Kilpatrick, 1982, 34–42; von Grunebaum, "Adab," *EAL* I:56; von Grunebaum, "Anthologies, Medieval," *EAL* I:94–96.

3. See Kilpatrick, "Adab," *EAL* I:56.

The Use of *Adab* in its Meanings in an Arabo-Islamic Context

A discussion of concepts and terms should not only pay attention to their meanings at different times, but they should also be examined in terms of their function and relationship to broader networks of concepts and beliefs. *Adab* has experienced wide semantic implications and was used in various ways in different circles, be they traditional, theological, or mundane contexts, which were influenced by social and cultural changes in Muslim societies from pre-Islam until the modern period.

Early Arabic dictionaries provide a natural starting point for the exploration of the components of this term and its functions at different levels. One of the early uses of *adab* is its association with the concept of *taʾdīb*, which embodies a form of training for those aspiring to acquire good character and manners and learn proper etiquette. This underlines how *adab* operates at the level of the functional aspects of applied morality. In the first Arabic dictionary, *Kitāb al-ʿAyn*, al-Khalīl b. Aḥmad al-Farāhīdī (d. ca. 175/791) says, "the *adīb* is the educator who educates others" (*muʾaddib yuʾaddibu ghayrah*) or "is educated by others" (*yataʾaddabu bi-ghayrih*).[4] He mentions the phrase "*addaba taʾdīban*," identifying a pre-Islamic use of *adab* to mean "correction" and "punishment." Thus, the nomads applied the word to the domestication of animals.[5]

The association of *adab* with educating someone about correct behavior and morality was preserved in poems, proverbs, and anecdotes that use *muruwwa*, a pre-Islamic term that combines manliness and virtuous conduct and was informed by tribal law and customs.[6] Al-Farāhīdī also links the root *ʾ-d-b* to "invitation to a banquet," an important quality for pre-Islamic Arabs, and the *adīb* to a "*ṣāḥib al-maʾduba*," where *al-maʾduba* or *al-maʾdaba* is a banquet, and the *ādīb* is the host who offers the invitation and entertains the guests.[7]

These two ancient associations of *adab*, with the concept of *taʾdīb* and as an "invitation to a banquet," were given a new emphasis with the coming of Islam in order to promote Islamic morals and literary sensibilities. This important development seems to have been overlooked by many modern scholars of Arabic literature until recently, as will be discussed later in this chapter. The ethics inspired by the Islamic revelation provided a more authoritative point of reference for *adab*, where religious and literary

4. Al-Farāhīdī, *Kitāb al-ʿAyn*, 85.

5. Cf. Bonebakker 1984, 405–410.

6. James Montgomery discusses the term *muruwwa* and its manifestation in classical Arabic poetry; see Montgomery 1986, 7; see also Neuwirth 2014, 76; Neuwirth 2017, 88n16.

7. See al-Farāhīdī, *Kitāb al-ʿAyn*, 85; Ibn Manẓūr, *Lisān al-ʿarab*, I:200–201; al-Fīrūzābādī, *al-Qāmūs al-muḥīṭ*, I:144.

elements and an aesthetic of scripture informed *adab*.[8] The Prophet Muhammad in a number of his sayings recognized that *adab* is associated with knowledge and the manners that are dictated by a divine source. For example, he is reported as saying, "My Lord has educated me, and so He excelled in educating me and I was brought up among the tribe of *Saʿd*" (*addabanī rabbī fa-aḥsana taʾdībī wa rubbitu fī banī Saʿd*).[9] In another *ḥadīth*, related by al-Ḥākim al-Nīsābūrī (d. ca. 405/1014) and attributed to Ibn Shihāb al-Zuhrī (d. ca. 124/742), the Prophet says, "Verily this knowledge (*ʿilm*) is "God's *adab*," through which He has educated his Prophet, and through which the Prophet has educated his community.'[10]

The intersection of religion and *adab* can be seen further in the utilization of the pre-Islamic notion of *adab* as "the invitation to a banquet" in early Islamic traditions and mystical literature. For example, in a number of *ḥadīth* the Qurʾān serves a similar function as the pre-Islamic meaning of *adab*, becoming the divine banquet sent by God to educate people and help them to refine their behavior. ʿAbd Allāh Ibn Masʿūd (d. ca. 32/652–653) narrates a *ḥadīth*: "Indeed the Qurʾān is the banquet of God [on earth], so you should learn from its banquet whatever you can" (*inna hadhā al-Qurʾān maʾdubatu'llāhi fataʿallamū min maʾdubatihi mā istaṭaʿtum*).[11]

The first/seventh-century allegory of the Qurʾān as a divine banquet providing the "nourishment" of knowledge, source of guidance, and a proof of God's divine generosity continued to be used by scholars from the third/ninth century onwards, and may have influenced the conceptualization of the role of the *adīb* as someone who invites people to religion and to achieve inner excellence, and thus the types of work that the *udabāʾ* produced.[12] This view of the *adīb* can be seen in numerous examples, including, Ibn al-Sikkīt (d. ca. 244/858) in the chapter on *al-daʿawāt* (invitations) in his *Kitāb al-Alfāẓ*, Aḥmad ibn Fāris al-Qazwīnī (d. ca. 395/1004) in his *Maqāyīs al-lugha*, and Muḥammad b. Aḥmad al-Qurṭubī (d. ca. 671/1272) in his *al-Jāmiʿ li-aḥkām al-Qurʾān*.[13] They either all cite the *ḥadīth* narrated by Ibn Masʿūd or cite oth-

8. For a thorough study of the role that Qurʾān's aesthetics play in *adab* works; Alshaar 2017, 1–58, and other chapters in the volume; see Bin Tyeer 2016. A discussion of these studies will be provided below.

9. Ibn al-Athīr, *al-Nihāya fī gharīb al-ḥadīth wa'l-athar*, I:4.

10. Al-Ḥākim al-Nīsābūrī, *Maʿrifat ʿulūm al-ḥadīth wa kamiyyat ajnāsih*, 247–248.

11. This *ḥadīth* is reported in different wordings in different collections, including al-Dārimī (d. 255/869), *Musnad al-Dārimī*, 2000, vol. IV, in the chapter entitled "On the Excellence of the Qurʾān" in the section on the merits of the one who reads the Qurʾān, *ḥadīth* no. 3358; see also *ḥadīth* nos. 3350 and 3365.

12. For further discussion of this point; see Alshaar 2017, 11–16.

13. See Ibn al-Sikkīt, *Kitāb al-Alfāẓ*, 1998, 456; Ibn Fāris, *Maqāyīs al-lugha*, 1946–52, I:74–75; al-Qurṭubī, *al-Jāmiʿ li-aḥkām al-Qurʾān* I:12.

ers who cited this *ḥadīth*.[14] Al-Rāghib al-Iṣfahānī (fl. 385/995) also provides a symbolic interpretation on *sūrat al-Māʾida* (Q 5:112–15) and mentions the Ṣūfī allegorical interpretation of these verses as referring to the realities of knowledge (*ḥaqāʾiq al-maʿrifa*). He links this interpretation to the Prophet's description of the "Qur'ān as the banquet of God on earth," drawing similarities between the *ḥadīth* and qurʾānic verses. This leads al-Iṣfahānī to say that "*adab* and *maʾduba* are seen as derived from the same origin (*aṣl*)" on the basis that both provide benefits, since the food of the *maʾduba* nourishes the body, while *adab* embodies knowledge that nourishes the soul.[15] In the same way, Muḥyī al-Dīn Ibn ʿArabī (d. ca. 637/1240) explains the relationship between the allegory of banquet and *adab* saying:

> God has commanded his servant to collect (*jamʿ*), and this is *adab*. *Adab* derives from banquet (*maʾduba*), which is coming together (*ijtimāʿ*) for food. Similarly, *adab* means to collect all that is good. The Prophet said: "God has taught me *adab*; meaning, He gathered all good things into me."[16]

Ibn ʿArabī explains further the many favors that God granted his Prophet Muhammad and describes how the latter acquired a perfect form of morality.[17]

The above discussion highlights a moral and educational function of *adab*, which seems to have been appropriated and utilized in a Muslim context to align its function and purpose with the ethics of the Qurʾān and its literary sensibilities.

The Qurʾān is held by members of the Muslim community as the premier text in Islamic culture, which engendered the growth and development of traditions and new cultural manifestations, with new aesthetic and poetic standards in literature, what Esad Duraković calls "the culture [of] the universe of the sacred text."[18] Mohammed Arkoun observed the psychological effect of revelation in Muslim societies, which he said evoked "collective emotions," that is, produced their social imaginary.[19] Furthermore, the transformation of the Qurʾān from oral to written text initiated a cultural shift, where an acknowledgment of the authority of writing over oral transmission was cultivated among members of the community.[20] With the writing

14. See further, Alshaar 2017, 11–13.
15. Sardār. 2002, 494–497.
16. See Muḥyī al-Dīn Ibn ʿArabī, *al-Futūḥāt al-makkiyya*, 640; cf. Alshaar 2017, 12–13.
17. For a further discussion of of Ibn ʿArabī's concept of *adab*, see Gril 1993, 228–263.
18. See Duraković 2015, xviii; cf. Alshaar 2017, 17.
19. See Arkoun 1988, 62–63; cf. Alshaar 2017, 18.
20. See Neuwirth 2017, 65–66.

down and codification of the Qurʾān and the collective acceptance of its authority, a much deeper awareness of writing as a medium for documenting ideas and preserving culture was produced. Muslims began to generate numerous texts in order to interact with the sacred scripture, which greatly influenced subsequent written productions.[21] From the outset, the Qurʾān challenged its immediate audience with reference to its style and aesthetic qualities, placing itself as a divinely revealed text above other forms of human production, including, poetry and soothsaying, both of which were associated with pagan practices. The collective acceptance of the superiority of the linguistic, literary, and rhetorical qualities of the Qurʾān by the Muslim community turned into a source of textual authority.

From the end of the second/eighth century up to the fourth/tenth century, Muslim scholars built on the qurʾānic *iʿjāz* (its inimitability) and developed it into a proper field of study to discuss the literary qualities of the Qurʾān and to affirm its superiority over all other forms of expression.[22]

The production of many manuals devoted to the study of the Qurʾān and its eloquence and literary qualities placed it in a primary position that necessarily attracted the attention of those interested in the art of writing, for example the *udabāʾ*, for most of whom the language of the Qurʾān was part of their training. Other explanations for why the Qurʾān was so important to the development of *adab* is the religious status of the Qurʾān and the community's daily interaction with the scripture. [23] The *udabāʾ* seemed to have been testing the boundaries of incorporating divine speech in their texts, which can tell us about the pursuit of *adab* and its exploratory nature.

As more Muslim traditions were put down in writing, the production of *adab* works developed along with the compiling of much *ḥadīth* literature in terms of their literary form and content, especially the *ḥadīth* compendia listed under the heading of *adab*.[24]

The cultural transformation in the Umayyad period (41/661–132/750) and the incorporation of the class of secretaries (*kuttāb*) into the system of administration influenced further the development of *adab*. These secretaries, which included individuals such as Sālim Abū l-ʿAlāʾ (d. ca. 126/743), ʿAbd al-Ḥamīd al-Kātib (d. ca.132/750), and ʿAbd Allāh Ibn al-Muqaffaʿ (d. ca. 139/756), introduced foreign elements by transmitting Greek and Persian traditions on ruling and morality, without excluding the importance of religious elements and pre-Arabic Islamic traditions, as will be discussed below. This resulted in a new semantic shift in *adab*, which came to mean "knowl-

21. Cf. Alshaar 2017, 18.
22. See Alshaar 2017, 16–20 ; see also Qāḍī and Mir, "Literature and the Qurʾān," *EQ* III:205.
23. For further explanation of these points, see Alshaar 2017, 17–24.
24. Cf. Sperl 2007, 459–486; see also Leder and Kilpatrick 1992, 2–26.

edge or rules of behavior and norms associated with a particular profession, discipline or class." An example of this new understanding is seen in *al-Adab al-ṣaghīr wa'l-adab al-kabīr* by Ibn al-Muqaffaʿ. This work starts by praising sound reason as a guide for people to reach goodness in this world and the next, including much advice based on the etiquette of the Sassanian court (224–651 CE).[25] Although the role of the secretarial class in developing *adab* should not be underestimated, some scholars, as will be discussed below, exaggerate the influence of the introduction of Iranian traditions into Arab culture by this class and consider it the starting point of *adab*.

Furthermore, during the Umayyad period especially, official state policy enforced Arabic as the language of the state, society and religion. Secretaries, authors, and public servants were advised to memorize the Qurʾān if they want to improve their language skills and acquire an eloquent style. The famous Umayyad secretary ʿAbd al-Ḥamīd al-Kātib (d. ca. 132/750)[26] advised secretaries to start by mastering the Qurʾān and its literary formulation, since he believed that repeated recitation of the Qurʾān led to an appreciation of the Qurʾān's literary formulation and moved one from the passive admiration of its art to the active imitation of it.[27] He encouraged secretaries to embellish their works with qurʾānic references to prove their talent and skill in appropriating qurʾānic language, formulations, and themes. He then advised them to build up knowledge of religious obligations as well as of the Arabic language. They were also advised to memorize poetry and acquire knowledge of mathematics, learn about the pre-Islamic histories of both the Arabs (including the famous Reports of the Days of the Arabs (*ayyām al-ʿarab*)) and the non-Arabs,[28] and to develop good handwriting. Ibrāhīm b. Muḥammad al-Shaybānī (d. ca. 298/911) also urged secretaries to gain efficiency in extracting appropriate verses from the Qurʾān and proverbial citations in order to enhance the artistic qualities of formal speech.[29] Thus, the practice of borrowing quotations or material from the Qurʾān (*iqtibās*) became common among the practitioners of *adab*, following the example of the Prophet and his early Companions, and seemed to have developed the style of *adab* writings.[30]

25. See Ibn al-Muqaffaʿ, *al-Adab al-ṣaghīr wa'l-adab al-kabīr*, 1960.

26. On ʿAbd al-Ḥamīd al-Kātib's use of the Qurʾān, see Wadād al-Qāḍī, "The Impact of the Qurʾān on the Epistolography of ʿAbd al-Ḥamīd," 1993.

27. See Latham, 1983, 167–179.

28. A number of scholars claimed that ʿAbd al-Ḥamīd and other secretaries tried to move away from the Arabic style and culture, a claim which is not substantiated by the sources, see further discussion below.

29. Al-Shaybānī, *al-Risāla al-ʿadhrāʾ*, 7.

30. For discussions on the practice of *iqtibās* see Sanni, 1998; van Gelder, 2002–3, 3–16; al-Qāḍī 1985, 99–148; Orfali and Pomerantz 2017, 191–219.

The meaning of *adab* as "knowledge or rules of behavior and norms associated with performing a particular profession, discipline or class" continued into the third/ninth century and beyond when it was used to describe the rules of behavior in a specific circle or discipline (*adab al-ṣuḥba*), the rules or culture needed to perform the function of a secretary (*adab al-kātib*), or the rules for behavior between master and disciple (*adab al-nafs wa 'l-dars*), or the rules of the teachers (*adab al-ʿālim wa l-mutaʿllim*), the rules for the reading of the Qurʾān (*adab qirāʾat al-Qurʾān*), or the rules of judges (*adab al-qāḍī*). This latter notion of *adab* in religious literature was first used by Abū ʿAbd Allāh Muḥammad b. Idrīs al-Shāfiʿī (d. ca. 204/820), who used the term *ādāb al-qāḍī* as a title for one of the sections in his *Kitāb al-Umm*.[31] The word *adab* was also frequently used as in chapter headings in many of the emerging *ḥadīth* compilations, discussing *adab* in relation to different religious practices and subject matters. The word was also used in *ḥadīth* circles in statements used for teaching instruction, such as, "this *ḥadīth* must be made available to the person who is being taught" (*hādhā al-ḥadīth yanbaghyī an yuʾṭā li- l-muʾaddab*).[32]

With the proliferation of many disciplines of learning and social groups, it seemed each group developed their own understanding of *adab* or proper moral code and behavior, which members of each discipline followed to express their sense of belonging to a specific discipline. Therefore, *adab* started to have wider social implications that cannot be limited to one specific meaning. The Ṣūfīs for example formulated their own branch of Ṣūfī *adab* since Ṣūfism is formed around *adab* (*al-taṣawwuf kulluhu ādāb*).[33] For each spiritual station (*maqām*), there is a form of *adab*, ethical behavior or etiquette, which corresponds to it and defines relationships between the members.[34] As discussed by Denis Gril, *adab* is embodied in Ṣūfism since both involve education (knowledge) for training and nurturing.[35] This underlines the link between the concept of *ta'dīb*, acquiring the knowledge one needs to master in order to engage in proper conduct or social etiquette (*adab al-ẓāhir*) and *tahdhīb*, refinement of soul and character or (*adab al-nafs*) and companionship (*adab al-ṣuḥba*).[36] This form of *adab* and Ṣūfism deal with knowledge (*ʿilm*) that leads to recognition (*maʿrifa*), and therefore they both deal with texts that include lived reports that were transmitted for their

31. See al-Shāfiʿī, *Kitāb al-Umm*, 299–300.

32. Cf. Wensinck 1936, 36–37.

33. For a collection of comprehensive studies on Ṣūfī *adab*, see Chiabotti, et al., 2016.

34. See Chiabotti, et al., 2016, 1.

35. See Gril 2016, 47–63.

36. For a discussion of the notion of *adab* in a range of Ṣūfī activities, see Abū Naṣr al-Sarrāj (d. ca.378/988), *Kitāb al-Lumaʿ*, 136–193.

moral value and put together in precise order to convey a specific function.[37] Thus, the *adīb* (a person of *adab*) is deeper in its ethical and moral connotations than only "politeness," as Stephan Guth suggested.[38]

At the beginning of the sixth/twelfth century, Ṣūfīs continued to develop their own institutions and topics related to *adab*, which figured in three types of discussions: the accomplishment of religious practices and proper attitude towards divine law (*adab al-sharīʿa*); proper attitudes towards others (*adab al- muʿāmalāt*); and attitudes towards God (*adab al-ḥaqq*).[39] Ṣūfī mystics used *adab* for their hermeneutical act of engaging with the reading of the Qurʾān (*adab al-Qurʾān*). This usage became evident in the writing of many Ṣūfī masters, including Rūmī's metaphor of "the Qurʾān as a bride" in his *Fīhi mā fīhi*, which Steffen Stelzer discussed as *adab* or proper behavior towards the divine words or the etiquette of a person towards God, since the divine word functions as intermediary between God and His creatures.[40] The last point shows how the meaning of *adab* in relation to the Qurʾān represents a connection between outer behavior and an attentive acknowledgement of the spirit of the Qurʾān and multiplicity of its meanings.

In the Abbasid period, widespread literacy and the "transformation from the predominantly oral/aural literary [culture] to the increasingly book-based and writerly [one]," as suggested by Shawkat Toorawa,[41] due to the availability of paper, which the Arabs learned from the Chinese, as well as the role played by intellectually curious caliphs who became devoted patrons of learning and scholarship, played a major role in the development of *adab* and culture. As a result, *adab* continued to acquire new connotations. In addition to its ethical and social associations, *adab* came to imply the sum of knowledge existing in this period.

More scholars generally identified themselves in this period on the basis of their commitments to the study of a specific discipline, which led to a self-imposed division of scholarly fields, resulting in a specific shift in the nature of knowledge that came to be conceived not simply in its abstract totality, but in a more restricted form in terms of the changes to specialized scholarship. Nevertheless, a wider approach that drew upon all available forms of knowledge and resisted specialization still existed.[42]

If one explores a number of Arabic foundational texts that are essential

37. See Keeler 2016, 63–102.

38. Cf. Francesco Chiabotti, et al. 2016, 5.

39. See also Erik, S. Ohlander, "Adab d) in Ṣūfism," *EI THREE* (Brill Online); cf. Alshaar 2017, 40–41.

40. See Stelzer 2017, 545–565.

41. See Toorawa 2005a, 2; cf. Toorawa 2005b, 303–304.

42. For a discussion on the intellectual practices and the different approach to knowledge in this period, see Alshaar 2015, 36–59.

in shaping the understanding of *adab* in this period, each of these texts leads to questions concerning "canon" and represents a unique element in the constituents of *adab* traditions. These texts also appear to reflect a form of curriculum or the types of knowledge that their authors thought are needed to achieve the form of *taʾdīb* required, stressing to various degrees the moral, linguistic, aesthetic, entertaining, intellectual, and educational function of *adab*.

For instance, in *Adab al-Kātib*, Ibn Qutayba (d. ca. 275/889) identifies *adab* with an encompassing moral curriculum that is linked to the developing Arabic disciplines in this period.[43] In his treatment of fourth/tenth-century works on the classification of knowledge, Wolfhart Heinrichs appears to affirm this view by noting "certain trends toward [the] establishment of *adab* as an autonomous field."[44] He states that during this period, *adab* is used in a wider intellectual context to signify a genre of anecdotal and anthological literature as well as a body of knowledge in the linguistic and literary fields that includes disciplines like grammar alongside its moral dimension as good behavior.[45]

This conception of *adab* in the pre-modern period, which avoids specialization, is also perceived in other works of Ibn Qutayba, who defined the *adīb* as the one who embraces all forms of knowledge, be it non-religious or religious, including the Book of God, *ḥadīth* and *fiqh*.[46] Ibn Qutayba set out to identify the stylistic and semantic peculiarities of the Qurʾān and to study its figurative language and its eloquence (*balāgha*). This knowledge is necessary for the *adīb* since the language of the Qurʾān was compared to other standards of Arabic literary speech and came to be seen as combining many meanings in a few words (*jawāmiʿ al- kalam*).[47] Thus, the *adīb* came to view the text of scripture as a powerful literary source and persuasive tool to influence readers.

This attempt by Ibn Qutayba to stress the importance of knowledge of the language and stylistic and literary features of the Qurʾān for the practitioner of *adab* could be seen as a response to a number of non-Arab secretaries and poets, such as Bashshār b. Burd (d. ca. 167/783 or 168/784), who driven by their professional pride and by anti-Arab sentiment (*shuʿūbiyya*), reportedly rejected the miraculous qualities of the Qurʾān and impugned its style.[48]

43. See Ibn Qutayba, *Adab al-kātib*, 5–20; cf. Al-Zabīdī, *Tāj al-ʿarūs*, II:12; see also Khalidi 1996, 108–111.

44. See Heinrichs 1995, 139.

45. Heinrichs 1995, 19–20.

46. See Ibn Qutayba, *Adab al-kātib*, 7, 13–14; see also Khalidi 2009, 104–105.

47. See Alshaar 2017, 18.

48. The *shuʿūbiyya* was an anti-Arab movement, which denied that Arabs should hold any intrinsic, privileged position, and some went so far as to deny the miraculous nature of the

These *adab* texts contained a specific kind of education, as well as a moral and intellectual curriculum addressed to a particular audience.[49] Ibn Qutayba, for example, in his *ʿUyūn al-akhbār* and *Adab al-kātib*, indicated that the main purpose of the types of materials that he selected was to allow readers to put knowledge into practice to refine their character and to acquire moral rectitude and virtue.[50] Thus, linking *adab* to the acquisition of knowledge that leads to virtue emphasizes the moral and educational functions of *adab*, which provide a basis for "practical ethics."[51]

Although for him all forms of knowledge share a single, underlying purpose (that is, the worship of God), he still honored knowledge – derived from the Qurʾān, the Prophetic traditions and the science of the Arabic language – as the essential component of *adab* and the model of piety.[52] The moral aspects of *adab* texts and particularly Ibn Qutayba's works have already been discussed by van Gelder, Sperl, and Khalidi, who notes that the division of the chapters in Ibn Qutayba's *Adab al-kātib* parallels and conceptually resonates with the *ḥadīth* collections found in the renowned *Ṣaḥīḥayn*.[53] In fact, *adab* compilations of the second/eighth and third/ninth centuries shared ethical orientations with the Qurʾān and certain texts handed down by religious traditions in terms of their concern for good conduct and personal virtue, and seem to have been molded by the character of these texts.[54] It may also be argued that Ibn Qutayba and other scholars also were influenced by the circulation of the first/seventh-century allegory of the Qurʾān as a divine banquet providing the "nourishment" of knowledge, goodness, and guidance. This influence brings a new emphasis to the pre-Islamic notion of *adab* as knowledge that should be practiced for the welfare of a person and society. This idea underlines an important aspect of classical *adab*, which is the link between knowledge (*ʿilm*) and *ʿamal* (action). The relationship between *ʿilm*, *ʿamal*, and *adab* has already been viewed by Rosenthal, who translated *adab* as "general knowledge," which included matters of ethics, morals, behavior, customs, and learning.[55]

This understanding of the binary between knowledge (*ʿilm*) and *ʿamal* (action) is also present in the writings of Abū ʿUthmān ʿAmr b. Baḥr al-Jāḥiẓ

Qurʾān and its style. On this movement see; Norris 1990, 31–47; see also Susanne Enderwitz, "al-shuʿūbiyya," *EI2* IX:513–516.

49. Cf. Alshaar 2017, 15; see also Sperl 2007, 459.
50. See van Gelder, "Ibn Qutayba," *EAL* I:361; Sperl 2007, 462; Khalidi 1996, 87–89.
51. Cf. Alshaar 2017, 15; cf. Sperl 2007, 459.
52. See Sperl 2007, 465.
53. See van Gelder, "Ibn Qutayba," *EAL* I:361; Sperl 2007, 462; Khalidi 1996, 87–89.
54. Cf. Leder and Kilpatrick 1992, 2.
55. Rosenthal 2007, 240–277.

(d. 255/868). In his introduction to *Kitāb al-Qiyān* (The Book of Singers), *adab* is used in reference to bodies of knowledge, for example, astronomy, geometry, medicine, and music, which should be seen as a system for the study of nature and society.[56] Across his writings, al-Jāḥiẓ also emphasized the educational function of *adab* and its personal and social dimensions, speaking of *adab* as a means of disciplining both the soul and society through the acquisition of knowledge and learning.[57] In this context, he highlights the value of religious traditions as an important source of knowledge to achieve this goal, something he shared with Ibn Qutayba. Finally, al-Jāḥiẓ uses *adab* to refer to the compilations of sayings by sages, both philosophers and prophets. [58]

In his *Risāla fī l-maʿād wa l-maʿāsh* (Epistle of the Next Life and this Life), which is also known as *Risāla fī l-akhlāq al-maḥmūda wa'lmathmūma* (Epistle on Praiseworthy and Blameworthy Characters), al-Jāḥiẓ links *adab* to the type of knowledge that could be used to derive benefit. This knowledge is an essential means suitable to promote ethics, as it draws on explanations of the next life, on religion, and in this life on aspects of how the world works, its organization, and the moral qualities and virtues that all cultures agree on their value for a person and society.[59] The interest in seeking to balance and integrate the views of religion (*dīn*) and the world (*dunyā*) to guide rulers and other privileged audiences was also evident in the advice literature written in Arabic and Persian known as "mirrors for princes" (*naṣīḥat al-mulūk*) as shown by Louise Marlow.[60] Authors of these texts provided their audiences with qurʾānic values and displayed a wide variety of approaches in their adoption of the sacred scripture. Fourth/tenth-century anthology authors also provided education on broad themes of morality, ethical personal conduct and virtues, refinement of the soul, and discussions of correct rulership to various caliphs and princes, who were largely the patrons of this body of literature. For example, Ibn ʿAbd Rabbih al-Andalusī (d. 328/940) described *adab* as a "goodly tree, with lofty branches, growing in good soil and bearing ripe fruits, so whoever takes his share of it [this tree i.e. *adab*] is heir to prophecy, and [acquires] the path (*minhāj*) of wisdom, and whoever holds fast to it will not feel lonely or estranged and will not go astray."[61]

Another aspect is how al-Jāḥiẓ thought of *adab* as eloquence (*balāgha*) and effective communication. This is the focus of his *al-Bayān wa'l-tabyīn*,

56. See al-Jāḥiẓ, *Rasāʾil al-Jāḥiẓ*, II:143–182; cf. Alshaar 2017, 9.

57. For a study of al-Jāḥiẓ's writings and thought, see Montgomery 1913. For al-Jāḥiẓ's approach to *adab*, *ḥikma* (wisdom) and history, see Khalidi 1996, 104–108.

58. Cf. Alshaar 2017, 9.

59. See al-Jāḥiẓ, *Rasāʾil al-Jāḥiẓ*, I:95; cf. Alshaar 2017, 9.

60. See Marlow 2017, 401–433.

61. See Ibn ʿAbd Rabbih, *al-ʿIqd al-farīd*, 1:2. Cf. Bray 2005, 14.

which aimed to achieve an intended message or meaning (*maʿnā*) through the use of eloquent and clear speech (*bayān*). The curriculum for training to achieve *bayān* include oratory (an important Arabic tradition), speeches, *ḥadīth* , and poetry. An important element in the composition of this book and others like it is not to bore readers and to keep them interested in the subject. In his definition of eloquence, al-Jāḥiẓ seemed to have engaged with theories that existed in his time.[62] In order to describe the different forms of lapses of or deformities of the tongue (*āfāt al-lisān*), the origin of language and the value of poetry, al-Jāḥiẓ used religious, religiously-oriented, and non-religious sources, including a selection of the best speeches of the Prophets, namely orations, *ḥadīth*, famous epistles, and poetry which he ascribed to different types of people, fools and wise people, sages and heretics, and Bedouins and urbanites. Thus, this form of *ta'dīb* or training in *bayān* leads to *adab* of the tongue: the use of eloquent speech as well, polite manners in addressing people, which resonates with the qurʾānic notion of a good word as a good tree (Q 14:24). In a century in which religious polemic and heated debates intensified about each and every field of knowledge, training in eloquence and rhetoric was a much needed curriculum in the field of Arabic sciences so that one was well-prepared to persuade and defeat. Thus, with the development of Arabo-Islamic society, even though *adab* was open to the influence of various sources of inspirations and tolerated different individual tastes, an *adīb* was more likely to "regard Islam as a cultural beginning," a constant invitation to explore the world and the human being.[63] An *adīb* would have had numerous forms of knowledge at his disposal and would have had recourse to a range of sources and multiple voices to build up his overall narrative, while continuing to consult religious materials.[64] Thus this attempt to continue to align *adab* with the Arabic and religious disciplines can be seen as a way to ensure a place for *adab* and the *adīb* within newly developing Islamic culture that was searching to define itself.

Thus, although some modern scholars such as Nallino, followed by Pellat and Gabrieli, draw rigid lines between human knowledge and religious knowledge in their definition of *adab*, as will be discussed in the following section, these two forms of knowledge cannot be separated and both provided a wealth of resources to the *udabāʾ* in classical Islam. In fact, *adab* texts provided their authors with a domain in which they exercised their intellectual curiosity, engaging not only with questions relating to the inclusion of

62. For a detailed and comprehensive study of Jāḥiẓ's theories of *bayān* and *balāgha*; see Montgomery 2006, 91–153.

63. For a comparison between the practitioner of *ḥadīth* and the *adīb*; see Khalidi 1996, 87.

64. Cf. Alshaar 2017, 15.

divine words in human speech and texts, but also to including divine words with those of Greek sages in their texts, allowing a dialogue between the two.

Building on this later point, one should consider the influence of Greek heritage and philosophy in the third/ninth and fourth/tenth century on producing new meanings and connotations of *adab*. One example is Ḥunayn b. Isḥāq's translation of the Aristotelian concept of "paideia" in the *Nichomachean Ethics* as *adab*. Greek culture widened the content of *adad* and introduced new themes and topics.[65] While the Persian secretarial class participated in the introduction of various prose genres and the pragmatic and functional aspects of *adab* style and writings as outlined above, the teaching of Greek sages and philosophers influenced the development of the subject of *ʿilm al-akhlāq* (knowledge of morality) and ethics generally. These philosophical materials were transmitted as fragments and assimilated by the *udabāʾ* in their texts alongside other materials including qurʾānic fragments in order to further a particular point of view or a particular theme. This act by which the *udabāʾ* would extract and transmit materials from earlier sources and authorities rather than their own words to express their views and to construct a certain narrative was a common practice in *adab* works in which didactic intention informed the narrative.

Furthermore, the interest in using philosophical ideas and citations led to the development of a new form of writing that combined philosophical thought with *adab* (*al-fann al-adabī*), which seemed to be a way of adhering to a literary form that was more common in court-sessions.[66] Scholars, including the Brethren of Purity, famously known as Ikhwān al-Ṣafāʾ and Abū Ḥayyān al-Tawḥīdī (circa 315–414/927–1023), who both seemed to have maintained a level of independence, endeavored to apply philosophy in society in different settings, such as, official courts, private sessions, and the book market (*sūq al-warrāqīn*).

Al-Tawḥīdī, particularly, an important litterateur and philosopher of the fourth/tenth century of Islam, was described by Yāqūt as "the philosopher of litterateurs and the litterateur of philosophers," "a *shaykh* among the Ṣūfīs" "the investigator (*muḥaqqiq*) of the *kalām* and the theologian (*mutakallim*) of the investigators," and "the leader of the eloquent."[67] This statement shows the difficulty of applying a single label to al-Tawḥīdī and his movement between different intellectual disciplines, including *adab*, philosophy, Ṣūfism and theology. Thus, it is fair to say that the intellectual interests of al-Tawḥīdī and the encyclopedic nature of his writings, in which opposition

65. On the influence of Greek culture on Arabic and Islamic traditions, see Goodman1983, 460–481.

66. See Rowson 1990, 50–92.

67. See Yāqūt, *Muʿjam al-Udabāʾ*, 15–11, cf. Alshaar 2010, 151.

between religion and philosophy could not exist, demonstrate the invalidity of the tendency of modern scholarship to separate belle-lettres and thought as though they were different genres in the context of fourth/tenth-century Islamic literature.[68]

In his *Risāla fī al-ʿUlūm* (On the [Classification of] Knowledge), al-Tawḥīdī attempted to reconcile various and separately conceived disciplines of knowledge and to assemble them into a cohesive framework, showing how they can be conceived in relation to one another. For him knowledge is noble in origin and this nobility applies to all its branches, whether religious or secular:

> If *ʿilm* is noble (*sharīf*) and the most noble (*ashraf*) of all things, then it follows that this universality (*al-ʿumūm*) is applicable to [all of its] class (*al-jins*), and this generalization entirely encompasses [both] the origin and the branch. This is because [the word] *al- ʿilm* with the definite article (*bil alif wa al-lām*) does not specify one [form of] knowledge (*maʿlūm*) rather than another.[69]

The knowledge that al-Tawḥīdī listed included Arabic religious sciences and logic and Greek philosophy. He then provided his holistic approach to knowledge by relating the Arabic religious sciences to a broader context, offering a view of perfection where knowledge of this science is integrated in a cohesive framework with logic:

> A person who has the facility of language (*lugha*), and is competent in grammar (*naḥw*), becomes the most skilful in [the art of] speech and will also prove adept at deriving (*taṣrīf*) meanings. He will also acquire further insight into the value of man, who is privileged over all animals, and becomes acquainted with the theologian's (*mutakallimūn*) deficiencies and gains insight into the manners of the jurists (*fuqahā'*) in [dealing with] an issue. If, after this, he were to speak some logic, he would exceed all rivals.[70]

Al-Tawḥīdī clarified this statement further by giving a short description of logic. He described it as an instrument that helps to evaluate how words convey meaning, whether they conform or deviate from a word's original meaning, and whether this meaning is presented in a clear, eloquent, or am-

68. See further discussion below.

69. Al-Tawḥīdī, "Risāla fī al-ʿUlūm," in *Rasāʾil Abī Ḥayyān al-Tawḥīdī*, 105–106; cf. Alshaar 2015, 77; cf. Alshaar 2010.

70. Al-Tawḥīdī, "Risāla fī al-ʿUlūm," 111.

biguous way. Therefore, logic purifies utterances and refines meanings and allows an understanding of their nuances.[71] For al-Tawḥīdī *adab* is a practice that requires tools and knowledge from different sources to materialize. Thus, an isolated approach to knowledge was no longer reasonable from the perspective of al-Tawḥīdī, who seemed to have provided his own type of intellectual inquiry that was based on the usage of all available knowledge.

By the time of the renowned ʿAbd al-Raḥmān b. Muḥammad Ibn Khaldūn (d. ca. 809/1406), the classification of *adab* as a branch of knowledge became more established. Ibn Khaldūn uses the term *ʿilm al-adab*, which belongs in the sciences of the Arabic language (*ʿulūm al-lisān al-ʿarabī*) together with grammar (*naḥw*), lexicography (*lugha*), and clarity and eloquence in spoken or written speech (*bayān*). Therefore, he defines *ʿilm al-adab* as a body of writings connected to the mastery of Arabic language, which eventually manifests itself in elegant poetic or prosaic compositions. This includes articulation, or eloquent expression rather than the exhaustive examination of contentious or debatable topics. Thus, this mastery can be achieved through the study of poetry and attendant anecdotes (*akhbār*), the canonical texts in religious studies (*ʿulūm sharʿiyya*), the Qurʾān and *ḥadīth*, and rhetorical devices known as *al-badīʿ*. Based on what he heard from his teachers in learning sessions (*majālis al-taʿlīm*), Ibn Khaldūn identified four core or canonical works that formed the curriculum of *ʿilm al-adab*: Ibn Qutayba's (d. 889) *Adab al-kuttāb* (or *Adab al-kātib*), al-Mubarrad's (d. ca. 898) *al-Kāmil*, al-Jāḥiẓ's (d. ca. 868) *al-Bayān wa l-tabyīn*, and Abū ʿAlī al-Qālī's (d. ca. 898) *al-Nawādir*.[72] Each of these books contains a specific type of education and represents a key element of *adab* whether moral, religious, intellectual, anecdotal, literary and eloquent, or entertaining. Therefore, they are the foundation for the study of *adab* and everything is secondary to them. To support the point of Ibn Khaldūn further, the wide reception and circulation of these canonical texts are evidence of how they were seen to be useful and valuable. For example, al-Jawāliqī (d. 1144) composed a commentary on Ibn Qutayba's *Adab al-Kātib,* and al-Qālī used his *Nawādir* to teach his students, and many other scholars narrated the text as well, including, al-Zibīdī (d.1790), and later an abridgement of *Nawādir* became available. These commentaries and abridgements became part of canon building and were prepared for students to facilitate teaching and learning in scholarly circles.

71. Al-Tawḥīdī, "Risāla fī al-ʿUlūm," 111. Al-Tawḥīdī provides similar views in three consecutive Muqābasāt dealing with language, grammar, and logic; see al-Tawḥīdī, *al-Muqābasāt*, 121–125, 126–128, 129–132.

72. See Ibn Khaldūn, *Tārīkh Ibn Khaldūn*, vol. 2, 1069–1070.

Modern/Western Scholarship on the Study of *Adab*

One of the main challenges in the study of *adab* is that pre-modern Muslim scholars used the category of *adab* to approach their own literary traditions, but this point often is not properly recognized in Western studies of *adab*. In addition, the wide social contexts of the term *adab* and its semantic complexity and various meanings that evolved gradually present difficulties for modern scholars who tend towards specializations and categorizations. Thus, many modern scholars of Arabic literature have different conceptions, definitions, and approaches for *adab* than the classical authors.

Given that the views of pre-modern scholars were closer to and more familiar with the contexts of the works produced, it is troubling that some modern studies are ready to either discredit them or view them through a modernistic lens that disregards their optimum position. A problem with some Western approaches in defining the *adab* corpus of literary traditions is that they import their understanding of this corpus from other cultural traditions.

Numerous scholars have attempted to resolve the above-mentioned difficulties concerning the study of *adab* by applying their own outside analogies or perspectives developed in European literary theory and Western scholarly categories. Concepts such as "belles-lettres" and "humanism" have been borrowed to analyze *adab* literary traditions, assuming that their core dynamic was a dichotomy between the "religious" on one side and the "profane," or the humanism of the elite, on the other. However, this raises major concerns about one culture borrowing a set of definitions and conceptions from another, and leads to questioning the suitability of approaching the subject of *adab* through Western categories.

Some scholars, including, Ilse Lichtenstädter and Seeger Bonebakker, consider *adab* a genre, containing works that bring knowledge to people in official contexts, for example, government officials (*kuttāb*) and to do it in an entertaining manner.[73] Others, such as Gustave von Grunebaum, Hilary Kilpatrick, and Bo Holmberg see *adab* as an approach to writing in which certain themes interact, or a style and a principle of form rather than a genre, or an array of materials.[74] Some researchers have had a more pragmatic approach. Charles Pellat, for example, stresses the purpose of *adab* in its social context and its function as a moral, social, and intellectual curriculum.[75] Wolfhart Heinrichs also identifies the meaning of *adab* and its significance in the con-

73. Lichtenstädter 1943, 33.

74. Von Grunebaum 1946, 255; Kilpatrick, "Adab," *EAL* I:56; von Grunebaum, "Anthologies, Medieval," *EAL* I:94–96; von Grunebaum 1982, 34–42; Holmberg 2006, 201.

75. Pellat 1964, 19–37.

text of the fourth/tenth century as "a genre of anecdotal and anthological literature, which serves as a quarry of quotable materials (*muḥāḍarāt*) for the bel-esprit."[76] Heinrichs, however, does not exclude the early meaning of *adab* as good and correct behavior, and he acknowledges the development of *adab* in the intellectual context of the developing fields of knowledge in the fourth/tenth century. He takes *abab* to encompasse the body of literary and linguistic knowledge presented by "*adab* disciplines" or *al-ʿulūm al-adabiyyah.*[77]

One influential theory is that *adab* is derived from inherited customary norms, which are informal values and modes of behavior that provide a level of training for members of a community. This theory seems to assume a secular context for the emergence of *adab*, but this idea overlooks the historical development and the religious elements of *adab* works.[78] This proposal was outlined initially by Karl Vollers and then developed by the Italian scholar Carlo Alfonso Nallino, who provided one of the most detailed Western analyses of the word.[79] Nallino suggests that *adab* derives from *daʾb* (pl. *adāb*), a recurrent term in pre-Islamic poetry, proverbs (*mathal*, pl. *amthāl*) and aphorisms (*ḥikma*, pl. *ḥikam*) that can be traced back to the concept of inherited customary norms (*sunna*) in old Arab traditions. These norms stressed the ethical and practical content of *adab* and evolved to mean education and nobility of character, then knowledge of a field of learning (excluding religious science), and finally its present definition as literature.[80]

Francesco Gabrieli, Fritz Meier, Charles Pellat, Gerhard Böwering, and Azartash Azarnoosh, for example, seem to adhere to these theories developed by Nallino.[81] Gabrieli and Goldziher before him identify *adab* with a general concept of *humanitas* by stressing further the secular context of *adab* in the Umayyad and ʿAbbasid periods which began to correspond to the "Latin urbanitas, the civility, courtesy, refinement of the cities in contrast to Bedouin uncouthness."[82] He at least stresses the similarity of the environment for *adab* to Roman culture. Gabrieli thus seems to be projecting enlightenment ideals, which held Greco-Roman culture in the highest regard also in his own the nineteenth and early twentieth-century European culture, onto Islamic civilization and its literary traditions.[83]

76. Heinrichs 1995, 119–120.
77. See Heinrichs 1995, 120.
78. Pellat 1969, 62–68.
79. Nallino 1948, 1–20.
80. Nallino 1948, 1–20.
81. Francesco Gabrieli, "Adab," *EI2* I:175–176; Meier 1999, 49–50; Pellat 1969, 62–68; Böwering 1983, 64; Vollers 1975, 180; Azarnoosh and Umar, "Adab," *Encyclopaedia Islamica*, 3:1–21.
82. See Gabrieli, "Adab," *EI2* I:175–176.
83. Cf. Heath 2009, 141.

Bonebakker, however, in his article "*Adab* and the Concept of Belles-Lettres," traces the diachronic development of the term from pre-Islamic times up to the twentieth century. He reviews earlier attempts at defining *adab* as a literary activity and critiques some of Nallino's findings, suggesting that *sunna* or custom was not the primary meaning of *adab*, but was merely one of the possibilities.[84] He shows that Nallino's findings are based on misuse and double interpretations of non-representative examples drawn from pre-Islamic poetry and the first century of Islam, and that by reanalyzing these poetic examples, other etymological meanings for *adab* appear. For instance, Bonebakker emphasizes the relationship in meaning of "customs" and of *maʾduba* as a "banquet in which the good customs of hospitality are respected," and the notion of the *adīb* as a "host who respects the good customs," as found in classical dictionaries and philological works between the second/eighth and fifth/eleventh centuries.[85] However, although he tried to acknowledge the social development of *adab*, he struggled to define it and restricted its use in the ʿAbbasid period to a form of "literary scholarship of a cultivated man presented in a systematic form."[86] This definition stresses education as a type of formal training based on certain methods and identifiable stages. However, this definition raises difficulties since Bonebakker appears to have excluded other meanings of *adab* within literary production, such as the original genre of *maqāmāt* and that of miscellaneous and unfinished scholarship, other philosophical *adab* works (*al-adab al-falsafī*), and manuals on *adab* that appeared in Sufī and other circles.

Tarif Khalidi associated *adab* with caliphal courts, literary salons, and the wealthy elite. In this context, the *adīb* was the gentleman scholar, who had proper education in all divisions of learning, refined character. He was an ornament to any salon, and provided materials to rulers interested in the theory and practice of politics. In this age of cultural transformation during the Umayyad and ʿAbbasid eras, religious sources and *ḥadīth* reports were replaced by *adab* books, which contained ample information and anecdotes concerning other nations and the antiquities of Arabia, and thereby were seen as more adequate sources for historical information than these other sources.[87] Bo Holmberg also acknowledged that the meaning of *adab* changed over time, highlighting important elements such as intellectual nourishment, manners, and education, but he still emphasized the content of the cultured literati élite with connection to the chancery and court con-

84. Bonebakker 1984, 405–410.
85. See al-Farāhīdī, *Kitāb al-ʿAyn*, VIII:85; Ibn Manẓūr, *Lisān al-ʿarab*, I:200–201; al-Fīrūzābādī, *al-Qāmūs al-muḥīṭ*, I:144.
86. Bonebakker 1990, 16–30.
87. Khalidi 1996, 83–86.

text, identifying two main functions of *adab*: to instruct and to entertain at the same time.[88] The emphasis on the secular court context underlines the idea of pragmatic non-religious *adab* writings, which were sponsored by the wealthy elites, and were open to the influence of other cultures and served to provide a curriculum of knowledge for the concerned audience, for example, rulers. Thus, it would be possible to say that Holmberg's emphasis on the court salon sessions as an engine for the production of *adab* may be influenced by a European affiliation of power with knowledge.

Furthermore, modern scholars seem to draw parallels with the Italian renaissance, projecting it upon the *adab* literature, making the two contexts the most flourishing eras of unimaginable cultural wealth and literary fertility, in which scholars, inspired by other cultures, introduced a curriculum for refinement, and new topics that urged them to perpetuate the more secular side of life. Although this perspective on the *adab* traditions highlights their formal educational function in the social discourse,[89] it fails to acknowledge the religious elements of *adab* works, and places *adab* and religious writing as opposites. This perspective is untenable in the pre-modern contexts where the humanistic tradition of *adab* is inextricably bound with the religious dimension that was implied in the engagement with the scripture as discussed in the previous section. In addition, associating *adab* with the caliphal court and the wealth of the elites places a greater importance on the form of patronized, traditional literary scholarship as the means for the production of *adab*, while overlooking other *udabāʾ*, who effectively displayed a level of independence and were not closely associated or tied to patrons, as discussed above.

The claim of the secular context of *adab* seems to reflect a lack of proper understanding and analysis of the dynamic system and the central themes that inspired the production of pre-modern literary writings and the educational and the moral values that it promoted,[90] as explained in the previous section. This attitude can be explained by a general tendency of a number of scholars to place a central importance on the influence of foreign cultures on the development of *adab* and literary traditions. Although, it is necessary to consider other influences that contributed to the development of *adab* in a wider context of cultural and civilizational encounters, one should not overlook its religious context and other indigenous elements that contrib-

88. See Holmberg 2006, 205.

89. For studies that explore the educational function of adab, see Samer Ali 2010, 33, who speaks of *adab* as a body of varied literary knowledge that a young littérateur must know; Bonebakker 1990, 16–30, who suggests that *adab* is the literary scholarship of a cultivated man presented in a systematic form.

90. Cf. Lichtenstädter 1943, 33.

uted to its formation. For example, Anastas al-Karmalī and Vollers proposed Greek origins for the word *adab*, Anastas al-Karmalī from the Greek construct *hēduepēs* 'sweet-voiced' (from *hēdus* 'sweet, agreeable', and *epos* 'speech'); Vollers from *edanos* 'edible'.[91] In *The Cambridge History of Arabic Literature: Arabic Literature to the End of the Umayyad Period*, a number of articles also discuss the influence of Persian, Greek, and Syrian traditions on Arabic literature.[92] Clifford Edmund Bosworth, for example, highlights the importance of the influence of Persian traditions,[93] and considers the translation of *Kalīla wa Dimna,* which was originally written in Pahlavī, into Arabic by ʿAbd Allāh Ibn al-Muqaffaʿ (d. ca. 139/756) as the starting point of the Arabic prose writings and "mirrors for princes" literature.[94] The importance of this work is undeniable since it introduced a narrative of sayings and anecdotes attributed to animals and underlined the performance aspects of the literature as an attractive tool to educate in morality and to teach in an entertaining manner. Many also drew attention to the growing need in this period to produce a universal form of *adab* that is familiar to a wider group of people and to meet the taste of a cosmopolitan population, like those of the ʿAbbasid society. Nevertheless, this perspective on *adab* underestimates other prose elements, such as pre-Islamic Arabic sermons, fables, and legends, which were transmitted orally and were inseparable from the thought of the Arabs.[95] The importance of pre-Islamic Arabic traditions, including, the history and anecdotal traditions of the *Days of the Arabs* as an indispensable component of the education of the *adīb* was noted by pre-modern practitioners of *adab* themselves, including, ʿAbd al-Ḥamīd al-Kātib. Unlike claims made by modern scholars, including Azartash Azarnoosh, who may have been driven by nationalistic sentiments to overemphasize the influence of Persian traditions on *adab* and its practitioners, ʿAbd al-Ḥamīd did not move away from the Arabic style,[96] but attempted to offer a coherent training program for those aspiring to acquire the art of writing and *adab*, one which synthesized religious and Arabic traditions with non-Arab elements.[97]

Furthermore, the treatment of *adab* as "belles-lettres" in the sense of (beautiful, entertaining, or refined literature) reflects Western scholars' cultural understanding of "what literature is." Their understanding is influ-

91. Cf. A. Azarnoosh and S. Umar, "Adab," *Encyclopaedia Islamica*, 3:2.

92. See Bosworth 1983, 483–496; Goodman 1983, 460–482; Ebied 1983, 497–501.

93. For examples of these studies; see Gibb 1962, 62–73; Enderwitz, "Adab b) and Islamic Scholarship in the ʿAbbāsid Period," in *EI THREE* (Brill Online).

94. See Bosworth 1983, 488.

95. On fables and legends in pre-Islamic and early Islamic times, see Norris 1983, 374–386.

96. See A. Azarnoosh and S. Umar, "Adab," *Encyclopaedia Islamica*, 3:1–21.

97. See above discussion.

enced by theories of literature developed in the eighteenth century, when the term itself came into existence. In the eighteenth century, the transition from traditional to modern rhetoric and the attempt to unite belles-lettres and rhetoric and find common ground between them in terms of taste, style, criticism, and forms of discourse, by scholars such as Adam Smith and Hugh Blair, influenced modern perspectives on the study of literature and literary forms of discourse, placing more emphasis on style and arrangement rather than invention or content.[98] Narration, as put by Smith, is a "discourse that related actions as they happened, a type of communication that had the dual purpose of entertaining and instructing its audience without any persuasive intentions."[99] In this context, the most important rhetorical art is style, in which the ethical and aesthetic appeal of the text shifted from an instrument of persuasion to an instrument of style.[100]

All these modern studies resulted in a plurality of views, with each addressing certain dimensions of *adab,* while excluding others of what premodern scholars would have considered *adab.* The Western understanding of literature and its development in a context of separation between the religious and the secular is not faithful to the context of pre-modern context of *adab*, where boundaries between the two spheres are blurred. Furthermore scholars, including, Stefan Sperl and Stephan Guth have already discussed the fallacies associated with this approach and called for a better critical approach to *adab* and its development.[101]

Another problem common in Western *adab* scholarship is the division of the literary traditions into belles-lettres (beautiful in style and entertaining) and technical (in the sense of specialist) works. This division imposes an artificial distinction between literature and thought, and is exemplified by volumes 2 and 3 of *The Cambridge History of Arabic Literature* (1990), which are entitled respectively *ʿAbbasid Belles-Lettres and Religion, Science and Learning in the ʿAbbasid Period.* These categories seem to reflect neither the perception of knowledge nor the practice of writing held by the classical authors from this period, such as Ibn Qutayba and al-Jāḥiẓ who, as discussed above, viewed *adab* as encompassing the sum of knowledge existing in their time.

In fact, these divisions between literature and thought seem to be an outcome of a modern tendency for specialization, and it could well also explain why certain attitudes towards the literary traditions were dominant in the European imagination that defined Arabic literary culture. For instance,

98. On the role of Adam Smith in rhetorical history, see Carter 1988, 3.
99. See Smith in Carter 1988, 5.
100. Carter 1988, 11.
101. Sperl 2007, 459–486; see also Guth 2010, 9–30.

Antoine Galland's translation in the eighteenth century of the popular folk -tales of *Thousand and One Nights* (or what is referred to as *The Arabian Nights*) captivated the interest of European scholars who saw this work as representative of a typical and genuine Arabic literary tradition.[102] These folk tales were circulated in oral culture until they were written down in the fifteenth century and were not considered as part of the traditional upper literary culture, but were composed for public use and circulation. They also seem to have reflected an image of the culture as one that is erotic and primitive, which seemed to have satisfied the European fantasy of the Arabs and their culture.

Thus, the interest that some Western writers took in works such as *Thousand and One Nights*, while ignoring many Arabic masterpieces in which literature and thought were essential in the formation of the texts, seems to be the result of their attempt to stereotype the East and its literature as irrational, exotic, inferior, and under-developed, and the West and its ideas as the starting point to elaborate topics, theories, concepts, and accounts concerning the Orient, its people, customs, and so on.[103] Furthermore, the interest in these folk tales as representative of Arabic literature seemed to be associated with the growing spread of Western ideas associated with disciplines, such as anthropology, folklore, narratology, and the attempt to write about non-European literary traditions from a European perspective.

It is noteworthy to mention that that attempt to write about non-European literary traditions from a European perspective extends to other fields of studies, including philology, which, as Sheldon Pollock claimed, may have been informed by political and colonial projects, while overlooking the historicity of the subject of philology and its multiple realizations and local inflections in various non-Western traditions.[104]

It could even be argued that the modern understanding of literature as imaginative or fictional writing is a relatively modern one, that came into being after the beginning of the nineteenth century. Prior to this "literature" in English (and the analogous terms in European languages) meant "writings" or "book knowledge."[105]

Badawī has already emphasized that *adab* should be approached as the kind of activities that were "either morally and spiritually edifying or else

102. Cf. Holmberg 2006, 180.

103. See Said 1978, 3; see also Muḥammed A. al-Daʾmī 1998, 1–11. For a discussion on Said's reading of colonial discourse in literary texts and a comparison between his approach and that of Gibb, see Allan 2012, 172–196.

104. For a critical study of the current issues in the study of philology and its future, see Pollock 2009, 931–961.

105. Cf. Günther 2005, xviii.

entertaining through mastery of language and verbal skills."[106] This seems more faithful to the context of classical scholars discussed above. In his analysis of al-Jāḥiẓ's art of epistolary, Peter Heath also spoke of *adab* as a literary production and acknowledged the difficulty of considering it as a form of literature (translating it as belles-lettres) since it is, quoting Fedwa Maltil-Douglas, a "polysemous" concept.[107] For Heath, this understanding of *adab* as literature resulted from the attempt of textually oriented scholars to move quickly to define the exact scope of materials used to train participants of literary *adab* (texts) and to study their authors. Bonebakker, for example, although he recognized that the semantic connotations of *adab* changed over time, still focused on the meaning of *adab* in a specific literary context as a form of literary activities. By so doing, he appears to have overlooked the broader social contexts of which these literary activities were part.[108]

Thus, an understanding of *adab*, should be grounded in the pre-modern context, which is a context broader, as suggested by Heath, than that of literary studies. This would require a comprehensive approach that is not only based on a primarily textual and philological examination of a specific meaning, but also one that considers the broader social implications of the idea of proper education.[109] Thus, there are questions relating to the aspects of *adab* in the social domain as well as the didactic, curricular, and emulative function of *adab* texts: who wrote them, how they were transmitted, and who decided upon their usage. These questions bring a better understanding of *adab* as a participatory social activity and an analysis of the sources in their intellectual contexts.

In recent scholarship, there has been an increasing awareness of the need for such an indigenous Arabo-Islamic approach that widens the scope of *adab*. In his introduction to his thematic volume *Ideas, Images, and Methods of Portrayal*, Sebastian Günther used the term "literature" in an inclusive rather than an exclusive way.[110] The articles in his volume included a larger category of exemplary Arabic writings and thought in the pre-modern period rather than merely the main form of classical Arabic belles-lettres. Günther added that this inclusive understanding of literature considers the historicity of classical Arabic literary scholarship by not confining its scope to fictional or imaginary prose. *Adab* dealt with moral, ethical, and intellectual concerns of pre-modern Arabic-Islamic culture, including stud-

106. Badawī 2001, 10.
107. Heath 2009, 136.
108. Heath 2009, 136.
109. See Heath 2009, 137.
110. Günther 2005, xviii.

ies that are literary and non-literary in nature. Those non-literary texts are excellent sources for literary analysis for their elegant use of language, sophisticated structure, and rhetorical qualities.

Other scholars, including Montgomery and Arkoun have already emphasized the importance of leaving behind this arbitrary division between literature and thought, or literary and non-literary texts.[111] In a number of his articles, Montgomery offers a more balanced reading of the pre-modern literary works, where he discusses the intellectual themes and motives that formed the writings of classical authors, such as, al-Jāḥiẓ, showing how he provided in his *adab* writings a form of his own brand of Muʿtazilī theology in the subjects that he introduced.[112] Likewise Montgomery reassess André Miquel's theories of the development of geographical writings in relation to the predetermined idea of *adab*, which he brought to Ibn Khurradādhbih's works and attempted to justify on their basis. According to Montgomery, applying this modern approach of the division between technical (systematic and analytical) and non-technical writing led to the isolation of these texts from their historicity and paid no attention to the perspective or objective of their authors.

This divide also assumes a distinction between two types of audiences: the bureaucratic, self-fulfilling class and the cultured, inquisitive one. Montgomery considers this dichotomy artificial within the ʿAbbasid era, since many of those who wrote *adab* texts were at some point connected with the class of secretaries.[113] Thus, a separation between the secretariat and culture seems artificial in this time period.

These artificial categories in the study of *adab* do not take into account the intentions of the authors and the complex factors that contribute to the making of their texts in their own environment. This point has been highlighted already by a number of scholars, including Julia Bray, who discussed the "mythical function" of *adab* texts, which she explained in the motifs that led to the production or preservation of books in the early stages.[114] She recognizes the social function and historical significance of *adab*, arguing that fiction and myth play a role in the formation of ʿAbbasid *adab*. Therefore, the *adīb* should be considered as a "mythographer," since he can assign meaning to his task by selecting and arranging materials in a way unique to his text.[115] This same point is also made by Philip Kennedy, who considered the rhetorical aspect of *adab* and its relationship to fiction or the blending

111. See Arkoun 1993, 129–130.
112. See Montgomery 2006, 129–130.
113. See Montgomery 2005, 180–181.
114. Bray 2005, 2.
115. Bray 2005, 8.

between fiction and reality when reflecting on the definition of *adab* and the variety of literatures that it encompasses.[116] He suggested that this type of rhetoric is similar to that which informs some fiction found in historical or historicized writings.[117] Therefore, when dealing with *adab* texts, it is essential to view them as a form of "historicized writing," recognizing the relationship between the rhetorical and the historical.

In her study of *Literature as History*, Julie Scott Meisam also demonstrated the difficulty of separating literature from thought. She makes a connection between *adab* and pre-modern historical writings embellishment. This persuasive writing of history was also acknowledged by Gibb and von Grunebaum who argued that the writing of history in the fourth/tenth century was conducted by secretaries and officials, who seemed to have introduced greater attention to style and led to the increasing "literarization" of historical writings.[118]

Furthermore, some recent research, which critically assessed Arabic historiography in an attempt to separate facts from fiction, claimed that many historical accounts and anecdotes are "fictions" passed off as history.[119] This assessment could be due to the orality of the culture and to the nature of the transmission of knowledge at the time and to the fact that many early scholars who transmitted historical accounts from earlier authorities had their own political and theological positions, which seem to have affected the mode of writing and the presentations of these accounts.[120]

Thus, the division of the literary traditions into belles-lettres and technical writing is not faithful to the context of pre-modern Arabic literary traditions, where attention to style and eloquence was a major preoccupation for scholars of the time. In that culture, fluid boundaries sometimes existed between different forms of intellectual productions, between transmission and the creation of texts, and the compiling of reports, their arrangements, and the acts of interpretation and designation of meanings, which led to the allusive nature of writing in this period.

Adab and Humanism

Another area of debate is the term "humanism," which some scholars who study the wider corpus of Islamic culture impose on *adab* literature. A close assessment of "humanism" is necessary in order to evaluate the contrasts

116. For an exploration of the complex modes in which textual activities model reality and introduces paradigms of conduct and perception; see Drory 2000; Drory 1994, 146–164.

117. Kennedy, 2005, xii.

118. Cf. Meisam 2000, 16n8.

119. Cf. Meisam 2000, 15.

120. Cf. Meisam 2000, 15.

that have been imposed on the literature using the term, such as scientific enquiry versus religious teaching, theoretical ethics versus practical ethics, and the social versus the personal in the context of the writing of scholars. In her book, *Ethics in Islam,* Nuha Alshaar discusses the application of "humanism" on the writings of Abū Ḥayyān al-Tawḥīdī and his contemporaries and questions the separation of literature and thought in this context.[121] She assesses the ways in which the term shaped the analysis of scholars such as Joel Kraemer, Marc Bergé, George Makdisi, and Mohammed Arkoun in their treatment of al-Tawḥīdī and his contemporaries. Bergé, for example, has endeavored to integrate the ideas of many Muslim scholars into a Western narrative of the development of secular intellectual thought.[122]

Kraemer, influenced by previous scholars including Mez, Rosenthal, and Gibb, uses the term the "Renaissance of Islam," to describe what he saw as the rebirth of the scientific and philosophical legacy of Hellenic antiquity in the fourth/tenth century of Islam.[123] Kraemer uses al-Tawḥīdī's writings to gather information about the belles-lettrists, poets, secretaries, viziers, emirs, theologians, and philosophers, claiming that their humanist elements were the product of this Graeco-Arabic renaissance.[124] Kraemer distinguishes between two forms of humanism: literary humanism as epitomized by the word *adab* – the broad humanism of a litterateur, scribe or courtier, such as al-Tawḥīdī – and the philosophical type of humanism as represented by scholars like Abū Sulaymān al-Sijistānī (d. ca. 375/985).

However, difficulty arises from the use of the term humanism, which is malleable and has many connotations that depend largely on what it is contrasted to. Furthermore, as already highlighted by a number of scholars, there are serious concerns with the use of this term in Muslim contexts, because humanism may be considered a historically exclusive term since it emerged in Europe and North America and had a large role to play in the formation of Western cultural identity. The meaning of the term "humanism" developed in line with the political and intellectual dynamics of subsequent civilizations.[125] For example, in thirteenth- and fourteenth-century Italy, "humanism" became associated with the criticism of the various systems of religious authority in order to limit the power of the church and its use of supernatural arguments to control the rest of society, and the attempt

121. For a close analysis of this point, see Alshaar 2015, 4–8.
122. For further discussion of this point, see Alshaar 2015, 7.
123. See Mes 1937; Gibb 1962; Rosenthal 1975, 12- 13; cf. Kraemer 1986, 1.
124. Kraemer 1986, 2.
125. See Alshaar 2015, 6; see also Trinkaus 1983, 455–456; Key 2005, 80.

to promote a new vision of a person.[126] Kraemer projects this Italian context onto fourth/tenth-century Islamic ethics,[127] highlighting three features of this Islamic Renaissance – individualism, cosmopolitanism, and secularism – and claiming that the objective of the philosophers and litterateurs is to enable society to develop gradually from inherited belief. He stresses an opposition in the forth/tenth century of Islam between iconoclastic individuals and orthodox societal norms.[128]

Kraemer's use of humanism also led him to distinguish between literary and philosophical works and works on religious science.[129] On this basis, he suggests that an *adīb* must have taken the side of rationalism.[130] This supposed position of the *adīb* resulted in difficulties in classifying many authors of the period, leading Kraemer to consider many of them as standing in opposition to the religious orthodoxy of the time.[131] This consideration, however, does not reflect the spirit of the age since even when philosophical/*adab* works can be distinguished from religious works, such distinction cannot be applied to authors who wrote or studied both disciplines, such as Abū Ḥayyān al-Tawḥīdī or the Brethren of Purity. Thus it is misleading to apply the term humanism in the context of these authors, assuming artificial boundaries between secular scientific and religious enquiries.

Makdisi and Arkoun also use the lens of humanism to analyze the works of scholars of the third and fourth Islamic centuries. Makdisi equates humanism with *adab* by comparing the relationship of a number of practitioners of *adab* to religion. Arkoun defines three areas: a religious humanism where a desire to be united with God produces humility in action and perception; a literary humanism where *adab* in its wider classical meaning is associated with the power and wealth of the elite, but does not break with religion; and a philosophical humanism which is a mixture of the previous two, but is based on careful rational investigation of God, man, and the universe.[132] Like Kraemer, Makdisi and also Arkoun drew boundaries between *adab* and religion in the literary works of the fourth/tenth Islamic century *udabāʾ* (similar to the Italian humanists' attempts to criticize the Christian religious establishment) to find grounds for their use of the terms humanism and secularism in their analysis of the literature. When these boundaries were

126. See Trinkaus 1983, 455–456; Alshaar 2015, 6.
127. See Alshaar 2015, 6.
128. Kraemer 1986, 5–20.
129. Kraemer 1986, 10.
130. Kraemer 1986, 11.
131. Kraemer 1986, 16–25.
132. Makdisi 1990; Arkoun 1997, 607–609.

not clearly identified, Makdisi suggests a shared skepticism among scholars whom he describes as "humanists." Arkoun, conversely, leaves room for a religious humanism, which does not create an apparent opposition between *adab* and religion.[133]

As already suggested by a number of scholars, including Carter, the projection of scientific humanism onto Islamic traditions is narrower than the sources allow, and hinders the possibility of perceiving an indigenous and self-sustaining "Islamic humanism."[134] There are insufficient details to support the application simply of the term humanism, and other sources may disapprove its usage being too selectively defined and too rooted within a Western understanding of history.[135] Thus, the perspective of humanism lacks the ability to address the career of various scholars of the pre-modern period, such as al-Tawḥīdī, who were actively involved in the study of different fields of knowledge, religious and non-religious.

One could also say that looking at *adab* tradition from the perspective of humanism and the artificial boundary between religion and *adab* fails to reflect the unified perception of knowledge by classical scholars or the nature of their works as discussed above. It also fails to capture the multiplicity of knowledge, especially religion and philosophy that were both essential components in the development of ideas and in the making of *adab* texts in the pre-modern period. Thus, the artificial boundary between religion and *adab* goes against the conception of pre-modern *adab,* which avoided specialization as pointed out by classical scholars, such as Ibn Qutayba and al-Jaḥiẓ. These scholars saw that the function of *adab* is to provide a moral curriculum for the benefit of persons by the realization of all available forms of knowledge, religious or non-religious ones.

Inclusive and Not Exclusive Approach to *adab*

The need for a better understanding of the process of writing and literary forms in the pre-modern Islamic period has caused numerous scholars to move away from a traditional Western understanding and its dominance to a more inclusive approach that studies classical Arabic literature in broader contexts and as products of their own culture and intellectual environment,

133. Arkoun 1997, 607–609; cf. Alshaar 2015, 8; Key 2005, 81, 83.

134. See Carter 1989, 304–305. Oliver Leaman also suggests that the claim of the existence of centuries of struggle between traditionalism and rationalism is not faithful to the development of legal and theoretical discussions in classical Islam and puts forwards a misleading narrative of Islamic piety and salvation discourse; see Leaman 1999, 159–160.

135. For further information, see Lapidus 1988, 199; Ashtiany 1989, 131–133. Cf. Alshaar 2015, 9.

especially taking its relation to the Qurʾān into account. This movement responds to the gap in modern scholarship that has been reluctant to consider the Qurʾān in a literary context,[136] resulting in rigid dichotomies in academic research between the two fields of qurʾānic studies and literary studies.

Navid Kermani's *Gott is schön,* which appeared in English translation in 2014 under the title *God is Beautiful: The Aesthetic Experience of the Qurʾān,* comprehensively dealt with the aesthetic qualities of the Qurʾān. Recently, two publications, including, *the Qurʾān and Adab: The Shaping of Literary Traditions in Classical Islam,* edited by Nuha Alshaar, and *The Qurʾān and the Aesthetics of Pre-modern Arabic Prose,* by Sarah bin Tyeer, focused on the reception of the Qurʾān in *adab* genres and its relationship with pre-modern Arabic literary traditions as well as the influence of the aesthetic of the Qurʾān on pre-modern Arabic prose.

These two studies argue for the acute interaction between the sacred and the profane in the context of Arabo-Islamic pre-modern traditions. In her introductory chapter to the *Qurʾān and Adab,* Alshaar explores the idea of the Qurʾān as a text and its reception in works of *adab* and how the authors of these texts engaged with the literary and aesthetic elements and the language of scripture in their works. This interaction allowed for an exploration of the connection between literary discourse and the Qurʾān.

The articles in Alshaar's volume *The Qurʾān and Adab* reexamine the relation of scripture to humanistic traditions in classical Islam, in this case *adab. Adab* has generally been classified as belles-lettres, but this disconnects it from the body of religious literature and denies its inherent religiosity. This volume explored the various ways in which *adab* is linked to the Qurʾān by looking at this issue in different literary genres, including, poetry, oratory, and anthologies. Thus scholars of Arabic studies are invited to rethink the assumed dichotomy between sacred and profane literature. As has been shown, the *udabāʾ* used qurʾānic materials in their texts and often provided their own understanding of these materials to serve a particular purpose. Their work could open the question of genre in the pre-modern period and thus provide an opportunity to admit greater fluidity in some of the existing boundaries between various academic fields, such as Arabic literary studies and qurʾānic studies.

Sarah bin Tayeer's work highlights the Qurʾān's centrality in a discussion on the aesthetics of *adab,* and shows that studies of pre-modern literary traditions should take into account the literary, aesthetic, and religious contexts of these works. The study helps readers to understand the interplay of the sacred text and culture and how culture is encoded in a

136. See Angelika Neuwirth's in Bin Tayeer 2016, foreword.

text. As explained previously by Geert Jan van Gelder, although the scope of *adab* would not normally refer to the Qurʾān or the Prophetic traditions, including *ḥadīth*, these texts cannot be excluded from discussions if one is to acquire a proper understanding of the literary canon. Thus, the inextricable link between the tradition of *adab* and the religiosity of the scripture should not be overlooked.

Conclusion

This chapter establishes that the definition of *adab* could not in fact be a stable, fixed and unchangeable one across the ages – which may have certainly affected the way in which *adab* is sometimes treated as "literature." This misunderstanding, accordingly, is the offspring of another, an attitude that often treats pre-modern Arabic literary products as atoms in a void, and which isolates them from their Arabic literary system, literary milieu, and linguistic religious history and significance in favor of over-simplified interpretations.

Modern scholarship would do well to apply a comprehensive understanding of *adab* as a type of inquiry based on the realization of all available forms of knowledge as found in its early practitioners rather than imposing categories from Western context on the corpus of *adab*. *Adab* should be considered in its totality, including works in which the ideals of an *adīb* may not have been written in the most aesthetic and refined form. Therefore, it is important to apply a historical and sociological approach to the study of pre-modern *adab* texts, paying attention not only to questions related to authorial concerns, but also to the audience of these texts, and the history of their transmission.

This chapter has shown that the religious and secular were constantly intertwined, and that the dichotomy between them in the study of *adab* is largely artificial. Therefore, it is recommended to move away from a traditional Eurocentric model to a more inclusive approach that views classical Arabic literary products as closely connected with their social and intellectual environment, of which the Qurʾān was a foundational source. Key parameters and a new and better understanding of pre-modern *adab* will emerge by looking at the cultural milieu, literary systems, and the religious aesthetic and linguistic history of pre-modern *adab* texts. [137]

137. I would like to thank Dr. Lawrence Lahey, who read through a draft of this paper and offered helpful suggestions.

Bibliography

Primary Sources

ʿAbd Allāh Ibn al-Muqaffaʿ. 1960. *Al-Adab al-ṣaghīr wa'l-adab al-kabīr*. Beirut.

al-Dārimī, ʿAbd Allāh b. ʿAbd al-Raḥmān al-Tamīmī. 2000. *Musnad al-Dārimī*, 4 vols. Edited by Ḥusayn Salīm Asad al-Dārānī. Riyadh.

al-Farāhīdī, al-Khalīl b. Aḥmad. 1980–1985. *Kitāb al-ʿAyn*. Edited by Mahdī al-Makhzūmī and Ibrāhīm al-Sāmarrāʾī. 8 vols. Baghdad.

al-Fīrūzābādī, Muḥammad b. Yaʿqūb. 1884–1885. *Al-Qāmūs al-muḥīṭ*. Edited by Naṣr Hūrīnī. 4 vols. Cairo.

Ḥākim al-Nīsābūrī, 2003. *Maʿrifat ʿulūm al-ḥadīth wa kamiyyat ajnāsih*. Edited by Aḥmad b. Fāris al-Salūm. Beirut.

Ibn ʿAbd Rabbih. 1940–49. *Al-ʿIqd al-farīd*. Edited by Aḥmad Amīn, Aḥmad al-Zayn and Ibrāhīm al-Abyārī. 7 vols. Cairo.

Ibn ʿArabī, Muḥyī al-Dīn. 1980. *Al-Futūḥāt al-makkiyya*. 4 vols. Beirut.

Ibn al-Athīr, Majd al-Dīn Abū 'l-Saʿādāt al-Mubārak. 1963–1965. *Al-Nihāya fī gharīb al-ḥadīth wa'l-athar*. Edited by Maḥmūd Muḥammad Ṭanāhī and al-Ṭāhir Aḥmad al-Zāwī. 5 vols. Cairo.

Ibn Fāris al-Qazwīnī, Abū'l-Ḥusayn Aḥmad. 1946–1952. *Maqāyīs al-lugha*. 6 vols. Edited by ʿAbd al-Salām Muḥammad Hārūn. Cairo.

Ibn Khaldūn, ʿAbd al-Raḥmān b. Muḥammad. 1983. *Tārīkh Ibn Khaldūn*. Edited by Suhayl Zakkār and Khalīl Shiḥāda. 14 vols. Beirut.

Ibn Manẓūr, Muḥammad b. Mukarram. 1955–1996. *Lisān al-ʿarab*. Edited by Iḥsān ʿAbbās. 20 vols. Beirut.

Ibn Qutayba, ʿAbd Allāh b. Muslim. 1963.*ʿUyūn al-akhbār*. Edited by Aḥmad Zakī al-ʿAdawī. 4 vols. Cairo.

———. 1967. *Al-Shiʿr wa'l-shuʿarāʾ*. Edited by Aḥmad Muḥammad Shākir. Cairo.

———. 1982. *Adab al-kātib*. Edited by Muḥammad al-Dālī. Beirut.

Ibn al-Sikkīt, Yaʿqūb. b. Isāḥq, 1998. *Kitāb al-Alfāẓ*. Edited by Fakhr al-Dīn Qabāwa. Beirut.

———. 1958. *The Muqaddimah: An Introduction to History*. Translated by Franz Rosenthal. 3 vols. London.

al-Jāḥiẓ, Abū ʿUthmān ʿAmr b. Baḥr. 1964–79. *Rasāʾil al-Jāḥiẓ*. Edited by ʿAbd al-Sallām Hārūn, 2 vols. Cairo.

al-Qurṭubī, Muḥammad b. Aḥmad. 2006. *Al-Jāmiʿ li-aḥkām al-Qurʾān wa'lmubayyin li-mā taḍammanahu mina'l-sunnati wa āy al-furqān*. Edited by ʿAbd Allāh b. ʿAbd al-Muḥsin al-Turkī. 24 vols. Beirut.

al-Sarrāj, Abū Naṣr. 2001. *Kitāb al-Lumaʿ*. Edited by Kāmil Muṣṭafā al-Hindāwī. Beirut.

al-Shāfiʿī, Abū ʿAbd Allāh Muḥammad b. Idrīs. 2011. *Kitāb al-Umm*. Edited by Rifʿat Fawzī ʿAbd al-Muṭṭalib. 11 vols. Al-Manṣūra.

al-Shaybānī, Ibrāhīm b. Muḥammad. 1931. *Al-Risāla al-ʿadhrāʾ*. Edited by Zakī Mubārak Cairo.

al-Tawḥīdī, Abū Ḥayyān. 1968. *Rasāʾil Abī Ḥayyān al-Tawḥīdī*. Edited by Ibrāhīm Kīlānī, Damascus.

———. 1970. *al-Muqābasāt*. Edited by Muḥammad Tawfīq Ḥusayn. Baghdad.

Yāqūt, ʿAbd Allāh al-Rūmī al-Ḥamawī, 1928–1937. *Muʿjam al-Udabāʾ*. Edited by A. Rifāʿī. Cairo.

al-Zabīdī, Muḥammad Murtaḍā, 1966. *Tāj al-ʿarūs*. Edited by ʿAlī Hilālī. 25 vols. Kuwait.

Secondary Sources

Allan, M. 2012. "How *Adab* Became Literary: Formalism, Orientalism and the Institutions of World Literature." *Journal of Arabic Literature* 43:172–196.

Ali, S. 2010. *Arabic Literary Salons in the Islamic Middle Ages.* Notre Dame, IN.

Arkoun, M. 1988. "The Notion of Revelation: From Ahl al-Kitāb to the Societies of the Book." *Die Welt des Islams* New Series 28, no. 1:62–63.

——. 1997. *Nazʿat al-Ansana fī al-Fikr al-ʿArabī: Jīl Miskawayh wa al-Tawḥīdī.* London.

Alshaar, N. 2010. "An Analytical Reading of al-Tawḥīdī's Epistle: *on [The Classification of] Knowledge* (*Risāla fī al-ʿUlūm*)." In *Reflections on Knowledge and Language in Middle Eastern Societies.*161–185. Edited by Bruno De Nicola, Husain Qutbuddin, and Yonatan Mendel. Cambridge.

——. 2015. *Ethics in Islam: Friendship in the Political Thought of al-Tawḥīdī and his Contemporaries.* London and New York.

——. 2017. "Introduction: The Relation of Adab to the Qurʾān: Conceptual and Historical Framework." In *The Qurʾān and Adab: The Shaping of Literary Traditions in Classical Islam*, edited by Nuha Alshaar, 1–58. Oxford.

Ashtiany, J. 1989. "Humanism in the Renaissance of Islam: The Cultural Revival during the Būyid Age by Joel L. Kraemer, Review." *Bulletin of the School of Oriental and African Studies* 52.1:131–133.

Ashtiany, J., et al. (eds). 1990. *The Cambridge History of Arabic Literature: ʿAbbasid Belles-Lettres*. Cambridge.

Azarnoosh, A. and S. Umar. "Adab." *Encyclopaedia Islamica* 3:1–21.

Badawī, M. M. 2001. *A Short History of Modern Arabic Literature*. Oxford.

Bin Tyeer, S. 2016. *The Qurʾān and the Aesthetics of Pre-modern Arabic Prose.* New York.

Bonebakker, S, A. 1984. "Early Arabic Literature and the Term *Adab*." *Jerusalem Studies in Arabic and Islam* 5:389–421.
Bray, J. 2005. "'Abbasid Myth and the Human Act: Ibn ʿAbd Rabbih and Others." In *On Fiction and Adab in Medieval Arabic Literature*. Studies in Arabic Language and Literature, vol. 6. Edited by Philip Kennedy, 1–55. Wiesbaden.
——. 1990. "Adab and the Concept of Belles-Lettres." In *The Cambridge History of Arabic Literature, Vol. II: 'Abbasid Belles-Lettres*, edited by Julia Ashtiany, Thomas M. Johnstone, John D. Latham, Robert B. Serjeant and G. Rex Smith, 16–30. Cambridge.
Bosworth, C. E. 1983. "The Persian Impact on Arabic Literature." In *The Cambridge History of Arabic Literature: Arabic Literature to the End of the Umayyad Period*, edited by Alfred F.L. Beeston, et al., 483–496. Cambridge.
Böwering, G. 1983. "The *Adab* Literature of Classical Sufism: Anṣārī's Code of Conduct." In *Moral Conduct and Authority: The Place of Adab in South Asian Islam*, edited by Barbara Daly Metcalf. Berkeley, 62–91.
Carter, M. 1988. "The Role of Invention in Belletristic Rhetoric: A Study of the Lectures of Adam Smith." *Rhetoric Society Quarterly* 18.1:1–13.
——. "Review of Humanism in the Renaissance of Islam: The Cultural Revival during the Būyid Age." *Journal of the American Oriental Society* 109.2:304–305.
Chiabotti, Francesco, et al. 2016. *Ethics and Spirituality in Islam: Sufi Adab*. Leiden. Brill.
Al-Da'mī, M. A. 1998. "Orientalism and Arab-Islamic History: An Inquiry into the Orientalists' Motives and Compulsions." *Arab Studies Quarterly* 20.4:1–11.
Drory, R. 2000. *Models and Contacts: Arabic Literature and its Impact on Medieval Jewish Culture*. Leiden.
—— 1994. "Three Attempts to Legitimize Fiction in Classical Arabic Literae ture." *Jerusalem Studies in Arabic and Islam* 18:146–164.
Duraković, E. 2015. *The Poetics of Ancient and Classical Arabic Literature*. Translated by Amila Karahasanović. Abingdon.
Ebied, R. Y. 1983. "The Syrian Impact on Arabic Literature." In *The Cambridge History of Arabic Literature: Arabic Literature to the End of the Umayyad Period*, edited by Alfred F.L. Beeston, et al., 497–501. Cambridge.
Enderwitz, S. "Adab b) and Islamic Scholarship in the ʿAbbāsid Period." *EI THREE* (Brill Online).

Enderwitz, S. "al-Shuʿūbiyya." *EI2*, vol. IX:513–516.
Erik, S. Ohlander, "Adab in Ṣūfism." *EI THREE* (Brill Online).
van Gelder, G. J. 2002–3. "Forbidden Firebrands: Frivolous *Iqtibās* (Quotation from the Qurʾān) According to Medieval Arab Critics," *Quaderni di Studi Arabi* 20–21:3–16.
van Gelder. G. "Ibn Qutayba." *EAL* I:361.
Gril, D. 1993. "*Adab* and Revelation, or One of the Foundations of the Hermeneutics of Ibn ʿArabi." In *Muhyiddin ibn ʿArabi: A Commemorative Volume,* edited by Stephen Hirtenstein and Michael Tiernan, 228–263. Rockport.
Gril, D. 2016. "Adab et éthique dans le soufisme. Quelques constats et interrogations." In *Ethics and Spirituality in Islam: Sufi Adab*, edited by Francesco Chiabotti, et al., 47–63. Leiden.
Gabrieli, F. "Adab." *EI*[2], vol. I:175–176.
Gibb, H. A. R. 1962. "The Social Significance of the Shuubiya." In *Studies on the Civilization of Islam*, edited by Stanford J. Shaw and William R. Polk, 62–73. Princeton.
Goodman, L. 1983. "The Greek Impact on Arabic Literature" In *The Cambridge History of Arabic Literature: Arabic Literature to the End of the Umayyad Period*, edited by Alfred F.L. Beeston, et al., 460–482. Cambridge.
Günther, S. (ed.). 2005. *Ideas, Images, and Methods of Portrayal: Insights into Classical Arabic Literature and Islam*. Brill.
Von Grunebaum, G. 1946. *Medieval Islam: A Study in Cultural Orientation.* Chicago.
Guth, S. 2010. "Politeness, Höflichkeit, *Adab*: A Comparative Conceptual–Cultural Perspective." In *Verbal Festivity in Arabic and Other Semitic Languages*, edited by Lutz Edzard and Stephan Guth, 9–30. Wiesbaden.
Heinrichs, W. 1995. "The Classification of the Sciences and the Consolidation of Philology in Classical Islam." In *Centres of Learning: Learning and Location in Pre-Modern Europe and the Near East,* edited by Jan W. Drijvers and Alasdair A. MacDonald, 119–140. Leiden.
Heath, P. 2009. "Al-Jāḥiẓ, Adab, and the Art of the Essay." In *Al-Jāḥiẓ: A Muslim Humanist for our Time*, edited by Arnim Heinemann, et al. Würzburg.
Holmberg, Bo. 2006. "Literary History: Towards a Global Perspective: *Adab* and Arabic Literature." In *Literary History Towards a Global Perspective*, edited by Anders Petersson, Gunilla Lindberg-Wada, Margareta Petersson, and Stefan Helgesson., Berlin, 180–205.
Keeler, A. 2016. "The Concept of *Adab* in Early Sufism with Particular Reference to the Teaching of Sahl b. ʿAbdallāh al-Tustarī (d. 283/896)." In

Ethics and Spirituality in Islam: Sufi Adab, edited by Francesco Chiabotti, et al., 63–102. Leiden. .

Key, A. 2005. "The Applicability of The Term 'Humanism' to Abū Ḥayyān al-Tawḥīdī." *Studia Islamica* 100:71–112.

Khalidi, T. 1996. *Arabic Historical Thought in the Classical Period*. Cambridge.

——. 2009. *Images of Muhammad: Narratives of the Prophet in Islam across the Centuries*. New York.

Kennedy, P. 2005. *On Fiction and Adab in Medieval Arabic Literature*. Studies in Arabic Language and Literature, vol. 6, Wiesbaden.

Kilpatrick, H. 1982. "A Genre in Classical Arabic: The Adab Encyclopedia." In *Union Européenne des Arabisants et Islamisants 10th Congress, Edinburgh, September 1980, Proceedings. Edinburgh,* edited by Robert Hillenbrand, 34–42. Edinburgh.

——. "Adab." *EAL*, I:56.

——. "Anthologies, Medieval." *EAL* I:94–96.

Khouri, M. A. 1992. "Literature." In *The Genius of Arab Civilization: Sources of Renaissance*, 47–75. 3rd edition. New York and London.

Kraemer, J. 1986. *Humanism in the Renaissance of Islam: The Cultural Revival During the Būyid Age*. Leiden.

Latham, J. D. 1983. "The Beginning of Arabic Prose Literature: The Epistolary Genre." In *The Cambridge History of Arabic Literature: Arabic Literature to the End of the Umayyad Period,* edited by Alfred F. L. Beeston, et al., 167–179. Cambridge.

Leaman, Oliver. 1999. "Ibn ʿAqīl: Religion and Culture in Classical Islam by George Maqdisi: Review" *British Journal of Middle Eastern Studies* 26.1:159–160.

Lapidus, M. 1988. "Humanism in the Renaissance of Islam: The Cultural Revival during the Būyid Age by Joel L. Kraemer, Review." *The American Historical Review* 93.1:199.

Leder, S, and H. Kilpatrick. 1992. "Classical Arabic Prose Literature: A Researchers' Sketch Map," *Journal of Arabic Literature* 23.1:2–26.

Lichtenstädter, I. 1943. "On the Conception of *Adab*.' *The Moslem World* 33.1:33–38.

Makdisi, G. 1990. *The Rise of Humanism in Classical Islam and the Christian West: With Special Reference to Scholasticism*. Edinburgh.

Marlow, L. 2017. "Wisdom and Justice: the Reception of the Qurʾān in Some Arabic and Persian Mirrors for Princes." In *The Qurʾān and Adab: The Shaping of Literary Traditions in Classical Islam*, edited by Nuha Alshaar, 401–433. Oxford.

Meier, F. 1999. "A Book of Etiquette for Sufis." In *Essays on Islamic Piety and*

Mysticism, translated by John O'Kane, with the editorial assistance of Bernd Radtke, 49–50. Leiden.

Meisam, J. S. 2000. "History as Literature." *Iranian Studies* 33.1:15- 30.

Mez, A. 1937. *The Renaissance of Islam*. Translated by S. K. Bukhsh and D. S. Margoliouth. London.

Montgomery, J. 1986. "Dichotomy in *Jāhilī* Poetry." *Journal of Arabic Literature* 17:1–16.

——. 2005. "Serendipity, Resistance, and Multivalency: Ibn Khurradādhbih and his Kitāb al-Masālik wa-l mamālik." In *On Fiction and Adab in Medieval Arabic Literature*, edited by Philip F. Kennedy. Wiesbaden..

——. 2006. "Al-Jāḥiẓ's Kitāb al-Bayān wa al-Tabyin." In *Writing and Representation in Medieval Islam: Muslim Horizons*, edited by Julia Bray, 91–153. London.

——. 2013. *In Praise of Books*. Edinburgh.

Nallino, C. A. 1948. "La letteratura araba dagli inizi all'epoca della dinastia umayyade." In *Raccolta di scritti editi e inediti, Vol. VI: Letteratura, linguistica, filosofia, varia (Con biobibliografia di C. A. Nallino e indici analitici), a cura di Maria Nallino*, edited by C. A. Nallino, 1–20. Rome.

Neuwirth, A. 2014. *Scripture, Poetry and the Making of a Community: Reading the Qurʾān as a Literary Text*. Oxford.

——.2017. "The 'Discovery of Writing' in the Qurʾān: Tracing a Cultural Shift in Arab Late Antiquity." In *The Qurʾān and Adab: The Shaping of Literary Tradition in Classical Islam*, edited by Nuha Alshaar. Oxford.

Norris, H. T. 1990. "The *Shuʿūbiyya*." In *The Cambridge History of Arabic Literature, Vol. II: ʿAbbasid Belles-Lettres*, edited by Julia Ashtiany, et al., 31–47. Cambridge.

Norris, H. T. 1983. "Fables and Legends in Pre-Islamic and Early Islamic Times; Early Arabic Prose." In *Arabic Literature to the End of the Umayyad Period*, edited by A. F. L. Beeston, T. M. Johnstone, R. B. Serjeant, G. R. Smith, 374–386. Cambridge.

Orfali, B, and M. Pomerantz. 2017. "'I See a Distant Fire': Thaʿālibī's (d. 429/1030) *Kitāb al-Iqtibās min al-Qurʾān al-karīm*." In *The Qurʾān and Adab: The Shaping of Literary Traditions in Classical Islam*, edited by Nuha Alshaar, 191–219. Oxford.

Pellat, C. 1969. "Adab" *Dāʾirat al-maʿārif, Vol. VIII*. Edited by Fūʾād al-Bustānī, 62–68. Beirut.

Pollock, Sh. 2009. "Future Philology? The Fate of a Soft Science in a Hard World" *Critical Inquiry* 35.4:931–961.

Pettersson, Anders. 2006 "Introduction: Concepts of Literature and Transcultural History." In *Literary History towards a Global Perspective*, edited by Anders Pettersson, 1–33. Berlin.

Al-Qāḍī, W. 2017. "The Impact of the Qur'ān on the Epistolography of ʿAbd al-Ḥamīd b. Yaḥyā al-Kātib (d. 132/750)" In *The Qur'ān and Adab: The Shaping of Literary Traditions in Classical Islam*, edited by Nuha Alshaar, 341–380. Oxford; originally appeared in *Approaches to the Qur'ān*, edited by. G. R. Hawting and Abdul-Kader A. Shareef, pp. 285–313., London and New York, 1993.

——. 1985. *Bishr b. Abī Kubār al-Balawī: Namūdhaj min al-nathr al-fannī al-mubakkir fi'l-Yaman.* Beirut. .

Rosenthal, F. 1975. *The Classical Heritage in Islam.* Translated by Emile and Jenny Marmorstein. London.

——. 2006. *Knowledge Triumphant: The Concept of Knowledge in Medieval Islam.* Leiden.

Rowson, E. K. 1990. "The Philosopher as Littérateur: al-Tawḥīdī and His Predecessors." *Zeitschrift für Geschichte der Arabisch-Islamischen Wissenschaften* 6:50–92.

Said, E.W. 1978. *Orientalism.* New York.

Sanni, A. 1998. *The Arabic Theory of Prosification and Versification: On Ḥall and Naẓm in Arabic Theoretical Discourse.* Stuttgart.

Sardār, H. M. 2002. *Tafsīr al-Rāghib al-Iṣfahānī min sūrat al-nisā' āya 114 wa ḥattā nihāyat sūrat al-mā'ida.* Mecca.

Sperl, S. 2007. "Man's 'Hollow Core': Ethics and Aesthetics in *Ḥadīth* Literature and Classical Arabic *Adab.*" *Bulletin of the School of Oriental and African Studies* 70.3:459–486.

Stelzer, S. 2017. "'Serving from Afar': Jalāl al-Dīn al-Rūmī (d. 672/1273) on the *Adab* of Interpreting the Qur'ān." In *The Qur'ān and Adab: The Shaping of Literary Traditions in Classical Islam*, edited by Nuha Alshaar, 545–565. Oxford.

Toorawa Sh. M. 2005a. *Ibn Abī Ṭāhir Ṭayfūr and Arabic Writerly Culture: A Ninth-Century Bookman in Baghdad.* London.

——. 2005b. "Defining *Adab* by (Re) defining the *Adīb*: Ibn Abī Ṭāyfūr and Storytelling." In *On Fiction and Adab in Medieval Arabic Literature*, edited by Philip F. Kennedy, 303–304. Wiesbaden.

Trinkaus, Ch. 1983. *The Scope of Renaissance Humanism.* Ann Arbor, MI.

Wensinck, A. J., 1936. *Al-Muʿjam al-Mufahras li-Alfāẓ al-Ḥadīth al-Nabawī.* Leiden.

Vollers, K. 1975. *Katalog der islamischen, christlich-orientalischen, jüdischen und samaritanischen Handschriften der Universitäts-Bibliothek zu Leipzig.* Bissendorf, Osnabrück.

9

The Good, the Bad, and the Heretic in Early Islamic History[1]

Mushegh Asatryan

Introduction

LET ME HAZARD a broad generalization about a common error in the human sciences: considering what is not a thing as a thing. That is, granting the status of a separate entity to something whose existence as such is not warranted – beyond a word or two by which it is designated. Some such imagined entities have been "the Orient," "the West," "Islam," "nation," "civilization," and their use has been successfully critiqued in the last decades.[2] Yet the uncritical use of similar entities as separate categories of analysis persists, and in this essay I will study three, commonly recurring in studies of early Shīʿism: "community," "heresy," and "thought" (along with their synonyms such as "group," "deviation," "doctrine," and the like). In addition, I will study the type of historical canvas onto which these categories are often pasted, that is, the view of how these entities evolve over time.

The use of these categories in historical studies is not problematic per se, as long as each is clearly defined and demarcated. In many representative studies of early Shīʿism this is not the case, however, as each is frequently treated as a biological organism or a person, with one's own life history, volition, and agency. The history that is narrated for such entities is often distinctly teleological and reinforces their status as separate things. Moreover, each of these categories reinforces various biases derived from the primary sources, which in turn reinforce certain orthodoxies. On the one hand, this is the orthodoxy of Sunnism, which posits that the pristine and united Muslim community was from time to time disturbed when various

1. I would like to thank Adam Gaiser for his meticulous reading of an earlier draft of this essay, and for a number of excellent suggestions with regard to literature and methodology.

2. With regard to Islamic history, see al-Azmeh's (2012, 506–507) critique of "civilization" and related categories, and Morony's (2005, 9) critique of the reification of "culture."

factions, including Shīᶜism, split from it. On the other, it is the orthodoxy of the Twelver or Imāmī Shīᶜism, which is assumed to have been disturbed by the Sunnīs from the outside, and by some troublesome heretics from the inside.

In my essay I focus on writings on Shīᶜism covering the first four Islamic centuries, as they are based on a common set of texts interpreted through a number of shared historiographic tropes. To refer to this period, I will henceforth simply use the noun "Shīᶜism" and the adjective "Shīᶜī." In keeping with the focus of the volume, I will study scholarship produced in Western Europe and North America. I will leave aside the rather rich scholarship on early Shīᶜism produced in Iran, the Arab world, and Turkey, since my goal is to show how the ostensibly "outsider" scholarship of the West uncritically reproduces various "insider" biases found in the classical sources. My essay is divided into five parts. Each of the first four discusses one of the above-mentioned tropes (community, heresy, thought), in addition to the view of how they exist in time. The final section discusses how said four themes can be studied more fruitfully – through a more careful, and methodologically and theoretically informed reading of the primary sources.

Community

> An historical mass, in this sense, is one whose imputed distinctiveness, individuality, and indeed whose very name – the West, Islam, this "community" or that – is taken to subtend a culture so specific and irreducible as to be in itself constitutive of both the history and of the present condition of this mass...[3]

Muslims

The main building block on which the construction of Shīᶜī history rests is denoted by the noun "community" and its synonyms. The category itself may be perfectly acceptable as a unit of historical analysis, but only if clearly defined. The semantic field of the word is broad enough to indicate any type of social group united by any type of commonality, and the failure to clearly define it leads to a blurry image of Shīᶜī history. Various cognates of the term have been applied to the early Muslims in general, whose alleged primeval unity was disturbed by splits into various groups, among them the Shīᶜīs. Since the Muslim community was viewed as a single whole, disagreements over leadership or the emergence of sectarian identities have been viewed as "splits" and "divisions."

3. Al-Azmeh 2007, 7.

In 1901, Julius Wellhausen wrote that after the murder of ʿUthmān, Islam split into two parties, one under ʿAlī and one under Muʿāwiya. Despite the seemingly essentialist language, referring to the "split" (*spaltete sich*) which "Islam" underwent, the narrative that follows presents a rather historically sound account, with real people (not some elusive entities) fighting and disagreeing over political leadership, while articulating religious discourses.[4] Not so for much of the scholarship produced in the more than hundred years since the publications of his book. In text after text, "Islam" and "community" figure as unproblematic categories. Definitions are proposed sometimes, but more often their self-evidence is taken for granted. One scholar, for example, writes of a "consensus that culminated in the consolidation of Sunnism in early ʿAbbāsid times," and that the Shīʿīs stood outside that consensus.[5] A stark division between an incipient Shīʿism and a majority Sunnism is assumed to have permeated many aspects of life, and to have formed the rationale for the actions of many Shīʿī individuals.[6]

In his book tellingly entitled *Les schisms dans l'islam* (The Schisms in Islam), Henri Loust states that the battle of Siffīn "once again, shattered the unity of the community" (*l'unité de la communauté*).[7] "Once again," since there were presumably other such cases of breach of communal unity, but the nature of that unity remains unclear. One of the clearest (but not the most convincing) definitions of religious community is perhaps proposed by Hodgson, who, writing about the period leading to the emergence of Islam, states:

> Between Nile and Oxus ..., the rise of the confessional allegiances soon meant the organization of the whole population into many mutually exclusive rival religious bodies; that is, into *communities* which were religious rather than primarily territorial. It was as socially unthinkable to be associated with two or more such communities as to be associated with none.[8]

He then goes on to speak of a similar process after the emergence of Islam, which united "the bulk of the population of the region into one religious community."[9] The idea that Late Antique religious communities were

4. Wellhausen 1901, 55 ff.; in another of his works, however, Wellhausen (1902, 32) speaks of the decay of the unity of Muhammad's community.

5. Clarke 2004, 109, cf. also 119. What this "consensus" is, the author does not explain.

6. See Takim (2006, 116), who notes that Shīʿī compilers recorded *ḥadīth* "in contradistinction" to the emerging Sunnī *ḥadīth*, without invoking any direct or circumstantial evidence of any sort.

7. Laoust 1965, 12.

8. Hodgson 1974, 135.

9. Hodgson 1974, 146.

"exclusive" is problematic, as demonstrated by recent research. Equally problematic is the use of such language with regard to Islam, along with the assumption that the Muslim community sprang into existence with a readily-formed identity.[10] Heinz Halm, for example, writes without much elaboration of an "original Islamic community," as a translation of the qurʾānic term *umma*, as if it signified an actually existing, firmly unified group of people.[11] He then writes that this unity underwent a "split" which has never "healed," then adds that the war that followed "was the first difficult 'trial' (*fitna*) in the Islamic community – in which Muslim took up arms against Muslim."[12] The word "heal," and the characterization of the war as one where Muslim fights Muslim presupposes the existence of a solidly unified, pristine unity of the community which has been regretfully disturbed. It also presupposes that "Muslimness" was the primary component of the identity of those fighting. Recent scholarship demonstrates, however, that the boundaries of this community in that period were far from firm and impenetrable, and that the religious identity of this community as "Muslims" par excellence, far from certain.[13]

Patricia Crone's account of the first civil wars and the splits is more detailed but equally essentialist and vaguely worded. According to her, as a result of these wars, "the community" was "split" into "rival communities." She goes on to state the insular nature of each such community in much stronger terms than Halm, saying that their members tried to "insulate themselves in social terms," publicly declaring their loyalty to its imam and dissociating from "everyone else." The few examples that she provides fail to show how each such community dissociated itself *from everyone else*, or how it was socially insular. Further, because members of each such community viewed it as a vehicle for salvation (just how we know this, is never explained), "each was a potential sect." Slightly later she provides a definition of "sect," but it remains as vague as her "community." "Sects," for her, are "[1] bounded communities [2] identified by different views on religious questions." Even assuming that the second part of the definition is clear (it is not), the first part still leaves the definition wanting.[14]

10. See the useful discussion in Freidenreich (2011, 9) regarding the contrast between otherness prescribed by the educated elite and the actual practices of exclusion of religious communities; cf. also Sizgorich 2009, 31; Morony 1974, 8 and 134.

11. On the development of the term *umma* in later Islamic tradition, see Donner 1998, 160–166.

12. Halm 2004, 1, 4–7.

13. Al-Azmeh 2014, 367–430; Friedlaender 2011, 131–143; Hughes 2017; Donner 2002–2003.

14. Crone 2012, 25–27. Even if we assume that "bounded" refers to the social self-insulation on the part of the various sects-in-the-making described above, the definition still doesn't hold as she fails to demonstrate such complete insulation, as I showed.

A bit later still, Crone suggests that unlike the Shīʿīs and the Khārijīs, the *Jamaʿī* Muslims, who were later to form the basis of Sunnism, consciously *chose* to maintain the unity of the community. They "stuck to communal unity," "refused to form separatist communities," and "had high appreciation of communal togetherness."[15] The problems with this description are several. The simplest is the nature of documentation. We may never conceivably know that they consciously *stuck* with unity, *refused* to separate, or *appreciated* togetherness unless this is documented in the sources (granted that we all agree on what "unity" and "togetherness" mean, which we hardly do). The second problem is more theoretical: who are the "they" we are talking about? Some prominent men among these so-called *Jamaʿīs*? All of them? The majority? Even if we did possess some such first-person testimonies, written by some prominent *Jamaʿīs*, this would only mean that this is the position of the leadership. For no group of people, however defined, may want the same thing, and when dealing with past societies especially, we usually learn of the ideas and desires of the powerful and the lettered of a certain community, not all of its members. And even granted that both of the above conditions are miraculously met, that is, if we suddenly come into possession of a cache of letters from every single *Jamaʿī* from that period (which is pretty much everyone except the Shīʿīs and the Khārijīs, following Crone's logic); and if all (or, well, most) of them state that they want communal unity and togetherness, how do we understand what the meaning of these words are? Political unity? Doctrinal uniformity? Economic integration? All of the above? But Crone never specifies.

Shīʿīs

Once the pristine "Muslim community" is "divided," one of the main resulting groups, the "Shīʿī community" is granted by scholars the same ill-defined coherence as the Muslim one before it. Hence, the assumptions apparent in Halm's and Crone's passages are abundantly present in discussions of inner-Shīʿī developments. One is the default unity of this community, which is frequently established by equating the community and its leadership.[16] The

15. Crone 2012, 28.

16. Cf. Buckley's (1998, 184) argument that thanks to the unification of Shīʿī doctrine, the "integrity of the majority group of Shīʿa was largely maintained." It is firstly unclear what the author means by the "unification of doctrine," especially since the author is speaking about doctrine as articulated in the Shīʿī *ḥadīth* corpus, which contains notoriously diverse and sometimes contradictory views on various doctrinal points. The second fallacy is assuming that a unified doctrine implies a unified community.

second is the negative characterization of the "splits" into various "sects" that have occurred in it.[17] An example is Modarressi's famous work, *Crisis and Consolidation*,[18] which depicts the disagreements over the leadership in the early Shīᶜī community as a series of crises that were finally overcome thanks to the efforts of some brave individuals, despite the hindrances of the vicious heretics. The assumptions of such characterizations mirror the positions of established orthodoxies, especially apparent in the heresiographic literature, which assumes the unity of a pristine Muslim *umma* or a Shīᶜī community which sadly split into sects.[19] The uncritical use of indigenous classifications is apparent: they were in most cases written after the events and groups they purport to describe, they are overly schematic as each represents a particular sectarian, highly polemical and biased standpoint (Sunnī, Imāmī, Ismāᶜīlī, etc.), and as has been demonstrated, many of the "sects" described in such texts most probably never existed.[20] And even if one group or another did exist, they are all overly reified in the heresiologies, and the historian should approach such indigenous categories with a great deal of caution.[21]

Of course, there were surely groups of people who had shared theological beliefs, but we should be cautious in treating them as separate social entities, and when we do, we should clearly define their parameters to the

17. Sachedina (1981, 34) writes, for example, that "extremists" and "undisciplined Imamites" such as al-Ḥallāj and al-Shalmaghānī caused much "dissidence" in the face of the Imāmī community. If anything, their dissidence caused trouble to the leadership of the community (Abdulsater 2011, 317–318), but the unquestioning taking of the side of leadership and assuming it represents the view of the community as a whole, privileges those in power and replicates theological classifications. In his otherwise excellent book, Najam Haider (2011, 15) mirrors a similar bias, by noting that the multiplicity of ideas on the Imam's nature in the early Shīᶜī community lead to a "confusion," and that, moreover, this confusion lead to a proliferation of extremist ideas. Two unexamined presuppositions are apparent here. One is the negative view of a diversity of opinion, hence "confusion." The other is the negative view of the ideas of the *ghulāt* (since it is the confusion that allowed for the proliferation of their extremist ideas). Finally, as is frequently encountered in scholarship, the "extreme-ness" of the teachings of the extremists is taken as an absolute value, and not as a polemical classification. On the "extremists" (*ghulāt*), see below.

18. Modarressi 1993.

19. E.g. al-Nawbakhtī, *Firaq*, 2ff.; al-Ashᶜarī, *Maqālāt*, 2 ff.

20. E.g. Bausani 2000, 132; Lewinstein 1992, 76; for a detailed overview of Muslim heresiographic literature, see van Ess 2011; for a discussion of such "invented" sects, see the last section.

21. Cf. Lewinstein 1991; Najam Haider (2018, 210) rightly notes that "[t]here was no definitive moment where the Muslim community split into two irreconcilable factions; such a perspective was anachronistically posited by later Sunnī and Shīᶜī scholars."

extent possible.[22] Conversely, we should not assume that the official position of a group (if indeed there was one), recorded in later heresiographies and other primary sources, was necessarily shared by all of its members, as is frequently implied. Finally, the language of "division" and its description as "crisis" may not be apposite in such cases, as noted, since disputes over succession, disagreements over legitimacy, and related theological and political matters, are a normal part of any society. At the same time, seeming uniformity of opinion does not necessarily presuppose consensus or harmony. They may reflect that a central dogma (for example, who is the next Imam) has been enforced from above, but we may never be sure that all the members of a given community were in agreement, even if the primary sources tell us so. Disagreement may still exist, but if it is successfully suppressed, and if a central dogma has been successfully enforced, we may never hear about dissident voices as the sources may not deem them important enough to record. Thus describing divisions of opinion as "crises" is a distinctly theological, insider position reflecting the interests of those in power in a given community and the resultant biases of the primary sources.

The failure to clearly define the "unity" of the "community" has allowed scholars to generalize about all Shīʿīs what has been reported for just one or several persons, treating Shīʿism as a single personality with one's own will and decision-making capability[23] and exaggerating its "independence" from the rest of Muslims. Takim writes of an "independent Shīʿī community," which "asserted its autonomy from the mainstream Sunnī majority." What these independence and autonomy are, Takim defines as follows (citing no evidence): "In a sense, the 'ideal' Shīʿī community, maintaining religious and administrative independence from the political structure, existed within a hostile Sunnī majority."[24] Many of these speculations have no trace in the historical record.[25]

22. Najam Haider (2011; 2018) is the only scholar, to my knowledge, to meticulously study and demonstrate the emergence of the early Shīʿīs as a separate social group who marked their identity by ritual and sacred space.

23. Cf. Clarke's (2004, 119) use of "cautious community," which, given the overall logic of her exposition appears as a pretty literal use of the word and not a metaphor.

24. Takim 2006, 183.

25. If the meaning of "religious" independence of the community is more or less clear, the administrative independence of the Shīʿī community in ʿAbbasid times is plainly erroneous: not only the Shīʿīs, but their Imams lived within the ambit of the caliphal government and displayed no discernible degree of independence from its administrative edifice. They did at times collect funds for inner-communal purposes (Asatryan 2014), but this is no indication that they possessed any self-governance.

Mainstream

Aside from differentiating Shīʿism from what is without, scholars pass judgments on what was central or mainstream, and what was fringe or periphery within.[26] Abdulaziz Sachedina's picture of the relations between the (majority of) Shīʿīs and the Muslim majority is more irenic, but it is equally unexamined and essentialist, albeit with a different emphasis. Instead of the external enemy, that is, the hostile Sunnīs, it tries to distance the Shīʿīs from the enemy within, the heretical "extremists."

> The moderate Shīʿītes, who were later on to form the bulk of the Shīʿītes maintaining the Imamate of the twelve Imams, although insisting on the exalted status of the Imams and allegiance of the twelve successors of the Prophet, maintained relations with the community at large.[27]

The "moderate Shīʿītes," to whom Sachedina refers, are here juxtaposed to the so-called "extremist" Shīʿīs (*ghulāt*), called thus by heresiographers because of their divinization of (that is, their "extreme" devotion to) the Imams, in addition to some other beliefs later deemed heterodox. The demonization of the "extremists" as heretics took place after the lifetime of the Imams, and during the first two centuries of Islam they had formed the integral part of the Shīʿī community.[28] The anachronistic depiction of them as heretics, however, remains a common trope in scholarship. The assertion that the moderates maintained relations with the community at large (as opposed to the extremists) reflects an unexamined and incorrect assumption most likely coming from the heresiographic accounts; namely, that the extremists, unlike the moderates, were shunned by said community, which follows from the fact that later Sunnī and Shīʿī heresiographers condemn the extremists wholesale as heretics, while considering the "moderates," that is the Imāmīs, as orthodox. Being later back-projections, however, these statements indicate nothing about the actual relations between the moderates and the broader community on the one hand, and the extremists and the community on the other. Meanwhile, the toleration on the part of *some* Sunnī authors of the official theological positions of one group among Shīʿīs (the "moderates") is taken to indicate that the Sunnīs and those moderates maintained relations.

26. Both terms are used by Turner (2006, 185), with no stated criteria for separating fringe from center.

27. Sachedina 1981, 13.

28. See my discussion in Asatryan 2017.

Sachedina equates the Shīʿī community as a whole with its leadership. When speaking about famous "heretic" al-Shalmaghānī (d. ca. 322/934–935), Sachedina claims that the latter endangered the institution of *niyāba*, which refers to the leadership of the community in the absence of the Imam. Sachedina then states that the authority of the then deputy of the Imam was so great that many of the followers of al-Shalmaghānī abandoned him, prefacing this statement with "[f]ortunately for the Imamites."[29] Thus the author assumes that averting the danger to the leadership of the Imāmī community was *fortunate* for the Imāmites as a whole.

Ismail Poonawala likewise upholds an orthodox position and implicitly equates the community with its leaders, claiming that "dissident" groups such as the "Wāqifīs and the Ghulāt" posed a danger to the "mainstream Shīʿī community."[30] The dictionary definition of "dissident" is "disagreeing especially with an established religious or political system, organization, or belief,"[31] and indeed, both groups did disagree somewhat[32] with the established religious system, but not always with the political one. But if anything, this means they posed a danger to the orthodoxy of the community (if there was already one), or to its power structure, which is not the same as the community itself. Here one thinks of the Soviet government's branding of its political dissidents as "enemies of the *people*."

In Hossein Modarressi's account, the mainstream community assumes firm boundaries from the very outset. He frequently uses "community" or "mainstream community" to refer to those Muslims who held views which for later standards were orthodox. Sometimes this refers specifically to the Shīʿīs, sometimes to the "Muslim community" in general. From these, various types of heretics split every now and then because of their heterodox beliefs,[33] or because they decide to abrogate the *sharīʿa* and allow unlawful acts.[34] Modarressi arrives at this picture through the normative operation of *naming* those who in his view held the right beliefs as "mainstream" and "community," who held "unanimous" views on this or that idea; and of *naming* those who in his view deviated as "heretics." This operation of naming entails no argumentation and a very selective reading of the primary

29. Sachedina 1981, 95–96.

30. Poonawala 2001, 120.

31. https://www.merriam-webster.com/dictionary/dissident.

32. On the *wāqifa*, see Buyukkara 2000; on the *ghulāt*, and on their position in the society, see Asatryan 2017, especially the last chapter.

33. Modarressi 1993, 22, 90.

34. Modarressi 1993, 21. The uncritical acceptance of heresiographic reports to this effect is another problem apparent in the works of Modarressi and others, and I will discuss this below.

sources, disregarding or explaining away evidence which does not fit his purposes. Thus, in his article about the early debates on the authenticity of the Qurʾān, he notes that famous eighth-century "extremist" Mufaḍḍal al-Juʿfī (d. before 183/799) and some others were excluded from the mainstream community for their heretical tendencies "in their own times as well as later." In support he cites the derogatory remarks of two later Shīʿī doxographers, whose notices about this individual are extremely short and merely reflect the positions of then reigning orthodoxy.[35] Meanwhile, there is abundant evidence that Mufaḍḍal had extensive contacts with the Imams and other members of the community, and that he rendered the Imams important financial services, and was highly valued by them.[36] As to later tradition, Mufaḍḍal's image is still not unambiguously negative, as two of the foremost representatives of Imāmī orthodoxy, al-Ṭūsī (d. ca. 459–460/1066–1067) and Shaykh Mufīd (d. ca. 413/1032), both speak of him very fondly.[37]

In a similar vein, in his *Crisis and Consolidation*, Modarressi postulates that the "Imāmite community" "unanimously" rejected the views of the *mufawwiḍa* heretics.[38] On the simplest level, the fallacy in this statement has to do with a selective reading of the primary sources, as it disregards the fact that many an orthodox *ḥadīth* compiler collected traditions with content later deemed heretical – something that Modarressi himself notes and tries to explain away earlier on the same page and elsewhere.[39] The second problem is more broadly methodological. The impossibility of knowing whether a community held a unanimous opinion on a certain idea (granted that unanimity in any community is possible at all) has been discussed above, and will be elaborated in greater detail later. Of course, one may presume that the author here is referring not to every single person in it but to those whose opinions could stand for the entire community. Following the overall logic of his book, this might refer to the learned scholars who upheld views that in the author's opinion were orthodox. But this is equally problematic, as it privileges the views of a minority in power (even when that power was more symbolic than political), presuming that reigning orthodoxy reflects the views of the entire community. And indeed he does, as those people who, he admits, "even supported the cosmological theories of the Mufawwiḍa," were for Modarressi "heretical persons and sects."[40] And on a couple of occa-

35. Modarressi 1993a, 32.

36. Asatryan 2014; Asatryan 2017, 55–61.

37. al-Ṭūsī (d. ca. 459–460/1066–1067), *Ghayba*, 210; al-Mufīd (d. ca. 413/1032), *Irshād*, 288.

38. Modarressi 1993, 48–49.

39. The primary sources are too many to list. For references, see Amir-Moezzi 2011; Asatryan 2017, 75–78.

40. Modarressi 1993, 49.

sions, he speaks of "common people" who failed to understand the "divine interest" behind the Imam's decisions, or who were rude to the Imam despite the community's respect for him.[41]

The narrative of the existence of a solid and uniformly orthodox-minded community that split during the lifetime of Imams is problematic not just for the lack of evidence to prove this, but for the abundance of evidence to the contrary. It replicates heresiographic accounts about the neat divisions of sects, while sources of two other types, *ḥadīth* and biographical dictionaries (*rijāl* works) completely defy such classifications. There is much material showing that so-called heretical individuals had extensive contacts both with the Imams and the regular members of what Modarressi might term the "mainstream community,"[42] and there appears to have been no social division between the "heretics" and the "mainstream."

Heresy

Linda: I think Dennis just wants to be normal.
Mavis: Can we stop using the word "normal"?
Drac: Where we live now, he's normal!

Hotel Transylvania 2[43]

The Radical and the un-Islamic

The distinction that is established between "mainstream" and "heretical" Shīʿīs is always in favor of the dominant, Twelver or Imāmī branch of Shīʿism, mirroring both today's situation and medieval classifications of Shīʿī heresiographers and theologians. And once this distinction has been established, the "heretics," along with their beliefs and practices are invariably described in negative and emotionally charged terms as deviant, vulgar, crude, and radical. Some scholars even take the liberty to pass judgments on who was only "nominally Muslim"[44] and who was "authentically Islamic,"[45] whose teachings were "false"[46] or whose lifestyle was "un-Islamic"[47] – all of these qualities reflecting a distinctly theological stance.

This story is old, but it continues well into the present. In an article pub-

41. Modarressi 1993, 67–68.
42. Amir-Moezzi 2011, 216, 218; Asatryan 2017, 54–60.
43. See: https://en.wikiquote.org/wiki/Hotel_Transylvania_2.
44. Turner 2006, 181.
45. Madelung 2014a, 460.
46. Dakake 2006, 333.
47. Takim 2006, 11.

lished in 1938, Louis Massignon presented a very speculative account about the role of the *ghulāt* in early Islamic history.[48] He spoke of their social virulence (*virulence sociale*) and their toxicity for the state (*«toxicité» pour l'État*[49]) and, without recourse to any primary sources, assigned to them the principal responsibility for dislocating the caliphate and for replacing it with various local dynasties, such as the Būyids and the Ḥamdānids. He further blamed the infiltration of the Sunnī caliphate by extremist Shīᶜī functionaries for the "astonishing exacerbation of financial immorality," once again, citing no evidence. Such a scholarly approach to the early Shīᶜī heretics, based on dominant Shīᶜī and Sunnī views, was duly noted already in 1955 by Marshall Hodgson in his oft-cited article on early Shīᶜism:

> The term *Ghulât*, 'exaggerators,' was used by the later Twelver Shîᶜites, who liked to think of themselves as moderates, to designate as an extremist any other Shîᶜite whose ideas particularly shocked them. ... Islamists, both Muslim and Western, have had a way of absorbing the point of view of orthodox Islâm; this has gone so far that Christian Islamists have looked with horror on Muslim heretics for teaching doctrines which are taken for granted coming from St. John and St. Paul. Accordingly, the early Ghulât have received scant respect among Islamists, since they have been despised by both Sunnîs and Twelvers.[50]

This sober assessment of the historical record and of scholarly bias has had little acceptance in the writings about Shīᶜism since the publication of Hodgson's article.[51] Time and again, and without explanation, this or that idea is adjudged as "deviant," "extreme," or "radical,"[52] opposed to the mod-

48. Massignon 2009, 656–659.

49. The quotation marks notwithstanding, the meaning assigned by Massignon to the word seems to be rather straightforward.

50. Hodgson 1955, 4–5.

51. For a careful study of the semantic field covered by the words *ghulāt* and *ghuluww* (i.e. "exaggeration" as practiced by the *ghulāt*), see al-Qāḍī 1976; most recently, see also the detailed study of the term by Anthony (2018).

52. Cf. Poonawala 2001, 110; Sachedina 1981, 7, 8, 10, 34, 95: "radical," "extremists and undisciplined Imamites like al-Hallaj and al-Shalmaghani," who are called by these derogatory names with no explanation and presumably for being less than orthodox, juxtaposed to the orthodox Abu l-Qāsim al-Nawbakhtī, the third "agent" of the Hidden Imam, whose "astute leadership" the author praises for saving the developing doctrine of the Imamate of the Hidden Imam from being uprooted; see also Modarressi 1993, 4, 9, 22, 34, 35, 42, 43, 80: "radical splinter sect," "radical extremists," "extremist," "radical wing of the Shīᶜite community," "radical elements," and "unorthodox" (used without quotation marks); Madelung writes about the Kufan Imāmīyya being "plagued" by the activities of the *ghulāt*, or that several extremists "escaped" excommunication by the Imams, thus implying that the Imams were bound to excommunicate heretics like them, see Madelung 1988, 77, 80–81; Madelung 2014a, 458; Clarke 2004, 16; Momen 1985, 66, 182; Clarke 2001, 110, 120,

erate "mainstream," which term, once again, is used with no definition or clarification.[53] The violent acts perpetrated by some of the *ghulāt* rebels are referred to with the term "terrorism,"[54] and the justification of these acts as meritorious is taken as an index of the *ghulāt*'s alienation.[55]

Normative, heresiographic classifications of people into villains and heroes is once again uncritically reproduced by scholars. In most cases, this is done without much substantiation through recourse to the primary sources, and certainly with no recourse to the two original *ghulāt* writings available to scholarship for most of the twentieth century, *Umm al-Kitāb* since 1936, and *Kitāb al-Haft* since 1960 (and, a third one, *Kitāb al-Ṣirāṭ*, since 1995). One of the corollaries of the failure to read the *ghulāt*'s own writings, or to critically engage with the hyper-polemical and neatly classificatory accounts of heresiographers, is the taking at face value of the *ghulāt*'s alleged antinomianism, accompanied with the reification of what is termed "the law" or the "*sharīʿa*."[56] While the heresiographic descriptions of the *ghulāt*'s alleged antinomianism accuse them of all kinds of sexual and other vices (indiscriminate sex, refusal to pray and fast, and so on), what survives of their own writings conveys a much more nuanced picture, where only *some* religious commandments could be bypassed by those who have achieved a certain degree of perfection.[57] In fact, the abovementioned *Kitāb al-Haft* contains a full out refutation of the accusations of sexual licenses leveled against the *ghulāt*, which none of the scholars discussing the topic note.[58]

Measuring Sincerity

Scholarly discussions about the degree of people's sincerity are unproductive because they reflect a polemical stance. More importantly, they are meaningless since there is no conceivable way to measure sincerity, certainly not at the remove of more than a millennium. Yet unsubstantiated and emotionally charged speculations frequently appear in discussions about the motives and psychological states of various individuals. People

53. Modarressi 1993, 64; Turner 2006, 185; Jafri 2007, 289, 291; Clarke 2001, 94.

54. Tucker 2008, xviii, 52, 68, 71.

55. See Morony's otherwise excellent *Iraq after the Muslim Conquest* (2005, 502).

56. Cf. Dakake (2007, 9, passim), who speaks of the "crude" and "vulgar" antinomianism of the *ghulāt* as opposed to the more "subtle" and "less morally offensive" one found among "mainstream" lines of Shīʿī thought. What exactly the crude and vulgar types are, and how one can distinguish them from the subtler and less offensive ones, the author does not specify, and it is very clear that all of these adjectives are simply polemical judgments that convey no other meaning other than the negative judgments of the heresiographers; see also van Ess 1991, 316; Modarressi 1993, 21; Madelung 2014a, 460 (writing about the Nuṣayrīs); Crone 2012, 83.

57. For a discussion of these passages, see Asatryan, forthcoming.

58. Pseudo-Mufaḍḍal al-Juʿfī (183/799), *Kitāb al-haft wa l-aẓilla*, 145–146.

viewed as heretical are assumed to use the religious feelings of their followers merely for their selfish, nefarious purposes, and are described as "self-appointed amateurs"[59] merely "pretending" to perform miracles,[60] or "cynically" using certain ideas to advance their claims.[61] Sachedina writes about the late seventh-century rebel Mukhtār al-Thaqafī as a "shrewd" and "ambitious" person who "manipulated the genuine religious devotions of ordinary men."[62]

The actions of the *right* type of Shīᶜīs, meanwhile, are noble, selfless, pious, and never politically-motivated, and their religious devotions, *genuine*, as noted by Sachedina. "There can be little doubt that the self-sacrifice of this band of men [the *tawwābūn*] must be ascribed to religious zeal for the house of ᶜAlī rather than any political considerations,"[63] postulates Moojan Momen. The actions of the orthodox Imāmī *ḥadīth* transmitters have been characterized by one scholar as "hard work and tireless efforts" in "removing the doubts and uncertainties of the Imāmite community and persuading the Imāmites of the truth of their doctrine."[64] That the truth of *their* doctrine is *the truth*, *tout court*, is not even questioned, and these men are described as "faithful" and "courageous." And in trying to explain away the existence of (in his assessment) not-so-orthodox traditions in compilations of non-heretical authors, the same writer veers into a psycho-analytical explanation of their mindset, stating that they "themselves did not believe in the content" of these *ḥadīth*.[65] None of these qualifiers and assessments of state of mind and sincerity are ever explained or substantiated.

Reading Selectively

The selective use of primary sources is one way in which normative assessments of Shīᶜī history make their way into scholarship. For example, when studying what he views as the Imāmī Shīᶜī theology, Madelung rightly cautions against the use of heresiographic accounts.[66] When discussing the *ghulāt*, however, he does not hesitate to use the same (with a resultant grim picture of said "heretics").[67] When dealing with the extremely multifarious *ḥadīth* corpus,[68] scholars once again, with not even an attempt at an *isnād*-

59. Crone 2012, 83.
60. Tucker 2008, 67.
61. Buckley 2002, 129.
62. Sachedina 1981, 9–10.
63. Momen 1985, 63.
64. Modarressi 1993, 105.
65. Modarressi 1993, 48.
66. Madelung 2014, 465.
67. Madelung 1988, 7.
68. Cf. Amir-Moezzi and Jambet 2014, 104.

cum-*matn* analysis, assume traditions reflecting "orthodox" views to be factually reliable, and ones seemingly coming from "heterodox" quarters as "questionable" and unreliable "forgeries."[69]

A selective reading of primary sources is evident in the work of Modarressi, who unquestioningly accepts the reports that fit his purposes and dismisses the ones which do not.[70] Or, based on a single episode recorded in *ḥadīth* (which he chooses to accept as authentic), he concludes that the Imam Jaʿfar al-Ṣādiq (d. ca. 148/765) *always* supported one of his "moderate" supporters and rejected his enemies.[71] The numerous *ḥadīth* where the Imam speaks favorably of famous "heretic" Mufaḍḍal al-Juʿfī, recorded in the very same as well as other sources, are passed over in silence.[72] He goes a step further still, and now charges a source of being as unreliable because heretical, now cites it to advance his particular view. For example, in describing the penetration of Shīʿī literature by the writings of the *mufawwiḍa* (another term for the *ghulāt*[73]), Modarressi writes the following about one of the eponymous founders of the Nuṣayrī sect:

> Further material from works of the Mufawwiḍa, and *even* from the writings of *heretical* authors such as Ḥusayn b. Ḥamdān al-Khuṣaybī, were later introduced into the Imāmite literature by *populist* authors who tended to put together and offer whatever report in their judgement could strengthen the faith of the people in the Imāms although the authors themselves *could never guarantee the authenticity* of many reports or many of the sources they quoted.[74] (emphases mine)

69. Turner 2006, 176; in her otherwise well-researched work, Dakake (2007, 169) calls well-known "extremist" Mufaḍḍal al-Juʿfī a "problematic figure," without directly explaining why, but noting (perhaps in the way of explanation of his problematic nature), that he is widely seen as an unreliable transmitter in the Shīʿī tradition; see also Dakake's (2007, 173, 194) side-taking in favor of "mainstream" *isnāds* as opposed to "questionable" ones with no discussion why. Takim cautions that the *ghulāt* may have interpolated *ḥadīth* into Shīʿī collections, and as evidence cites reports from al-Kashshī's work, without noting that these likewise may be interpolations (Takim 2006, 62 and 196n88).

70. Modarressi 1993, 34, 38, 41, 43, 45, 47.

71. Modarressi 1993, 30–31. Similarly, when writing about the "pious and respected member of the Shīʿite community," Ḥujr b. Zāʾida al-Ḥaḍramī, Hossein Modarressi (2003, 272) simply assumes without much ado that the traditions where the Imam Jaʿfar al-Ṣādiq speaks of him critically were ascribed to the latter by the *mufawwiḍa* in order to discredit him.

72. For a discussion of these references, see Asatryan 2017, 54–60.

73. Modarressi distinguishes them from the *ghulāt* proper, but the sources do not support such a division, see Asatryan 2017, 98–111.

74. Modarressi 1993, 47.

Nor did the non-populist, "reliable" authors used by Modarressi "guarantee the authenticity of many reports" they cite, yet Modarressi unquestioningly uses them when he wishes. But this is not all. Some pages later, Modarressi does not hesitate to cite the writings of the selfsame "heretical author" al-Khuṣaybī (d. ca. 346/957 or 358/969) to claim that "the overwhelming majority of the Imāmites accepted Ḥasan al-ᶜAskarī (d. ca. 260/874) as the Imām."[75]

Amateurs and Professionals

Perhaps the most openly normative description of the *ghulāt* is found in Crone's *Medieval Islamic Political Thought*. She writes that for the *ghulāt*, "[t]o know the Imam as he really was one had to accept the claims of some self-appointed missionary."[76] She adds that "the Ghulāt hijacked the term imam to apply it ... to their Gnostic savior or other divine leader of the quasi-pagan type."[77] Later on she notes that the "Ghulāt everywhere tended to be religious amateurs drawn from the semi-literate world of villagers or petty urban people...."[78] The normative implications of these three passages are legion. The derogatory "some self-appointed" implies that in contrast to these heretics, *real* Muslims revered persons who were not self-appointed. (Implying, perhaps, that these other ones were either divinely- or at least popularly-appointed. None of the two points is verifiable through evidence and both reflect distinctly normative positions). That the *ghulāt* "hijacked" the term "imam" presumes that the orthodox Muslims did not, but they used it in its "correct" sense (correct, according to whom?). Why she calls their type "quasi-pagan" is unclear, but the fact that it is contrasted with the right, that is, *monotheistic* leaders of the true Muslims is apparent.

Finally, calling the "Ghulāt everywhere" semi-literate religious amateurs is not just a statement unsubstantiated in the primary sources. Had she consulted two of three then-available *ghulāt* writings, she could have detected a rather high degree of literacy and pretty good knowledge of the Qurʾān.[79] And the doxographic works telling about the biographies of *ghulāt* and other Shīᶜīs never, to my knowledge, mention the level of their literacy. If anything, they frequently list treatise after treatise composed by these

75. Modarressi 1993, 65.
76. Crone 2012, 83.
77. Crone 2012, 84.
78. Crone 2012, 96.
79. One of them, *Umm al-Kitāb*, survives in Persian, while originally composed in Arabic.

men.[80] Crucial here is their description as "religious amateurs," implying that the scholars articulating orthodox views were religious *professionals*.

Thought

The fact that ideas presuppose agents is very readily discounted, as the ideas get up and do battle on their own behalf.[81]

The Authentic and the Foreign

Just as groups are named and treated as self-evident entities, so are they often attributed particular sets of beliefs to which unity and immutability are assigned. Similar to the negative evaluation of splits within communities, doctrinal elements perceived to have come from outside of established orthodoxy, or from outside of Islam, are described in negative terms. This follows the logic of proclaiming the ready-made nature of Islam from the very inception, which sprung into existence with a complete set of teachings deriving from the Qurʾan,[82] un outdated view to say the least.[83] By the same token, Shīʿī thought or "the Shīʿī view" are sometimes assumed to represent the very teachings of the Imams, and are treated as a unified whole.[84] This purity is said to have been contaminated by accretions deemed "for-

80. E.g. al-Najāshī (d. ca. 450/1058–1059), *Rijāl*, 334; al-Kashshī, *Rijāl*, 271 and 481; al-Mufīd (d. ca. 413/1032), *al-Masāʾil al-sarawiyya*, 37; see also the list of the *ghulāt* writings surviving in fragments in the Appendix of Asatryan 2017, 179–181.

81. Skinner 1969, 11.

82. Takim 2006, 7.

83. For a history of the complex and gradual process of the emergence of the earliest Muslim cult, called here "Paleo-Islam," see Al-Azmeh 2014, 279–357 and, for a briefer account, Al-Azmeh 2018.

84. Clarke 2004, 112; Poonawala 2001, 115. Buckley (2007, 326) writes that the ʿAbbasids attempted to "usurp" Shīʿī principles and symbolism, which implies, on the one hand, that the Shīʿīs had certain inalterable principles, and on the other, that these were the preserve of the Shīʿīs alone, and that anyone else's espousal of some form of them could only be interpreted as usurpation. Tamima Bayhom-Daou's extremely well-researched articles on early Shīʿī thought commit, nevertheless, one fallacy: they claim that the thought of some early Shīʿī thinkers represented the "main" or the "prevalent" trend in Shīʿism at that time, without much demonstration, see Bayhom-Daou 2003, 74; Bayhom-Daou 2001, 190. Maria Dakake's contention that "the inaccessibility of the Imams certainly allowed a number of false teachings to flourish among certain extremist Shīʿīte groups" (Dakake 2006, 333) contains two fallacies. Most importantly, it assumes that the teachings of the Imams were true Shīʿī theology and ones that differed were false, which reflects not a historical but a theological stance. A further corollary of this stance is that the beliefs deemed "heretical" by later Imāmī standards are a priori assumed to have been distortions of the Imams' teachings – with no attempt at source-critical evaluation of the evidence.

eign," which were introduced by groups adjudged as heretical. Thus, Shīᶜism is treated as a biological organism, which accepts or repels foreign bodies or germs that present themselves in the form of ideas. And when these malicious ideas inflict the organism, they are said to exert mysterious influence over the actions and desires of people. To arrive at such a picture, scholars have cherrypicked evidence, generalized beyond the scope of available evidence, or have essentialized Islam and Shīᶜism, passing judgments about what is "foreign" and what is not.[85]

How to Identify Early Imāmī Theology?

Let us look at a recent article about early Shīᶜī theology by one of the foremost scholars of Medieval Islam, and Shīᶜism in particular, Wilferd Madelung. The focus of the article is clearly defined, and treats what the author calls "Early Imāmī Theology."[86]In achieving this goal, however, the author performs several operations which cast doubt on the result. First, in setting out to study this theology, he performs a selective reading of the primary sources. Second, based on this reading he presumes to arrive at what the teachings of the Shīᶜī Imams themselves have been, with no effort to critically assess the evidence. Third, having apparently arrived at an understanding of what the Imams themselves have taught, he presumes uniformity of doctrine among all of the Imams,[87] and furthermore, generalizes that the teachings of the Imams formed the basis of early Shīᶜī theology in general. Finally, he reads into the sources what is simply not there in order to support his points.

Madelung's aim in this article is, first, to present early Shīᶜī theology, implying that it was exemplified in the sayings of the Imams; second, that it

85. Madelung's discussion of the contacts between Zoroastrianism and Islam illustrates this approach well. He writes, without much elaboration, about the "motivation" of some of medieval Iran's religious movements (including Shīᶜism) (Madelung 1988, x). Then he goes on to speak of an "uncompromising antagonism" between Islam and Zoroastrianism (Madelung 1988, 1). While this personalized language may be interpreted as just a metaphor, the account that follows reveals Madelung's implicit assumptions when speaking about the two religions. Thus, he notes that despite this antagonism, in the eighth and ninth centuries a number of popular movements arose in Iran which "overtly mixed Persian and Islamic religious beliefs and motives" (Madelung 1988, 1). If two religions are antagonistic, how could elements from them be combined together, and combined "overtly" at that? The answer might lie in what Madelung considers as religion proper. This shows that for him, what counts for "Islam" and "Zoroastrianism" are the views of theologians and heresiographers, and that popular movements do not stand for religion proper. Note that in the passage where he speaks about their mixing of elements from the two religions, they are not called "religions," but "popular revolutionary movements" (what he then calls "Low Church").

86. Madelung 2014.

87. E.g. Madelung 2014, 467.

was essentially rationalist; and third, that "[t]he unambiguous affirmation of the primacy of reason over prophetic revelation in religion places early Imāmī theology close to the rationalist theology of the Muʿtazila."

The first problem with the article is a matter of definitions, namely, his oscillation in the article between what he calls "Early Imāmī Theology" and the "the doctrine of the Imams."[88] Beyond the fallacy of generalizing about *all* of early Shīʿī theology (based on mere scraps of cherrypicked evidence, which I will discuss in a moment),[89] it is unclear whether Madelung speaks of the theology of the Imams or of their followers. Both are legitimate topics of study but are by no means identical. In the article, however, they are now treated as one thing, now as two different ones. Thus at the beginning, Madelung rightly notes the problems with studying "early Imāmī Shīʿī theology" based on doxographical texts. He then suggests that

> The doctrine of the Imams, who did not participate in *kalām* debates but whose teaching was considered as authoritative and was elaborated by the Imāmī scholars, is never expressly quoted in these sources. The evolution of the teaching of the Imams must be examined primarily on the basis of Imāmī sources.[90]

Coming after the initial complaint about the state of research on Shīʿī theology, this implicitly suggests that Imāmī theology consists of the teachings of the Imams. Of course, Madelung duly notes that the Imams did not engage in theological disputes, and only responded when asked, leaving it to the theologians to elaborate their responses.[91] On the next page, however, he cites four *ḥadīth* related on the authority of, hence assumed to report the very words of, the fifth and the sixth Imams Muḥammad al-Bāqir (d. ca. 114/732) and Jaʿfar al-Ṣādiq, then suggesting that these represent "Imāmī theology."[92] Another page later, Madelung explicitly speaks of a "theology

88. Madelung 2014, 465.

89. Cf. general statements such as the "unambiguous affirmation of the primacy of reason over prophetic revelation in religion places early Imāmī theology," "[e]arly Imāmī theology was explicitly anti-Qadarī," "Imāmī theology, however, fully agreed," and "Imāmī theology rejected the concept of an eternal immutable will of God" (Madelung 2014, 466, 472, 473). Of course, the fallacy here is not that one or another of these statements is altogether incorrect, but that generalizations are made about all of Shīʿī theology deriving from a *ḥadīth* report or two.

90. Madelung 2014, 465.

91. Madelung 2014, 465.

92. Madelung 2014, 366. The full sentence comes after the fourth *ḥadīth* cited, suggesting that its conclusion is dictated by the content of the *ḥadīth*: "The unambiguous affirmation of the primacy of reason over prophetic revelation in religion places early Imāmī theology close to the rationalist theology of the Muʿtazila."

espoused by the Imams."[93] Throughout the article Madelung presents how various Shīʿī theologians were corrected or instructed by this or that Imam. The implication is now clear: after all, for Madelung the views of the Shīʿī Imams stand for "the early Imāmī Shīʿī theology," although the point is never stated directly. Ultimately, this is not just a failure on the author's part to define the terms of the discussion. By implying that the teachings of the Imams *are* Imāmī Shīʿī theology, he adopts a normative theological view, which treats of the opinions of the Imams as true theology, which their followers either succeeded or failed to successfully internalize. This, instead of looking at theology as a historical, dynamic, and evolving system.

Now, to show the "unambiguous affirmation of the primacy of reason," Madelung uses the first section of the first volume of *al-Kāfī*, one of the authoritative Shīʿī *ḥadīth* compilations by al-Kulaynī (d. ca. 329/941). It is entitled "The Book of Intellect and Ignorance" (*Kitāb al-ʿAql wa l-Jahl*), and according to him, it "renders highest praise to reason and rationality."[94] In confirmation, Madelung cites just four *ḥadīth* from the first volume of al-Kulaynī's *al-Kāfī*. Only one of these defines somewhat what it means by intellect – something with which people recognize God, His creation, and distinguish good from evil. The other three simply praise it. But even the *ḥadīth* that does define intellect does not make clear what kind of intellect it is, and what types of operations it uses to arrive at the knowledge of God. There is certainly no mention of the rationality that the author speaks of.[95] Nor do the remaining several dozen *ḥadīth* comprising this section of *al-Kāfī* speak of the type of rationalist discourse found in Muʿtazilī sources. In fact, one *ḥadīth* speaks of intelligence and its armies in openly superhuman terms, presenting it as the first of the spiritual entities created by God.[96] Yet Madelung, with the wave of a hand and without citing any evidence, dismisses the argument of some "modern historians of Imāmī thought" that these intellect and reason are superhuman, pushing it outside the pale of mainstream Imāmī Shīʿī theology:

> While such belief in a superhuman intelligence of the Imams may have been common among the extremist Shiʿa (*ghulāt*), the teaching of the Imams as presented by al-Kulaynī did not envisage the existence of a higher reason above "mere human reason."[97]

93. Madelung 2014, 367.
94. Madelung 2014, 466.
95. al-Kulaynī (d. 329/941), *al-Kāfī*, 1:53–73.
96. al-Kulaynī, *al-Kāfī*, 1:64–66.
97. Madelung 2014, 267.

Once again, the troublesome *ghulāt* are said to uphold views that deviate from the teaching of the Imams. Of course, to accept that these are *the teaching of the Imams*, we must grant that the handful of *ḥadīth* cherrypicked by Madelung from the work of just one among many early Shīʿī compilers are indeed authentically reported from the words of the Imams. We must also grant, furthermore, that the countless *ḥadīth* presenting alternative (sometimes "heretical") ideas relating to intellect and other issues, found in the work of the selfsame al-Kulaynī and others, are only *falsely* attributed to them.[98] There is abundant evidence of just such views in the Shīʿī *ḥadīth* corpus.[99]

Apart from speculations about the essential Shīʿī position on reason, Madelung's discussion includes, for example, the statement that "Imāmī theology ... fully agreed with the Muʿtazilī thesis that God's justice requires that His reward and punishment must be based on responsibility, capability (*istiṭāʿa*) and free choice of the human agents."[100] A large number of *ḥadīth*, meanwhile, articulate an alternative worldview.[101]

The historical study of *ḥadīth*, the so-called *isnād*-cum-*matn* analysis, has now a rather long history in Islamic studies. Madelung, however, simply assumes that the *ḥadīth* he has selected for his purposes are authentic, presenting them as the very words of one or another of the Imams, something he does elsewhere as well.[102] The existence of alternative views attributed to the very same or other Imams in the very same or other compilations is simply passed over in silence. The stories Madelung cites are assumed to represent *the* words of the Imams, and the theological view of *all* the Imams are assumed to be largely the same.[103]

Influence and Contamination

Outside the circles of the "orthodox," Imāmī Shīʿism, systems of thought are likewise treated as essential entities, which largely lead an insular existence and are sometimes contaminated through contact with one another. For example, in his discussion of the history of an early Ismaili source, *Kitāb al-Kashf*, Heinz Halm notes the existence in it of several elements from an-

98. For a similarly uncritical approach to use of *ḥadīth* in trying to determine what the Imams have said, see Dakake 2006, 335.

99. Amir-Moezzi 1994, 6–13; Amir-Moezzi 2011, 193–210.

100. Madelung 2014, 472.

101. E.g., Dakake 2007, 141–145.

102. Madelung 2014a, 459

103. The problematic nature of such an approach is further compounded by the possibility of censorship that classical Islamic texts may have undergone through centuries.

other tradition. One such element is, for example, the idea of reincarnation, abundantly documented in the teachings of the *ghulāt*. Halm's conclusion is that initially, the chapters of the Ismāʿīlī text where these foreign elements are found were authored by the *ghulāt*, and persisted "despite an Ismāʿīlī redaction" (*trotz der ismailitischen Redaktion*).[104] This conclusion reflects Halm's assumption that the teachings of the Ismāʿīlīs and the *ghulāt* each possessed a number of distinct, essential qualities. For example, he notes that "the Ismāʿīlīs firmly reject reincarnation" (*die Ismāʿīlīya die Seelenwanderung strikt verwirft*),[105] citing a passage from the work of one author, al-Kirmānī, to that effect, despite the rather well-documented evidence that some Ismāʿīlīs did believe in *tanāsukh*.[106] Ultimately, I disagree with Halm's analysis not because there have been Ismāʿīlīs who, despite his statement, believed in it. Rather, his assumption of the essential qualities of one branch of Shīʿism or another have lead him to conclude that the only reason why the elements considered to belong to one group exist in the text of another is that these are the remnants of the teachings of one tradition in the text of another, the result of mingling or contamination. A closer, more discursively attuned reading reveals, however, that the references to the transmigration of souls and some other *ghulāt* teachings are not the result of an unsuccessfully erased borrowing from, but polemic against, the *ghulāt*.[107]

"Influence" is not always described in such neutral terms. Thought deemed "heretical," permeating either just Shīʿism or Islam in general, is at times quite directly seen as a negative impact or even a disease, from which orthodox forms of Islam have tried to rid themselves – sometimes successfully, sometimes not. This is another instance where the hegemonic positions of Muslim orthodoxy are uncritically reproduced. One category which scholars use to describe the teachings of the *ghulāt*, without much elaboration, is "Gnosticism."[108] For example, in his book entitled *Die islamische Gnosis*, Heinz Halm writes that early Islam had to contend with the penetration of Gnostic elements under an Islamic guise, which tried to alter the teaching of the Qurʾān and to give it a distinctly Gnostic meaning. The groups that arose as a result of this onslaught of Gnosticism were the

104. Halm 1978, 150, also 165.

105. Halm 1978, 150.

106. al-ʿUmarī (d. ca. 749/1349), *Masālik al-abṣār*, 77–78; Landolt 2001, 77; cf. Walker 1993, 98–99; de Smet 2013, 77–108.

107. I discuss these passages in my article, Asatryan 2019.

108. E.g. Turner 2006, 185, who writes that "messianism and gnosticism ... were ever present in *ghālī* thought"; cf. also Tucker 2008, 136, speaking of a "Gnostic character"; Lapidus 2014, 139, writing that the defeat of al-Mukhtār's uprising "prompted a turn to gnosticism," and that Gnosticism "generated a large number of Shiʿi sects."

Shīʿī *ghulāt* and the Ismāʿīlīs. These elements were decidedly foreign, and the young Islam had initially no developed theology to counter this penetration.[109] This interaction between foreign and authentically Islamic teachings is described almost as the interaction between biological organisms, or an organism and a disease, to which the former may either resist or may not.

Patricia Crone speaks of the category of "Gnosticism" in much more directly biological terms. She writes of it as a positively established type of religiosity that exists across various religious traditions. She describes it as a "virus" or a "code," which can attack any established form of religion and "subvert it to its ends." After being "rampant" in Iraq, it was "picked up" by Muslims, who, according to her narrative, were the Shīʿī *ghulāt*.[110] The category "Gnosticism" is not unproblematic already with regard to its original use in reference to the early Christian milieu.[111] But Crone does not acknowledge this, and even broadens the scope of its use, creating an entire "type" of religiosity that can exist across religions. Then – like an individual with one's own volition and nefarious designs – it is said to subvert them for its purposes. For what *purposes* and why *subvert*, and what this subversion entails, we never learn.

A biological metaphor is found in Tucker's account of the *ghulāt*'s history. He claims that in the teaching of early Shīʿī "extremist" and rebel Mughīra b. Saʿīd (d. ca. 119/737) one may see the "germ" of "revolutionary violence later associated with the terrorist wing of the *Nizārīs*."[112] This metaphor comes with an added assumption that certain ideas have decided control over people's motives and actions. Using metaphors in historical narratives is not a problem in itself, as long as the metaphorical sense is laid bare and the actual implications of the term are made clear. Here, however, the word "germ" is only a metaphor in a very limited sense, for this passage implies that indeed, as with a real germ, the idea of violence was sown in Islamic thought by Mughīra, and that it came to full bloom in the practices of the Nizaris.

This allegory may indicate several things, none of which is historically plausible, (if we grant, of course, that individuals and groups resort to violence *not* for gaining resources, for political influence, because of personal conflicts, and other mundane reasons, but solely because they have been somehow impacted by the violent ideas of an earlier group). First, it

109. Halm 1981, 10–11, 14–15.
110. Crone 2012, 80–82.
111. Williams 1996; Burns 2018; King 2003.
112. Tucker 2008, 70.

indicates that the Nizaris somehow learned about the violent practices of Mughīra and, inspired by them, decided to try them out. Second, it indicates that the Nizaris could *only* learn about the violent ideas from a Muslim (presumably because they were Muslim and Mughīra was Muslim). The third conclusion seems the most speculative, but Tucker's essentialist language[113] suggests just such a view, namely, that once having "entered" Islam, religious ideas somehow become part of the general Islamic lore across time and across space. Thus, Tucker sees no need to show the concrete material itineraries – texts, codices, roads, people – through which ideas get from one person to another, from Mughīra to the Nizaris. The final implication of Tucker's statement is the most ideological. How do we know that the violence perpetrated by the "terrorist wing of the *Nizārīs*" comes from the germ sown by Mughīra and not, say, the 'Abbasid armies, the Seljuks, or the Daylamīs – all of whom were much closer at hand? My hunch is that, because for Tucker they both were "heretics," and "Shī'ī" heretics at that, they were somehow similar.[114]

Sameness

Finally, ideas are assumed not only to sow seeds that germinate centuries later, but they are said to persist through time, identical and unchanged. Writing about the introduction of Ṣūfī ideas into Shī'ī philosophical thought, Hossein Modarressi notes that the resultant notion of the Imams' existential authority (*al-wilāya al-takwīniyya*) "was virtually the same as the Mufawwiḍa's cosmological theory on the authority of the 'first creature' or the 'perfect man' in the creation and supervision of the world." And those who have supported the concept to its full logical conclusion "must be regarded as the true heirs to the Mufawwiḍa ... because their doctrines are identical."[115] The problem with this statement is positing the identity of two ideas, articulated in two different sets of texts, centuries apart, in completely different intellectual, religious, political, cultural environments. The polemical intent of Modarressi's passage,[116] to use Sajjad Rizvi's words, is quite clear.

113. Noting, for example, that the doctrines of the early *ghulāt* rebel groups were "destined to have a lasting influence upon groups all the way to the present," Tucker 2008, xv.

114. I note Tucker's problematic use of "terrorist" below.

115. Modarressi 1993, 49.

116. Rizvi 2014, 394.

Shīʿism in History

> It is more productive to think in terms of what Muslims did than in terms of what Islam did ...[117]

In his *En Islam Iranien*, Henri Corbin famously criticized the historical study of Shīʿism. Instead, he advocated for a phenomenological approach, which would focus on the way religion is experienced by the faithful themselves, thereby allowing us to discover its transhistorical essence.[118] This view of a substance inherent in Shīʿī history which remains the same across time has been expressed in scholarship in various degrees of explicitness.

As I discussed above, scholars have viewed Shīʿism as a single community with a "mainstream" with firm boundaries, which were sometimes disturbed by various heretical groups. They have also assigned some essential ideas both to this mainstream and to the heretics, and have posited that the former were sometimes contaminated by the latter, but largely kept their essential distinctiveness. This has led the scholars to assign to Shīʿism an essential substance whose history is an unbroken continuity. Sometimes the features of this essence are described without recourse to the passage of time. But even when time comes into the picture, their history is written up as a coherent story, with a beginning and an end almost naturally given, with its heroes and villains, its crises and reliefs, where the transhistorical essence is now activated, now goes dormant, and now raises its head again. A well-made story, to use Hayden White's phrase, "with central subjects, proper beginnings, middles, and ends, and a coherence that permits to us to see 'the end' in every beginning."[119]

Shīʿism is thus treated as an individual, with a life-history of one's own who persists, along with his essential characteristics, throughout centuries. In the process, the passage of time loses importance, and scholars frequently discuss various historical stages of Shīʿism as if it is the same thing throughout. Following this logic, they bring examples from one historical era to illustrate a point relating to another, or use the atemporal present tense to speak about Shīʿism in general. As in the discussions of "community" and "thought," such a story simply reproduces the discourses of reigning orthodoxy, and adds nothing to our understanding of the dynamics of historical continuity and change in religious traditions.

But this is not the whole problem. A questionable historiographic trope,

117. Morony 2005, 6.
118. Corbin 1971, xvi –xix, 44, 222; for a study of Corbin and his intellectual milieu, see Wasserstrom 1999.
119. White 1987, 24.

abundantly found in several authoritative accounts of Shīʿī history, is summarized in Hayden White's last phrase – seeing the end in the beginning. Namely, this refers to writing history in a manner that suggests only one pre-ordained roadmap for Shīʿism's progress, which various crises and villains have tried to distort to no avail. It is implicitly or explicitly assumed that many of the events and processes that have taken place had to take place of necessity.

The most ahistorical of modern writings on Shīʿism is perhaps Takim's discussion of what he calls "the Shīʿī holy man"[120] (preceded by an equally ahistorical discussion of the Ṣūfī holy man[121]). The discussion is written in the atemporal present tense. For example, the author notes that "The *wilāya* enables the imam to provide salvation to his followers...," or that "Shīʿism posits the spiritual authority of the imam to be predicated on two main features...."[122] Indeed, the characteristics of the Shīʿī holy man are described as if they do not change over time. Thus, in his (rarely documented) speculations about this or that characteristic of Shīʿī holy men, he cites sources ranging from Shīʿī *ḥadīth* recorded in the early centuries of Islam, to the collections of sermons attributed to Imam ʿAlī compiled in the tenth century, to a twentieth- century guide to pilgrimages. [123] In citing the latter, the author notes that it "epitomizes the genre of salutations offered to the Imams,"[124] with no reference to time or place, then cites a twentieth-century Shīʿī jurist's words to the effect that "those buried in Najaf will not be punished in the grave."[125] Any attempt to historically contextualize and discursively analyze such statements is missing, and every now and then, the author offers overtly theological positions.[126]

120. Takim 2006, 76.

121. Takim 2006, 37–56.

122. Takim 2006, 57.

123. The book is al-Sayyid Husayn Talib's *Guide to Ziyarat: Selected Supplications*, which was translated by Takim and published in English in 2000. I did not have access to the book itself, but the following website provides information about the book's first appearance: http://khatoons.com/guide-to-ziyarat-selected-supplications-iraq-iran-and-syria.html.

124. Takim 2006, 65.

125. Takim 2006, 67.

126. He speaks of the "competence and special understanding" of the Imams' disciples, or of the transfer of the Imams' supernatural attributes to their disciples. In his discussion of the characteristics of the holy man in Islam, he notes this: "Extraordinary powers, together with the inability of the laity to experience the numinous directly, mean that the elements of awe, fascination, and captivation that ensue from a direct experience of the numinous are transferred to the holy man. This is because the mediation and extraordinary powers of the holy man enable ordinary people to experience something of the awe and majesty of the numinous in him. In many instances, people are captivated and inexorably drawn to the holy man himself since he becomes the vehicle for experiencing the numinous," Takim 2006, 40, 90, 135.

Jafri explicitly speaks of the idea of the linear continuity of Shīʿī history in his *The Origins and Early Development of Shiʿa Islam*:

> The history of a people of every branch, be it political, cultural, religious, or constitutional, is an unbroken continuity. No religious or political organization nor any particular viewpoint within a religious tradition can be properly understood without due reference to its first tangible appearance.[127]

True to this principle, Jafri speaks of the "dormancy" in the history of Shīʿī Islam during the period of Abū Bakr's and ʿUmar's caliphates. This presupposes that, indeed, there is an unbroken continuity of Shīʿism between ʿAlī's lifetime and its later manifestations, and that, like a biological organism, it is at times dormant and at times wakes up – a trope familiar from discourse on the history of modern nations.[128]

Sachedina and Modarressi offer similarly teleological accounts of Shīʿī history, viewing it as an unbroken line whose itinerary has been virtually predestined, and using a fair amount of theologizing in the meantime. Like Takim, the former frequently uses the atemporal present and now refers to the Shīʿītes or Imāmī Shīʿītes, now to Shīʿism, now to the undefined "Shīʿī piety" and the "Imamite spiritual edifice,"[129] or uses the generalizing adjective "Shīʿī," with no reference to the passage of time, historical circumstance, social context, or to real human beings. For example, he writes:

> al-Mahdi's rule personifies the chiliastic vision of *the Shiʿites*, who *believe* that all their dreams will come true 'when God will place his ... hand on the heads of the people, through which He will bring their intellects together'. The *Shiʿites will*, as a result of this blessing, be able to use the accumulated experience of mankind to remove imperfections in their society.[130] (emphases mine)

Alongside treating Shīʿism and Shīʿīs as a transhistorical essence, the author speaks of Shīʿī history as a story with a single possible ending which has been "destined"[131] from the outset. Despite the efforts of its inner enemies, that is, the heretics,[132] or its external enemies, that is, the various inimical dynasties,[133] Imāmī religion nevertheless survives into the present

127. Jafri 2006, 27.
128. Anderson 1991, 195.
129. Sachedina 1981, 13, 173, 174, 180–183.
130. Sachedina 1981, 173–174.
131. Sachedina 1981, 181.
132. Sachedina 1981, 98.
133. Sachedina 1981, 181.

time. Once again, blaming the various internal enemies for trying to subvert, or indeed destroy, Shīᶜī religion, reflects a thinly veiled recycling of an insider, hegemonic discourse presupposing only one possible *true* form for Shīᶜism.

Elsewhere, Sachedina is much more open about his theological commitments. He writes about the establishment of a "spiritual link in the lives of the Imamites," then discusses the Shīᶜī community's "historical responsibility of establishing a true Islamic rule." He concludes the book with a sentence openly implying the special role of the Hidden Imam, noting that his deputyship, "direct or indirect, provided the crucial guardianship of [the Shīᶜī] community."[134]

In Modarressi's account, the predestinarian views of Shīᶜī history are mixed with openly theological positions. Thus on the one hand, the author writes in a way suggesting that the later history of Imāmī Shīᶜism was inherent in the earlier period. On the other, he supports this with statements that suggest active theological commitment to the truth of the Imāmī Shīᶜī doctrine. The entire story of Shīᶜism is presented as the struggle of orthodox Shīᶜism against various detractors in the form of heretics, who unsuccessfully try to introduce incorrect elements into its teaching. In the meantime, whenever the opinions of the community regarding the leadership or certain theological positions vary, the author characterizes them as a "crisis" (note the title of his book), "chaos," or "turmoil."[135] Implicit here is the notion that there can be only one correct position on matters of leadership or theology.

Modarressi also implies that Shīᶜī history could only unfold the way it did. For example, he writes:

> When viewed from a distance, the history of the Imāmate from the ascension of Ḥasan al-ᶜAskarī through the Minor Occultation seems to have been *a period of preparation* for the future transformation, an intermediary state in which the Imāmite community evolved procedures for solving its doctrinal and legal problems without the authority of a present Imām.[136] (emphasis mine)

The passage suggests, without specifying how, that the community somehow sensed the impending disappearance of Muḥammad al-Mahdī and its future without a present Imam. Elsewhere, in a much more openly theological passage, he attributes prescience not to the community as a whole,

134. Sachedina 1981, 183.
135. Modarressi 1993, vii, 60, 76.
136. Modarressi 1993, 70.

but just to the Imam. He writes that the eleventh Imam Ḥasan al-ʿAskarī changed his style in answering legal questions "[c]learly for the purpose of preparing the community for the situation it was going to experience in the imminent future."[137]

Modarressi's theological commitments come to the fore in several other passages as well. For example, he tries to justify the excessive spending of one of the Imam's associates in the face of criticisms he had received by noting that common people were unable to understand "the divine interest behind the Imām's decisions."[138] And explaining the introduction of the non-Imāmī concept of *mahdī* into Shīʿī circles, he openly states that it is possible that the concept was "revealed by God to the Prophet and via him to the Imāms."[139]

In narrating the victorious march of orthodox Imāmism, the author openly takes sides. For example, at one point he writes about the "doctrinal turmoil" that the community could experience if left without a living Imam. "Fortunately," he continues with relief, the twelfth Imam was born and the turmoil was avoided. The conclusion to the story of occultation is described in rather triumphant and theologically committed terms. Thanks to the circulation of certain *ḥadīth*, doubts and uncertainties regarding the "*truth* of Twelver Shīʿism doctrine" in the community dissipated (emphasis mine). All of this, thanks to the "hard work" of "faithful" and "courageous" Imāmī transmitters of *ḥadīth*.[140]

As I tried to show above, treatments of Shīʿism in history commit the fallacy of suggesting that the story was destined to unfold the way it did. They also once again reproduce reigning discourse about the correctness of the orthodox, Imāmī Shīʿism. In doing this, scholars describe every multiplicity of opinion within the Shīʿī community as a "crisis" or "chaos," and every dissenting voice as a "heresy," ready to "destroy" or "uproot" the only possible, true version of religion.[141] And the eventual victory of the dominant school of Shīʿism is celebrated as its survival despite the vicissitudes of time and the detractions of its enemies.

137. Modarressi 1993, 69.
138. Modarressi 1993, 67.
139. Modarressi 1993, 89n195.
140. Modarressi 1993, 105.
141. For these formulations see, Modarressi 1993, vii et passim; Sachedina 1981, 98.

Philology, Theory, History: Moving Forward

> A gestural inclusion that seems to welcome theory (usually offered in the preface or introduction or footnotes to an empirical study) only to ignore its implications in the work that follows.[142]

> Without an anchor in empirics and philosophically sophisticated methods of analysis, theorizing in the study of religion risks degenerating into fictionalizing and omphaloskepsis.[143]

The four tropes found in scholarship on early Shīᶜism – community, heresy, thought, and teleological history – all reflect a distinctive insider approach. They take at face-value heresiographic classifications of Islam into sects and groups, and privilege those that have attained the status of orthodoxy. Within the groups, they privilege the views of those with influence above the views of those without. In what follows, I would like to suggest alternative ways to studying these four themes. On the one hand, these comprise a more critical and thorough study of the historical record, and on the other, greater engagement with recent advances in the social sciences, religious studies, and studies of discourse. Using insights from these fields of knowledge in historical studies – either derisively or smugly (but seldom neutrally) called by the term "theory" – has caused much controversy. Let me, therefore, say a few words about my understanding of how "theory" and study of the historical record could be approached, with special reference to the materials covered in my essay.

In historical studies, the use of what is called "theory" is at times viewed with suspicion and regarded as a useless pastime as opposed to the solid study of primary sources.[144] Proponents and opponents of the use of theory have offered various critiques of one another.[145] On the one hand, the former charge that some scholars use the uncritical application of "theory" as a license for groundless philosophizing, without due attention to the prima-

142. Kleinberg et al. 2018, 7.

143. Blum 2017, 21.

144. An articulation of this trend is, for example, Marwick 1995.

145. E.g. White 1987; Clark 2004; most recently, Kleinberg et. al. 2018. On the usefulness of anthropological insights in the study of history, see Davis 1981; Robert Darnton's preface to the revised edition of his *The Great Cat Massacre* is another interesting, if brief, meditation on the subject, see Darnton 1984, xv-xix. Needless to say, what I here call "proponents of theory" and its "opponents" are not homogeneous schools of thought, each with a unified set of methods and presuppositions.

ry sources.[146] The latter, among other things, charge traditional historians (and here I include scholars of Islam and of religion in general) of taking the categories of their analysis for granted (such as gender, class, religion, magic, civilization, myth[147]), or of falling prey to the lure of a well-ordered narrative.[148] The materials I surveyed demonstrate that if one uncritically uses theory, by merely "stuffing" the material of the primary sources into a theoretical framework adopted without much reflection, this may lead to a similar situation as does abstention from theory in favor of what may appear as meticulous study of primary sources. For example, Liyakat Takim's study, ostensibly based on Weber's sociology of religion, is as full of theological pre-commitments, an uncritical use of various categories of analysis (for example, "holy man"), and ahistorical essentializing language, as any of the other works surveyed which do not cite any "theory." Good examples are Sachedina's book, essentially based on the study of primary sources, or the much more richly primary-source based (visually at least, in the form of thick footnotes) *Crisis and Consolidation* by Modarressi.

Ultimately, no theory should be used as a mathematical formula or as a mold into which data may be stuffed. As the above examples show, neither theory nor the study of primary sources alone, nor both together, have cognitive value if done uncritically and carelessly. Citing what counts as "theory" is no license to advance claims that are not supported through the careful study of the historical record.[149] Nor is knowledge of the past readily apparent in the primary sources.

This should not, of course, lead us to methodological agnosticism. Instead, it should make us humbler in our claims, making us think twice before generalizing what we know of just one person onto an entire "community," or extrapolating the content of one text onto an entire "tradition." As I see it, theoretically informed study of history and religion comprises a more careful reading of the primary sources, and a more careful, and modest in its claims, interpretation of the historical data. This should comprise, among other things, a careful consideration of one's analytical categories and units

146. E.g. Donner 2013, 15 –16; LaCapra 2004, 270.

147. E.g. Kleinberg et al. 2018; Smith 2004; McCutcheon 1997; Lincoln 1999.

148. Megill 2007, 66, 77; Roberts 1996; White 1987.

149. For a discussion of the pitfalls of overemphasis on theory, see Blum 2017, where he insightfully notes that theory "must be restrained in order to maintain its intellectual integrity" (21). He further writes that "[a]cknowlgement of the fact that theory does not produce an exact representation of the world that it seeks to explain does not imply that the scholar enjoys unconstrained poetic license, but that she is faced with a continual task of revision and refinement" (24). For a scathing critique of what Blum calls "unconstrained poetic license," see Donner 2013, 15–16; see also the useful discussion in Morony 2005, 12 –13, on the limits of the applicability of social-scientific theory in studying history; cf. also LaCapra 2004, 261.

of analysis.[150] For our purposes, these categories and units are "community," "heresy," "thought," and the image of how history unfolds. So let me dwell on each separately, and show how they could be, or have been, studied more fruitfully.

The main premise upon which the discussion of "community" is based is the existence of social divisions along doctrinal lines. The result of such imaginary divisions are some nebulous communities, assumed to function as self-contained units, and attributed uniformity of doctrine. Because such units are ill-defined, scholars treat them as they wish, now as communities with firm boundaries, now as more malleable entities. The assumption in both is that all members of said unit have some kind of a consensus about religious doctrine. And even when there is no consensus, those who fall outside of what is adjudged as "mainstream" are explained away as deviants. Two fallacies are apparent in such an approach. A careless reading of the historical record, which leads to overgeneralization, and normative assumptions about what is right and wrong.

I do not wish to spend time on the latter, as it is apparent to most of us scholars of history and religion that we are not here to judge who is the right type of Muslim and who is not. I would like to focus on the first point instead. Most of the information about certain "communities" in early Islamic times, whether religious, ethnic, or other, relies on the classifications found in the primary sources, chiefly heresiographies, but also historical chronicles and the like. These sources usually tell us that so-and-so was a Shīʿī or a Khārijī, or that so-and-so had a number of followers who shared his beliefs. Following their lead, scholars uncritically reproduce these categories, then write about them as if they were self-sufficient entities. Several untested assumptions are apparent here: first, that the followers of each sectarian leader shared his beliefs; second, that each group of people was held together by these shared beliefs first and foremost; and third, that the people who followed the person and shared his beliefs formed some kind of a social entity. Exactly what kind of entity is rarely defined, but scholarly accounts treat them as units with clearly defined boundaries.

A more critical approach to the primary sources, coupled with studies in discourse and related fields caution us to approach ready-made, socially and doctrinally unified categories primarily as constructions of their authors – heresiographers, theologians, or chroniclers. Discourse analysis teaches us that descriptions of the world and classifications of people and objects does not present a mirror image of the world, but often actively constructs a ver-

150. For a discussion of what is called "reflexivity" in social sciences, see Somers 1999, 132–135.

sion of it.[151] These versions of reality, moreover, are constructed in such a way as to advance the interests of the writer or his group. Thus, even when a heresiographer or a chronicler classifies a certain number of people as professing a certain sectarian identity, this does not automatically mean that there was a separate group of people, a "community," to whom this refers. And when he writes of them as immoral and deviant heretics, we may be almost sure that he is advancing his own version of orthodoxy and blaming them as deviants. Lumping people into categories is a useful tool to categorize and to exclude.

Sometimes heresiographers simply invented sects, by adding to the name of their alleged founder the Arabic suffix *-iyya*.[152] A quite typical example of a collection of such "*-iyya*"s is the heresiography by medieval author Muḥammad b. Saʿd al-Azdī al-Qalḥatī, entitled *Kitāb al-Kashf wa l-bayān fī sharḥ iftirāq al-firaq wa l-adyān*. Thus, alongside such broad categories as the Imāmiyya, referring to the Imāmīs, he lists much smaller units such as the Bayāniyya or the Manṣūriyya. On the other hand, he attaches *-iyya* to the names of Shīʿī theologians Hishām b. al-Ḥakam, creating a Hishāmiyya, or to the name of Nuʿmān al-Aḥwal, known as Ṣāḥib al-Ṭāq, creating a Nuʿmāniyya. Regardless of whether some of these groups existed or not (the Imāmiyya and the Manṣūriyya certainly did), these three types of *-iyya*'s refer to three different categories of groups. In the first case, it refers to a large number of people holding more or less uniform beliefs over a long period of time, and (supposedly) unified by these beliefs and a certain group identity. In the second case, it refers to the followers of a rebel who (allegedly) shared his beliefs, but who, after his demise most probably ceased their existence as a separate group. And in the third case, it refers to the friends or followers (*aṣḥāb*) of a certain character who was known for his theological views, but who most likely did not form any kind of social unit comparable to the Imāmīyya or the Manṣūriyya.[153]

Furthermore, even when a group of people who followed a certain sectarian individual did exist, what we mean by "group" is lightyears from clear. Take the example of any of the leaders of the *ghulāt* uprisings that

151. Potter 1996 studies the uses of discursive language in live conversation, but many of his arguments are very pertinent to our material; an extremely broad range of discursive practices, including ones found in premodern texts, are studied by Bruce Lincoln in Lincoln 2014 and Lincoln 2012.

152. Lewinstein 1992, 76; I am grateful to Adam Gaiser for drawing my attention to this work.

153. On *Kitāb al-Kashf wa l-Bayān*, see van Ess 2011, 960–970. I am grateful to Majid Daneshgar for bringing my attention to this text, and for kindly sending me a scanned copy of the manuscript GMS 97, kept in the Sir George Grey Special Collections, Auckland Libraries, New Zealand.

took place in the first half of the eighth century, the Khaṭṭābiyya (lead by Abū l-Khaṭṭāb al-Asadī), the Mughīriyya (lead by Mughīra), or the Bayāniyya (lead by Bayān b. Samᶜān). Each of these individuals espoused a version of the beliefs of the *ghulāt*, and had a number of people who followed him. Each of these *-iyya*'s could be called a group in a very conventional sense, however. While we know what its leader professed, we have a very vague idea about the beliefs of his followers. And even when the sources do report on the beliefs of the followers as well (such as those of the Khaṭṭābiyya), we may never be sure whether the heresiographer is simply extrapolating the beliefs of the leader onto the entire group of people who followed him, or whether all or some of them did indeed believe in what their leader believed. Furthermore, the followers of each of these leaders may have joined them for any number of reasons – social, economic, or other – much more mundane than the sharing of common beliefs (although one does not rule this out too).[154] But scholars take the words of heresiographies and other sources at face value, implying frequently that the sole reason for the unity of a group was their religious doctrine.[155]

Now for the notion of the social unity of a group. The followers of the leaders noted above could have joined them for just a short period, for a number of personal reasons, and religious conviction need not have been the primary one. Conversely, sharing a common set of beliefs with a large group of people does not necessarily indicate the existence of a distinct social entity. Indeed, there is evidence showing that people of various convictions, some "heretical" some "orthodox," freely mixed with each other in eighth-century Kufa.[156]

When moving on to larger units, such as the "Shīᶜī community" as a whole (or even to Muslims, Christians, Jews, etc.[157]), similar problems persist, as the existence of firm social boundaries between groups professing

154. A good example of such an invented sect is the "Mufaḍḍaliyya," called after the name of its alleged founder Mufaḍḍal al-Juᶜfī. Several partially overlapping and brief reports about them are preserved in the works of al-Ashᶜarī, *Maqālāt*, 12; al-Baghdādī (d. ca. 429/1037), *Farq*, 249–250; al-Isfarāyinī (d. ca. 471/1078–9), *Tabṣīr*, 112; al-Shahrastānī (first half of the sixth/twelfth century), *Milal*, 1:122–123; and Abū Tammām (fl. fourth-tenth century), *al-Shajara*, 122–123. Yet the numerous accounts about Mufaḍḍal found in *ḥadīth* sources betray no trace of the existence of a group of people who could conceivably be called a sect. The accounts are too many to list; for a discussion, see Asatryan 2017, 46–61.

155. Najam Haider cautions against such an approach in Haider 2011, 229 and Haider 2018. For an extremely insightful discussion of early Islamic sectarianism in general, see Gaiser 2017, 68–73. In particular, Gaiser notes that "sect identification remains but one aspect of a larger, and malleable, patchwork of individual and group identifications that might include nationality, race, ethnicity, language, profession, family, and even geography." (69).

156. See e.g. Amir-Moezzi 2011, 218–219; Asatryan 2017, 55–60.

157. Hughes 2017; Morony 1974; Sizgorich 2009.

differing religious beliefs is far from established. As I discussed above, it is assumed that already during the lifetime of the Imams, there was a distinct Shīʿī community with some degree of doctrinal uniformity. Those who fell outside of it are viewed as "splits." Once again, the two unexamined assumptions emerge: consensus about religious belief on the one hand, and the notion that those who shared this consensus were a distinct social entity. We do have information about the religious teachings of the Shīʿīs (*some* Shīʿīs) in those times in the form of *ḥadīth*, but they are very diverse, which reflects multiplicity of doctrine during the time of the Imams. Yet scholars pick one set of beliefs found in these accounts and claim that they were shared by the entire community. Two fallacies are apparent here, both privileging the positions of "orthodoxy" and prestige: a selective reading of the primary sources, and the extrapolation of the ideas of a limited number of individuals onto the entire community. The first fallacy follows the lead of later standards of orthodoxy, discarding everything that later heresiographs viewed as heretical. And the second one privileges those who held the position of influence within the Shīʿī community – namely, those whose accounts survived until our times.

A contemporary example suggests itself. Surely, an attentive observer today may detect that people who call themselves "Muslims" in the West speak many languages, have diverse cultures, wear different types of clothing, and practice and interpret Islam in widely divergent ways. Sometimes they live in closely knit urban communities, sometime they attend the same mosque, sometimes neither. Some are doctors, some are taxi drivers, and one is the mayor of a major European capital. With regard to the main precepts of Islam we see the same diversity, as some Muslims pray and some do not, some fast during Ramadan, while others drink alcohol. Yet if someone in the far future stumbles upon a batch of today's newspapers that discuss these people by using the blanket term "Muslim," he/she may gain the impression of a homogeneous social group with uniform practices and beliefs, and with strictly delineated boundaries. Conversely, if one finds a promotional booklet disseminated by a mosque in today's Canada, one may gain the impression that all that Muslims think about – all of them – are interreligious dialogue or women's rights, whereas this may only reflect the (real or professed) views or concerns of just a few people among the community leaders. The Muslim dentist who happens to attend that mosque may or may not share those ideas, and may have completely different concerns on his mind. I suggest that we should read heresiographies as the informed observer would read today's newspaper, and *ḥadīth* as the booklet disseminated by the mosque.

I should note that I do not rule out the existence of any Shīᶜī groups in early Islamic times which had more or less uniform beliefs, and which functioned as separate social entities. But the existence of such groups should in each case be carefully demonstrated based on a minute study of the historical evidence and cannot be simply assumed based on presumably shared beliefs. Furthermore, the scholar should lay bare the nature and shortcomings of the primary sources she/he uses. One book which departs from the uncritical treatment of "groups" in early Islamic history is Najam Haider's *The Origins of the Shīᶜa*, as it meticulously demonstrates the emergence of the earliest Shīᶜī identities, and carefully describes the ways in which such identities were marked, ritual and sacred space.[158] Importantly, while the author does take insights from social-theoretical literature, such as works drawing on Bourdieu's *Distinction*, it does not dominate his narrative. Indeed, all of the arguments are based on a meticulous study of the primary sources.

The problems with the notions of "heresy" and "orthodoxy" stem from presuppositions similar to the above. That the emotive and negative valuation of heresies is a distinctly polemical, heresiographical stance seems evident, but because scholars overtly or implicitly reproduce it time and again, it is worth dwelling upon. It rests on the notion of a unity of the "mainstream," whether doctrinal or social, or both. Put differently, this view presupposes "society as an integrated totality, within which cosmology and social structure support and reflect each other."[159] Alongside, negative meaning is attached to divisions or disagreements over doctrine or leadership, hence any type of disagreement is viewed as a vicious attack on a pristine unity. The polemical accounts aside, the historical record simply does not support such a view. Doctrinal diversity need not indicate social fragmentation, nor is (apparent) doctrinal uniformity an index of social cohesion. And even if such a uniformity is established, it does not mean that all of the members of a certain community willfully accept it. If anything, it indicates a successful imposition of orthodoxy, hence an exercise of power. As noted by Sewell in his discussion of the concept of uniformity in culture, integration is more a matter of the exercise of power rather than the expression of a common ethos, and cultural consensus, even when achieved, "is bound to hide suppressed conflicts and disagreements."[160]

Thus, during Jaᶜfar al-Ṣādiq's lifetime there was a range of views about

158. Haider 2011; for a shorter formulation, see Haider 2018.

159. Asad 1986, 352.

160. Sewell 1999, 53–54; in anthropology, see Vincent Crapanzano's critique of the reification of "Balinese subjectivity at cockfights" in the work of Clifford Geertz (see Crapanzano 1986, 74).

the nature of the Imam's authority, views which later heresiographers classified as either heretical or orthodox. Yet the Imam had no problem having followers and close associates among holders of many. This does not necessarily mean that the Shīʿī community was fragmented. And if it was, the lines of demarcation need not have necessarily followed doctrinal divisions, as Haider shows us.[161] Conversely, the fact that "heretics" such as al-Shalmaghānī were put to gruesome death does not necessarily mean that the Shīʿī community as a whole found their views abhorrent. It simply indicates that they did not get along with the *leadership* of the Shīʿī community.[162] Hence, positing that they were killed because they deviated from the "mainstream" privileges the narrow personal interests of the Shīʿī leadership over the entire community. Once again, scholars give preferential treatment to those in power. Meanwhile, we should keep in mind that heresy and orthodoxy are constructs which reflect configurations of power at one historical point or another, and are not absolute entities or values.[163]

Similarly polemical are the evaluations of some of the actions of the "heretics" as "terrorism" or "magic."[164] Why the *ghulāt*'s violent acts were terrorism and, say, the Fāṭimids' (ultimately successful) military efforts to establish themselves in North Africa were not, is not self-evident. After all, as is all too clear from the contemporary discourse on terrorism, one person's terrorist is another's freedom fighter. It is equally unclear why the *ghulāt*'s attempts to justify their actions are said to indicate their alienation,[165] or anything at all. Hardly anyone would think that the Muslim attempts to frame their conquests as *futūḥ* is a sign of their alienation or some other ill. All entities who commit violence – governments, sects, rebels – valorize theirs and demonize their opponent's. One's own conquest of another's territory is "discovery" or "liberation," and one's own war is "holy." Conversely, the conquest of one's own land is "occupation," and rebellion against one's state is "mutiny" or "terrorism." That many of these discourses are framed in religious terms, as Bruce Lincoln reminds us in his "Theses on Religion and Violence," should cause us no wonder.[166] The same can be said about

161. Haider 2011.

162. Abdulsater 2011, 317–318.

163. In the apt formulation of Asad, "'Heresy' is first and foremost the product of a power process in which *Truth is authorized* and *Error anathematized*," see Asad 1986, 356, which is a detailed discussion of the issue of heresy with regard to medieval European history. See also Asad 2009, 22. For a discussion of a similar classification with regard to Mazdakism in Late Antique Iran, see the excellent article by Rezakhani (2014).

164. The references are noted above, in the section "Heresy."

165. Morony 2005, 502.

166. Lincoln 2006, 93–95; for a penetrating study of religious and other discourses related to violence and conflict in general, see Lincoln 2006.

terming some of the actions of the *ghulāt* as "magic." Jonathan Smith's study of the use of this category in scholarly discourse shows that it is always an uncritical reproduction of indigenous, polemical uses of the term. Like in the case with "terrorism" and "heresy," the opposition "magic" and "religion" is simply an exercise in othering and never a neutral description.[167] The polemical context of the accusations of magic becomes clear in many excerpts from *ghulāt* writings, which refute the accusations of magic leveled against them, and re-describe their own actions as divine miracles.[168]

Just as human collectives are constructed, classified, then treated as individuals or organisms, so is what scholars call "thought" or "theology," a system of religious ideas pertaining to one or another of the abovementioned "communities." The thought of a particular group is assigned a unity and a coherence, and when elements from the teachings of one "community" are found in that of another, one possible solution suggests itself: contamination or influence. Furthermore, just as there are "mainstream" communities and their teachings, there are also "heretical" teachings that try to contaminate the purity of the former.

Scholarship written in the tradition of religious studies, discourse analysis, and intellectual history once again suggests that a much more fruitful approach is to look at individual texts as discourses expressing the desires, fears, aspirations of, as well as pressures on, individual authors,[169] and not as an expression of an essential Imamī-ness, Sunnī-ness, or something else. In the brilliantly simple expression of Peter Burke, in studying texts we must try to understand "who wants whom to remember what, and why."[170] Two discourses produced in seemingly the "same" tradition and expressing seemingly the "same" doctrines may be written with completely different goals in mind, responding to completely different circumstances. For discourses are produced in response to external circumstances such as social pressures, the interests of their authors, as well as other, competing discourses.[171] Anthropological studies of discourse, furthermore, tell us that the configuration of power has a distinct impact on how discourses are formulated.[172]

167. Smith 2014.

168. I study these passages in Asatryan 2017, 84–88.

169. A useful place to start, especially when reading religious texts, is Bruce Lincoln's "How to Read a Religious Text" (Lincoln 2012), along with Lincoln 2014 and other works by the same author; see also Skinner 1969, 37–38, 49–50.

170. Burke 1997, 56. The phrase refers to what he calls "social memory," but keeping this in mind is helpful in studying any type of discourse.

171. Asad 2009, 10; Rose 1999, 228–229; Sewell 1999, 135; Bakhtin, 1987.

172. Scott 1990; for a study of how political persecution impacts the art of writing, see Strauss 1952.

Thus, to point out several "important" common features between one or more texts and a tradition or school, then postulate that these texts belong to it, does not tell us much. Nor are the two iterations of a religious doctrine the "same" – no more than the two different people articulating it are.[173] And none is more "original" than the other. We may grant, of course, that the conventional meaning of "originality" may suggest the degree to which an individual text uses elements not found in its predecessors.[174] However, both the discourse-analytical study of live conversation, and the study of ancient royal inscriptions tell us otherwise. It is frequently the seemingly unimportant details – turns of phrase, logical emphases, uses of vocabulary – that may tell us about the unstated goals and the interests its author tries to advance.[175]

Nor is a study of "foreign" contaminations or influences of one tradition by another, the way it is customarily done in Islamic studies, very informative. Furthermore, positing influence may amount to an ideological stance rather than an analytical procedure. As Hussein Abdulsater shows us, studies of influence frequently establish a hierarchy between the two presumed parties, contrasting them in terms of "originality versus imitation, genuineness versus spuriousness."[176] In the case of scholarship reviewed above, there is a reverse hierarchy, but the ideological implication remains.

Traditionally used approaches reify the tradition or the school on the one hand, and ignore the circumstances of the composition of individual texts, and the goals of the discourses articulated in them on the other. To study a text fruitfully, one ought to learn about the circumstances of its composition, the social position of its author, the amount of power he/she held, the types of pressures he/she experienced, and the interests that were involved. One should also learn about discourses expressed in other texts, which the text in question tries to refute, compete with, or interact with in

173. Skinner 1969, 38.

174. This is apparently the meaning assigned to "original" by Madelung (1970, 27) in his article on "Imamism and Muʿtazilite Theology."

175. In his discussion of conversation analysis, Jonathan Potter notes that it is the seemingly small details of conversation, such as intonation, which do much important "work" in communication, see Potter 1996, 58. Of course, the texts historians of Shīʿism are dealing with are written, hence they lack the specifics of oral delivery. Still, the logic of the argument still holds, as written texts also contain small, seemingly unobtrusive details, which may nevertheless matter in delivering nuances of meaning that are informed by the author's and the (perceived) audience's relations, the power dynamic involved in the situation, and so on. For a minute study of the importance of small details in written sources, in this case, Achemenid royal inscriptions, see Lincoln 2007, 10–11. To make sense of a passage, he writes, "it must be read against others to which it is related, and even the smallest variations in form can contain nuances of great importance."

176. Abdulsater 2017, 6; see also King 2003, 220–223, with regard to the early Christian milieu.

some other ways. In regards to "borrowing," it is true that elements from one text or tradition do find their way into another text or tradition. But to posit influence and be done with the job explains little. First of all, that seemingly the "same" idea is the result of influence and not coincidence has to be carefully established by looking at concrete contacts between individuals, itineraries of texts, and other material ways an idea can travel from one place to another. Secondly, "borrowing" or "mixing" may have extremely revealing political implications which merit exploring, as shown, for example, by Jonathan Smith in his study of Maori myth.[177] Finally, one should take into consideration that the published or manuscript versions of texts that we hold in our hands today have likely undergone a process of censorship throughout the long years of their transmission.[178]

Let me bring two examples of how a contextually attuned reading of a religious text differs from the more traditional one.[179] One is the abovementioned text studied by Heinz Halm, entitled *Kitāb al-Kashf*, one of the earliest Ismaili writings. It seemingly shares several elements with the teachings of the *ghulāt*. Following the logic of reified thought,[180] Halm has concluded that these elements are the remains of an unsuccessfully erased *ghulāt* substratum. A more careful reading, however, reveals that the text represents its

177. Smith 1982.

178. For a study of the main ways in which Islamic texts have been censored, see Daneshgar 2018; for a general discussion of censorship, see Darnton 2014, 229–243.

179. I would like to note several recent works which eschew the reification of religious groups and schools of thought, studying Shīʿī *ḥadīth*, historical narratives, and theology through a historical lens. The broadest in coverage is Najam Haider's *Shīʿī Islam: An Introduction* (2014). Despite being called an introduction, this book raises some important methodological questions regarding how historical and theological discourses produced by various Shīʿī groups could be approached. Haider studies the vision of the past among the main Shīʿī communities in trying to understand the role it plays in constructing each community's vision of itself. Two monographs bring important insights to the study the Shīʿī *ḥadīth* materials. Its shortcomings noted above notwithstanding, Maria Dakake's *Charismatic Community* (2007) convincingly explores the kind of social world they collectively articulate. And Andrew Newman's *Ḥadīth as Discourse between Qum and Baghdad* (2000) examines several early Shīʿī *ḥadīth* compilations, analyzing their content and structure for the work each was doing for the community where it was produced. Two recent monographs, finally, study the period after the occultation of the Twelfth Imam. Hussein Abdulsater's *Shīʿī Doctrine, Muʿtazili Theology* (2017) is a detailed examination of the thought of Shīʿī theologian al-Sharīf al-Murtaḍā (d. ca. 1044). Apart from conducting a minute study of al-Murtaḍā's doctrine, Abdulsater investigates his social and intellectual milieu, and analyzes the ways in which his oeuvre was an attempt to construct an independent Shīʿī identity. And through a study of several biographies of the twelve Imams, Matthew Pierce's *Twelve Infallible Men* (2016) explores the type of communal identity and social ideals their authors were articulating.

180. E.g. his postulation, against ample evidence, that the teaching of metempsychosis is foreign to Ismaili thought, see above.

author's polemic against another discourse, that of the *ghulāt* relating to the transmigration of souls and similar matters.[181] Here is an example of one author trying to distance his group from the beliefs of another, who during the composition of the text were condemned by many Muslims as heretical. The interests of the author are apparent. Another example is the question of Christian elements in Nuṣayrī thought. In his monograph on the Nuṣayrīs, Yaron Friedman discusses at some length these Christian elements in the teachings of the Nuṣayrīs, ultimately to reject Christian influence on Nuṣayrism by positing that the elements that seem Christian are only so on the superficial level, and that overall, Nuṣayrī thought rejected Christianity.[182] In doing this the author makes judgments as to what counts for profound Christian influence and what does not. For example, in studying the text by early Nuṣayrī author Muḥammad b. ʿAlī al-Jillī (d. after 399/1009) entitled *al-Risāla al-masīḥiyya*, which describes the nature of Christ by using both Christian and Muslim imagery, Friedman notes that it may serve to reject the hypothesis of Christian influence on Nuṣayrism. He does not explain why, but the examples that he brings suggest that for him, this "influence" is not Christian enough.[183] In his discussion, the author reifies Christianity, by passing judgment on what is truly Christian and what is not (the apocryphal writings are apparently not). Then he reifies Nuṣayrism, by presenting two authors living a long time apart as representing "Nuṣayrī religion," with no attention to individual circumstance. To present a historically more plausible explanation of how elements resembling Christian teachings can be accounted for when found in Nuṣayrī texts, we should refrain from asking the simplistic question, "did Christianity influence Nuṣayrism – yes or no?" Instead, we should treat individual texts as the creation of individual agents with their distinct interests and circumstances. In the case of al-Jillī, for example, one should explore to the extent possible whether there were Christians in his environment, and what his (or the Nuṣayrī community's) relations with those Christians were.[184] We should further explore the min-

181. I discuss this in detail in Asatryan 2019.

182. Friedman 2012, 225–227.

183. Friedman 2012, 226–227; he also notes that through this operation, the author tried to establish an "*artificial* mystical bond between Nuṣayrism and Christianity" (emphasis mine) implicitly suggesting the existence of *true* mystical bonds between religions.

184. The writings of al-Jillī's near contemporary author al-Ṭabarānī (d. 426/1034–1035) show that at that point, the relations between the Nuṣayrīs (some Nuṣayrīs at any rate) and certain Christians may have been good. Thus in his law manual, he accords the Christians a high value, and another, eleventh-century anonymous epistle discusses why the Christians are closer to being believers than the Jews; see al-Ṭabarānī, *al-Ḥāwī*, 91–92 and id., *Jawhariyya*, 36; *Majmaʿ al-akhbār*, 57.

ute configuration of elements deemed Christian with regard to Muslim ones in his text, to see whether he is trying to establish some type of a hierarchy between the two, or whether he treats them in some other way. And we should examine whether, or how, the types of relations between these elements reflect the relationships between al-Jillī or the Nuṣayrīs with the Christians at that particular moment.[185] Not all of these questions may be answered sufficiently, but instead of leading to undue speculation and generalization, these limitations should be acknowledged.

Earlier I discussed how the vision of history constructed by some scholars suffers either from timeless essentialization, or from an overly teleological linearity, which implies only one possible way in which events and processes could unfold. Hayden White's criticism of creating well-ordered narratives – with clear, as if naturally given beginnings and conclusions, where the end is implicit in the beginning – was noted above. First of all, such narratives give the progression of events the logical coherence it does not have – by making things simply "fall into place."[186] For our purposes there is more, however. In several authoritative histories of Shīᶜism, the seemingly logical march of events is narrated in such a way as to privilege reigning orthodoxy, by viewing just one group of people, the Imāmī or Twelver Shīᶜīs, as its heroes. And among these, furthermore, we only learn about the elites, who stand for everyone else in what is described as the Imāmī community. The powerless or the illiterate are either not mentioned or are assumed to go with the flow. During its march, Imāmism is assailed by various villains – the nebulous "Sunnīs" from the outside, and by the vicious "heretics" from the inside. But it always *inevitably* survives and emerges, strong and victorious.[187]

By uncritically adopting the polemical position of the written sources mostly left by those who have attained the powerful status of orthodoxy, scholars achieve a skewed image of the history of early Shīᶜism. For this approach ignores the dynamic ways in which societies and religious traditions change over time and perpetuates the fiction of an eternally unchanging Islam.

185. Bruce Lincoln's "How to Read a Religious Text" is a brilliant example of a study of a religious text that combines an analysis of historical circumstance with discursive elements of a text, see Lincoln 2012; see also Spiegel 1999; for a discussion of how premodern texts have been, and could be, approached by historians, see Clark 2004, 156–185.

186. Megill 2007, 65–66, see also 77.

187. For a critique of this type of historical narration in the study of Islam, see Al-Azmeh 2007, 49. For a discussion of the problematic nature of the term "Sunnism" in early Islamic history, see Gaiser 2017, 66.

Bibliography

Abdulsater, H. 2011. "Dynamics of Absence: Twelver Shīʿism during the Minor Occultation." *Zeitschrift der deutschen morgenländischen Gesellschaft* 161:305–334.

——. 2017. *Shiʿi Doctrine, Muʿtazili Theology: al-Sharīf al-Murtaḍā and Imami Discourse*. Edinburgh.

Abū Tammām. 1988. *Kitāb al-Shajara*. Edited by W. Madelung and P. E. Walker as *An Ismaili Heresiography*. Leiden.

Amir-Moezzi, M. A. 1994. *The Divine Guide in Early Shiʿism: The Sources of Esotericism in Islam*. Translated by D. Streight. Albany.

——. 2011. "Knowledge is Power: Interpretations and Implications of the Miracle in Early Imamism." In *The Spirituality of Shiʿi Islam: Beliefs and Practices*, 229–193. London.

—— and C. Jambet. 2014. *Qu'est-ce que le shî'isme?* Paris.

Anderson, B. 1991. *Imagined Communities: Reflections on the Origin and Spread of Nationalism*. London.

Anthony, S. 2018. "Ghulāt (Extremist Shīʿīs)." In *Encyclopaedia of Islam, Three*. 2007. Leiden.

Asad, T. 1986. "Medieval Heresy: An Anthropological View." *Social History* 11.3:345–362.

——. 2009. "The Idea of an Anthropology of Islam." *Qui Parle* 17.2: 1–30.

Asatryan, M. 2014. "Bankers and Politics: The Network of Shiʿi Moneychangers in Eighth-Ninth Century Kufa and their Role in the Shiʿi Community." *Journal of Persianate Studies* 7:1–21.

——. 2017. *Controversies in Formative Shiʿi Islam: The Ghulat Muslims and their Beliefs*. London.

——. 2019. "Early Ismailis and Other Muslims: Polemics and Borrowing in *Kitāb al-Kashf*." In *Intellectual Interactions in the Islamic World: The Ismaili Thread*, edited by O. Mir-Kasimov, 273–298. London.

——. forthcoming. "Of Wine, Sex, and Other Abominations: Accusations of Libertinism in Early Islamic Iraq."

al-Ashʿarī, A. Ḥ. 1929–1933. *Maqālāt al-islāmiyīn*, edited by H. Ritter. Istanbul.

al-Azmeh, A. 2007. *The Times of History: Universal Topics in Islamic Historiography*. Budapest.

——. 2012. "Civilization as a Political Disposition." *Economy and Society* 41.4:501–512.

——. 2014. *The Emergence of Islam in Late Antiquity: Allāh and his People*. Cambridge.

——. 2018. "Paleo-Islam: Transfigurations of Late Antique Religion." In A

Companion to Religion in Late Antiquity, edited by J. Lössl and N. J. Baker-Brian, 345–368. Hoboken, NJ.

al-Baghdādī, ʿA. Q. n.d. *al-Farq bayn al-firaq*. Edited by Muḥammad Muḥī al-Dīn ʿAbd al-Ḥamīd. Cairo.

Bakhtin, M. 1987. "The Problem of Speech Genres." In *Speech Genres and Other Late Essays*, edited by Caryl Emerson and Michael Holquist, 60--102. Austin.

Bausani, A. 2000. *Religion in Iran: From Zoroaster to Baha'ullah*. Translated by J. Marchesi. New York.

Bayhom-Daou, T. 2001. "The Imam's Knowledge and the Quran According to al-Faḍl b. Shādhān al-Nīsābūrī (d. 260 A.H./875 AD)." *Bulletin of the School of Oriental and African Studies* 64.2:188–207.

——. 2003. "Hishām b. al-Ḥakam (d. 179/795) and his Doctrine of the Imām's Knowledge." *Journal of Semitic Studies* 48.1:71–108.

Blum, J. 2017, "On the Restraint of Theory." In *Theory in a Time of Excess*, edited by Aaron Hughes, 21–31. Sheffield.

Buckley, R. 1998. "On the Origins of Shīʿi Ḥadīth." *The Muslim World* 88.2:165–184.

——. 2002. "The Imām Jaʿfar al-Ṣādiq, Abū'l Khaṭṭāb and the Abbasids." *Der Islam* 2002:118–140.

——. 2007. "The Morphology and Significance of Some Imāmī Shīʿite Traditions." *Journal of Semitic Studies* 52.2:301–334.

Burke, P. 1997. "History as Social Memory." In *Varieties of Cultural History*, 43–59. Ithaca.

Burns, D. "Gnosticism, Gnostics, and Gnosis." In *The Gnostic World*, edited by G. Trompf, G. Mikkelsen, and J. Johnson, 9–25. London.

Buyukkara, M. 2000. "The Schism in the Party of Mūsā al-Kāẓim and the Emergence of the Wāqifa." *Arabica* 47.1:78–99.

Clark, E. 2004. *History, Theory, Text: Historians and the Linguistic Turn*. Cambridge, MA.

Clarke, L. 2001. "Introduction [to Part 2]." In *Shīʿite Heritage: Essays on Classical and Modern Traditions*, edited by Linda Clarke, 93–101. Binghamton.

——. 2004. "Faith and Unfaith in Pre-Occultation Shīʿism: a Study in Theology and Social History." *Islam and Christian-Muslim Relations* 15.1:109–123.

Corbin, H. 1971. *En Islam Iranien: Aspects spirituels et philosophiques; 1. Le Shîʿisme deodécimain*. Paris.

Crapanzano, V. 1986. "Hermes' Dilemma: The Masking of Subversion in Ethnographic Description." In *Writing Culture*, edited by James Clifford and George E. Marcus, 51–76. Berkeley.

Crone, P. 2005. *Medieval Islamic Political Thought*. Edinburgh.
Daneshgar, M. 2018. "Censored Manuscripts, Censored Intellects: Can we Trust the Past?" *Mizan*, April 23. http://www.mizanproject.org/censored-manuscripts-censored-intellects/.
Dakake, M. 2007. *Charismatic Community: Shiʿite Identity in Early Islam*. Albany.
——. 2006. "Hiding in Plain Sight: The Practical and Doctrinal Significance of Secrecy in Shiʿite Islam." *Journal of the American Academy of Religion* 74.2:324–355.
Davis, N. 1981. "The Possibilities of the Past." *Journal of Interdisciplinary History* 12.2:267–275.
Darnton, R. 2014. *Censors at Work: How States Shaped Literature*. New York.
——. 1984. *The Great Cat Massacre and Other Episodes in French Cultural History*. New York.
De Smet, D. 2014. "La transmigration des âmes. Une notion problématique dans l'ismaélisme d'époque Fatimide." In *Unity in Diversity: Mysticism, Messianism and the Construction of Religious Authority in Islam*, edited by Orkhan Mir-Kasimov, 77–110. Leiden.
Donner, F. 1998. *Narratives of Islamic Origins: The Beginnings of Islamic Historical Writing*. Princeton.
——. 2002–2003. "From Believers to Muslims: Confessional Self-Identity in the Early Islamic Community." *Al-Abhath* 50–51:9–53.
——. 2013. "MESA Presidential Address 2012: MESA and the American University." *Review of Middle East Studies* 47.1:4–18.
Freidenreich, D. 2011. *Foreigners and their Food: Constructing Otherness in Jewish, Christian, and Islamic Law*. Berkeley.
Gaiser, A. 2017. "A Narrative Identity Approach to Islamic Sectarianism." In *Sectarianization: Mapping the New Politics of the Middle East*, edited by N. Hashemi and Danny Postel. 61–75. Oxford.
Haider, N. 2011. *The Origins of the Shīʿa: Identity, Ritual, and Sacred Space in Eighth-Century Kūfa*. Cambridge.
——. 2014. *Shīʿī Islam: An Introduction*. Cambridge.
——. 2018. "The Myth of the 'Shīʿī Perspective': Identity and Memory in Early Islam." In *Routledge Handbook on Early Islam*, edited by Herbert Berg, 209–222. London.
Halm, H. 1978. *Kosmologie und Heilslehre der frühen Ismāʿīlīya: Eine Studie zur islamischen Gnosis*. Wiesbaden.
——. 1982. *Die islamische Gnosis: die extreme Schia und die ʿAlawiten*. Zurich.
——. 2004. *Shiʿism*, 2nd ed. Translated by Janet Watson and Marian Hill. New York.
Hodgson, M. 1955. "How Did the Early Shīʿa Become Sectarian?" *Journal of the American Oriental Society* 75:1–13.

——. 1974. *The Venture of Islam*, vol. 1. Chicago.
Hughes, A. 2017. "Religion without Religion: Integrating Islamic Origins into Religious Studies." *Journal of the American Academy of Religion* 85.4:1–22.
——. 2017. *Shared Identities: Medieval and Modern Imaginings of Judeo-Islam*. Oxford.
al-Isfarāyinī, Abū l-Muẓaffar. 1373/1955. *al-Tabṣīr fī l-dīn*. Edited by Muḥammad Zāhid b. al-Ḥasan al-Kawtharī. Cairo.
al-Kashshī, A. ᶜA. M. 1427/2006. *Rijāl*, edited by J. al-Qayyūmī al-Iṣfahānī. Qum.
King, K. 2003. *What is Gnosticism?* Cambridge, MA.
Kleinberg, E., J. W. Scott, and G. Wilder. 2018. "Theses on Theory and History." *Theory Revolt*, August 11. http://theoryrevolt.com/download/WildOnCollective_Theses-Booklet.pdf.
al-Kulaynī, Muḥammad b. Yaᶜqūb. 1431/2009. *al-Kāfī*, vol. 1. Edited by M. Jaᶜfar Shams al-Dīn. Beirut.
LaCapra, D. 2004. *History in Transit: Experience, Identity, Critical Theory*. Ithaca.
Landolt, H. 2001. "Introduction to the Translation [of *Kashf al-Maḥjūb*]." In *An Anthology of Philosophy of Persia*, edited by Seyyed Hossein Nasr with Mehdi Aminrazavi, 2:74–82. Oxford.
Laoust, H. 1965. *Les schismes dans l'islam*. Paris.
Lapidus, I. 2014. *A History of Islamic Societies*, 3rd ed. Cambridge.
Lewinstein, K. 1991. "The Azāriqa in Islamic Heresiography." *Bulletin of the School of Oriental and African Studies* 54.2:251–268.
——. 1992. "Making and Unmaking a Sect: The Heresiographers and the Ṣufriyya." *Studia Islamica* 76:75–96.
Lincoln, B. 1999. *Theorizing Myth: Narrative, Ideology, and Scholarship*. Chicago.
——. 2006. *Holy Terrors: Thinking about Religion after September 11*. 2nd ed. Chicago.
——. 2007. *Religion, Empire, and Torture: The Case of Achaemenian Persia, With a Postscript on Abu Ghraib*. Chicago.
——. 2012. "How to Read a Religious Text." In *Gods and Demons, Priests and Scholars: Critical Explorations in the History of Religions*, 5–15. Chicago.
——. 2014. *Discourse and the Construction of Society: Comparative Studies of Myth, Ritual, and Classification*. 2nd ed. Oxford.
Madelung, W. 1970. "Imamism in Muᶜtazilite Theology." In *Le Shiᶜisme imāmite*, edited by T. Fahd, 13–29. Paris.
——. 1988. *Religious Trends in Early Islamic Iran*. Albany.
——. 1989. "The *Hāshimiyyāt* of al-Kumayt and Hāshimī Shiᶜism." *Studia Islamica* 70:5–26.

——. 2014. "Early Imāmī Theology as Reflected in the *Kitāb al-Kāfī* of al-Kulaynī." In *The Study of Shiʿi Islam: History, Theology and Law*, edited by F. Daftary and G. Miskinzoda, 465–474. London.

——. 2014a. "Introduction [to Theology]." In *The Study of Shiʿi Islam: History, Theology and Law*, edited by F. Daftary and G. Miskinzoda, 455–463. London.

Majmaʿ al-akhbār. 2008. In *Silsilat al-turāth al-ʿalawī*, edited by Abū Mūsā and Shaykh Mūsā, 8:7–161. Lebanon.

Marwick, A. 1995. "Two Approaches to Historical Study: The Metaphysical (Including 'Postmodernism') and the Historical." *Journal of Contemporary History* 30.1:5–35.

Massignon, L. 2009. "Recherches sur les Shîʿites extrémistes à Baghdad à la fin du troisième siècle de l'Hégire." In *Écrits mémorables*, edited by Christian Jambet et al., 2:656–659. Paris.

McCutcheon, R. 1996. *Manufacturing Religion: The Discourse on Sui Generis Religion and the Politics of Nostalgia*. New York.

Megill, A. 2007. *Historical Knowledge, Historical Error: A Contemporary Guide to Practice*. Chicago.

Modarressi, H. 1993. *Crisis and Consolidation in the Formative Period of Shiʿite Islam*. Princeton.

——. 1993a. "Early Debates on the Integrity of the Qurʾān: A Brief Survey." *Studia Islamica* 77:5–39.

——. 2003. *Tradition and Survival: A Bibliographical Survey of Early Shīʿite Literature*. Oxford.

Morony, M. 1974. "Religious Communities in Late Sasanian and Early Muslim Iraq." *Journal of the Economic and Social History of the Orient* 17.2:113–135.

——. 2005. *Iraq after the Muslim Conquest*. 2nd ed. Piscataway.

al-Najāshī, Aḥmad b. ʿAlī. 1431/2010. *Rijāl*. Beirut.

al-Nawbakhtī, Abū l-Ḥasan. 1931. *Firaq al-shīʿa*. Edited by H. Ritter. Istanbul.

Newman, A. 2000. *The Formative Period of Twelver Shīʿism: Ḥadīth as Discourse Between Qum and Baghdad*. London.

Pierce, M. 2016. *Twelve Infallible Men: The Imams and the Making of Shiʿism*. Cambridge, MA.

Poonawala, I. 2001. "The Imām's Authority during the Pre-Ghaybah Period: Theoretical and Practical Considerations." In *Shīʿite Heritage: Essays on Classical and Modern Traditions*, edited by Linda Clarke, 103–122. Binghamton.

Potter, J. 1996. *Representing Reality: Discourse, Rhetoric and Social Construction*. London.

Pseudo-Mufaḍḍal al-Juʿfī. 1981. *Kitāb al-haft wa l-aẓilla*. Edited by ʿĀrif Tāmir. Beirut.

al-Qāḍī, W. 1976. "The Development of the Term *Ghulāt* in Muslim Literature with Special Reference to the Kaysāniyya." In *Akten des VII. Kongresses für Arabistik und Islamwissenschaft*, edited by A. Dietrich, 295–319. Göttingen.

al-Qalhatī, M. b. S. n.d. *Kitāb al-Kashf wa l-Bayān fī Sharḥ Iftirāq al-Firaq wa l-Adyān*. Sir George Grey Special Collections, Auckland Libraries, New Zealand [GMS 97].

Rezakhani, Kh. 2014. "Mazdakism, Manichaeism and Zoroastrianism: in Search of Orthodoxy and Heterodoxy in Late Antique Iran." *Iranian Studies* 48.1:1–16.

Rizvi, S. 2008. [Review of Dakake 2007]. *Journal of Qurʾanic Studies* 10.2:98–101.

——. 2014. "Seeking the Face of God: The Safawid *Ḥikmat* Tradition's Conceptualizaion of *Walāya Takwīniyya*." In *The Study of Shiʿi Islam: History, Theology and Law*, edited by F. Daftary and G. Miskinzoda, 391–410. London.

Roberts, G. 1996. "Narrative History as a Way of Life." *Journal of Contemporary History* 31.1:221–228.

Rose, S. 1999. "Cultural Analysis and Moral Discourses: Episodes, Continuities, and Transformations." In *Beyond the Cultural Turn: New Directions in the Study of Society and Culture*, edited by Victoria Bonnell and Lynn Hunt, 217–238. Berkeley.

Sachedina, A. 1981. *Islamic Messianism: The Idea of the Mahdi in Twelver Shiʿism*. Albany.

Scott, J. 1990. *Domination and the Arts of Resistance: Hidden Transcripts*. New Haven.

Sewell, W. "The Concept(s) of Culture." In *Beyond the Cultural Turn: New Directions in the Study of Society and Culture*, edited by Victoria Bonnell and Lynn Hunt, 35–61. Berkeley.

al-Shahrastānī, A. F. 1415/1994. *Kitāb al-Milal wa l-niḥal*, 2 vols. Edited by A. ʿA. al-Saʿīd al-Mandūh. Beirut.

al-Shaykh al-Mufīd. 1399/1979. *Irshād*. Edited by Ḥ. al-Aʿlamī. Beirut.

——. 1413/1992. *al-Masāʾil al-sarawiyya*. Edited by Ṣ. ʿAbd al-Ḥamīd. n.p.

Sizgorich, T. 2009. *Violence and Belief in Late Antiquity: Militant Devotion in Christianity and Islam*. Philadelphia.

Skinner, Q. 1969. "Meaning and Understanding in the History of Ideas." *History and Theory* 8.1:3–53.

Smith, J. 1982. *Imagining Religion: From Babylon to Jonestown*. Chicago.

——. 2004. "Trading Places." In *Relating Religion: Essays in the Study of Religion*, 215–229. Chicago.

Somers, M. 1999. "The Privatization of Citizenship: How to Unthink a Knowledge Culture." In *Beyond the Cultural Turn: New Directions in the Study of Society and Culture*, edited by Victoria Bonnell and Lynn Hunt, 121–161. Berkeley.

Spiegel, G. 1999. "History, Historicism, and the Social Logic of the Text." In *The Past as Text: The Theory and Practice of Medieval Historiography*, 3–28. Baltimore.

Strauss, L. 1952. *Persecution and the Art of Writing*. Westport.

al-Ṭabarānī, Maymūn b. al-Qāsim. 2006. *Kitāb al-ḥāwī fī ʿilm al-fatāwī*. In *Silsilat al-turāth al-ʿalawī*, edited by A. Mūsā and Shaykh Mūsā, 116–3:45. Lebanon.

——. 2006. *Al-Jawhariyya al-kalbiyya*. In *Silsilat al-turāth al-ʿalawī*, edited by A. Mūsā and Shaykh Mūsā, 40–3:19. Lebanon.

Takim, L. 2006. *Heirs of the Prophet: Charisma and Religious Aurthority in Shiʿite Islam*. Albany.

Turner, C. 2006. "The 'Tradition of Mufaḍḍal' and the Doctrine of the *Rajʿa*: Evidence of *Ghuluww* in the Eschatology of Twelver Shiʿism?" *Iran: Journal of the British Institute of Persian Studies* 44:175–195.

al-Ṭūsī, Muḥammad b. al-Ḥasan. 1965/1385. *Kitāb al-Ghayba*. Edited by Ā. B. Tihrānī. Najaf.

al-ʿUmarī, Shihāb al-Dīn. 1985. *Masālik al-abṣār fī mamālik al-amṣār*. Edited by A. F. Sayyid. Cairo.

van Ess, J. 1991. *Theologie und Gesellschaft in 2. und 3. Jahrhundert Hidschra*, vol. 1. Berlin.

——. 2011. *Der Eine und das Andere: Beobachtungen an islamischen häresiographischen Texten*. Berlin.

Walker, P. 1991. "The Doctrine of Metempsychosis in Islam." In *Islamic Studies Presented to Charles J. Adams*, edited by Wael B. Hallaq and Donald Little, 219–238. Leiden.

Wasserstrom, S. 1999. *Religion after Religion: Gerschom Scholem, Mircea Eliade, and Henry Corbin at Eranos*. Princeton.

Wellhausen, J. 1901. *Die religiös-politischen Oppositionsparteien im alten Islam*. Berlin.

——. 1902. *Das arabische Reich und sein Sturz*. Berlin.

White, H. 1987. "The Value of Narrativity in the Representation of Reality." In *The Content of the Form: Narrative Discourse and Historical Representation*, 1–25. Baltimore.

Williams, M. 1996. *Rethinking "Gnosticism": An Argument for Dismantling a Dubious Category*. Princeton.

10

Ismāʿīliyya and Ismāʿīlism: From Polemical Portrayal to Academic Inquiry

Khalil Andani

There is hardly an aspect of the Islamic community, especially in its earlier period, which was not touched in one way or another by the presence of Ismāʿīlism.[1]

Seyyed Hossein Nasr*

THIS CHAPTER ASSESSES the state of academic scholarship on the Ismāʿīlī Muslims in terms of the methodological categories of theology, polemic, and academic scholarship and presents two critical arguments on the state of the field.[2] The earliest Western scholarship on the Ismāʿīlīs began in the eighteenth and nineteenth century, largely based on hostile polemical accounts written by their adversaries, resulting in the proliferation of anti-Ismāʿīlī polemic under the guise of academic scholarship. This gave rise to rather sensationalist accounts of the Nizārī Ismāʿīlīs as a secret society of tricksters who consumed hashish and carried out systematic assassinations. A more holistic academic approach to Ismāʿīlī studies began in the early twentieth century and has proven quite successful in advancing the field, as Ismāʿīlī studies progresses at a staggering pace. At the same time, however, a tendency best described as "academic-polemic" continues to hamper academic treatments of select Ismāʿīlī topics, particularly the historical origins of the Fatimid Caliphate and the career of Aga Khan I in colonial India. This is evident in how certain authors simply mirror or privilege anti-Ismāʿīlī polemical narratives in an uncritical manner while marginalizing or omitting important historical evidence that contravenes their arguments.

Second, Ismāʿīlī studies as a field takes for granted the existence of an intelligible entity called "Ismāʿīlism" as its ostensible object of study but

1. Nasr 1977, 1.

2. In many ways, this chapter is the sequel to my two articles surveying Ismaili studies scholarship, see note 6.

there is yet to be a critical interrogation of the origins, construction, and problems with "Ismāʿīlism" as a category of analysis. I show that Ismāʿīlism is either explicitly or implicitly being defined as a sectarian religious ideology consisting of one or more essentialist doctrines, centered on allegiance to and recognition of the religious authority of the Ismāʿīlī Imams . As employed by many scholars, Ismāʿīlism is a reified sui generis entity, somehow transcending history and manifesting through various instances or "species" of historical Ismāʿīlī movements, communities, and theologies. I show that Ismāʿīlism presently conceived as an analytical and taxonomical category fails to cohere with many examples of historical Ismāʿīlī phenomena and needs to be reconceptualized.

The chapter proceeds as follows: first, some definitions and examples of the theological, polemical, and academic approaches to the study of Islam and the Ismāʿīlīs in particular; second, an analysis of "academic-polemical" approaches that still weigh heavily in the academic study of Ismāʿīlī history, particularly with respect to the origins of the Fatimids and the religio-political career of Aga Khan I; third, a critical analysis of how the concept of "Ismāʿīlism" arose as a reified sectarian category in Ismāʿīlī studies scholarship; fourth, an argument as to why Ismāʿīlism as currently defined is problematic and incoherent both in terms of accounting for historical Ismāʿīlī "insider" self-definitions as well as Ismāʿīlī phenomena among non-Ismāʿīlī Muslim thinkers; fifth, preliminary considerations on how Ismāʿīlism as an analytical object can be redefined in future studies.

The Ismāʿīliyya: A Short History

> This name [Ismāʿīliyya] designates those whose [spiritual] ancestry goes back to Mawlānā Ismāʿīl ibn Jaʿfar al-Ṣādiq, ibn Muḥammad al-Bāqir, ibn ʿAlī Zayn al-ʿĀbidīn, ibn al-Ḥusayn al-Taqī, ibn ʿAlī al-Murtaḍā al-Waṣī. This is our inherent name.[3]
>
> ʿAlī b. Muḥammad b. al-Walīd

The designation "Ismāʿīlīs" (*Ismāʿīliyya*) refers to several Shīʿī communities who believe in the existence of an Imamate (*imāma*), a divinely-ordained office of religio-political leadership and spiritual guidance succeeding the Prophet Muḥammad, which continues in a specific descendants or "Imams" issuing from ʿAlī b. Abī Ṭālib and Fāṭima bint Muḥammad through the lineage of Ismāʿīl b. Jaʿfar al-Ṣādiq (d. ca. after 138/755). The figure of the Imam according to some early Shīʿī movements was revered as the heir of

3. ʿAlī b. Muḥammad b. al-Walīd (d. 612/1215), quoted in Virani 2007, 200.

Muḥammad's spiritual knowledge and authority; the possessor of the true interpretation and hidden meanings of the qurʾānic revelation; a pre-existent light that God created prior to the physical world; and continuously divinely-inspired through celestial beings including the Holy Spirit and the angels.[4]

Muslim heresiographical and doxographical writings, composed mostly by non-Ismāʿīlīs, refer to the Ismāʿīlīs as one among many schismatic parties (*firāq*, sing. *firqah*) whose origins lie in the disagreement among Shīʿī groups over the rightful successor to Imam Jaʿfar al-Ṣādiq (d. 148/765). Most sources indicate, either explicitly or implicitly, that al-Ṣādiq had designated his second eldest son Ismāʿīl as the Imam to succeed him. But Ismāʿīl, by most accounts, died before his father and this plunged the Shīʿī followers of al-Ṣādiq into a succession crisis upon his own death. Those groups that recognized the Imamate of Ismāʿīl and/or his lineal descendants beginning with his son Muḥammad were designated as the *Ismāʿīliyya*.[5]

The history of the earliest Ismāʿīlīs in the latter half of the second/eighth century is obscure due to the lack of documentary sources, necessitating some historical reconstruction concerning the early period using later sources; it is possible that the original Ismāʿīlī groups were Kūfan Shīʿīs.[6] The extant works that describe the activities of the Ismāʿīlīs come from the late third/ninth century and the early fourth/tenth century. From these sources, it may be gleaned that an active, highly organized, and clandestine Ismāʿīlī Summons, self-designated as *daʿwat al-ḥaqq* (the summons of truth) and *al-daʿwat al-hādiyya* (the rightly-guided summons) and carried out by numerous *duʿāt* ('summoners', sing. *dāʿī*), was being directed by three generations of hereditary leaders based in southwestern Persia and Salamiyya. This Ismāʿīlī Summons began to find success in Yemen, Iraq, Bahrain, and North Africa in the late third/ninth century. As reported in extant sources, the Ismāʿīlī summoners invited Muslims to the recognition of an Imam from the descendants of the Prophet that would soon rise and overthrow the Abbasids; this eschatological Imam was designated as the *Mahdī* (the rightly guided one) and the *Qāʾim* (the eschatological riser). The Summons also imparted highly intricate theological, cosmological, and hermeneutical doctrines through different levels of teaching and initiation, partly resembling those of later Ṣūfī brotherhoods. At the end of the third/ninth century, the hereditary leader of the Ismāʿīlī Summons, ʿAbd Allāh al-Mahdī (d. ca. 322/934), openly disclosed that he and his ancestors had been the heredi-

4. On this Imamological doctrine, see Amir-Moezzi 1994, 2011.

5. Madelung 2018, 62–67.

6. For the historical summary of the Ismailis in the next few paragraphs, see Andani 2016a, 2016b.

tary Imams in direct succession to Imam Jaʿfar al-Ṣādiq; he revealed himself as the present Imam and the first in a series of divinely-ordained *Mahdī*s.

The success of the Ismāʿīlī Summons led to the establishment of the Fatimid Caliphate (909–1171) in which a Shīʿī Imam claiming descent from the Prophet's *Ahl al-Bayt*, beginning with ʿAbd Allāh al-Mahdī, ruled as both Imam and Caliph over a large empire. This Fatimid period facilitated numerous developments in Ismāʿīlī law, theology, philosophy, and socio-political activity. Through both the Fatimid Caliphate and the Ismāʿīlī Summons, which was active in Syria, Persia, Central Asia, and India, the Ismāʿīlīs presented their own Shīʿī vision of Islam and offered a religio-political challenge to the emerging Sunnī traditions of Islam represented by the Abbasid Caliphs and the *ʿulamāʾ*. As a result, numerous polemical treatises were written against the Fatimids and many Ismāʿīlī populations beyond the Fatimid empire were persecuted. Upon the death of al-Mustanṣir (d. 487/1094), reckoned as the eighth Fatimid Caliph and the eighteenth Ismāʿīlī Imam, the Ismāʿīlīs split into two groups over the identity of this Imam's successor. The Mustʿalī Ismāʿīlīs regarded al-Mustanṣir's younger son, Aḥmad al-Mustʿalī (d. 495/1011) as the next Imam, whom the powerful Fatimid vizier al-Afḍal had swiftly placed on the Fatimid throne in a coup d'état. The Mustʿalī Ismāʿīlīs recognized two more Imams following Mustʿalī until their twenty-first Imam, al-Ṭayyib, presumably disappeared as an infant in about 526/1132. The Ṭayyibī Ismāʿīlīs accepted the concealed al-Ṭayyib and his descendants as their Imams and henceforth followed the leadership of a chief *dāʿī* (*dāʿī muṭlaq*) as the deputy of the concealed Ṭayyibī Imams. Over the next eight centuries, the Ṭayyibī Ismāʿīlīs experienced further schisms over the rightful holder of the *dāʿī muṭlaq* office and the three major Ṭayyibī Ismāʿīlī communities today are the Dāʾūdī Bohras, the Sulaymānī Bohras, and the ʿAlawī Bohras, each of whom is led by a different line of *dāʿīs.*

The Nizārī Ismāʿīlīs recognized the Imamate of Nizār b. al-Mustanṣir (the official heir-designate to the Fatimid Caliphate and Imamate) and his descendants. The Nizārī communities, based in Syria, Persia, Central Asia, and India, cut ties with the Fatimid dynasty after Nizār's failed revolt and formed their own independent Nizārī Ismāʿīlī summons. The Nizārī Imamate continued among the descendants of Nizār (d. 488/1095), who eventually migrated to Persia and found refuge in the Nizārī fortress state under the central authority of Alamut. Following the Mongol defeat of the Nizārī state in 654/1256, the Nizārī Ismāʿīlīs survived mainly through practicing tactical dissimulation (*taqiyya*) in the guise of Sunnīs, Ṣūfīs, Twelvers, and sometimes Hindus. The Nizārī Imams eventually rose out of obscurity and became involved in Iranian politics in the eighteenth century. The forty-sixth Imam,

Ḥasan ʿAlī Shāh (d. 1298/1881) was given the title Āqā Khān ('Aga Khan') by Faṭh ʿAlī Shāh Qājār (d. 1769/1834). The succeeding Nizārī Ismāʿīlī Imams all carry the title of Aga Khan with the current Imam, the forty-ninth in the series, being Shāh Karīm al-Ḥusaynī Aga Khan IV (b. 1936) – who has become internationally recognized for his humanitarian work and promotion of pluralism.

The first scholars that studied the Ismāʿīlīs, their history, and their theologies were eighteenth- and nineteenth-century Orientalists, who relied on the hostile and inaccurate portrayals of the Ismāʿīlīs produced by Sunnī polemicists and medieval European writers. This Orientalist discourse depicted the Ismāʿīlīs as a secret society of heretics and fanatics, who were a menace of Muslim history. It was only with the British "re-discovery" of the Nizārī Ismāʿīlīs in Persia and India under the then leadership of Ḥasan ʿAlī Shāh Aga Khan I that portrayals of the Ismāʿīlīs began to shift. The recovery of actual Ismāʿīlī historical, theological, and devotional writings in the early twentieth century helped ignite the beginning of the modern academic study of the Ismāʿīlīs. In support of this new scholarly agenda, Sulṭān Muḥammad Shāh Aga Khan III (d. 1957) patronized the Ismāʿīlī Society of Bombay, which funded the research and publications of Vladimir Ivanow, a pioneer scholar of Ismāʿīlī studies. Likewise, in 1977, Aga Khan IV established the Institute of Ismāʿīlī Studies, which has become the premier academic institution for Ismāʿīlī studies in terms of manuscript collection, editions, translations, research, and publications.

Studying the Ismāʿīlīs:
Theology, Polemics, and Academic Analysis

> We need to make it one of our principal tasks to situate the texts we study within such intellectual contexts as enable us to make sense of what their authors were doing in writing them.[7]
>
> Quentin Skinner

This volume takes as its point of departure the existence of at least three approaches to scholarship on Islam: the theological, the polemical, and the academic. All three approaches can be intellectually rigorous and contribute valuable insights about a given subject. But these approaches are differentiated by: a) their end goals, b) their ontological and epistemic commitments, and c) their methods of analysis and argument. I define theology as a con-

7. Skinner, quoted in Coffey and Chapman 2009, 2.

structive hermeneutical process in which a person produces and responds to meaning through a set of deep personal commitments concerning the interrelationship between the self, the world, and reality.[8] A theological approach to the study of Islam and the Ismāʿīlī traditions in particular entails a commitment to the existence of God, a spiritual realm of celestial beings (intellects, souls, angels), and the authority of certain institutions, such as the Prophets, the Ismāʿīlī Imamate, the Qurʾān, the Ismāʿīlī Summons, etc. An Ismāʿīlī theology constructs, expounds, or relies on truth claims centered on these theological commitments; as a method of analysis, Ismāʿīlī theology draws evidence from philosophical argument, the authoritative sources of the Ismāʿīlī tradition including the guidance of the Ismāʿīlī Imamate, and personal experience. A theological approach still has immense analytical value because it demonstrates how Ismāʿīlīs conceived, understood and practiced their intellectual and religious traditions. A polemical approach to the study of the Ismāʿīlīs, meanwhile, is one that seeks to attack and undermine normative Ismāʿīlī commitments and present alternative commitments, whether theological or otherwise. As noted below, there are numerous examples of anti-Ismāʿīlī polemic produced throughout history. Sometimes, an author may inadvertently engage in polemic without the intention to do so by uncritically relying on sources that advance a polemical agenda. Polemics have a great deal of historical value and may be analyzed in terms of how Ismāʿīlī traditions were (mis)represented by their antagonists and how these representations influenced other discourses.

The academic approach to the study of Ismāʿīlī Muslim history and thought is quite different from the theological and the polemical. Quentin Skinner, a leading thinker of the Cambridge School of intellectual history, describes the goal of an academic approach to the history of ideas as follows:

> We need to make it one of our principal tasks to situate the texts we study within such intellectual contexts as enable us to make sense of what their authors were doing in writing them. My aspiration is not of course to enter into the thought-processes of long-dead thinkers; it is simply to use the ordinary techniques of historical enquiry to grasp their concepts, to follow their distinctions, to appreciate their beliefs and, so far as possible, to see things their way.[9]

8. My definition of theology is based on Clooney 2001 and Nguyen 2018. I do not use "theology" solely in the sense of *ʿilm al-kalām*, which is only one kind of theology in an Islamic context.

9. Skinner, quoted in Coffey and Chapman 2009, 2.

Skinner's approach, which emphasizes both situating agents and understanding their intellectual productions on their own terms, is suitable for the academic study of Islam. Islam is best approached, not as a fixed set of beliefs, rituals, and activities, but as an ongoing hermeneutical process in history through which Muslim agents living across time and space interpret their reality, create meaning, and construct their selves in terms of the Revelation to Muḥammad; in doing so, they constitute Islam in its various forms while also being affected by their interpretations of Islam.[10] As Jacques Waardenburg frames it, "if Islam interprets reality, it is itself continuously reinterpreted by its believers, adherents and sympathizers."[11] An academic approach to the study of Islam is an analytical inquiry into *how* and *why* Muslims are constructing Islam in the way they do and *what* meanings they are creating, with the goal of being able to "see things their way." Academic analysis is *not* concerned with constructing, prescribing, supporting, or refuting the truth-claims made by Muslim actors and thereby differs from both theology and polemics in this respect. Instead, an academic approach aspires to fully comprehend and describe the myriad of ways in which Muslim agents and others construct Islam with due regard to their manifold contexts.

The academic study of Islam is really the study of Muslim historical actors and this requires an interdisciplinary arsenal of theories and methods. Various academic disciplinary frameworks such as history, sociology, anthropology, ethics, philosophy, philology, literature, intellectual history, etc. are based on metaphysical and epistemic assumptions concerning the nature of empirical reality, human agency, the criteria of historical truth, the nature of evidence, etc. In this respect, there is a certain kinship between theological and academic approaches to Islam. Timothy Fitzgerald, who has devoted many pages to differentiating theology from the historical study of religion, admits as much:

> All paradigms rest on metaphysical assumptions including my own... These issues of how we look at the world and how we should interpret institutions take place within a framework of metaphysical assumptions which always need to be explicit. In this sense we are not different from theologians.[12]

We must also bear in mind that academic and analytical claims about a religious tradition are normative in relation to a community of scholars and

10. This conception of Islam is based on Ahmed, 2015.
11. Waardenburg 2007, 34.
12. Fitzgerald 1997, 97.

a wider human culture. Kevin Schilbrack observes that "no form of thinking is normatively neutral. Norms are in this sense an ineliminable part of culture as such.... All thinking is normative or value-laden, and there is no privileged neutral view."[13] A recent example of how even historical analysis registers as normative is Shahab Ahmed's conceptualization of Islam in his *What is Islam.*[14] Even though Ahmed's methodology was historical, analytical, and hermeneutical, he was widely interpreted as making normative claims, due to the subject matter and comprehensive scope of his analysis.[15]

It is tempting to brand theological approaches as "insider" and polemical and academic approaches as "outsider." While this division of labor seems rather neat, the reality is more complex. Insiders may launch a polemic against their own religious tradition; Asghar Ali Engineer's writings on the Bohra Ismāʿīlīs perhaps exemplify this approach.[16] Insiders may perform an academic analysis of some aspect of their own religious tradition while drawing on their insider positionality to enrich their work; Daryoush Mohammad Poor's *Authority Without Territory* is an academic study of the modern institutions of the Ismāʿīlī Imamate in which the author's self-admitted insider position granted him the "critical intimacy" to draw new patterns, connections, and insights into his analysis.[17] Outsiders can also make seemingly theological or normative claims concerning another religious tradition or its institutions; Christian authors, among others, have made normative claims about "what the Qurʾan really means" for centuries.[18] These interpenetrations and permutations of various insider, outsider, polemical, and academic approaches is perhaps nowhere more applicable than the field of Ismāʿīlī studies.

A great deal of historical "insider" Ismāʿīlī literature – theological treatises, legal works, poetry, prayers, historical accounts, hymns – composed by pre-modern Ismāʿīlī Imams, *dāʿīs,* and believers has been recovered, edited, and translated and we could classify this Ismāʿīlī literature as broadly theological in orientation. There is also a long-established tradition of Muslim writers attacking the Ismāʿīlīs and accusing them of all sorts of theological and moral infamies. These authors include Ibn Rizām (ca. 340/951), Akhū Muḥsin Muḥammad b. ʿAlī (d. ca. 374/985), Ibn al-Nadīm (d. ca. 385/995–388/998), ʿAbd al-Jabbār (d. ca. 415/1025), Abū l-Qāsim al-

13. Schilbrack 2012, 113–114.
14. Ahmed 2015.
15. See the various responses to Ahmed in Fuerst and Peterson 2016.
16. Engineer 1980.
17. Poor 2014, 24–25.
18. As documented in Bazzano 2016.

Bustī (d. ca. 420/1029), the ʿAbbāsid Caliph al-Qādir (d. ca. 422/1031), Abū Bakr Muḥammad al-Bāqillānī (d. ca. 403/1013), Abū Ḥāmid al-Ghazālī (d. ca. 505/1111), and Āṭā Mālik Juvaynī (d. ca. 681/1283), among others.[19] These writings fall in the category of "outsider" polemic while also being "insider" theology with respect to the traditions they come from, such as Twelver, Zaydī, or Sunnī Islam . There is also a tradition of European writing on the Ismāʿīlīs stemming from Crusader accounts, which was largely based on a further exacerbation of anti-Ismāʿīlī polemic. These European narratives originated the sensational "Assassin legends" concerning the Nizārī Ismāʿīlīs being hashish eaters carrying out assassinations under the spell of their "Old Man of the Mountain."[20]

The "outsider" academic study of the Ismāʿīlīs technically begins with Orientalist scholarship in the eighteenth century. During this time, Orientalist scholars remained unaware of the existence of contemporary Ismāʿīlī communities. Thus, this early scholarship overwhelmingly portrayed the Ismāʿīlīs and their beliefs based on the anti-Ismāʿīlī polemic of the above Sunnī scholars, the inaccurate European writings perpetuating the "Assassin legends", and the personal biases of certain Orientalist writers. Joseph von Hammer-Purgstall (d.1856) published a popular book on the Nizārī Ismāʿīlīs in which he promoted a highly distorted narrative about them based on Marco Polo's stories. Reflecting Sunnī polemics, Crusader mistruths, and his personal bias against secret societies in the wake of the French Revolution, Von Hammer-Purgstall described the Nizārī Ismāʿīlīs as "that union of imposters and dupes, which ... undermined all religion and morality."[21] Silvestre de Sacy (d. 1838) endorsed the popular but *fictitious* claim that the Nizārī Ismāʿīlīs consumed hashish in some manner and echoed the anti-Fatimid rhetoric coined by Sunnī polemicists when he relied on Akhū Muḥsin's hostile account of Ismāʿīlī origins.[22] Thus, much of the Orientalist scholarship on the Ismāʿīlīs was a strange hybrid of the academic and the polemic; it was "academic-polemic" in aspiring to be academic but resulted in the promotion of polemical views. It was Jean Baptiste L. J. Rousseau (d. 1831) who first alerted the Europeans to the existence of Nizārī Ismāʿīlīs in Syria and Iran, where he confirmed the existence of their forty-fifth Imam Shāh Khalīl Allāh (d. 1232/1817) residing in the village of Maḥallāt.[23]

19. A good summary of these authors up to the end of the fifth/eleventh century is in Lika 2018, 38–60.

20. The genealogy of the Assassin narratives is studied in Daftary 1994.

21. Daftary 2007, 25.

22. Daftary 2007, 24–25.

23. Daftary 2007, 27.

A more rigorous academic discourse of Ismāʿīlī studies formed partly in response to this older "academic-polemical" approach and this was due to the recovery of authentic Ismāʿīlī "insider" writings in the early twentieth century. Thus, in reading pioneer scholars of the Ismāʿīlīs like Vladimir Ivanow (d. 1970), Asaf A. A. Fyzee (d. 1981), Husayn Hamdani (d. 1962), Zahid ʿAli (d. 1958), Paul Casanova (d. 1926), Marshall G. Hodgson (d. 1968), Henry Corbin (d. 1978), Rudolf Strothmann (d. 1960), Muhammad Kamil Husayn (d. 1961), and Samuel M. Stern (d. 1969), one finds an approach that is both academic and receptive along the lines proposed by Skinner. Much of their early work consisted of editing, translating, and expounding Arabic and Persian Ismāʿīlī texts, thereby setting the foundation for later scholars. Academic scholarship on the Ismāʿīlīs has continued through succeeding generations of scholars, including Ismail K. Poonawala, Abbas Hamdani, Wilferd Madelung, Heinz Halm, Paul E. Walker, Hermann Landolt, Farhad Daftary, Arzina Lalani, Ali Asani, Azim Nanji, Verena Klemm, Shin Nomoto, Daniel De Smet, Tahera Qutbuddin, Shainool Jiwa, Shafique N. Virani, and others. To date, most of the academic work on the Ismāʿīlīs consists of historical analytical studies of specific Ismāʿīlī figures, texts, or periods, such as the Fatimid Caliphate, the Nizārī Ismāʿīlī polity in Persia, the post-Mongol period, the Tayyibis in Yemen, and the modern Nizārī Ismāʿīlī and Bohra communities. The field also includes some excellent literary and philological analysis of specimens of Ismāʿīlī literature in Arabic, Persian, and South Asian languages. There have also been a few political, sociological, and anthropological studies of specific Ismāʿīlī communities in modern times. The study of Ismāʿīlī theology, philosophy, and hermeneutics is less developed but is now progressing at a renewed pace. Recent contributions in this area of study include the work of David Hollenberg, Jamel Velji, Elizabeth Alexandrin, and Sayeh Meisami.

Ismāʿīlī studies scholarship as recognized in the academic domain generally remains free of theological and overtly apologetic studies. The few theologically oriented works produced in modern times only have circulation within the Ismāʿīlī community and, most recently, on the internet. The production of modern "insider" Ismāʿīlī theological expositions began in the late nineteenth century and continued into the twentieth century, with the writings of Shihāb al-Dīn Shāh al-Ḥusaynī (d. 1302/1884), Fidāʾī Khurasānī (d. 1342/1932), and a number of short works by Ismāʿīlī missionary-scholars such as the famous *Nūram Mubīn* (1936), a history of the Ismāʿīlī Imams written in Gujarati by Ali Muhammad Chunara.[24] More recent Ismāʿīlī theological studies include the writings of Nizārī Ismāʿīlī preachers (*wāʿẓīn*) like the late

24. On these authors and works see Beben 2017 and Asani 2011.

Abualy A. Aziz (d. 2008)[25] and Kamaluddin Ali;[26] the writings of the Ismāʿīlī mystical theologian Allamah Nasir al-Din Hunzai (d. 2017), who was extremely prolific in reviving a modern form of medieval Neoplatonic Ismāʿīlī theology and has an immense following;[27] the Ismāʿīlī Secondary Level Curriculum textbooks that provide a normative religious education to the Nizārī Ismāʿīlī community;[28] and the online and print publications of Ismaili Gnosis, which present a contemporary academically informed discourse of Ismāʿīlī theology and philosophy, akin to modern Christian theology, for Ismāʿīlī and non-Ismāʿīlī readers alike.[29] To this group of theological studies, one may also add the recently published *Faith and Ethics: The Vision of the Ismāʿīlī Imamat* by M. Ali Lakhani, which is a metaphysical exposition of the present Aga Khan's teachings.[30] What these studies have in common is that they either rely upon or expound Ismāʿīlī theological claims, such as the existence of an absolute transcendent God, the divine revelation of the Qurʾān, the divine authority of the Ismāʿīlī Imams, a teleological portrayal of Ismāʿīlī history, and further Ismāʿīlī theological and ritual commitments. In general, these insider theological presentations constitute a separate "track" of Ismāʿīlī scholarship and remain separate from the academic field of Ismāʿīlī studies proper. If anything, contemporary presentations of Ismāʿīlī theology merit further academic analysis, as they have been virtually ignored in modern scholarship. The time is also ripe for a more sophisticated Ismāʿīlī constructive theology to enter into those domains of modern academia that welcome such approaches, as is the case with Christian theology.

Academic-Polemical Approaches in Ismāʿīlī Studies: Fatimid Origins and the First Aga Khan

> They [the Ismāʿīlīs] said: "Our method will be to choose such a man as will help us in our doctrine. We shall claim that he belongs to the "People of the House" (ahl al-bayt).... Now their aim in all that was power and domination.[31]
>
> Abū Ḥāmid al-Ghazālī

25. Aziz 1985 and 2005.
26. See the list of titles online in Kamaluddin Ali Muhammad 2017.
27. See the list of his books online in the Institute for Spiritual Wisdom and Luminous Science 2017.
28. See the titles online at The Institute of Ismaili Studies 2016.
29. Ismaili Gnosis 2018 (online) and Ismaili Gnosis 2016 (print).
30. Lakhani 2017.
31. Al-Ghazālī (d. ca. 505/1111), tr. McCarthy 1980, 184.

> Doubts concerning the 'Alid extraction of the Ismā'īlīs need to be taken seriously. Contemporaries of the Fāṭimids were unanimous in disputing their descent from Jaʿfar al-Ṣādiq.[32]
>
> Heinz Halm

Despite the progress made from the early academic polemic of the nineteenth century, some degree of polemic endures in the study of the Ismāʿīlīs on a small number of important issues. One paramount example in which the specter of polemical discourse remains at large is the scholarly treatment of the origins and genealogy of the Fatimid Imam-Caliphs.

As documented in historical studies, the Fatimids declared themselves as direct descendants of the Prophet Muḥammad through ʿAlī b. Abī Ṭālib and Fāṭima bint Muḥammad from the inception of their Caliphate in 297/909; but, like other dynasties, they did not release their complete genealogy in public. The first Fatimid Imam-Caliph, ʿAbd Allāh (ʿUbayd Allāh) al-Mahdī, reportedly sent a letter to the Ismāʿīlīs of Yemen, where he traced his Fatimid ancestry from ʿAbd Allāh b. Jaʿfar al-Ṣādiq and maintained that he and his ancestors constituted a continuous succession of Imams. He further revealed that the preaching of the "Ismāʿīlī" Summons towards the Imamate of "Ismāʿīl" and the eschatological appearance of "Muḥammad b. Ismāʿīl" had been a "cover" to veil the identity of the real Imams descended from ʿAbd Allāh b. Jaʿfar al-Ṣādiq from persecution. The source of this declaration is a letter of al-Mahdī composed in the early fourth/tenth century and reproduced from memory by a high-ranking Ismāʿīlī *dāʿī*. If it is authentic (and it appears to be), al-Mahdī's letter registers as the earliest evidence of the Fatimid account of their own ancestry and should ideally be given priority over later sources.[33] However, al-Mahdī's declaration came as a shock to a segment of Ismāʿīlīs who, for various reasons, had been expecting the return of Muḥammad b. Ismāʿīl as the messianic *Qāʾim* and *Mahdī*. Decades later, the Fatimid Imam-Caliph al-Muʿizz sought to address this issue and presented the dynasty's genealogy in somewhat different terms, maintaining that they were descended from Muḥammad b. Ismāʿīl and recognizing the latter's Imamate and eschatological role. This version became the "official" Fatimid genealogy in the dynasty's public and internal *daʿwa* discourse. This move was likely prompted by al-Muʿizz's efforts to reach out to the Eastern Ismāʿīlīs in Persia and Iraq who had rejected al-Mahdī's claim to the

32. Halm 2004, 162.

33. The letter was first published and translated in H. Hamdani 1958. Then A. Hamdani and de Blois published a new edition and analysis based on more manuscripts in Hamdani and de Blois 1983.

Imamate and the strategy seems to have worked.[34] Except by H. Hamdani, A. Hamdani and de Blois, and Madelung, al-Mahdī's letter and its implications for historically validating Fatimid genealogy have not been seriously considered.

Meanwhile, the Abbasids and their partisan scholars began to manufacture an alternative genealogy of the Fatimids, attempting to link the emerging dynasty to scurrilous origins. The premier courtier and companion to the Abbasid Caliphs, Muḥammad b. Yaḥyā al-Ṣūlī (d. ca. 335/947), presented a calumnious genealogy of the first Fatimid Imam-Caliph and claimed that ʿAbd Allāh al-Mahdī was descended from a heretic (*zindīq*) named Sālim, who hailed from ʿAskar Mukram.[35] In the next few decades, the anti-Ismāʿīlī polemicists Ibn Rizām (d. ca. 340/951), Akhū Muḥsin Muḥammad b. ʿAlī (d. ca. 374/985), and Ibn al-Nadīm (d. ca. 385/995–388/998) circulated a "black legend" that the ancestors of the Ismāʿīlī and the Fatimid Imam-Caliphs were "Dayṣānī" (Bardesanian) heretics named Maymūn al-Qaddāḥ and his son ʿAbd Allāh b. Maymūn, who allegedly hatched the Ismāʿīlī religion as a conspiracy to destroy Islam from within. This defamatory story of the "Qaddāḥid" ancestry of the Fatimids evolved further when the Abbasid Caliph al-Qādir issued the Baghdad Manifesto in 402/1011, incorporating these various polemical layers in asserting a heretical, infidel, Zoroastrian, and Dayṣāni pedigree for the Fatimids. By the late fourth/tenth century, the "Qaddāḥid" narrative had even penetrated Ismāʿīlī and Zaydī circles and the Fatimid Imam-Caliph al-Muʿizz and *dāʿī* Ḥamīd al-Dīn al-Kirmānī (d. after 411/1020) were forced to issue refutations of it.[36]

In this respect, portraying the Fatimids as heretics (*zindiqa*), Daysanians, infidels, or atheists, came to function as an enduring polemical trope in Sunnī historiography. With the destruction of Ismāʿīlī literature and persecution of the Ismāʿīlīs for several centuries, this "black legend" subsisted in Sunnī Muslim writings and was picked up by nineteenth century Orientalist scholars like Silvestre de Sacy and M. J. de Goeje. In the end, the "Qaddāḥid" black legend was thoroughly refuted and put to rest by Ivanow in 1946, who showed that Maymūn al-Qaddāḥ and his son were transmitters of traditions from Imam Muḥammad al-Bāqir and Jaʿfar al-Ṣādiq and had nothing to do with the Ismāʿīlīs, having lived long before them. Nevertheless, modern scholarly discussion of the Fatimids' pedigree remains contaminated with polemical overtones very much in the line of early Orientalist scholarship.

Overall, what the Fatimid and anti-Fatimid writings agree on is that the

34. Daftary 2007, 166.
35. Jiwa 2017, 33.
36. Daftary 2007, 101–105.

pre-Fatimid Ismāʿīlī Summons was led by three generations of hereditary leaders – called ʿAbd Allāh (d. ca. 212/827–828), Aḥmad b. ʿAbd Allāh, and the two brothers Muḥammad b. Aḥmad (d. ca. 286/899) and al-Ḥusayn b. Aḥmad (d. ca. 268/881–82) – and that the Fatimid Imam-Caliph ʿAbd Allāh al-Mahdī was the son of al-Ḥusayn. The disagreement lies over the origins of the Fatimid ancestor ʿAbd Allāh – was he a descendant of Jaʿfar al-Ṣādiq, Maymūn al-Qaddāḥ, or someone else? The issue has grave implications for theology as well, because direct lineal descent from ʿAlī b. Abī Ṭālib via Jaʿfar al-Ṣādiq is a necessary condition for the Fatimids' claim to the Imamate and the contemporary claims to religious authority by the Ṭayyibī *dāʿīs* and the Nizārī Ismāʿīlī Imams.

Among modern Ismāʿīlī studies scholars, the origins of the Fatimids remains a contentious issue. As I have recounted elsewhere, one group of historians including Ivanow, Husayn Hamdani, Abbas Hamdani, Jiwa, Walker, and Daftary generally support the claim that the Fatimid Ismāʿīlī Imam-Caliphs were historically directly descended from the Prophet Muḥammad through Jaʿfar al-Sāḍiq based on their examination of the evidence, historical and otherwise. However, these scholars have not yet compiled a comprehensive case for this affirmation. Meanwhile, another group of scholars including Heinz Halm, Michael Brett, and Omert Schrier remain skeptical about the integrity of the Fatimid lineage.[37] They regard it respectively as Ismāʿīlī sectarian propaganda, a mythic Fatimid claim to sacred history whose veracity cannot be determined, or the result of the wishful enthusiasm of the Fatimid supporters.[38] This skepticism springs from the fact that most of the written sources concerning the Fatimid lineage – both for and against – stem from the mid-to-late fourth/tenth century onward and reflect the partisan interests of their authors. There also seems to be an underlying bias among these scholars to the effect that any positive historical valuation of the Fatimid genealogy can only arise from theological or apologetic agendas. Thus, when Prince Peter Hagop Mamour authored a book in defense of the ʿAlid lineage of the Fatimids from a source critical perspective, Brett claimed that Mamour was an Ismāʿīlī (he does not appear to be) and dismissed his contribution as polemical.[39] All of this appears rather incongruent given that both Halm and Brett provide an otherwise evenhanded treatment of Fatimid religio-political rule in their publications.

In my estimation, this skeptical scholarly orientation toward Fatimid

37. Andani 2016a, 199–200.

38. Halm 1996, 8–10, 156–157; 2004, 162–163; Brett 2001, 29–48; Schrier 2006.

39. Mamour 1934; Brett 2001, 30. I have seen no evidence that Mamour is an Ismāʿīlī. But even if he was, his book's method is source critical and certainly not theological.

origins, proceeding as it were from hermeneutics of suspicion, mirrors medieval anti-Fatimid polemic and suffers from at least four historical and methodological problems. First, this approach dismisses altogether the Ismāʿīlīs' perspective on the genealogy of their Imams, including al-Mahdī's early letter, as unreliable and then overstates the historical value of anti-Ismāʿīlī polemical narratives. For example, Halm relied on reports from Ibn Rizām to suggest that the Fatimids are descended from ʿAqīl b. Abī Ṭālib.[40] He also seriously considered the claim of Abū Bakr Muḥammad al-Sūlī (d. 336/946), the close companion and courtier of the Abbasid Caliphs, that the Fatimids are descendants of a non-Arab "heretic" (*zindīq*).[41] Al-Ṣūlī's version is merely the earliest layer of anti-Fatimid polemic that later snowballed into the more elaborate narratives of later writers.[42] It remains unclear why Halm grants these anti-Fatimid and pro-Abbasid versions of Fatimid origins an aura of respectability while wholly rejecting Ismāʿīlī writings on the genealogy of their own Fatimid Imam-Caliphs as "blatant propaganda."[43] Meanwhile, Schrier attempts to revive the long debunked "black legend" of ʿAbd Allāh b. Maymūn al-Qaddāḥ as the progenitor of the Fatimids by taking the claims of Ibn Rizām and Akhū Muḥsin at their word and interpreting the Fatimid efforts to refute this myth as evidence of its historicity.[44] In all of these proposals, there is an evident lack of critical objectivity as scholarly preference is highly skewed towards anti-Ismāʿīlī polemical sources over Ismāʿīlī sources.

While it is certainly true that many Sunnī scholars contested or remained agnostic about the Fatimid lineage claims, their political support for the Abbasids and an emerging Sunnī orthodoxy often underlined these contestations. The Abbasids only issued the Baghdad Manifesto in the fifth/eleventh century after the Fatimids had made serious political and religious inroads into their territories and as a part of al-Qādir's strategy to brand himself as the guardian of Sunnī Islam. Accordingly, the medieval historians Ibn Khaldūn (d. 809/1406) and al-Maqrīzī (d. 845/1442) bluntly charged many of the detractors of the Fatimids with historical bias due to their harboring pro-Abbasid agendas. Ibn Khaldūn opined that those who slandered the Fatimids did so based on "stories that were made up in favor of the weak Abbasid caliphs."[45] Two passages containing al-Maqrīzī's critical comments are worth quoting in full, where he observes that only the "easterners"

40. Halm 1996, 10.
41. Halm 1996, 8–9; Halm 2004, 162–163.
42. Jiwa 2017, 33.
43. Halm 2004, 162.
44. Schrier 2006.
45. Ibn Khaldūn (d. 809/1406), quoted in Jiwa 2017, 57.

of Baghdad and Syria launched dubious attacks on the Fatimids while the Egyptian chroniclers refrained from such aspersions:

> What you will realise about the majority of the attacks against them [the Fatimids] is that the despicable reports, especially those pertaining to expelling them from the Muslim fold *(ahl al-Islam),* are seen only in the books of the easterners, of the Baghdadis and the Syrians.
>
> It is clear to those who have delved into the sciences of his day that the latter are much prejudiced against the Fatimid caliphs and say abominable things about them, despite the fact that their knowledge of the conditions in Egypt is extremely limited. Often, I have seen them relating in their histories, events in Egypt, stories which are not accepted by intelligent scholars and rejected by those skilled and informed about the history of Egypt. The people of each region know best about their own events, and so the Egyptian historians know best about what took place there.[46]

Given the theological and polemical bias of many Iraqi and Syrian detractors of the Fatimids, the historian of the Fatimids must exercise caution in adopting their claims. In doing so, the modern historian would be applying the same critical due diligence as his or her predecessors like Ibn Khaldūn and al-Maqrīzī.

Secondly, Halm, Brett, and Schrier all fail to consider several prominent medieval Muslim voices who affirmed and sometimes defended the Fatimids' claim to ʿAlid descent based on their own investigation. This omission paints a distorted picture of how the Fatimids were perceived by the wider public. For example, Halm urged his readers to take the doubts about the ʿAlid lineage of the Fatimids seriously because the *Ashrāf* (acknowledged blood descendants of the Prophet) and their ʿAlid *naqībs*, a prominent social group responsible for verifying the ʿAlid genealogy of various claimants, would never portray a legitimate ʿAlid as an imposter. Halm then cited the opposition of merely one member of the Syrian *Ashrāf*, the highly polemical Akhū Muḥsin, to create the impression that the entirety of *Ashrāf* disputed the lineage of the Fatimids.[47] And yet nothing could be further from the truth. The public perception of the Fatimid lineage was never as one-sided as this.

For one thing, Sharīf Akhū Muḥsin's account of Fatimid origins was simply copied from Ibn Rizām and was not the result of his own genealogical

46. Al-Maqrīzī (d. 845/1442), quoted in Jiwa 2008.
47. Halm 2004, 162.

research. Furthermore, it is evident that many of the *Ashrāf* of Egypt, the *Ashrāf* of Mecca and Medina, the Buyid *Amīr* ʿAḍud al-Dawla (d. ca. 372/983), and at least one member of the *Ashrāf* of Baghdad, the famous Sharīf al-Raḍī (d. ca. 406/1015), acknowledged the ʿAlid lineage of the Fatimid Imam-Caliphs.[48] The *Ashrāf* of Mecca and Medina endorsed the Fatimid genealogical claims in the Friday prayers during the fourth/tenth century. A delegation of Ḥasanid *Ashrāf* from Ḥijāz and Yemen journeyed to North Africa and declared the Fatimid Imam-Caliph al-Muʿizz as the *Qāʾim* of the *Ahl al-Bayt.*[49] The Ḥasanid *Sharīf* of Mecca, al-Ḥasan b. Jaʿfar (d. 430/1038), endorsed the ʿAlid Ḥusaynid lineage of the Fatimid Imam-Caliph al-ʿAzīz (d. 386/996) in a sermon delivered before the Ḥijāzī *Ashrāf* in front of the Kaʿba. He first adorned the Kaʿba in a shroud of Fatimid white and then praised the Fatimid Imam-Caliphs as "the sons of al-Ḥusayn."[50]

The case of the Sharīf al-Raḍī is especially significant because he is alleged to have signed the Abbasid Baghdad Manifesto denouncing the Fatimids as imposters. But Ibn Athīr, al-Maqrīzī, Ibn al-Jawzī, and Idrīs ʿImād al-Dīn all report that the Sharīf rebuked the Abbasid Caliph al-Qādir by composing the poem below in praise of the Fatimid Imam-Caliph al-Ḥākim:

> [Why should] I bear humiliation in the land of the enemy, when in Egypt the Caliph is an 'Alid.
> His father is my father, his friend (*mawlāhu*) is my friend (*mawlāy*),
> if the distant stranger bears malice for me.
> That which ties my neck to his neck, is the sayyid of all men, Muḥammad and 'Alī. [51]

The way Sharīf al-Raḍī evokes the familial ties binding the Baghdad *Ashrāf* and the Fatimids in Egypt is of immense significance. Not only does al-Raḍī testify to the reigning Fatimid Imam-Caliph as an ʿAlid in all three verses, he allusively speaks to his own intention of emigrating to Egypt. Thus, Ibn Athīr wholly rejected the claim that al-Raḍī signed the Baghdad Manifesto in the first place.[52]

In addition to the prominent personalities mentioned above, several Muslim historians including Ibn Ḥammād (d. ca. 628/1230), Ibn al-Tuwayr (d. ca. 617/1220), Ibn Ẓafīr (d. ca. 630/1233), Ibn Athīr (d. ca. 630/1233), Ibn

48. Andani 2016, 200.
49. Jiwa 2016, 10–11.
50. Jiwa 2016, 18–19.
51. Sharīf al-Raḍī (d. ca. 406/1015), quoted and translated from several primary sources in Jiwa 2017, 41.
52. Ibid., 79.

ʿAbd al-Ẓāhir (d.ca. 692/1293), Ibn Khaldūn (d. ca. 809/1406), al-Maqrīzī (d. ca. 845/1442), Ibn Taghrībirdī (d. ca. 874/1470), and other Egyptian writers affirmed the Fatimids' lineage from the Prophet.[53] By not even mentioning these important figures who agreed with the Fatimid claims to prophetic ancestry, Halm, Brett, and Schrier create an inaccurate portrayal of the reception of Fatimid claims among wider Muslim society.

Thirdly, when certain scholars frame the extant textual evidence for Fatimid genealogy as being partisan and therefore less reliable, they do not acknowledge that the contemporaries of the Fatimids that affirmed their prophetic genealogy sometimes did so based on a different epistemological framework than modern textual historicism. For example, while the Fatimids never published their full genealogy, this did not prevent Ismāʿīlī *dāʿīs* like Ḥamīd al-Dīn al-Kirmānī or al-Muʾayyad al-Shīrāzī (d. ca. 470/1078) from trying to convince Buyid *amīrs* to give allegiance to the Fatimid Imam-Caliphs as the legitimate heirs of the Prophet, and expecting to succeed in these efforts. Evidently, it was realistic to believe that a Muslim ruler with broad Shīʿī sympathies could accept the Fatimid Imam-Caliphs as legitimate bodily descendants of Muḥammad without actually knowing or textually proving every name in their ʿAlid-Fatimid lineage. This could only be possible if certain supra-historical truths (from theology, metaphysics, philosophy, lived social reality) informed their historical perspective and we find this approach reflected in Kirmānī's treatise, "The Shining Lamps Illuminating the Proof of the Imamate" (*al-maṣābīḥ fī l-ithbāt al-imāma*).[54]

In this work, Kirmānī first proves the general existence in the world of an infallible divinely-guided Imamate in the lineage of the Prophet using theological arguments and then uses a deductive process of elimination to specify his master, the Fatimid Imam-Caliph al-Ḥākim, as the only possible candidate for this Imamate.[55] In this treatise, there is no attempt by Kirmānī to prove al-Ḥākim's Fatimid descent from the Prophet; this is taken for granted despite the Baghdad Manifesto issued only a few years earlier. Kirmānī, a gifted intellectual well versed in logic and philosophy, surely could not have expected to win over a Buyid *amīr* to the Fatimid cause if his Imam's genealogy was widely doubted, hotly contested or lacked what most regard as objective evidence. In one section, Kirmānī offered a hybrid theological-historical argument for the continuation of the ʿAlid lineage to the present time: he reasoned that if a divinely-guided Shīʿī Imam like Jaʿfar al-

53. Andani 2016, 200; Walker 2003, 86–89; Jiwa 1992, 57–58. Ibn Taghrībirdī's position is more ambiguous, but he traced the lineage of his teacher al-Maqrīzī back to ʿAlī b. Abī Ṭālib through the Fatimid Caliphs, as reported in Walker 2003.

54. Kirmānī, tr. Walker 2007.

55. Kirmānī, tr. Walker 2007, 100–111.

Ṣādiq historically designated one of his sons as the succeeding Imam, then the latter must always have at least one line of descendants that endures to the present time among whom the true Imam exists.[56] In this way, Kirmānī assures the historical continuity of the Ismāʿīlī Imamate for himself and his readers by first establishing the Imamate's necessary existence in the world through logical-theological argument and then deducing further "historical facts" from that premise to conclude that al-Ḥākim alone is the true Imam.[57] Certainly, Kirmānī's method here is theo-philosophical and only partly historical; I am not suggesting that modern historians adopt it. But the fact that medieval Ismāʿīlīs and non-Ismāʿīlīs could and did accept Fatimid claims to a prophetic genealogy in this manner without seeing its physical or textual evidence demonstrates that a perceived lack of extant documentary evidence for the Fatimid lineage then and now does not indicate its falsity in the eyes of their contemporaries. The perceptive comments of Ivanow, made decades ago, still hold true on the above point:

> The absence of detailed biographies of the ancestors of al-Mahdī is explained by the Ismāʿīlī sources as the result of their having lived in strict disguise.... Thus the long "blank" period in the story of the Imams, living in such conditions, cannot reasonably be taken as valid proof of the falsity of their claims to continuous succession from their original ancestor Ismā'īl b. Ja'far. We do not know how, and by what proofs they used to convince their followers as to the genuineness of their claims. But our ignorance does not constitute a "legal proof" of the futility of their case. It seems that it would be far more suspicious if they had had a consistent and clear-cut story, prepared to satisfy the legitimate curiosity of their followers and of outsiders.[58]

Fourthly, the documented history of the Fatimid Caliphate shows that the Imam-Caliphs exercised religious, social, and political agency in relation to their subjects, allies, rivals, and other influential parties in ways that could only be possible for bona fide descendants of the Prophet Muḥammad. In other words, the Fatimids did not merely assert their ʿAlid lineage, they "enacted" it in practical terms. On this very note, Walker observes that the question of genealogy was not a real issue in terms of the Fatimids' rule over and relationship to their subjects:

> To the extent that uncertainty about their genealogy made their rule more difficult, it must, of course, be taken into account. However,

56. Kirmānī, tr. Walker 2007, 105–108.
57. Kirmānī, tr. Walker 2007, 126.
58. Ivanow 1942, 43–33.

> that conclusion should be established first. A considerable amount of evidence that the Fatimids were treated by their subjects as caliphs and imams with a reasonable genealogical claim to be descendants of the Prophet argues against it. The caliphs, moreover, evidently preferred not to provoke such controversies.[59]

Examples of the Fatimids exercising agency as descendants of the Prophet include their relationships with the Idrīsids of North Africa, the *Ashrāf* of the Ḥijāz, the Egyptian *Ashrāf* following the Fatimid expansion into Egypt, the Buyids in the course of diplomacy, and other tribal chiefs in various regions. A great deal of research has discussed how the descendants of the Prophet, known as the *Ashrāf,* constituted a distinct, socially elevated, and charismatic class of individuals in medieval Muslim societies and were often holders of special functions, rights, and privileges. The Idrīsids were an ʿAlid Ḥasanid dynasty legitimized through a Zaydī Shīʿī model of the Imamate. The Fatimids ended Idrīsid rule in Fez in the mid fourth/tenth century but retained some of the Idrīsid princes as governors. Based on his prophetic pedigree, the Imam-Caliph al-Muʿizz forged a special relationship between the Fatimid Caliphate and the Idrīsid princes. He evoked their mutual familial kinship and thus accorded the Idrīsid nobles elevated status in the Fatimid court. Even the Idrīsid *Ashrāf* involved in rebellions were granted special treatment by the Imam-Caliph due to their shared ʿAlid lineage. At the same time, the Imam-Caliph emphasized the importance of obedience to the divinely-appointed Imam as a condition for the Idrīsids to maintain their noble prophetic lineage.[60]

An even greater example of the Fatimids enacting their ʿAlid descent was when al-Muʿizz successfully mediated a violent conflict between two Ḥijāzī *Ashrāf* clans, the Banū Ḥasan and the Banū Jaʿfar, in 348/959–960, and also sent blood money to resolve their feud. It is hardly conceivable that the Fatimid Imam-Caliph's personal intervention would have been welcome or effective if he had been regarded as an imposter. Shortly after, the Ḥasanid *Amīr* Jaʿfar b. Muḥammad al-Ḥusaynī took control of Mecca and proclaimed the Fatimid Imam-Caliph as the legitimate ruler. The *Ashrāf* of Mecca and Medina continued to acknowledge the authority of the Fatimids until 454–455/1062–1063.[61]

The Fatimids' relationship with the Egyptian *Ashrāf* during their expansion into Egypt is an eminent example of Fatimid agency derived from broader recognition as descendants of the Prophet. As Jiwa observes, the

59. Walker 2002, 188.
60. Jiwa 2016, 8–9.
61. Jiwa 2016, 10–11.

Fatimids' close relationship with the Egyptian *Ashrāf* rested squarely upon their shared familial ties:

> The mediation of the *ashrāf* was arguably one of the most instrumental factors in securing a generally peaceful Fāṭimid entry into Egypt, a point of major significance in understanding the Fāṭimid-*ashrāf* dynamic. The fact that the notables of the surviving Egyptian administration and the military delegated to these members of the *ashrāf* the authority to negotiate the vested interests of the Egyptian nobility with the Fātimid commander suggests that the Egyptian notables were drawing on the shared kinship of the *ashrāf* with al-Muʿizz.[62]

Two of the delegates that met the Fatimid general Jawhar upon his entry into Egypt and negotiated the *amān* (guarantee of safety) were members of the *Ashrāf*. The Sharīf Abū Jaʿfar Muslim al-Ḥusaynī served as a key mediator between the Fatimids and the Egyptian public in the publication of the *amān*.[63] One version of this *amān* even refers to the Fatimid Imam-Caliphs as the family (*ahl*) of Sharīf Muslim. He also led the Egyptian *Ashrāf* in receiving the Imam-Caliph al-Muʿizz and was the first to speak to him. In the ensuing conversation, al-Muʿizz asked Sharīf Muslim about the wellbeing of the *Ashrāf* and went on to involve them in his administration.[64] It is reported that al-Muʿizz publicly addressed the Egyptian *Ashrāf* as follows: "O members of my family and my cousins from the progeny of Fāṭimah, you are my kin and you are the amour (*al-ʿudda*)." Likewise, the Sharīf Muslim expressed his inclination for the Fatimids when he said: "I wish my father and my grandfather had seen al-Muʿizz, for they would have been proud of him. I cannot compare any of the Umayyad or ʿAbbāsid caliphs with him."[65]

Later when the Fatimid Imam-Caliph al-ʿAzīz engaged in diplomatic dispatches with the Buyid dynasty, the *Amīr* ʿAḍud al-Dawla explicitly recognized al-ʿAzīz's Fatimid descent in his letter to the Imam-Caliph. As reported by the historian Ibn Taghrībirdī (d. ca. 874/1470), the Buyid *Amīr* "had written a letter to him [al-ʿAzīz] acknowledging in it the excellence of the *ahl al-bait* and confirming to al-ʿAzīz that he was from that pure source. He addressed him [al-ʿAzīz] as *al-ḥaḍrat al-sharīfa* and words to that effect." In his response to the Buyid *Amīr*, al-ʿAzīz reiterated his Fatimid ʿAlid descent numerous time, referring to Muḥammad as his forefather and Muḥammad's

62. Jiwa 2016, 15.
63. Jiwa 2016, 14.
64. Jiwa 2016, 15–16.
65. Jiwa 2016, 17.

pure progeny as his ancestors.[66] Two other noteworthy examples of Fatimid dominance stemming directly from their ʿAlid lineage consist of cases where the chiefs of two Iraqi Bedouin principalities recognized Fatimid religio-political authority in 401/1010. The ʿUqaylid chieftain Qirwāsh, ruling over Mosul, proclaimed his allegiance to the Fatimid Imam-Caliph al-Ḥakim bi-amr Allāh and endorsed his ʿAlid pedigree explicitly in his *khuṭba*. He spoke of ʿAlī b. Abī Ṭālib as the "father of the rightly guided Imams" and the Fatimid Caliph as the "Imam of the age, fortress of the faith, master of the ʿAlid *daʿwa* (*ṣāhib al-daʿwa al-ʿalawiyya*) and prophetic religion," and Commander of the Faithful.[67] At the same time, ʿAlī b. Mazyad, the chief of the Mazyadids in southern Iraq, issued similar proclamations recognizing the Fatimids. All of this created what Walker calls a "Fatimid noose" surrounding Baghdad. These Fatimid incursions into the Abbasid heartland, along with their popularity among a rioting Shīʿī populace chanting "Yā Ḥākim, Yā Manṣūr" in 398/1008, prompted al-Qādir to issue the Baghdad Manifesto as a denunciation of the Fatimids.[68]

The above examples evidence that the Fatimids were certainly able to influence, exercise authority, forge relationships, and express agency in relation to a wide array of Muslim socio-political actors and parties in a manner only appropriate for actual descendants of the Prophet. While this certainly does not provide a textual demonstration of their claims, these social facts go a long way in depicting how the Fatimids' pedigree was perceived and received by their contemporaries. Ibn Khaldūn argued the same point in his *Muqaddima* when he asserted the legitimacy of the Fatimids as descendants of Muhammad against claims to the contrary:

> The ('Ubaydid-Fatimid) dynasty lasted uninterruptedly for about two hundred and seventy years. They held possession of the place where Ibrahim (Abraham) had stood and where he had prayed, the home of the Prophet and the place where he was buried, the place where the pilgrims stand and where the angels descended (to bring the revelation to Muhammad). Then, their rule came to an end. During all that time, their partisans showed them the greatest devotion and love and firmly believed in their descent from the imam Ismail, the son of Jaʿfar as-Sadiq. Even after the dynasty had gone and its influence had disappeared, people still came forward to press the claims of the sect.... Had there been doubts about their pedigree, their followers would not have undergone the dangers involved in supporting them. A sectarian does not manipulate his own affairs, nor sow confusion

66. Jiwa 1992, 59.
67. Jiwa 2017, 48.
68. Jiwa 2017, 46.

> within his own sect, nor act as a liar where his own beliefs are concerned.[69]

In sum, a polemical posture still looms large when it comes to discussions of the origins and ancestry of the Fatimid Imam-Caliphs. Future approaches to Fatimid origins would fare better by aiming for more balance in weighing Ismāʿīlī and polemical sources, providing a more comprehensive picture of how the Fatimids' lineage claim was received by non-Ismāʿīlī scholars, considering the Fatimids' Ismāʿīlī followers' approach to validating their lineage, and focusing on the power and agency the Fatimids were able to exercise through wider acceptance of their genealogy.

A more recent academic study that seems to exemplify an "academic-polemical" approach to study of the Ismāʿīlīs is *The Aga Khan Case* by Teena Purohit.[70] While Purohit's study displays some merit in its deconstruction of colonialist frames of sectarian religious categories, her overall approach polemicizes the history of the Aga Khans and the narratives of Khoja tradition through gross misrepresentations of both.

In the famous Aga Khan Case tried in the High Court of Bombay in 1866, a small minority of the Khoja caste group challenged the Imam Ḥasan ʿAlī Shāh Aga Khan I's authority as the Ismāʿīlī Imam and alleged that the Khoja caste was Sunnī instead of Ismāʿīlī Muslim. It should be noted that the plaintiffs in the Aga Khan Case resorted to the anti-Ismāʿīlī polemic discussed above to paint the Aga Khan and the Ismāʿīlīs as heretics and fanatics throughout history. In the end, the documentary evidence presented by the Aga Khan's defense counsel demonstrated the Khoja community's longstanding spiritual allegiance and recognition of the Aga Khan and his ancestors as their Imams. The defense presented original letters, ledgers, circulars, and witness testimony showing that an overwhelming majority of the Khoja caste in Bombay and other areas had steadfastly recognized the Aga Khan and his ancestors as their Imams and spiritual masters for generations, having regularly remitted tithes to them as a religious duty and embarked on risky pilgrimages to the Imams' residence in Persia.[71] The Court ruled in the Aga Khan's favor, concluding that the Khojas were a Hindu caste that had been converted to the faith of Shīʿī Ismāʿīlī Islam centuries previously and remained under the spiritual authority of the Aga Khan.

From the very beginning, Purohit makes several erroneous claims about Aga Khan I to obscure his identity as the Imam of the Ismāʿīlīs and conceal the longstanding historical relationship between the Khoja caste and the Nizārī Ismāʿīlī Imams in Persia. She incorrectly alleges that the Aga Khan's

69. Ibn Khaldūn, tr. Franz Rosenthal 1958, vol. 1.
70. Purohit 2012.
71. See Howard 1895.

father, Imam Shāh Khalīl Allāh (d. 1232/1817), was "the first Isma'ili Imam to appear almost five centuries after the fall of the last Isma'ili stronghold of Alamut," when various sources report about Ismāʿīlī Imams engaging in religious and political activities long before this Imam.[72] Purohit misleadingly claims that Aga Khan I was not the "official Imam" of the Ismāʿīlīs before 1866 and that Ismāʿīlīs worldwide had been developing traditions autonomously without the guidance of the Ismāʿīlī Imams;[73] in actual fact, the Ismāʿīlī Imams had been in contact with various communities since the Anjudan revival in the eighth/fifteenth century. For these reasons, Daniel Beben, who recently edited and translated the Persian memoirs of Aga Khan I, has remarked that Purohit's "analysis of the historical background of the Aga Khan and his relationship to the Ismāʿīlīs of South Asia demonstrates a number of omissions and severe oversimplifications."[74]

Purohit's denial of any historical connection between the Ismāʿīlī Imams in Persia and the Khojas of India is likewise contradicted by documentary evidence going back to the seventeenth century, including eyewitness testimony from Khayrkhwāh-i Harātī (fl. tenth/sixteenth century), letters from the Ismāʿīlī Imams, historical evidence of Khoja pilgrimages to the Imams, and Khoja tomb inscriptions in the Nizārī Imams' mausoleum in Persia.[75] Purohit also reverses the historical facts about the Aga Khan Case by portraying the plaintiffs as the "caste leaders" of the Khojas,[76] when in reality these plaintiffs were but a small dissident group that had been expelled from the Khoja caste by unanimous vote on three separate occasions in 1835, 1848, and 1861.[77]

Purohit's reading of the Khoja *gināns* is deeply problematic due to her exclusive focus on Vashnavi frames and failure to engage with the literature's polythetic symbolic frameworks, which include Indo-Muslim, Ṣūfī, Sant, and Bhaktī discourses.[78] She interprets the *Das Avatar ginān* to be about a Twelver Shīʿī hidden Imam in occultation and thereby denies the tradition's historical connection to the Ismāʿīlī Imams.[79] But her argument collapses

72. Purhoit 2012, 19.

73. Purohit 2012, 22.

74. Beben 2018, 14.

75. For a discussion of this evidence, see Beben 2018, 25. See also Daftary 2007, 457–459.

76. See Purohit 2012, 4, 24, 28, 34, for her repeated naming of the plaintiff party as the "Khoja leaders."

77. See Daftary 2007, 474–475 for the sequence of events leading to the dissident group being dismissed from the Khoja communal body.

78. On the multilayered symbolic discourse of the *gināns*, see Asani 2002, 1–53. On the bridal symbolism in the *gināns*, see Asani 2002, 54–70.

79. Purohit 2012, 11, 63–69.

when one simply notes that many other *ginān*s identify the figure of the *avatara, shaāh, satguru, qāʾim, nar,* or *swāmī* with a historical Ismāʿīlī Imam – such as Qāṣimshāh (d. ca. 771/1369–1370), Islāmshāh (d. ca. 829/1425–1426), Mustanṣir billāh II (d. ca. 885/1480), Abū Dharr ʿAlī (tenth/sixteenth century), Shāh Nizār (d. ca. 1722), or Shāh Khalīl Allāh (d. ca. 1232/1817).[80] Based on her highly selective approach to the literature, Purohit claims that the "throne" (*takht*) in the *ginān*s signifies an absent awaited messianic figure, which the Aga Khans supplanted with a new idea of a living Imam. In actual fact, the throne image in the *ginān*s and Persian Ismāʿīlī literature is a potent symbol for the office of the living Ismāʿīlī Imamate, which is why other *ginān*s depicted a historical Ismāʿīlī Imam sitting upon a throne.[81] In the end, Purohit's polemical approach to the Aga Khans, the Ismāʿīlīs, and the Khoja *ginān* tradition, akin to the very colonialist spirit she seeks to denounce, ultimately talks over and silences the communal memory of the Khojas, who always regarded their *ginān*s as the compositions of their *pir*s (preacher-saints) sent by the Nizārī Ismāʿīlī Imams in Persia to guide them.

Apart from the reservations given above, the study of the Ismāʿīlīs in the academic domain is in a healthy state in terms of methodology. However, there are issues of a broader theoretical nature. Every academic field reaches a state where scholars must take a step back and reflect on the nature of their object of study. In this case, the object of study in Ismāʿīlī studies is an amorphous and elusive entity called "Ismāʿīlism."

The Construction and Conceptualization of "Ismāʿīlism" in Modern Scholarship

> Ismāʿīlism is one such response integral to the overall Shia perspective which seeks to comprehend the true meaning of the Islamic message, and trace a path to its fulfilment.[82]
>
> The Institute of Ismāʿīlī Studies

80. For the mentions of Qāṣimshāh and Islāmshāh, see the translations in Kassam 1995, 192–193, 345. For the mentions of Mustanṣir billāh and Abū Dharr ʿAlī, see the translations in Virani 1995, 21, 33. For the name of Shāh Nizār, see the translation in Shackle and Moir 1992, 98–101. For the name of Shāh Khalīl Allāh, see Shackle and Moir 1992, 87. On a related note, Purohit neglects to attend to the genealogy of Ismaili Imams recited by the Khojas in their daily prayers, a portion of which (up to Shāh Nizār) is shared with the Imamshāhī group.

81. For an Ismāʿīlī Imam depicted on the "throne" in the *ginān*s, see *Anant Akhado*, verses 45–47, 101, 275–277, 350, 441, transliterated in Ḥasan Kabīr al-Dīn 1995; Shackle and Moir 1992, 77; Virani 1995, 32; For the throne image in Persian literature, see Virani 2007, 14, 174.

82. Institute of Ismaili Studies 2018.

Just as Shahab Ahmed's *What is Islam?* marked a watershed moment in scholarly debates over the definition of "Islam" in Islamic studies, the Islamic studies subfield known as Ismāʿīlī studies is in dire need of a similar intervention. The term "Ismāʿīlism" is frequently used in modern scholarship in a variety of ways without a clear definition or conceptualization. For example, it is very common to see mention of Ismāʿīlism generally and its many compounds like "Fatimid Ismāʿīlism," "Nizārī Ismāʿīlism," "philosophical Ismāʿīlism," "Persian Ismāʿīlism," "Satpanth Ismāʿīlism," etc. throughout academic literature.[83] The problem is that we still lack a clear sense of what "Ismāʿīlism" is supposed to be. In this section, I will argue that Ismāʿīlism in modern scholarship is being defined as a sectarian ideological object, constituted either by a combination of historical Ismāʿīlī doctrines or by allegiance to and submission to the religious authority of the Ismāʿīlī Imams. The roots of this sectarian ideological construction of Ismāʿīlism can be found in the 1866 Aga Khan Case mentioned earlier, where the plaintiff and defense lawyers sparred over various portrayals of the Aga Khan and the Ismāʿīlīs ranging from arch heretics to sectarian Shīʿī Muslims. This sense of Ismāʿīlism qua sectarian ideology came to underlie the field of Ismāʿīlī studies and continues to plague scholarly discourse. In what follows, I show that Ismāʿīlism as a scholarly object of investigation came about through reifying one or more historical Ismāʿīlī doctrines, such as the divine authority of a specific line of Imams.

The Construction of Ismāʿīlism in the Colonial Court

> 'Ismāʿīlī Studies' now represents an epistemological entity in its own right, carving out as well as facilitating understanding of at once a Fatimid cultural past as well as a Muslim universality for the global Ismāʿīlī community.[84]
>
> Soumen Mukherjee

One of the most prominent and influential definitions of the Ismāʿīlīs stems not from scholarship, but from the outcome of the 1866 Aga Khan Case mentioned earlier. In the twenty-four day trial, the plaintiffs painted Shīʿī Islam and its Ismāʿīlī interpretation as a form of heresy recently brought by the Aga Khan and imposed upon the Khojas; they asserted that the Khojas had been Sunnī Muslims since their conversion by Pīr Ṣadr al-Dīn in the fourteenth

83. For examples of this frequent usage, see Daftary 2007 and more recently, Hollenberg 2016.

84. Mukherjee 2017, 53–54.

century and that the Aga Khan and his followers were heretics descended from the infamous "Assassins" of medieval lore.[85] In building their case, the plaintiffs drew upon available Orientalist "academic-polemical" scholarship and anti-Ismāʿīlī polemic produced by Sunnī Muslim writers. In response to the plaintiffs' arguments, the Aga Khan's defense counsel, Edward Irving Howard, presented a highly impressive and lengthy discourse directed towards two distinct ends: first, to offer a moral and historical rehabilitation of the Aga Khan and the Ismāʿīlīs; second, to demonstrate the longstanding spiritual ties between the Aga Khan, his ancestors, and the Khoja caste.[86] In his defense speech, whose published version spans over one hundred pages, Howard provided a historical narrative tying together various phases of Shīʿī and Ismāʿīlī history, including the early period of Jaʿfar al-Ṣādiq, the Fatimid Caliphate, the Nizārī polity centered in Alamut, the post-Mongol Nizārīs, the Aga Khan and his ancestors in Persia, and the Khojas. In order to make the history of the Ismāʿīlīs more intelligible to the colonial judge, he liberally employed analogies between Ismāʿīlī beliefs and Christian ideas, evoking notions like the papacy, Catholics, Protestants, papists, etc. Howard also addressed and refuted some of the polemical portrayals of the Ismāʿīlīs produced by the likes of Ibn Riẓām, al-Ghazālī, al-Juvaynī, and the Orientalist scholar von Hammer-Purgstall. He extolled the Fatimid Caliphate as an example of Ismāʿīlīs making positive contributions to Islamic civilization and morally defended the targeted assassinations carried out by the medieval Nizārī Ismāʿīlīs besieged by Sunnī armies by drawing analogies with the divinely-sanctioned violence in the Old Testament. Termed the "Howardian Moment" by Soumen Mukherjee, Howard's discourse represents a turning point in Western perceptions of the Ismāʿīlīs. His speech amounted to a scholarly intervention against older polemical scholarship and his arguments prefigured many of the academic, historical, and critical analyses that today constitute the field of modern Ismāʿīlī studies.[87]

The real problem in terms of scholarly categorization stems from the framework employed by Justice Arnould in delivering the Aga Khan Case judgment. His ruling revolved around five questions as quoted below:

> First: What are Sunnīs as distinct from Shi'as?
>
> Secondly: Who and What are the Shi'a Imami Ismāʿīlīs?
>
> Thirdly: Who and what is the first defendant, the Aga Khan?
>
> Fourthly: Who and what are the Khojas and what are and

85. Asani 2011, 105–106.
86. Howard 1895.
87. Mukherjee 2017, 53–76.

have been their relations with the first defendant and his ancestors?

Fifthly: What have been the relations of the first defendant, Aga Khan, with the particular community to which the relators and plaintiffs belong, viz., the Khoja community of Bombay?[88]

To the first question, the judge defined Sunnī Muslims as the "orthodox" Muslims, followers of the *Sunna* or tradition, who profess the *Shahāda*: there is no god except God and Muḥammad is the messenger of God. He defined the Shīʿī Muslims as those who affirm, in addition to the *Shahāda*, that "ʿAlī the companion of Muḥammad is the Vicar of God" and regard ʿAlī as having almost equal status to the Prophet Muḥammad. He further described the meaning of the word *Shīʿa* as "separatists."[89] After a few pages outlining Sunnī-Shīʿī differences in belief, history and ritual, the judge defined the Shīʿī Imami Ismāʿīlīs as:

> those among the Shi'as who hold Ismail, the seventh in descent from 'Ali to have been the last of the Revealed Imams; and who also hold that, until the final manifestation of Ali (who as an incarnation of God) is to come before the end of all things to judge the world – the *musnud* [throne] of the Imamate (or in Latin idiom the office of Supreme Pontiff) is rightfully held by an hereditary succession of unrevealed Imams, the lineal descendants of 'Ali through Isma'il.[90]

The judgment then proceeded to trace the history of the Ismāʿīlīs and their Imams through various historical periods to the person of the present Aga Khan based on the sources and testimony available to him. The judge then declared that

> His Highness Aga Khan, Mahallati is the hereditary Chief and unrevealed Imam of the Isma'ilis – the present or living holder of the Musnud of the Imamate – claiming descent in direct line from 'Ali, the Vicar of God, through the 7th (and according to the Isma'ili creed), the last, of the Revealed Imams – Isma'il, the son of Jaʿfar al-Sadiq.[91]

After analyzing the traditions, history and religious practices of the Khojas and summarizing witness testimony, the judge ruled that the Khojas were:

> A sect of people, whose ancestors were Hindu in original; which was

88. Purhoit 2012, 49.
89. Arnould 1866, 5.
90. Arnould 1866, 7.
91. Arnould 1866, 10.

> converted and has throughout abided in the faith of the Shi'a Imami Isma'ilis; and which has always been and still is bound by ties of spiritual allegiance to the hereditary Imams of the Isma'ilis.[92]

The Aga Khan Case judgment issued by the High Court of Bombay is important for a number of reasons, and other scholars have assessed its impact in terms of the British colonial practice of categorizing their subjects into discrete religious groups.[93] Prior to the ruling, while the Khojas certainly harbored beliefs and practices expressing their Shīʿī Ismāʿīlī allegiance, they did not self-identify using the term "Ismāʿīlī"; they chiefly identified using indigenous Indic categories like caste or *panth*. The Bombay High Court, however, formed its judgment through reification, "mentally making religion into a thing, gradually coming to conceive it as an objective systematic entity."[94] In doing so, the Court abstracted a set of Khoja beliefs and commitments from their way of life and gave these a label in terms of categories like Muslim, Hindu, Sunnī, Shīʿī, Ismāʿīlī, etc. Thus, the text of the judgment presented the Khojas as "originally Hindus of the trading class" who were subsequently "converted by Pir Sadr al-Din about 400 years ago" to Ismāʿīlī Islam.[95]

Asani best summarizes how the case judge privileged a framework of religious sectarian categories, informed by Western scholars of Islam, over and above the testimony of the Khojas themselves:

> He carefully sifted through the evidence he had gathered from witnesses, looking for elements that he could fit within the framework of the categories "Islam," "Muslim," "Hindu," "Shīʿa," and "Ismāʿīlī" deduced from the scholarship of Western historians of Islam. He regarded these experts as authorities who had objective knowledge of the subject and were, he felt, more reliable than the Khoja practitioners themselves.[96]

The judgment exerted a decisive influence upon the academic study of the Ismāʿīlīs that began in the next century because it presents the first modern definition of "Ismāʿīlī" that would later permeate the field of Ismāʿīlī studies. It first defines Shīʿī Islam as a religious sect in opposition to the Sunnī Islam, termed as the orthodox form of Islam. The Ismāʿīlīs were then situated as a subsect of the Shīʿa and distinguished from them by their rec-

92. Arnould 1866, 21.
93. See Asani 2011.
94. Smith 1991, 52.
95. Arnound 1866, 21–22.
96. Asani 2011, 107.

ognition of a line of Imams from Ismāʿīl, son of Jaʿfar al-al-Ṣādiq. Next, the judgment also puts forth, for the first time in Western literature, a historical narrative of an unbroken lineage of Ismāʿīlī Imams through history around which the Ismāʿīlī sect coalesces, develops, and is ultimately defined. The religious identity of the Khojas was then determined to be Ismāʿīlī solely by the caste's religious and spiritual ties to the Aga Khan and his ancestors.

We can regard this definition of "Ismāʿīlī" outlined in the Aga Khan Case judgment – a commitment of spiritual allegiance to the Ismāʿīlī line of Imams throughout its entire history – as the earliest construction of what will later be called "Ismāʿīlism" in academic literature. Nile Greene concurs when he writes that

> [i]n order to recognize rather than gloss over the discontinuity of Isma'ili history in the manner of many scholarly apologetics it therefore makes sense to speak of the Agha Khan and his sons as the modern producers of a "Neo-Isma'ilism."[97]

As it will be seen, the Ismāʿīlī definition and historical narrative canonized in the Aga Khan Case judgment prefigures how "Ismāʿīlism" emerges as a taxonomical category in the Western scholarship beginning in the next century.

Definitions of Ismāʿīlism in Modern Scholarship

> What may be suggested is to regard as belonging to Ismāʿīlism all sectarian developments in Shīʿīte Islam whose doctrine is built around what we may conventionally designate by a term, borrowed from organic chemistry, "the Ismāʿīlī radical."[98]
>
> Vladimir Ivanow

Following the Aga Khan Case judgment, Ismāʿīlism has been reified and defined in essentialist terms within Western academic studies published through the twentieth century and well into the present day. While it is impossible to survey every single such work, several examples from seminal scholars in Ismāʿīlī studies will suffice to demonstrate this claim. In general, "Ismāʿīlism" is presented as a static religious ideology, intelligible entity, or sectarian Muslim movement traversing time and space since its origins in the eighth century while also branching out into several Ismāʿīlī subsects. The content of Ismāʿīlism is defined in scholarship either in terms of several

97. Green 2011, 157.
98. Ivanow 1963, 5.

theological doctrines or in terms of a single doctrine – belief in and allegiance to the Ismāʿīlī Imams. The term "Ismāʿīlī" is then used to describe any phenomena that expresses Ismāʿīlism as defined.

The earliest conceptualization of Ismāʿīlism as a scholarly category is based on a taxonomy of sects. Evidently, the idea of Ismāʿīlism as a sect was a defining parameter in the Aga Khan Case judgment. The judgment used the word sect numerous times to describe the Shīʿī Muslims, the Ismāʿīlī Muslims, and the Khojas. We can better understand why the Bombay High Court cast its definition of the Ismāʿīlīs in sectarian terms by recalling that the plaintiffs first invoked the sectarian model in a negative light. They alleged that the Khojas of Bombay were actually Sunnī Muslims while the Shīʿī Islam of the Aga Khan was a sectarian heresy. This left the defense no choice but to respond on a sectarian playing field in which Sunnī Islam stood as normative orthodox Islam. Therefore, the emerging definition of Ismāʿīlī from the Aga Khan Case represents, at best, a makeshift and provisional definition adopted for the purposes of legal defense. The sectarian frame not only endured but infiltrated early Ismāʿīlī studies scholarship. In 1923, De Lacy O'Leary published a book on the Fatimid Caliphate in which he constantly referred to the "Ismāʿīlian sect" of Shīʿī Islam.[99] Framing Ismāʿīlism as the "sect of a sect" successfully cordons off Ismāʿīlī history and thought from the rest of Muslim history, philosophy, and literature. Such separatist notions are expressed in the Church-sect typologies of Max Weber. Weber defined a church as "a compulsory and comprehensive institution." The church "embraces the whole society, and in general you enter it by being born into it." But a sect is "a voluntary and elective association (*verein*): you are in it by choice – yours and its." A sect is a "community of personally charismatic individuals."[100] Perhaps some of the deployments of the term "sect" in Western scholarship on Islam occur due to how the term *firqah*, used by medieval Muslim scholars to designate various groups with political and theological views, is being translated into English. Nevertheless, Marshall Hodgson reminds us that "sect" and *firqah* are by no means the same thing and should not be equated:

> But to use the word "sect" wherever a Muslim writer used the word *firqah* produces odd misconceptions. A person could maintain a given viewpoint on the imamat, one on questions of metaphysics of *kalām*, and one on *fiqh* law.... Note that the conventional distinction between "orthodox Islam" and "the sects" is at best dubious.[101]

99. O'Leary 1923.
100. Cook 1999, 273–274.
101. Hodgson 1974, 67.

Despite these reservations, David Hollenberg based his recent study of Ismāʿīlī revelatory hermeneutics or *taʾwīl* on a sectarian reading of Ismāʿīlism. Drawing on Weber's ideas as interpreted by later thinkers, Hollenberg consistently speaks of "Ismāʿīlism" in the third/ninth and fourth/tenth centuries as "a millenarian sect" and interprets Ismāʿīlī literature in the same light. This led Hollenberg to conclude that the primary purpose of Ismāʿīlī *taʾwīl*, as a method of interpretation, was to engender a sectarian ethos of exclusive identity and create ideological tension between the Ismāʿīlī "sectarians" and the rest of the Muslims. As a corollary of his argument, Hollenberg interpreted the jurisprudence (*fiqh*), public ritual, coinage, architecture, and ceremony of the Fatimid Caliphate as pan-ʿAlid or partisan Shīʿī rhetoric as opposed to expressions of Ismāʿīlī commitments. Evidently, a sectarian conception of Ismāʿīlism is rather narrow and necessarily excludes a great deal of meaningful Fatimid Caliphal discourse.[102]

If Ismāʿīlism is a sect in the Weberian sense, then Ismāʿīlism can only represent a deviation from the default "church," where the latter is exemplified by the Sunnī majority; except that there was no such thing as a consolidated and internally reconciled majoritarian Sunnī tradition of Islam until the fifth/eleventh century at the earliest. Characterizing Ismāʿīlism as a sect fails to acknowledge the contested process of orthodoxy construction in the Sunnī context, in which various Sunnī political, theological, and legal orientations could easily be framed as "sects" using the same logic as Hollenberg. Why should the Ashʿarīs, Muʿtazilīs, Ḥanbalīs, or Ḥanafīs qualify as "schools" while only the Ismāʿīlīs count as a "sect"? In the end, the difference seems rather arbitrary and reflects value judgments on the part of the historian. Adam Gaiser, more than anyone else, argues extensively that the typology of Weberian "sects" is inappropriate in the context of Islamic history and should be discarded: "Clearly, the analytical church-sect-cult categories discussed above are not much help in characterizing early intra-religious divisions among Muslims."[103]

In recent studies of the Ismāʿīlīs there has been some movement away from framing the different branches of Islam as sects and instead referring to them as "communities of interpretation." Daftary contextualizes the appearance of various Sunnī and Shīʿī branches over history and geography as the emergence of communities of interpretations, each trying to understand and interpret the message of Islam in their own distinctive manners.[104] He further warns that articulating the history and doctrines of Sunnī and Shīʿī communities in terms of orthodoxy and heterodoxy amounts to imposing

102. Hollenberg 2016, 1–34.
103. Gaiser 2017, 67.
104. Daftary 1996.

Christian categories on Muslim phenomena and should be jettisoned. While "communities of interpretation" is certainly a more appropriate frame than the sectarian models, the question of what distinctive interpretations of Islam qualify a community to be labeled as "Ismāʿīlī" and what contents or concepts comprise "Ismāʿīlism" remains in need of analysis.

The earliest instance of the term "Ismāʿīlism" in the English language occurs in the work of Vladimir Ivanow, the acknowledged pioneer of modern Ismāʿīlī studies. In his 1922 article titled "Ismailitica," Ivanow used the word Ismāʿīlism several times in four pages through remarks inquiring about the "origin of Ismāʿīlism."[105] Bernard Lewis then published *The Origins of Ismailism* in 1940 and conceived of Ismāʿīlism as an "interconfessional" ideology that recognized and incorporated the truths of several religions and tended toward relativism.[106] In *A Creed of the Fatimids* published in 1936, Ivanow construed that "Ismāʿīlism never was uniform as a doctrine, but presented the picture of a bunch of parallel local movements which agreed in the main tenets, but greatly differed in details."[107]

In this early stage, it seems that Ivanow's concept of Ismāʿīlism was based on the reification of certain doctrines or tenets. In the preface to his 1942 *Ismaili Tradition Concerning the Rise of the Fatimids,* Ivanow provided an introductory definition of Ismāʿīlism as a sectarian Shīʿī movement whose central tenet centered around the figure of the Imam:

> The central and fundamental ideal of Ismāʿīlism, also common to various Shīʿīte sects, was the ultimate triumph of Islam as the sole religion of the world, the ultimate union of mankind in "one flock under one shepherd", i.e. the Imam from the house of the Prophet, who alone can guide long suffering humanity to a righteous and peaceful life, filling the earth with justice and equity ever as much as it has always been filled with injustice, oppression, and bestiality.[108]

As his studies progressed Ivanow's characterization of Ismāʿīlism and its tenets became more specific. Finally, in his 1963 *Ismaili Literature,* a widely acclaimed publication in its time, Ivanow provided his most developed and nuanced conceptualization of Ismāʿīlism in both historical and doctrinal terms. He began by presenting Ismāʿīlism as the story of a single ideological movement whose doctrines develop in various directions through different phases in history:

105. Ivanow 1922, 60–64.
106. Lewis 1940.
107. Ivanow 1936, 2.
108. Ivanow 1942, xvii.

> The story of Ismāʿīlism is composed of "phases," some running parallel to others, and some developing in sequence, directly or after a certain "leap." It is something like the metamorphoses of the egg, caterpillar, chrysalis, butterfly – the substance and individuality intrinsically the same, but forms markedly different. But taken as a complex of interconnected phenomena it may to a great extent permit us to grasp the nature of this ideology as a whole by supplementing what is incomplete in one "phase" by observation of an analogous development in another. Thus the only way is to choose as an object of study the whole group of cognate phenomena in its entirety.[109]

The above description articulates a vision of Ismāʿīlism as a reified entity in history – like an egg developing into a butterfly – sprouting diverse offshoots and movements. It also betrays a teleological worldview where Ismāʿīlism should ideally evolve according to a certain historical trajectory.

In the next paragraph, Ivanow went on to characterize the unity of Ismāʿīlism as an ideological movement with diverse manifestations and evolutions in history by comparing it to the idea of a "radical" from organic chemistry. His remarks are worth quoting in full:

> Now the question arises as to what we should regard as a "cognate" development, as far as Ismāʿīlism is concerned? What may be suggested is to regard as belonging to Ismāʿīlism all sectarian developments in Shiʿite Islam whose doctrine is built around what we may conventionally designate by a term, borrowed from organic chemistry, "the Ismāʿīlī radical." This is the indissoluble combination of five dogmatic principles which, as what is called "radical" in chemistry, form a "unit," which may be itself combined with other ideas and their complexes, but always inseparably, as if forming an "irresolvable element." It consists of: strict monotheism, belief in periodical Apostolic missions of great prophets, Imamat as a further development of the preceding, *daʿwat* or missionary function of the Imam, and *ta'wil* or revelation of the inner implications of scripture and forms of worship. All these form the basic and essential, indispensable structure of the "radical." In practical life it is quite possible to observe various deviations from such ideal structure. Some ingredients may be fading, and some abnormally overdeveloped – this is what may be designated as occasional or heretical tendencies, especially in a backward milieu.[110]

109. Ivanow 1963, 5.
110. Ivanow 1963, 5.

Ivanow saw Ismāʿīlism as an ideology, termed the "Ismāʿīlī radical," with a core and unchangeable essence and manifesting certain properties. This ideology is an objective essence consisting of five doctrinal elements: radical monotheism, the idea of Prophethood through history, the Imamate, the *daʿwa* (summons) and the revelatory hermeneutics (*taʾwīl*) of Islam. It is true that all five elements are among the major themes discussed in Ismāʿīlī doctrinal literature going back to the tenth century. But Ivanow reified these five elements as "basic and essential" in that they form an "indispensable structure," an idea he expresses by using the analogy of the "indissoluble" radical from organic chemistry. Even when some of these five elements do not manifest prominently in a certain period or context, Ivanow maintained that all five elements are nevertheless present and only fail to appear due to some extrinsic factor, such as heresy or "backwards" intellectual contexts. Although Ivanow proposed this model in 1963, I have not yet come across any other attempts to define Ismāʿīlism in such a precise fashion, besides Hollenberg's study noted earlier. Even then, Ivanow's model of Ismāʿīlism seems to have evaded critical analysis and is not explicitly referenced in later scholarly discussions. In fact, contemporary Ismāʿīlī studies literature seems to be devoid of any discussions about Ismāʿīlism as a scholarly category. Nevertheless, recent studies continue to speak of Ismāʿīlism as a reified entity carrying certain doctrines through history and manifesting in different forms.

Scholars following Ivanow continued to write about the history and thought of the Ismāʿīlīs in terms of a sectarian ideology called Ismāʿīlism. In a 1972 article, Samuel M. Stern wrote that "Ismāʿīlism was founded in the middle of the third century of the Hijra, i.e. the middle of the ninth century A.D., as an underground revolutionary movement, aiming at the overthrow of the 'Abbasid caliphate."[111] Among the next generation of scholars, Aziz Esmail and Azim Nanji provide a historical narrative and doctrinal survey of Ismāʿīlism in their 1977 chapter, "The Ismailis in History." Their chapter defines Ismāʿīlism in the following way:

> Ismāʿīlism embodies a complex of attitudes – attitudes towards such fundamental questions as the nature of truth and how truth can best be attained through proper organisation of society – which can be traced back to the lifetime of Prophet Muhammad and the period immediately following his death. These attitudes came to be centred around the figure of Imam ʿAli, the Prophet's cousin and son-in-law, who was also closely associated with him right from the beginning of

111. Stern 1983, 234.

> his prophetic mission. The nature of the doctrine which evolved out of these attitudes will be considered further below. The implication that the essential origins of the Ismāʿīlīs lay in a dynastic dispute centring on the figure of Imam Ismāʿil, rather than in attitudes going back to the beginnings of Islam, is reflected mostly in non-Ismāʿīlī polemical writers, such as Ibn Rizam, al-Nawbakhti, al-Qummi, al-Ashʿari, al-Busti, etc.[112]

Esmail and Nanji's description of the nature of Ismāʿīlism, as comprising "attitudes" about "the nature of truth and now truth can best be attained through proper organization of society" that go back to the Prophet Muḥammad, is an improved version of the ideological model first proposed by Ivanow. Developed Ismāʿīlī doctrine, in their view, is what evolved out of these primordial "attitudes" through historical and intellectual processes. They also rejected the sectarian framing of Ismāʿīlism as merely emerging from an Imamate succession dispute. However, their chapter went on to define the central features of Ismāʿīlism in terms of the same doctrines noted by Ivanow: obedience to the Imam, the distinction between the exoteric and the esoteric, cycles of prophethood, the advent of the messianic figure called the *Qāʾim,* the radical transcendence of God, etc. They also provided a historical schema of phases in which Ismāʿīlī history and thought develops. Thus, the Esmail-Nanji concept of Ismāʿīlism is a refinement and elaboration of the basic structure first put forth by Ivanow.

Farhad Daftary, in the course of his many works on Ismāʿīlī history published over the last three decades, employs the term Ismāʿīlism in a variety of ways. In his 2004 published bibliography of Ismāʿīlī studies, Daftary spoke of Ismāʿīlism in numerous places and contexts. In the preface he remarks that "Ismāʿīlism is defined rather broadly here to cover what some scholars designate more specifically as Fatimid studies, including Fatimid political history, institutions, art and archaeology."[113] He speaks of an "opening phase" of Ismāʿīlism followed by the Fatimid period as its "golden age."[114] In terms of Ismāʿīlī practices and the individual believer, Daftary refers to "initiation into Ismāʿīlism" through an oath of fealty.[115] Following Paul Walker, Daftary describes the philosophical expositions of certain Persian Ismāʿīlī philosophers as "philosophical Ismāʿīlism."[116] He then speaks of a develop-

112. Esmail and Nanji 1977, 228–229.
113. Daftary 2004, xii.
114. Daftary 2004, 6–20.
115. Daftary 2004, 16–17.
116. Daftary 2004, 29.

ment beginning in the fifteenth century in which "a type of coalescence had emerged between Persian Ṣūfism and Nizārī Ismāʿīlism."[117] The above examples showcase the multitude of ways the term Ismāʿīlism continues to be employed. The term is used to denote the Ismāʿīlī movement or *daʿwa*, certain kinds of Ismāʿīlī doctrine, Ismāʿīlī intellectual traditions, and Ismāʿīlī history as a whole. One is left with the idea that there are several iterations, manifestations or species of a universal genus called Ismāʿīlism within different historical, cultural, and intellectual contexts. This seems very similar to the Ivanow-Esmail-Nanji model but what precisely Ismāʿīlism entails in a taxonomical sense remains to be seen. What exactly makes something an instance of "Ismāʿīlism"?

In *The Poetics of Religious Experience*, Aziz Esmail presents a somewhat different concept of Ismāʿīlism than what he and Nanji had proposed two decades prior. Esmail expresses some caution about the term "Ismāʿīlism," noting how the use of an -ism implies a uniform body of thought and doctrine – something not true of Ismāʿīlī writers throughout history:

> In speaking about "Ismailism," one has to be careful, as with "Islam," to make relevant distinctions and qualifications. The suffix "ism" may suggest a uniform body of doctrines, whereas in fact, apart from allegiance to the Ismaili Imamate, the thought-forms, temperaments, and intellectual caliber of Ismaili authors differ widely. Secondly, the same suffix, with its suggestion of a self-contained doctrinal system, implies a sealed compartment, as it were, within the intellectual history of Islam. Nothing could be further from the truth.[118]

Esmail's remarks are certainly valid as to the inappropriate use of the term Ismāʿīlism as some mass ideology or body of universal ideas manifesting over time and space. At the same time, Esmail has isolated and reified a single belief that he sees as common to all Ismāʿīlī thinkers, communities, and traditions – allegiance to the Ismāʿīlī Imamate. Esmail's above position, appearing in an essay published by the Institute of Ismāʿīlī Studies, also speaks to the "insider" theological orientation of the modern Ismāʿīlī community.

Both the term Ismāʿīlism and its definition in terms of allegiance to the Imamate have been appropriated by modern Ismāʿīlī authors including the Aga Khans. The later speeches and writings of Aga Khan III refer to the religion of his community as Ismāʿīlism.[119] The Institute of Ismāʿīlī Studies uses

117. Daftary 2004, 67.
118. Esmail 1998, 49.
119. Aga Khan III 1954, 1955.

Ismāʿīlism as the official designation of the Ismāʿīlī Muslim interpretation of Islam.[120] As shown in the studies of Steinberg and Poor, the institution of the Ismāʿīlī Imamate and the authority of the present Imam form the cornerstone of contemporary Ismāʿīlī institutional and communal discourse. Throughout normative Ismāʿīlī communal literature, recognition and allegiance to the Ismāʿīlī Imam is presented as the essence of Ismāʿīlism and the bond that unites a culturally and ethnically diverse Nizārī Ismāʿīlī community spread across the globe.[121] Thus, Ismāʿīlism – originally an outsider scholarly category – has become embedded within insider communal discourse and self-identity.

In summary, we can see at least three concrete conceptualizations of Ismāʿīlism in academic literature. As the first model, Ivanow conceived Ismāʿīlism as an ideological movement founded in the seventh century and moving through history into the present time. While Ismāʿīlism's beliefs, doctrines, and practices evolve throughout history under the influence of historical, intellectual, and cultural contexts, Ivanow specifically regarded Ismāʿīlism's core or essence as comprised of five key doctrines – radical monotheism, the mission of the prior Prophets, the Imamate, the *daʿwa,* and revelatory hermeneutics (*taʾwīl*). His analogy of Ismāʿīlism's ideology with organic chemistry's "radical" betrays the way in which Ismāʿīlism is being conceived as an unchanging essence. The second model, of Nanji-Esmail, which appears to be followed implicitly by Daftary, views Ismāʿīlism as the embodiment of certain attitudes about the nature of truth and its implementation in society, where historical Ismāʿīlī doctrines are developments of these attitudes within various contexts. The third model is where Esmail presents allegiance to the Ismāʿīlī Imamate as the essential content of Ismāʿīlism, while rejecting any notion of doctrinal uniformity among historical Ismāʿīlī communities.

The purpose of the above discussion was to lay out the intellectual genealogy of the concept of Ismāʿīlism and the category Ismāʿīlī from the nineteenth century to the present time. One clearly notices a progression as the Ismāʿīlīs are first defined as sectarian movement, followed by the definition of Ismāʿīlism as an ideology or communal interpretation with certain essential features. The prevailing concepts of Ismāʿīlism are plagued by two taxonomical features: monothetic taxonomy and essentialism. In the opening chapter of *Imagining Religion,* Jonathan Z. Smith raises the issue of how scholars apply taxonomy to the study of religion. As he notes, most scholars define religion and its various categories (including particular religions and

120. Institute of Ismaili Studies 2018.
121. See the analyses and examples of Steinberg 2011 and Poor 2014.

their branches) in a monothetic way. A monothetic taxonomy focuses on a single feature and determines the correct category to which a given phenomenon belongs based on the presence or absence of that feature. In doing so, the scholar treats that feature as a sine qua non – the *that without which* – the category no longer holds. Drawing on the example of biology, Smith cites example questions such as "does it have chlorophyll or not?", "if it has chlorophyll, does it have true flowers or not?" etc. Such a monothetic taxonomy works by asking binary questions until the phenomenon in question logically falls into the appropriate category.[122]

Smith's observations apply to the way the High Court of Bombay determined the religious identity of the Khojas of Bombay. The entire judgment depends on how the judge framed the first two questions: *First: What are Sunnīs as distinct from Shias? Secondly: Who and What are the Shia Imami Ismāʿīlīs?* This effort to determine what differentiates Sunnī Muslims from Shīʿa Muslims, and further, how Shīʿa Ismāʿīlī Muslims differ from other Shīʿa is very much an exercise in monothetic taxonomy. As noted above, the judge's answers to these questions demonstrate how, in his eyes, there is but one key feature differentiating the Sunnī and the Shīʿa and the Ismāʿīlī Shīʿa from the Twelver Shīʿa . For the High Court of Bombay, what makes the Shīʿa sect different from the Sunnī is their affirmation that ʿAlī is the Vicar of God. Similarly, the key and defining feature of the Ismāʿīlī sect is the claim that "the Imamate (or in Latin idiom the office of Supreme Pontiff] is rightfully held by an hereditary succession of unrevealed Imams, the lineal descendants of ʿAlī through Ismaʿīl."[123] For Smith, this approach "gives a taxonomy for particular religious traditions by identifying a single trait which is held to reveal the 'essence' of that tradition" and yields results that are "arbitrary and poorly defined."[124] Smith would be equally unimpressed by Ivanow's proposal, which frames Ismāʿīlism as the indivisible or "indissoluble" union of five key dogmas, centered upon the figure of the Imam, evolving through history akin to the development of the caterpillar's journey toward becoming a butterfly. While Ivanow's model of five doctrinal elements is technically not monothetic, it falls into the same essentialist trap that the Aga Khan Case judgment exemplified. For Ivanow, the five doctrinal elements – strict monotheism, prophethood, Imamate, *daʿwa*, and revelatory hermeneutics (*taʾwīl*) – must always be in union for Ismāʿīlism to be Ismāʿīlism. Even if one or two features fail to obtain at one point in history, this is merely a "heretical tendency" or "decay," and the essence of

122. Smith 1982, 2–3.
123. Arnould 1866, 7.
124. Smith 1982, 7.

Ismāʿīlism remains unchanged regardless of its historical, geographical, and cultural manifestations.

The Esmail-Nanji-Daftary model of Ismāʿīlism as a set of primordial attitudes constituting a genus, which is then embodied in specific instances over history (Fatimid Ismāʿīlism, philosophical Ismāʿīlism) equally implies an essential or core body of "attitudes" or perspectives that constitutes Ismāʿīlism. Esmail's formulation of Ismāʿīlism, although offered implicitly in his critique of the implied doctrinal uniformity exemplified by his predecessors, makes "allegiance to the Ismāʿīlī Imamate" the single shared characteristic that unites the otherwise disparate discourses of Ismāʿīlī authors. This means that the "essence" of Ismāʿīlism as a category is allegiance to the Ismāʿīlī Imamate. This conceptualization is actually a return to the Aga Khan Case judgment that concluded that the Khojas of Bombay are a group of Shīʿī Ismāʿīlīs "which has always been and still is bound by ties of spiritual allegiance to the hereditary Imams of the Ismāʿīlīs." In a certain way, definitions of Ismāʿīlism in Ismāʿīlī studies scholarship have come full circle.

Shortcomings of Current Conceptualizations of Ismāʿīlism

Of the three models of Ismāʿīlism discussed above, Esmail's "thin" conceptualization of Ismāʿīlism as allegiance to the Ismāʿīlī Imamate may offer the most viable solution. Unlike the Ivanow or Esmail-Nanji-Daftary models, Esmail's model is the least extended in terms of essentialist features. Thus, one could just take allegiance to the Ismāʿīlī Imams as the essential feature of Ismāʿīlism as a category and Ismāʿīlī as a designation, while admitting several branches or "species" of Ismāʿīlism with their unique doctrines, practices and traditions as influenced by history, culture, socio-political contexts, etc. Accordingly, one can coherently speak of "Fatimid Ismāʿīlism," "philosophical Ismāʿīlism," "Alamut Ismāʿīlism," or "Satpanthi Ismāʿīlism" as further extensions and developments from the basic or "core" Ismāʿīlism whose essential feature is allegiance to the Imams.

This method, however, quickly runs into its own problems. A properly historical approach to the Ismāʿīlī belief in the Imams and the Imamate reveals that Ismāʿīlīs of various times, cultures, and locations conceived the figure of the Imam in a myriad of mutually contradictory ways. The "Imamology" articulated in historical Ismāʿīlī literature ranges from regarding the Imam as a divinely guided descendent of the Prophet who establishes justice, a divinely-inspired guide to esoteric knowledge, the rightful Caliph of the Prophet, an earthly manifestation of Neoplatonic cosmic principles, a human manifestation or *avatara* of God, and a modern spiritual leader who undertakes humanitarian work in his expression of Islamic ethics. For these reasons, Walker and Madelung concluded that belief or allegiance to the Imamate cannot serve as a unifying characteristic of historical Ismāᶜīlī interpretations:

> Surely, if any single concept brought all of the Ismāᶜīlīs together, it was their fundamental attachment to the line of imams they accepted. Yet, when Wilferd Madelung, the first modern investigator with access to a substantial range of the early Ismāᶜīlī literature, attempted to verify the doctrine of the imamate and the messiah in each of the successive phases of the history of the movement, he found that the literature produced by the *daᶜwa* offered no consistent teaching on these issues. In fact, the doctrine appeared to change over time, evolving according to circumstances. He discovered, moreover, that at any given time there were important variations between the views of one faction and another.[125]

Even if it is true that every Ismāᶜīlī community throughout history retained some form of belief in a line of Ismāᶜīlī Imams, they conceived the role and nature of the Imam in divergent ways due to the vastly different intellectual, theological, and symbolic frameworks in which their visions of the Imam were deeply embedded and invested with meaning. Thus, making the Imamate the defining feature of Ismāᶜīlism privileges one characteristic of Ismāᶜīlī worldviews over others. It also relegates some very important phenomena – like the Neoplatonic cosmologies employed by certain Ismāᶜīlī philosophers or the Indic motifs and symbolism in the Khoja tradition of *ginān*s – to the status of mere window dressing that remains incidental to Ismāᶜīlī religious identity, faith, and self-conception. Furthermore, defining Ismāᶜīlism in terms of allegiance to the Ismāᶜīlī Imamate easily slides into portrayals of Ismāᶜīlism as mere "authoritarianism" and "conformism" (*taqlīd*).

The inadequacy of defining Ismāᶜīlism solely through allegiance to the Ismāᶜīlī Imamate is further evident when testing it against some of the ways that Ismāᶜīlīs historically defined themselves and described their religious orientation. As it turns out, Ismāᶜīlīs throughout history designated their communities and their religious commitments in much wider terms than mere allegiance to the Ismāᶜīlī Imams. Virani's comments on this issue are instructive:

> In fact, the Ismāᶜīlīs did not call their religion "Ismāᶜīlism." This was a name given to them by the early heresiographers, notably al-Nawbakhti and al-Qummi. They referred to themselves simply as

125. Walker 1993, 9.

> the Faith of Truth (*din al-haqq*) or the Summons to the Truth (*da'wat al-haqq*). The fifteenth-century Ismāʿīlī author, Bu Ishaq Quhistani, states quite plainly that "the people of the Truth are the people of the Summons." Such designations remained common even when the community spread to South Asia, where it came to be known as the Path of Truth (*satpanth*).[126]

When the Ismāʿīlī authors use designations like Summons to the Truth, Faith of Truth, People of Truth, and People of the Summons as self-referents, they are clearly depicting the essence of their faith and their identity in far richer and much deeper terms than mere "allegiance to the Ismāʿīlī Imamate." This is not the place to enter into an analysis of the meaning and context of terms like *daʿwa, dīn,* or *ḥaqq*, but it suffices to say that "allegiance to the Ismāʿīlī Imams" fails to capture the rich scope and arena of meaning signified by the terms used by the Ismāʿīlīs themselves. This is not to deny that the authority of the Ismāʿīlī Imams held great importance for the Ismāʿīlīs; but they clearly conceived the Imams' authority as part of a more holistic onto-cosmological and epistemic framework, in which notions of truth (*ḥaqq*) and the esoteric reality (*bāṭin*) were of prime importance. Several more examples drawn from Ismāʿīlī literature throughout the centuries helps further illustrate the magnitude of this point. Abū Yaʿqūb al-Sijistānī (d. ca. 361/971) refers to his Ismāʿīlī community as the "people of the truth" (*ahl al-ḥaqīqa*) and the "people of inner realities" (*ahl al-ḥaqāʾiq*) respectively.[127] Sunnī Muslim theologians of various schools labelled their own schools of thought using similar terms. In the official decrees and literature of the Fatimid Caliphate, the members of the Ismāʿīlī *daʿwa* were called the "believers" (*al-muʾminūn*) and the "friends of God" (*awliyāʾ Allāh*) while non-Ismāʿīlī Muslims were simply called *al-muslimīn*.[128] The Fatimid jurist al-Qāḍī al-Nuʿmān (d. ca. 363/974) explained how the sphere of *islām* (submission), which all Muslims participate in, is represented by a large circle; but the sphere of *imān* (faith) was a smaller elite circle within the larger circle of Islam.[129] Nāṣir-i Khusraw (d. ca. 481/1088), the Persian Ismāʿīlī philosopher, poet, and *dāʿī*, refers to his community using a variety of designations including the Shīʿa, the people of revelatory hermeneutics (*ahl al-taʾwīl*), the sages of true religion (*ḥukamā-ye dīn-e ḥaqq*), and the people of divine support (*ahl al-taʾyīd*).[130] Naṣīr al-Dīn Ṭūsī (d. ca. 672/1273) designates the Nizārī

126. Virani 2007, 71–72.
127. Virani 2007, 146.
128. Daftary 2005, 76.
129. Hamdani 2006, 67.
130. Khusraw 2012.

Ismāʿīlīs of his day as the followers of authoritative instruction (*taʿlīmiyyān*) due to the fact that the Ismāʿīlīs were famous for putting forth a rational dialectical argument demonstrating humankind's permanent need for an infallible instructor (*muʿallim*) to reach knowledge of God.[131]

Just as the Ismāʿīlīs did not designate themselves as "Ismāʿīlī" for several centuries, they never described their religion as "Ismāʿīlism." The term most often used, *dīn*, is an Arabic word with multiple layers and contexts of meaning. Accordingly, *dīn* has been translated as "obligation," "faith" "law," "obedience," and "religion" within the context of its Ismāʿīlī usage.[132] Notwithstanding the contested nature of the term "religion" and its problematic genealogy in Western thought, it suffices to note that the early Ismāʿīlīs conceived *dīn* as a multifaceted socio-political and spiritual program with the double aim of establishing a just society and affecting a personal transformation for the adept through the spiritual realization of the absolute oneness of God through the mediation of the Ismāʿīlī Imam. As described in *The Master and the Disciple,* a pre-Fatimid Ismāʿīlī initiation text originating in the late ninth century, the *dīn* espoused and practiced by the Ismāʿīlīs (referred to as *ahl al-dīn*) encompasses three distinct levels: the exoteric (*ẓāhir*), the esoteric (*bāṭin*), and the esoteric of the esoteric (*bāṭin al- bāṭin*). The exoteric layer or *zahir* refers to the scripture, scriptural symbols, and laws enjoined upon human beings for their conduct and actions in the physical world. The esoteric layer or *bāṭin* refers to the inward spiritual content that the outward symbols and practices signify – and this includes the members, doctrines, and practices of the Ismāʿīlī *daʿwa.* The third and deepest layer, the *bāṭin al- bāṭin,* is called "the *dīn* of God" and is the "essential reality" (*ḥaqīqa*) of the exoteric and esoteric dimensions of *dīn.*[133] While the figure of the Imam is mentioned throughout this work, as in many other Ismāʿīlī works through the medieval period, a consistent feature of Ismāʿīlī literature is the comprehensive worldview within which the Ismāʿīlīs situated their socio-political aspirations and spiritual ideals, including those connected to the figure of the Imam. The conceptualization of Ismāʿīlism as allegiance to the Ismāʿīlī Imams fails to capture a great deal of these themes.

The Ismāʿīlīs only gradually adopted "Ismāʿīlī" as a self-designation during pre-modern times in the context of responding to anti-Ismāʿīlī polemics. In 487/1094, al-Ghazālī published a highly polemical treatise against the Ismāʿīlīs at the request of the ʿAbbasid Caliph. In the course of this polemic, al-Ghazālī employed various names to describe the community, some of

131. Tusi 1998, 30.
132. Calderini 1993.
133. Jaʿfar b. Manṣūr al-Yaman (d. ca. 349/960) 2001, 90–94.

them derogatory and others derived from his predecessors in polemics. His list of names included Bāṭiniyya, Qarāmita, Ismāʿīliyya, and Taʿlīmiyya.[134] An Ismāʿīlī response to al-Ghazālī's polemic was penned by the fifth *dāʿī muṭlaq* of the Ṭayyibī Ismāʿīlīs, ʿAlī b. Muḥammad b. al-Walīd (d. ca. 612/1215). In his treatise, al-Walīd accepted the designation "Ismāʿīliyya" by reorienting the term and investing it with positive meaning:

> This name designates those whose [spiritual] ancestry goes back to Mawlana [*sic*] Ismaʿil ibn Jaʿfar al-Sadiq, ibn Muhammad al-Baqir, ibn ʿAli Zayn al-ʿAbidin, ibn al-Husayn al-Taqi, ibn ʿAli al-Murtada al-Wasi. This is our inherent name. It is our honour and our glory before all of the other branches of Islam, because we stand on the Path of the Truth, in following our guides the Imams. We drink at an abundant fountain, and we hold firmly to the guiding lines of their walaya. Thus they cause us to climb from rank to rank among the degrees of proximity [to God] and excellence.[135]

While al-Walīd agreed with the appropriateness of the term Ismāʿīlī, even referring to this as "our inherent name," he was quick to expand the deeper meaning and signification of the term. The word "Ismāʿīlī," in al-Walīd's view, does not only mean spiritual allegiance or ancestry going back to the Imam Ismāʿīl b. Jaʿfar. Its meaning revolves around ideas of truth (*ḥaqq*), spiritual guidance, *walāya*, and proximity to God. None of these are captured if the term Ismāʿīlī only signifies allegiance to the Ismāʿīlī Imams. A tenth/fifteenth-century Nizārī Ismāʿīlī author, writing in a period when the Ismāʿīlīs had already adopted the term Ismāʿīlī as their label, reminds his readers that "the imamate was transmitted from Mawlānā Jaʿfar al-Ṣādiq to Imam Ismāʿīl, may peace be upon us from both of them, even though, in truth, all the Imams are one and there is a change only in form, not in meaning or reality."[136] The way that these Ṭayyibī Ismāʿīlī and Nizārī Ismāʿīlī authors interpret the Ismāʿīlī label demonstrates their focus on domains of meaning that lie deeper than mere allegiance to the Ismāʿīlī Imamate.

The above analysis has hopefully demonstrated why defining Ismāʿīlism in essentialist terms as allegiance to the Ismāʿīlī Imams is no longer viable. When the defining parameter of Ismāʿīlism is only allegiance to the Ismāʿīlī Imam, then various facets of the worldviews, doctrines, and self-designations of the Ismāʿīlīs – *ḥaqq* ('truth'), *ḥaqīqa* (reality), *bāṭin* (esoteric), *daʿwa* (summons), *taʾwīl* (revelatory hermeneutics) and *taʾyīd* (divine inspiration),

134. Virani 2007, 199.
135. ʿAlī b. Muḥammad b. al-Walīd (d. ca. 612/1215), quoted in Virani 2007, 200.
136. Virani 2010, 204.

dīn, *walāyah*, proximity to God, etc. – risk being marginalized as non-essential or unimportant features or even ignored altogether.

Ismāʿīlī Phenomena Beyond the Ismāʿīlī Imamate

The problematic nature of conceptualizing Ismāʿīlism in essentialist terms as allegiance to the Ismāʿīlī Imams is further underscored when this model is examined against several historical phenomena uncovered by recent scholarship. These consist of cases where figures with uncertain or clear lack of allegiance to the historical Ismāʿīlī Imams have adopted and adapted what are otherwise Ismāʿīlī doctrines, cosmologies, and hermeneutical methods into their worldviews. In other words, we have a case of Ismāʿīlī doctrines, hermeneutics, and theologies bereft of any sure allegiance to the Ismāʿīlī Imams. In order to illustrate the challenge posed by these cases, we refer to them respectively as follows: Anonymous Ismāʿīlīs, Jewish Ismāʿīlism, and Andalusi-Ismāʿīlī Cosmologies. In these cases, the "thin" conceptualization of Ismāʿīlism as allegiance to the Ismāʿīlī Imams would exclude them from being classified as Ismāʿīlī phenomenon. But the centrality of Ismāʿīlī ideas to the thought of these figures shows, rather, that there is a problem with the "thin" conceptualization itself and not the phenomena in question.

"Anonymous Ismāʿīlīs": Ikhwān al-Ṣafāʾ and al-Shahrastānī

The Ikhwān Al-Ṣafāʾ (The Brethren of Purity), the authors of the famous Epistles (*rasāʾil*) dating to sometime between the late third/ninth and late fourth/tenth centuries and operating in Basra, have challenged scholars due to the difficulty in determining their exact religious affiliation. The arguments concerning their precise religious identity centers upon whether they were Ismāʿīlīs and what kind of Ismāʿīlīs they were. The opinions include those of Abbas Hamdani, who regards the Ikhwān as Ismāʿīlī *dāʿīs* of the late third/ninth or early fourth/tenth century preparing the groundwork for the Fatimid revolution; Yves Marquet, who sees the Ikhwān as pro-Fatimid writers active throughout the fourth/tenth century; Samuel Stern and Wilferd Madelung, who believe the Ikhwān were an Ismāʿīlī faction that did not recognize the Fatimids and believed in Muḥammad b. Ismāʿīl as the last and awaited Imam; and Ian Richard Netton, who does not regard the Ikhwān as Ismāʿīlīs of any kind.[137] All of the scholarly debate about the Ikhwān's religious affiliation remains wholly oriented around their view of the Ismāʿīlī Imamate. Hamdani's argument for the Ikhwān's Ismāʿīlī affiliation hinges, in large part, on the idea of the Imamate presented in their Epistles and,

137. The viewpoints are summarized in Ebstein 2013, 28–29.

likewise, Netton's argument rejecting their affiliation is based on "the essential nature of the Imamate to the Ismā'īlis, and the inferior role allocated to the Imamate by the Ikhwān."[138] Netton particularly refers to the fact that the Ikhwān seem to give more prominence to the idea of a collective brotherhood possessing the necessary spiritual and moral leadership qualities as opposed to a hereditary ʿAlid Imamate as grounds for rejecting their Ismāʿīlī identity. Such a methodology and conclusion presume the essentialist conceptualization of Ismāʿīlism as allegiance to the Ismāʿīlī Imamate and completely downplays the other features of the Ikhwān's worldview that could be used to argue *for* their Ismāʿīlī allegiance. On this point, Michael Ebstein convincingly argues that the Ikhwān's approach to spiritual and political leadership, although more humanistic with less emphasis on the Imamate (they never speak of an "Ismāʿīlī" Imamate), nevertheless displays clear Shīʿī Ismāʿīlī themes and ideas:

> Contrary to the opinion of Ian Netton, I do not think that the universal-humanistic approach of the Ikhwan excludes their Shīʿī-Ismāʿīlī identity; this identity is proven by many Shīʿī-Ismāʿīli motifs which are found in the Ikhwān's oeuvre. In my view, the Ikhwān indeed belonged to the Shīʿī-Ismāʿīlī milieu, but chose to interpret their own Shīʿī-Ismāʿīlī beliefs in a unique way, different from that of most other contemporary Shīʿī-Ismāʿīlī scholars.[139]

Ebstein's argument for the Ismāʿīlī identity of the Ikhwān does not rely on their emphasis or lack of emphasis on the doctrine of Imamate, but rather on the numerous other Ismāʿīlī themes in their work – such as their Neoplatonic cosmogony, their concept of Prophethood in terms of seven cycles, or their notion of the human being as the microcosm. In this respect, his work represents a promising template for a new approach.

Another boundary case in terms of Ismāʿīlī allegiance is found in the famous Muslim theologian and heresiographer ʿAbd al-Karīm al-Shahrastānī (d. ca. 547/1153). Shahrastānī was a prominent intellectual in Sunnī Muslim circles, holding a position in the Nizāmiyya College in Baghdad, and was once considered by Western scholars as an orthodox Sunnī Ashʿarī thinker. However, the most recent scholarship on Shahrastānī's life and thought has inferred that he secretly professed Ismāʿīlī Islam. What is interesting for taxonomical purposes is the evidence that several scholars, including Guy Monnot, Wilfred Madelung, Diana Steigerwald, and Toby Mayer, have mobilized to demonstrate Shahrastānī's Ismāʿīlī convictions. For example,

138. Netton 1980.
139. Ebstein 2013, 180.

Madelung first drew attention to the way Shahrastānī critiques Ibn Sīnā's ontology and theology in his *Book of the Wrestling Match* (*Kitāb Muṣāraʿat al-Falāsifa*) by means of a radical apophatic theology that accords with Ismāʿīlī apophatic theology.[140] Mayer refers to this text as "among the works most evidential of the author's Isma'ili links."[141] Most of the evidence supporting Shahrastānī's Ismāʿīlī affiliation consists of the theological, exegetical, and philosophical positions he takes in several works, including his esoteric Qurʾān commentary, heresiography, and *majālis* (lectures). Shahrastānī, to be sure, never mentions in any of his known works that he has allegiance to an Ismāʿīlī lineage of Imams or that he is a member of the Ismāʿīlī *daʿwa*. The closest he comes is his claim that there is a "present, living, current Imam" (*al-imām al-ḥāḍir al-ḥayy al-qāʾim*) on earth as opposed to an awaited hidden Imam of the Twelver Shīʿa.[142] All of this demonstrates how the category of Ismāʿīlism, if assessed *only* in terms of allegiance to the Ismāʿīlī Imams, would fail to be useful in Shahrastānī's case. Scholars have only been able to *infer* an Ismāʿīlī presence in Shahrastānī's works because they have analyzed his thought in terms of Ismāʿīlī theological positions and commitments apart from the Imamate. What this tells us is that a proper taxonomy of Ismāʿīlism as a category must reach beyond allegiance to the Ismāʿīlī Imams as its defining feature.

"Jewish Ismāʿīlism": Maimonides and R. Nathanel ben al-Fayyūmī

While the Ikhwān and Shahrastānī represent "border cases" where their allegiance to the Ismāʿīlī Imams is probable or at best inconclusive, two medieval Jewish thinkers provide a noteworthy case of Ismāʿīlī phenomena present within the worldview of those who have no allegiance to the Ismāʿīlī Imamate. However, these developments have been mainly discussed in the field of Jewish intellectual history. Ebstein observed that "various studies by scholars in the areas of Jewish thought and *Kabbalah* have demonstrated the existence of Ismāʿīlī traces in medieval Jewish writings, in al-Andalus and elsewhere."[143] Moses Maimonides (1138–1204), one of the most prolific and influential thinkers in the history of Jewish thought stands as a foremost example of this. Alfred L. Ivry was among the first scholars to shed light on the Ismāʿīlī ideas and doctrines present in Maimonides' theology, noting "an entire pattern of sympathy which Maimonides harbors towards Ismāʿīlī

140. Madelung 1977.
141. Mayer 2009, 13.
142. Mayer 2009, 18.
143. Ebstein 2013, 21.

methodology and even doctrine."[144] In a chapter titled "Isma'ili Theology and Maimonides' Theology," Ivry observes how Maimonides engages with and incorporates a number of Ismāʿīlī ideals, doctrines, and theological positions. These include a radical apophatic theology which sees a series of negations as the only way to affirm the absolute oneness of God; the concept of *taqiyya* or religious dissimulation and the Ismāʿīlī teaching methodology; the concept of the *nāṭiq* (speaker-prophet), who apprehends spiritual truth and expresses it in human language in the form of law, which Maimonides applies to Moses; and the necessity of the *walī* or esoteric interpreter of prophetic revelation.[145]

Certain Jewish thinkers in Yemen after Maimonides display what some scholars have called "Jewish Ismāʿīlism" or "Ismāʿīlized Judaism."[146] The most notable case of "Jewish Ismāʿīlism" is found in the work of Rabbi Nathanel ben al-Fayyūmī (d. ca. 1165), a leading Jewish scholar in Yemen. Ronald C. Kiener's seminal article on Nathanel Ben al-Fayyūmī begins with an explicit summary of this phenomenon:

> A Rabbinic authority in 12th century Yemen, R. Nethanel ben al-Fayyūmī (author of the work entitled Bustān al-ʿUqūl), penetrated to no small degree into what we presently regard as the esoteric theology of Islamic Ismāʿīlism. We shall see how he deftly employed Ismāʿīlī cosmology, prophetology, and hermeneutics in defense of Rabbinic Judaism. Thus it is in this limited but fully accurate sense that I write of a "Jewish Ismāʿīlism." I hope to show that R. Nethanel's response to the Ismāʿīlī *daʿwa* of his day was itself cast in a typically Ismāʿīlī theological world-view.[147]

The many cases of what Jewish studies scholars call "Jewish Ismāʿīlism" can only cause us to rethink the conceptualization of Ismāʿīlism/Ismāʿīlī employed by most scholars in the field of Ismāʿīlī studies. None of the Jewish thinkers referenced above, including Maimondies, R. Nathanel and many others, possess allegiance to an Ismāʿīlī Imamate of any kind. And yet their writings bear the influence of, and in some cases, are permeated with Ismāʿīlī theological and cosmological ideas. While Ivanow and others believed that the "radical monotheism," concept of prophethood, doctrine of Imamate, *daʿwa*, and *taʾwīl* of the Ismāʿīlīs constituted an indivisible whole, the Jewish case shows that these elements are indeed separable, with Jewish think-

144. Ivry in Wasserstrom 2014, 144.
145. Ivry 1995, 284–294.
146. Wasserstrom 2014, 135.
147. Kiener 1984, 249.

ers carefully incorporating some elements and not others. If Jewish studies scholars are able to coherently speak of such a thing as Jewish Ismāʿīlism, then it calls for a reconsideration of what ultimately constitutes Ismāʿīlism when allegiance to the Ismāʿīlī Imams is clearly absent.

Andalusi-Ismāʿīlī Cosmologies: Ibn Masarra and Ibn al-ʿArabī

Recent research comparing the Ismāʿīlī thought of the Ikhwān al-Ṣafāʾ and the Fatimid Ismāʿīlī philosophers with the Andalusian Sunnī mysticism of Ibn Masarra (d. ca. 319/931) and Ibn al-ʿArabī (d. ca. 638/1240) by Ebstein should provide a shocking but far-reaching tremor through our efforts to retain the prevailing narrow conceptualization of Ismāʿīlism. Ebstein's thorough textual analysis shows that Ibn Masarra and Ibn al-ʿArabī developed "a certain type of mystical-philosophical thought in the Islamic tradition different from the Ṣūfism or *taṣawwuf* prevalent in the Eastern Islamic world."[148] Terming this thought as Sunnī Andalusi mysticism, Ebstein demonstrates how the Andalusi mystics share five important theological, cosmological and soteriological doctrines with medieval Ismāʿīlī thinkers: a Neoplatonic cosmogony rooted in the Word or Command of God, the esoteric interpretation of letters, the concept of *walāya* and the Friends of God (*awliyāʾ Allāh*), the idea of the Perfect Man, and the schema of parallel worlds.[149] In terms of the Neoplatonic cosmogony based on the concept of the Word or Will of God, Ebstein emphasizes how Ismāʿīlī authors "contributed greatly to the formation of a new and unique Neoplatonic tradition, distinct from other Neoplatonic traditions in the Islamic world of that period."[150] Ebstein concludes from his findings that:

> The Ismāʿīlī tradition played a significant role in the formation of the intellectual world from which both Ibn Masarra and Ibn al-ʿArabī emerged. Despite the fact that these two authors were doubtlessly influenced by other, diverse sources – such as the Quran and *Hadith*, Arabic theology and philosophy, and, in the case of Ibn al-ʿArabī, by Ṣūfism as well – the Ismāʿīlī tradition helped shape the unique intellectual climate in North Africa and al-Andalus from which Ibn Masarra and Ibn al-ʿArabī derived.[151]

Ebstein's findings show us how Ismāʿīlī doctrines, pertaining to cosmology, scriptural hermeneutics, and the Imamate, can exert a decisive influence in

148. Ebstein 2013, 3.
149. Ebstein 2013, 231.
150. Ebstein 2013, 76.
151. Ebstein 2013, 232.

the formation of a distinct Sunnī mystical tradition found in Ibn al-ʿArabī and other Andalusi mystics, even when the latter have no allegiance to the Ismāʿīlī Imamate. As he notes after his conclusion,

> [n]owhere in their writings can one find an expression of the most essential and fundamental tenet of the Shīʿī-Ismāʿīlī belief – the recognition of ʿAlī ibn Abī Ṭālib and his descendants, the *imāms,* as the sole legitimate leaders of the Islamic community.[152]

If the presence of distinctively Ismāʿīlī doctrines in Maimonides, R. Nathanel, and others allow us to speak of "Jewish Ismāʿīlism" then it would not be at all inappropriate to speak of an "Andalusi Ismāʿīlī" worldview which underlies the thought of Ibn Masarra and Ibn al-ʿArabī. To offer another important example, the Sunnī mystical theologian al-Ghazālī appropriated a number of Ismāʿīlī positions from Nāṣir-i Khusraw on cosmology, theology, and prophecy and integrated them into his own esoteric worldview despite strongly rejecting the Ismāʿīlī Imamate's claims to religious authority.[153] In all of these cases one is confronted with Ismāʿīlī theological or cosmological positions held by Jewish and Sunnī Muslim mystics which do not involve any allegiance to the Ismāʿīlī Imamate.

The above examples – the Ikhwān al-Ṣafāʾ, al-Shahrastānī, "Jewish Ismāʿīlism," "Sunnī Andalusi-Ismāʿīlī" or "Ghazālian-Ismāʿīlī" cosmology – show the inadequacy of how Ismāʿīlism is currently framed in much of contemporary scholarship. To the above cases, we could add two examples already noted in Ismāʿīlī studies scholarship: the first is the confluence and cross-pollination of Nizārī Ismāʿīlī thought and Ṣūfī terminology into a "Ṣūfico-Ismāʿīlī" discourse in Persia from the ninth/fourteenth century onward.[154] This shared discourse culminated in certain Nizārī Ismāʿīlī Imams being affiliated with the Niʿmatullāhī Ṣūfī order in Iran during the eighteenth and nineteenth centuries.[155] The close and intertwined relationship between Nizārī Ismāʿīlī and Ṣūfī ideas even prompted certain Nizārī communities in Persia and Central Asia to revere some famous Ṣūfī poets as belonging to their own community, due to which the Nizārīs recited their poetry as part of their congregational ritual practice:

> As a result of their close relationship with Ṣūfism in post-Alamut times, the Nizārīs have regarded some of the greatest mystic poets of Persia as their co-religionists, and selections of their works have been

152. Ebstein 2013, 234.
153. Andani 2018.
154. For examples of this, see Asani 2002, 91 and Lewisohn 2003.
155. Daftary 2007, 461–463.

> preserved by the Nizārīs of Badakhshan and Persia. In this category, mention may be made of Sanāʾī (d. ca. 535/1140), Farīd al-Dīn ʿAṭṭār (d. ca. 627/1230), and Jalāl al-Dīn Rūmī (d. 672/1273), as well as lesser known Ṣūfī personalities such as Qāṣm al-Anwār (d. ca. 837/1433). The Nizārīs of Badakhshan also consider ʿAzīz al-Dīn Nasafī as a co-religionist.... The Nizārī Ismāʿīlīs of Persia, Afghanistan and Central Asia have continued to use verses of the mystical poets of the Iranian world in their social and religious ceremonies.[156]

Apart from the elevation of ʿAlī, who is a revered figure in Ṣūfism, one certainly would not find allegiance to the Ismāʿīlī Imamate being asserted in the verses of Sanāʾī, ʿAṭṭār, or Rūmī. Nevertheless, various Nizārī communities perceived their Ṣūfī poetry as expressions of their own Ismāʿīlī commitments, which indicates that what is today called "Ismāʿīlism" was historically much broader than allegiance to the Imamate. The second case would be the Khojas of South Asia mentioned earlier, whose eclectic hymns (*gināns*) and ritual practices incorporated Indo-Muslim, Ṣūfī, Ismāʿīlī, Bhakti, Sant, and Vaishnavi symbols, which then went on to influence other religious movements in South Asia.[157] These various examples demonstrate the lack of coherence between the essentialist concept of Ismāʿīlism as allegiance to an Ismāʿīlī Imamate and the various other theologies, cosmologies, symbols, poetry, and discourses that historically register as "Ismāʿīlī." The idea of Ismāʿīlism as a sectarian movement or essentialist ideology with several branches evolving through history must be jettisoned in favor of a more expansive taxonomy that can accommodate a diverse array of Ismāʿīlī phenomena.

Rethinking Ismāʿīlism: Future Considerations

While fleshing out a new conceptualization of Ismāʿīlism is beyond the scope of this chapter, I will briefly suggest some conceptual frames that can assist future efforts toward this end. The goal of such reconceptualization must be to define Ismāʿīlism as an analytical object in a way that accounts for historical Ismāʿīlī phenomena in all their diversity and mutual contradiction. Accomplishing this feat calls for at least three modifications to the models surveyed above.

First, in a reversal of the old sectarian frames, Ismāʿīlism should be defined within the context of a historically-grounded and analytically coherent conceptualization of Islam. This means that certain scholarly defi-

156. Daftary 2007, 420.
157. On the Satpanth tradition of the Khojas, see Asani 2002 and 2011.

nitions of Islam as law (*sharīʿa*), civilization, theology (*kalām*), creed (*ʿaqīda*), or a modern notion of religion based on Christian analogues will not be adequate. The historical experience of the Ismāʿīlīs as a minority community seldom possessing political power, evolving their theological positions over time through various symbolic frameworks, and emphasizing the esoteric over the exoteric (to the point of partially abolishing the law) does not "fit" into these paradigms. A more promising conceptualization of Islam into which Ismāʿīlism could be situated is Shahab Ahmed's definition of Islam as a hermeneutical process of meaning-making through engaging the Pre-Text, Text, and/or Con-Text of the Muhammadan Revelation.[158] Although Ahmed's otherwise well-argued and encyclopaedic study happened to marginalize Shīʿīsm and Ismāʿīlism entirely, his concept of Islam ironically may provide the most welcoming framework in which to reconceptualize Ismāʿīlism as a type of Islamic hermeneutic. Another reasonable alternative to positing Ismāʿīlism as a sectarian movement is Adam Gaiser's notion of a "narrative identity model," which approaches intra-Muslim religious diversity as a set of evolving narratives through which a community constructs, interprets, and makes sense of its social world.[159]

Second, Ismāʿīlism should not be defined in terms of an essence comprised of doctrinal positions – including the Ismāʿīlī belief in the Imamate. The foregoing has shown that even conceptualizing Ismāʿīlism solely in terms of allegiance to the Imamate fails to cohere with various historical Ismāʿīlī phenomena. If anything, allegiance to the Ismāʿīlī Imamate may be a preliminary description of many Ismāʿīlī phenomena but fails to be exhaustive. To use an analogy, affirmation of the *Shahāda* ("there is no god but God and Muḥammad is His messenger") may be a *description* common to all Muslims, but it hardly holds as a *definition* of Islam. This is because Muslims understood the meaning of the *Shahāda* within their own differing historical, cultural, theological, cosmological, and symbolic frameworks; likewise, Ismāʿīlīs throughout time and space conceived their relationship to the Ismāʿīlī Imamate within diverse semiotic worlds in which "the Imam" meant different things to different communities. If not in terms of its content, what viable option remains to conceptualize Ismāʿīlism? Instead of regarding it as a monolithic set of doctrines or theological positions, the solution seems to lie in conceiving Ismāʿīlism as a process enacted by historical agents, including Ismāʿīlī individuals and communities. As noted by Ahmed, "one of the most important corrective notions to have emerged in the scholarly literature is the theoretical proposal that we should seek to

158. See Ahmed 2015, Chapter 5.
159. See Gaiser 2017, 61–75.

conceptualize Islam as and in terms of process."[160] A "processual" model of Ismāʿīlism holds several advantages over an "essence" model. It would acknowledge that Ismāʿīlīs historically constructed and continue to construct Ismāʿīlism through various intellectual, ritual, cultural, social, and creative engagements, and direct more attention to their actions instead of abstracting doctrines and beliefs. Of course, more work is required to determine the nature and parameters of this process. A possible starting point on this front is Talal Asad's proposal of defining Islam as a discursive tradition, meaning "a historically evolving set of discourses, embodied in the practices and institutions of Islamic societies and hence deeply imbricated in the material life of those inhabiting them."[161] How and whether Asad's "discursive tradition" can apply to the case of Ismāʿīlism remains to be determined.

Finally, a solution to the problem of monothetic essentialism in conceiving Ismāʿīlism may be found in Jonathan Z. Smith's proposal that scholars adopt a "polythetic" mode of classifying religious phenomena. Smith described this approach as follows:

> In this new mode, a class is defined as consisting of a set of properties, each individual member of the class to possess "a large (but unspecified) number" of these properties, with each property to be possessed by "a large number" of individuals in the class, but no single property to be possessed by every member of the class. If the class contained a large population, it would be possible to arrange them according to the properties possessed in common in such a way that each individual would most closely resemble its nearest neighbor and least closely resemble the farthest.[162]

Smith derived the above polythetic method from biology but observed that it is equally applicable to the study of religion. In *Imagining Religion,* Smith simulated a polythetic taxonomy with respect to Judaism in two ways. In the first case, he picked one taxic indicator seen as "an internal agent of discrimination" – circumcision in this case – and mapped its trajectory and treatment through early Jewish material.[163] In the second case, Smith selected a sample of material from early Judaism – funerary inscriptions – and noted the various terms and elements in which Jewish identity was indicated in this material.[164] The results were surprising. Circumcision turned out to be inconsistent as an indicator of Jewishness and therefore unten-

160. Ahmed 2015, 116–117.
161. Asad quoted in Anjum 2007, 662.
162. Smith 1982, 4.
163. Smith 1982, 9.
164. Smith 1982, 15–18.

able as a measure of "normative Judaism."[165] The findings of the second case revealed "a set of characteristics largely centered on the synagogue which may be used as one cluster toward the eventual polythetic classification of Judaism."[166] In effect, the above survey of Ismāʿīlī literature revealed a similar finding with respect to allegiance to the Imamate in relation to Ismāʿīlism.

Such a polythetic approach to taxonomy would be greatly valuable for the study of the Ismāʿīlīs. Carrying out this operation would require a book-length study to present, so what follows is meant to be a simulation to show what the polythetic taxonomy of Ismāʿīlism *could* look like. The source material to be surveyed would consist of recognized Ismāʿīlī traditions (theological, philosophical, devotional, ritual, poetry) through the centuries as these constitute a bulk of what scholars are cataloguing, editing, translating, and analyzing. It would also include examples from the above Muslim thinkers whose Ismāʿīlī affiliation is uncertain or absent but whose worldviews contain Ismāʿīlī influences. Some of the distinctive taxa to be mapped through this material could be the following:

1. Absolute transcendence of God
2. Cosmogony that posits spiritual intermediaries between God and the Universe
3. Cyclical Prophetology (for example, *nāṭiq, asās, tanzīl, sharīʿa*)
4. Imamology (for example, *walāya, imāma, qāʾim, avatara*)
5. The Summons (*daʿwa*) to the Truth
6. Distinction between the *ẓāhir* and *bāṭin* and the method of *taʾwīl*
7. Cosmology of hierarchical and parallel worlds (that is, physical, spiritual, religious worlds)
8. Establishment of justice through a socio-political order
9. Eschatology (*qiyāma*) centered on the parousia of the Mahdī/Qāʾim
10. Spiritual transformation of the human soul

The above list of taxa is suggestive, not exhaustive, and only given here for illustrative purposes. A full and complete analysis would select a sample of Ismāʿīlī literature with due account to historical period, cultural context, intellectual milieu, and geographical location. The next step would be to arrange each phenomenon, group of phenomena, or current of Ismāʿīlī discourses based on the taxa contained within it. In theory, it would be pos-

165. Smith 1982, 14.
166. Smith 1982, 18.

sible to classify and assess all the various Ismāʿīlī movements, discourses, traditions, and currents in accordance with this polythetic taxonomy and thereby speak of various kinds of Ismāʿīlism without granting normativity to any particular strand. It should also be remembered that the full list of taxa, such as the sample given above, do not in any way constitute the "essence" of Ismāʿīlism. Nor does it follow that any specific taxa – such as allegiance to the Ismāʿīlī Imamate – amount to the "essence" of what the term Ismāʿīlī entails. This would allow scholars to meaningfully speak of "early Ismāʿīlism," "Fatimid Ismāʿīlism," "Jewish Ismāʿīlism," or "Satpanthi Ismāʿīlism" without falling into essentialism on one hand or total ambiguity on the other.

Conclusion

The theological, polemical, and academic approaches to the study of Islam in general and the Ismāʿīlīs specifically are distinct discursive projects with mutually conflicting goals, assumptions, and methodologies. Initially relying on medieval anti-Ismāʿīlī polemical writings, the Orientalist study of the Ismāʿīlīs in the eighteenth and nineteenth centuries began with the proliferation of "black legends" about the Ismāʿīlīs and amounted to polemics in the guise of academic study. A more integral academic approach to the history and thought of the Ismāʿīlīs over the last several decades has accomplished a great deal to remedy these problems and re-orient the field, although polemical tendencies continue to plague some historical approaches to the Fatimids and the modern Aga Khans. At the same time, Ismāʿīlī studies faces theoretical issues in terms of the construction and employment of the very category of "Ismāʿīlism." The latter term has been straightjacketed by reification, sectarian frameworks, monothetic taxonomies, and essentialist definitions such that "Ismāʿīlism" fails to adequately describe the fullness of historical Ismāʿīlī phenomena. A more coherent definition may be formulated by framing Ismāʿīlism as a form of hermeneutics instead of a sect, conceiving Ismāʿīlism as a process as opposed to an essence, and employing a polythetic taxonomy when classifying various Ismāʿīlī phenomena. Verifying Nasr's claim, that "there is hardly an aspect of the Islamic community, especially in its earlier period, which was not touched in one way or another by the presence of Ismāʿīlism," will ultimately depend upon whether scholars employ a coherent concept of Ismāʿīlism in the first place.

Bibliography

Aga Khan III, S. M. Sh. 1954. "Islam, The Religion of My Ancestors." Published online at The NanoWisdoms Archive. http://www.nanowisdoms.org/nwblog/1225/.

——. 1955. "Platinum Jubilee Ceremony, Material Intelligence and Spiritual Enlightenment." Published online at The NanoWisdoms. http://www.nanowisdoms.org/nwblog/1250/.

Ahmed, Sh. 2015. *What Is Islam? The Importance of Being Islamic*. Princeton.

Amir-Moezzi. M. A. 1994. *The Divine Guide in Early Shi'ism*. Albany, NY.

——. 2011. *The Spirituality of Shi'i Islam*. London, New York.

Andani, Kh. 2016a. "A Survey of Ismaili Studies (Part 1): Early Ismailism and Fatimid Ismailism." *Religion Compass* 10.8:191–206.

——. 2016b. "A Survey of Ismaili Studies (Part 1): Early Ismailism and Fatimid Ismailism." *Religion Compass* 10.11:269–282.

——. 2018. "The Merits of the Bāṭiniyya: Al-Ghazālī's Appropriation of Ismāʿīlī Cosmology." *Journal of Islamic Studies* 29.2:181–229.

Anjum, Ovamir. 2007. "Islam as a Discursive Tradition: Talal Asad and His Interlocutors." *Comparative Studies of South Asia, Africa and the Middle East* 27.3:656–672.

Arnould, Joseph. 1866. *Judgment by The Hon'able Sir Joseph Arnould in The Kojah Case Otherwise Known As The Aga Khan Case, Printed At the Bombay Gazette*. Bombay.

Asani, Ali. S. 2002. *Ecstasy and Enlightenment*. London.

——. 2010. "From Satpanthi to Ismaili Muslim." In *A Modern History of The Ismailis*, edited by F. Daftary, 95–128. London.

Aziz, Abualy A. 1985. *Ismaili Tariqah (Part I)*. Toronto.

——. 2005. *Ismaili Tariqah (Part I)*. Vancouver.

Bazzano. E. 2016. "Normative Readings of the Qur'an: From the Premodern Middle East to the Modern West. *Journal of the American Academy of Religion* 84.1:74–97.

Beben, D. 2017. "The Fatimid Legacy and the Foundations of the Modern Nizārī Imamate." In *The Fatimid Caliphate: Diversity of Traditions*, edited by F. Daftary and Sh. Jiwa, 192–223. London.

Beben, D. and D. Mohammad Poor. 2018. *The First Aga Khan*. London, New York.

Brett, M. 2001. *The Rise of the Fatimids*. Leiden, Boston.

Calderini, S. 1993. "*ʿĀlam al-Dīn* in Ismāʿīlism: World Of Obedience Or World of Immobility?" *Bulletin of the School of Oriental and African Studies* 56.3:459–469.

Chapman, A, J. Coffey and B. S. Gregory. 2009. *Seeing Things Their Way: Intellectual History and Return of Religion*. Notre Dame.
Clooney, F. X. 2001. *Hindu God, Christian God: How Reason Helps Break Down the Boundaries Between Religions.* New York.
Cook, Michael. 1999. "Weber and Islamic Sects." In *Max Weber and Islam*, edited by T. E. Huff and W. Schluchter, 273–280. New Brunswick, New Jersey.
Daftary, F. 1994. *The Assassin Legends: Myths of the Ismāʿīlīs*. London, New York.
——. 2004. *Ismaili Literature*. London, New York.
——. 2005. *Ismailis in Medieval Muslim Societies*. London, New York.
——. 2007. *The Ismāʿīlīs: Their History and Doctrines.* Second Edition. Cambridge.
——. 2012. *Historical Dictionary of The Ismāʿīlīs*. Lanham, MD.
——. 2015. "Diversity in Islam: Communities of Interpretation." In *The Muslim Almanac*, 1st ed., 161–73. Detroit.
Ebstein, M. 2013. *Mysticism and Philosophy in Al-Andalus*. Amsterdam.
Engineer, A. 1980. *The Bohras*. Delhi.
Esmail, A. 1998. *The Poetics of Religious Experience*. London.
Esmail, A., and A. Nanji. 1977. "The Ismaʿilis in History." In *Ismāʿīlī Contributions To Islamic Culture*, edited by Seyyed Hossein Nasr. Tehran.
Fitzgerald, Timothy. 1997. "A Critique of "Religion" as a Cross-Cultural Category." *Method and Theory in the Study of Religion* 9.2:91–110.
Fuerst, I. M., and K. Peterson. 2016. *What is Islam? Forum*. August 19. https://marginalia.lareviewofbooks.org/islam-forum-introduction/.
Gaiser, A. 2017. "A Narrative Identity Approach to Islamic Sectarianism." In *Sectarianization: Mapping the Politics of the New Middle East,* edited by N. Hashemi and D. Postel, 61–75. London.
Green, N. 2011. *Bombay Islam*. Cambridge.
Halm, H. 1996. *Empire of the Mahdi*. Leiden, New York.
——. 2004. *Shiʿism*. 2nd ed. New York.
Hamdani, A., and F. de Blois. 1983. "A Re-Examination of al-Mahdī's Letter to the Yemenites on the Genealogy of the Fāṭimid Caliphs." *Journal of the Royal Asiatic Society* 2:173–207.
——. 1995. "A Critique of Paul Casanova's Dating of the *Rasa'il Ikhwan Al-Safa'*." In *Mediaeval Ismāʿīli History and Thought*, edited by F. Daftary, 145–152. Cambridge.
Hamdani, S. A. 2006. *Between Revolution and State*. London, New York.
Hamdani, H. F. 1958. *On The Genealogy of the Fatimid Caliphs*. Cairo.

Ḥasan Kabīr al-Dīn. "Anant Akhado." The Heritage Society. http://ismaili.net/heritage/node/13075.
Hodgson, M. G. S. 1974. *The Venture of Islam*. Chicago.
Hollenberg, D. 2016. *Beyond the Qurʾān: Early Ismāʿīlī Ta'wīl and the Secrets of the Prophets.* Columbia.
Howard, E. I. 1895. *The Shia School of Islam and its Branches, Especially that of the Imamee-Ismailies.* Bombay.
Ibn Khaldūn. 1958. *The Muqaddimah: An Introduction to History*. Translated by and F.Rosenthall. 3 vols. London. http://www.muslimphilosophy.com/ik/Muqaddimah/
Institute for Spiritual Wisdom and Luminous Science. 2017. http://www.monoreality.org/books/books-english/.
Institute of Ismaili Studies. 2016. "The IIS Secondary Curriculum." https://iis.ac.uk/curriculum/secondary-curriculum/.
——. 2018 "The Ismaili Imamat." https://iis.ac.uk/about-us/Ismaili-imamat.
Ismaili Gnosis. 2016. "Beyond Creator and Universe: From Pandeism to Ismaili Muslim Neoplatonism." In *Pandeism: An Anthology,* edited by K. Mapson, 374–425. Winchester.
Ismaili Gnosis. 2018. "Ismaili Gnosis." https://Ismailignosis.com/
Ivanow, V. 1922. *Ismailitica*. Calcutta.
——. 1936. *A Creed of The Fatimids*. Bombay.
——. 1942. *Ismaili Tradition Concerning the Rise of The Fatimids*. London, Calcutta, Bombay.
Ivanow, V. 1963. *Ismaili Literature*. Tehran.
Ivry, A. L. 1995. "Isma'ili Theology And Maimonides' Philosophy." In *The Jews of Medieval Islam: Community, Society, And Identity*, edited by D. Frank, 271–300. Leiden.
Jiwa, Sh. 1992. "Fāṭimid-Būyid Diplomacy During the Reign of Al-'Azīz billāh (365/975–386/996)." *Journal of Islamic Studies* 28.3:57–71.
——. 2008. "Historical Representations of a Fatimid Imam-caliph: Exploring al-Maqrizi's and Idris' writings on al-Muʿizz Li Din Allah." December 15. https://iis.ac.uk/academic-article/historical-representations-fatimid-imam-caliph-exploring-al-maqrizi-s-and-idris-writings-al-mu-izz.
——. 2016. "Kinship, Camaraderie, and Contestation: Fāṭimid Relations with the Ashrāf in the Fourth/Tenth Century." *Journal of the Medieval Mediterranean* 28.3:242–264.
——. 2017. "The Baghdad Manifest o (402/1011): A Re-Examination of Fatimid-Abbasid Rivalry." In *The Fatimid Caliphate: Diversity of Traditions*, edited by F. Daftary and Sh. Jiwa, 22–79. London, New York.

Kamaluddin, A. M., and Z. K. 2017. "Kamalzar Collections." October 20. http://www.kamalzar.com/.
Kassam, T. R. 1995. *Songs of Wisdom and Circles of Dance*. Albany.
Kiener, R. C. 1984. "Jewish Ismāʿīlism in Twelfth Century Yemen: R. Nethanel ben al-Fayyūmī." *The Jewish Quarterly Review* 74.3:249–266. DOI: 10.2307/1454196.
Kraemer, J. L. 2008. *Maimonides: The Life and World of One of Civilization's Greatest Minds*. Crown Publishing Group.
Lakhani, M. A. 2017. *Faith and Ethics: The Vision of the Ismaili Imamat*. London.
Lewis, B. 1975. *The Origins of Ismailism*. New York.
Lika. E. 2018. *Proofs of Prophecy and the Refutation of the Ismāʿīliyya*. Berlin, Boston.
Madelung, W. 1977. "Aspects of Isma'ili Theology: The Prophetic Chain And The God Beyond Being." In *Ismāʿīlī Contributions To Islamic Culture*, edited by S. H. Nasr, 53–65. Tehran.
——. 2018. "The Imamate in Early Ismaili Doctrine." *Shii Studies Review* 2.1–2:62–155.
Mamour, P. P. H. 1934. *Polemics on the Origin of the Fatimi Caliphs*. London.
McCarthy, R. 1980. *Freedom and Fulfilment*. Boston.
Mukherjee, S. 2017. *Ismailism and Islam in South Asia*. Cambridge.
Nasr, S. H. 1977. *Ismāʿīlī Contributions to Islamic Culture*. Tehran.
Nasir-i Khusraw. 2012. *Between Reason and Revelation*. Translated by E. L. Ormsby. London, New York.
Netton, I. R. 1980. "Brotherhood versus Imāmate: Ikhwān al-Ṣafā'and the Ismāʿīlīs." *Jerusalem Studies in Arabic and Islam* 2:253–262.
Nguyen, M. 2018. *Modern Muslim Theology*. Lanham.
O'Leary, De Lacy. 1923. *A Short History of The Fatimid Khalifate*. London.
Poor, D. M. 2014. *Authority without Territory*. New York.
Purohit, T. 2012. *The Aga Khan Case*. Cambridge, MA.
Schilbrack, K. 2012. "The Social Construction of 'Religion' and Its Limits: A Critical Reading of Timothy Fitzgerald." *Method and Theory in the Study of Religion* 24:97–117.
Schrier, O. J. 2006. "The Prehistory of the Fatimid Dynasty: Some Chronological and Genealogical Remarks." *Die Welt des Orients* 36:143–191.
Shackle, C., and Z. Moir. 1992. *Ismaili Hymns from South Asia*. London.
al-Shahrastānī, Muḥammad ibn ʿAbd al-Karīm. 2009. *Keys to The Arcana*. Translated by T. Mayer. Edited by M. 'A. Adharshab. Oxford.
Smith, J. Z. 1982. *Imagining Religion*. Chicago.
——. 1996. "A Matter of Class: Taxonomies of Religion." *Harvard Theological Review* 89.4:387–403.

Steinberg, J. 2011. *Isma'ili Modern: Globalization and Identity in a Muslim Community*. Chapel Hill.
Tusi, N. M. 1998. *Contemplation and Action*. Translated by S. J Badakhchani. London, New York.
Virani, Sh. N. 1995. *The Voice of Truth: Life and Works of Sayyid Nūr Muḥammad Shāh, a 15th/16th century Ismāʿīlī Mystic*. Master's Thesis. McGill University.
——. 2007. *The Ismailis in The Middle Ages*. Oxford.
——. 2010. "The Right Path: A Post-Mongol Persian Ismāʿīlī Treatise." *Iranian Studies* 43.2:197–221.
Waardenburg, J. J. 1995. *Muslims as Actors*. Berlin, New York.
Walker, P. E. 1993. *Early Philosophical Shiism*. Cambridge.
——. 2002. *Exploring an Islamic Empire: Fatimid History and Its Sources*. London, New York.
——. 2003. "Al-Maqrīzī and the Fatimids." *Mamlūk Studies Review* 7/2:83–97.
——. 2007. *Master of the Age*. London, New York.
Wasserstrom, S. M. 1995. *Between Muslim and Jew: The Problem of Symbiosis under Early Islam*. Princeton, NJ.
al-Yaman, Jaʿfar ibn Mansur, and James Winston Morris (editor and translator). 2001. *The Master and The Disciple*. London, New York.

11

Studying Ṣūfism Beyond Orientalism, Fundamentalism, and Perennialism

Mahdi Tourage

Introduction

THE GOAL OF THIS CHAPTER is to push the study of Ṣūfism outside the parameters of dominant scholarship. It will highlight the ways in which scholarship on Ṣūfism is a product and producer of specific discourses. I will point out several limitations that characterize modern scholarly studies of Ṣūfism, especially one of the most coherent and systemic forms of it, known as "Perennialist philosophy" (*al-ḥikmat al-ʿatīqa/khalida*). These limitations include the romanticizing of Islamic intellectual history through their selective readings of premodern mystical ideas as well as misrecognizing modernity and their own location within it. They also assume an originary universal subject hidden beneath the surface of all religions. It is possible to see these limitations as a deliberate move to dispel the myth of Orientalists' modern "discovery" and classification of Ṣūfism, Muslim fundamentalists' assaults on it, and secular modernists' decrying of it. We can even imagine some benefits in positing a pre-existing subject within Ṣūfism as the kind of strategic self-essentializing that is advocated in some postcolonial circles. However, assuming fixed boundaries between presumably holistic premodern and irredeemably diseased modern subjects presupposes a universal subject that is recognizable and accessible only to a few who are capable of perceiving it. The critiques of the constructed nature of the Perennialists' position (and its violent impact on real-life experiences) are then dismissed as products of secular western epistemologies and alien to Islam. It is in this context that scholarship on Ṣūfism often overlooks its inherent inconsistencies and goes on to insist on Ṣūfism's recoverable internal coherence, which is argued to have been disrupted only by unprecedented external forces.[1] Even defining the term *taṣawwuf*, translated as Ṣūfism, has been an impossible task from very early on in Islamic history. Ambiguity

1. Hodgson 1974, 97.

of terminology, play on words, the richness of Arabic language and its reverberations in other Muslim languages and the "mysterious" character of mysticism all contribute to the impossibility of defining Ṣūfism (not to mention the veracity of the claims of mystical experiences).[2]

To contest these limitations imposed on the studies of Ṣūfism I will situate Ṣūfism within the postmodern theories of subjectivity, specifically putting Lacanian psychoanalysis and the work of Jalāl al-Dīn Rūmī (d. ca. 1278) in a creative conversation with one another. I will begin with noting a few studies that have shown that more than any other social science psychoanalysis is an apt tool for projects that un-cover contingencies operative in the studies of mystical concepts. This will be followed by a brief discussion of Lacan's theory of signification, which I will argue uniquely parallels the concerns of a premodern Ṣūfī like Rūmī with the formation and dissemination of the subject of his mystical enterprise. Aside from being a "medievalist," specific features that make Lacan's theory particularly relevant to the studies of Ṣūfism will be discussed. The most important of these features are his formulation of desire, which functions like esoteric secrets in a mystical context. As will be argued, esoteric secrets are characterized by the lack of a definite referent in the process that produces them, just as desires are essentially unsatisfiable; both remain radically indeterminable subjects.

Drawing these parallels is not to turn Ṣūfism into a postmodern theoretical work or Lacan's writing into a form of occult mysticism, but to dispute the dominant scholarships that assume an insurmountable tension between postmodern theories and studies of Ṣūfism. That tension, I will conclude, is in fact to be found in many modern scholarly studies of Ṣūfism that authorize only a specific modality of knowledge production. The result they hold to be ahistorical Truth transcending cultural and historic contingencies. In drawing similarities between a premodern Ṣūfī and the postmodern theoretical concerns with the construction of subjectivity and the process of knowledge production I pursue several goals related to the study of Ṣūfism. I will argue that fixation of rigid boundaries between post- and pre-modern processes of subject-formation as a stable foundation for the study of Ṣūfism is not tenable. I also aim to demonstrate the relevance of theoretical/conceptual resources offered by Ṣūfism for a better understanding of modern subjectivities, not in the ways of new age spirituality, but one that is rooted in the epistemic-hermeneutical link between the Lacanian theoretical framework and resources of Ṣūfism. My goal here is to open up ways of differently reimagining subjectivities; and to unsettle the presumption of a

2. Schimmel 1975, 3–22.

need for maintaining a spatial or epistemological other (such as Europe, or postmodernity/feminism) against which scholarly studies of Ṣūfism can be conveniently positioned.

Situating Studies of Ṣūfism

The modern European study of Ṣūfism is entangled with colonialism. The early European scholars of Ṣūfism are characterized as Orientalist outsiders standing in contrast to the insiders' representations of Ṣūfī tradition.[3] If certain European scholars of Ṣūfism are the external other of Ṣūfism,[4] a second group, Muslim puritanical "fundamentalists" who violently reject Ṣūfism in favor of an earlier "Golden Age" of Islam are posited as its internal other. The violence of this strand of Islam was evident from its early days when Muḥammad ibn ʿAbd al-Wahhāb destroyed the Ṣūfī tombs and shrines of central Arabia, a trend that finds continuity in the actions of Taliban and the Islamic State of Iraq and Syria (ISIS).[5] A third approach to Ṣūfism, that of the secular modernists, equally hold Ṣūfism responsible for the backwardness of Muslims. Also relevant to the study of Ṣūfism are efforts by popular Ṣūfī community leaders like Hamza Yusuf. A white male American convert to Islam, Yusuf favors the Moroccan Shaykh Zarrūq (d. ca. 1493) as the key to the reform of Islam in America after September 11, 2001.[6] Propelled by his popularity (to a large part due to his white, male, convert status[7]) Yusuf is an active player in restoring a balance to various dimensions of contemporary experience of Islam such as "law, Ṣūfism, and humanist intellectual rigor."[8] To the discussion of the place of Ṣūfism in post-9/11 era we should add the political discourse of repositioning Ṣūfism as a template for domesticating Muslim subjectivities. For example, Gregory Lipton has argued that refashioning Ṣūfism in the post-9/11 political climate is a political move aiming to decouple Ṣūfism from Islam's ritualistic formalism for the purpose of negotiating an acceptable place for American Islam.[9]

Aside from these approaches are those which posit Ṣūfism as a pre-

3. For a discussion of these early Orientalist scholars of Ṣūfism (such as Edward Lane, John P. Brown, Sir William Jones, Sir John Malcolm, James William Graham), see Ernst 1997, 2–31.

4. Not all European scholars of Islam and Ṣūfism are considered its external other, some are considered "good" or insider Orientalists and some "bad" ones. See Varisco 2007, 40–62.

5. See Kugle 2007, 280.

6. Kugle 2006.

7. Tourage 2013.

8. For a discussion of Yusuf adopting Zarrūq's methodology for training followers, see Kugle 2006, 15–16.

9. Lipton 2011.

existing given in order to dispel Orientalists' "discovery" of it, Muslim fundamentalists' assaults on it, secular modernists' decrying of it, and other politically expedient exploitations of it. Dubbed Perennialists or Traditionalists, they claim that the universal core of Ṣūfism can be recovered, for example through its representatives, traditions and textual evidence. This recovery is imperative to their project of addressing modernity, which they consider to be an irreversibly failed project. Their assessment of modern civilization as "monstrous deviation" leads them to argue for accessing the "immutable principles" of tradition as "holistic solutions."[10] They claim there is an originary universal subject hidden beneath the surface of all religions, which nourishes mystics and seekers of all ages. Because they separate the presumably holistic premodern and irredeemably modern subjects, the universal subject of Ṣūfism, they argue, is recognizable and accessible only to the few who are capable of perceiving it (presumably themselves). True to their elitist stance they dismiss critiques of their constructed position by arguing that such critiques are irrelevant products of modern western epistemologies and alien to Ṣūfism. They overlook internal tensions in the development of Ṣūfism and inconsistency at the core of its postulates and premises.

The Perennialists and the Study of Ṣūfism

The blind spots of the Perennialist approach to Ṣūfism have been examined and critiqued in several studies.[11] Here I will note some of the relevant points to the study of Ṣūfism. First, in its enthusiasm for vindicating the character of Islamic thought, Traditionalism romanticizes Islamic intellectual history by conveniently ignoring "the abominations and splits that have occurred in the history of Islamic societies."[12] For example, Mehrzad Boroujerdi has shown that the glorification of religious cultures of past societies precludes Seyyed Hossein Nasr, one of the preeminent proponents of Perennialist philosophy, from deliberating on the state of intolerance, decadence, misery, repression, excommunication, banishment, theological persecutions and executions, and ignorance rampant in those societies.[13] Michael Muhammad Knight puts it best:

> Contemporary Muslim intellectuals who present themselves as voices of capitalized Tradition against what they see as diseased modern life,

10. Lumbard 2009, xiv.
11. Shaikh 2012; Lipton 2018.
12. Boroujerdi 1996, 128.
13. Boroujerdi 1996, 128–129.

> such as Seyyed Hossein Nasr and Hamza Yusuf, are not time travelers. They have never seen the premodern world that they promote to their constituencies (despite Yusuf's narrative of the Mauritanian desert as a place that time forgot), but can only promote a simplified, exoticized, and ultimately self-referential image of classical Islam, just as Euro-American New Agers might fetishize and commodify India or Tibet as lands of "spirituality."[14]

Second, their exoticizing of the premodern world is predicated upon their misrecognition of modernity. Nasr's critique of modernity for example, is characterized by Boroujerdi as more troubling than his glorification of premodern Islamic history. He writes that Nasr's understanding of the modern world is "quite subjective and ahistorical," failing "to appreciate the reasons for the philosophical uneasiness that landed the Enlightenment movement in the first place and the inventiveness that has since sustained it."[15] Boroujerdi continues: "Nasr criticizes the age of modernity while he forgets that historical consciousness is itself a product of the modern subjective mind."[16] The solution offered by Nasr for what he views as "a profound crisis within the modern world in all domains," lies in Perennial philosophy, which he argues provides the highest truths and highest form of knowledge.[17] In its crisis-based diagnosis of modernity, fear of modern philosophy's demise by postmodernism, feminism, and activism, insisting on class, gender, and racial hierarchies as profoundly inherent in a divine/natural order, Nasr's *A Young Muslim's Guide to the Modern World* is comparable to such popular works as Jordan Peterson's *12 Rules for Life: An Antidote to Chaos*. Similarly, both prescribe return to "Ancient wisdom,"[18] or "primordial and perennial"[19] past in order to alleviate the modern "desperation of meaninglessness" and alienation. The inception of these two works can be traced back to social movements such as the mythopoetic men's movement and earlier social and economic upheavals of the late nineteenth century.[20] However, not withstanding its major shortcomings (for example its proto-scientific suggestions that are rooted in nostalgia for rugged individualism), Peterson's book at least offers practical advice for its intended audience.

14. Knight 2017, 166–167.
15. Boroujerdi 1996, 128–129.
16. Boroujerdi 1996, 129.
17. Nasr 2003, 191, 207.
18. Peterson 2018, 368.
19. Nasr 2003, 6.
20. For a discussion of Peterson's lineage among "healers of modern man's soul," such as Mircea Eliade and Joseph Campbell, and political ramifications of their work on studying ancient mythology, see Mishra 2016.

Examples could be found in his advocating self-discipline, taking personal responsibility, and as ridiculous as it might sound, correcting one's posture.[21] Nasr's book, however, evokes a nostalgia for the perfection of an idealized Islamic past in the face of the West's slow demise. Examples include his assertions that in Islamic history "there has always been the participation of the people in government through specifically Islamic channels," therefore the Muslim world did have its own form of "democracy;" or it is difficult in the traditional Islamic dress to be an agnostic or atheist.[22]

Third, Traditionalists hold their philosophy to be perennial, transcending historical contingencies and not a product of a specific historical moment. The late Swiss German writer and the Shaykh (spiritual leader) of the first traditional European Ṣūfī order, Frithjof Schuon (d. 1998) is a good example. Schuon is ranked among the greatest Ṣūfī masters of the past and present and often compared to the most influential Ṣūfī sage, Muhyiddīn Ibn ʿArabī (d. 1240). His doctrine of Perennialism is widely considered to be based on Ibn ʿArabī's "Unity of Being." A mythologized status is accorded to him by the academy's prestigious names: some have considered him to be the man who "directly 'apprehended the Truth,'" or who "seems like the cosmic intellect itself," "unaffected by the limitations of historical circumstances."[23] However, as Gregory Lipton has shown, far from being a universal timeless Truth traced back to Ibn ʿArabī, Schuon's Perennial philosophy is a product of the nineteenth-century Eurocentric "Aryan myth" of racial superiority.[24] Some traditionalists have even pushed to impose a mystical force onto the course of history. Worth noting here are Julius Evola's unsuccessful attempt to guide the Fascist regime that governed Italy toward Traditionalism, and the Romanian Traditionalist Mircea Eliade who has been accused of involvement with the Romanian Iron Guard.[25] The Traditionalists in its Shīʿī version, for example Seyyed Hossein Nasr, had some involvement in the nationalist project of the Shah's regime in pre-revolutionary Iran. Ali Mirsepassi has shown that their political affiliations were born out of the substance of their Heideggerian thought, not political opportunism.[26] Elsewhere he has also argued that their critique of modernity is similarly rooted in the Heideggerian counter-Enlightenment movement that called for return to the absolute authority of tradition.[27]

21. Peterson 2018, 25–26.
22. Nasr 2003, 197, 113.
23. Lipton 2017, 263, 264.
24. Lipton 2017.
25. Sedgwick 2004, 109–117.
26. Mirsepassi 2017.
27. Mirsepassi 2011.

The Universal Perfect Man

Related to the Perennialists' foundational claims to have a unique access to the Truth and immutable universal principles are their selective readings of pre-modern mystics and their ideas (the fourth point). Similar to their romanticizing of Islamic intellectual history, they overlook premodern mystics' social, political and cultural realities – as if these Ṣūfī authorities and their ideas stood outside of their time and space. One example to note here is the often-repeated concept of the Universal Perfect Man (*al-insān al-kāmil*), a doctrine that gained prominence through Ibn ʿArabī's work.

William Chittick, one of the leading contemporary authorities on Ṣūfism (writing as an "insider") frames this concept in terms of a fundamental polarization of the universe into microcosm and macrocosm. The latter is universe, and the former is man, who reflects divine names and qualities.[28] The knowledge of the whole universe is possible only through man's knowledge of himself. The Universal Perfect Man is "the perfect human model" whose inward reality is the inward reality of the whole universe.[29] To give concrete reality to this abstract doctrine it is anchored in the person of the Prophet Muḥammad. He is considered to be "the most perfect manifestation of the Universal Man."[30] Since there is no evidence of this doctrine in the Qurʾān, Chittick relates a saying (*ḥadīth*) of the Prophet as the proof of his state of perfection as the Universal Man: "The first thing created by God was my light (*nūrī*)."[31] How this *ḥadīth* with its dubious authenticity and varying versions ("The first thing created by God was my spirit") is the proof for this doctrine is not explained. Further proof is provided by referring to the numerous Ṣūfī saints who are considered to have embodied such perfection. Since they supposedly did reach this state, Chittick argues, they were familiar with its meaning "in a concrete manner" even though they did not articulate it in the same terms as Ibn ʿArabī.[32] Chittick relates a few lines of poems by Jami, the Ṣūfī poet of fifteenth-century Persia, as further elaboration and support. He goes on to note that since these three lines by Jami are originally words uttered by ʿAlī, the Prophet's cousin and son-in-law, it proves that doctrine of the microcosm and the macrocosm was known earlier on in Islamic history.

28. Chittick 2005, 49. The Universal Perfect Man has been explained by a few other scholars as well. However, I have chosen Chittick because he discusses it in relation to Jalāl al-Dīn Rūmī's work. For other explanations of this doctrine, see Burkhardt 2008, 89; Izutsu 1983, 247–260.

29. Chittick 2005, 50.

30. Chittick 2005, 50.

31. Chittick 2005, 50.

32. Chittick 2005, 51.

The complexity of the doctrine of the Universal Perfect Man is explained through the use of literary devices and philosophical reasoning such as paradox and apophasis (saying through unsaying) and mirror analogy.[33] In itself this doctrine is a fascinating case for studying the history of ideas. We can even appreciate the polemical expediency of the assertion that Prophet Muhḥammad was the perfect embodiment of the Universal Man – though as it has been pointed out by Muslim feminist thinkers, the gendered bias of this assertion will not fit well with the claimed universality of the Islamic message.[34] This appreciation (and its critique) can be extended to devotional sectarian considerations of the Shīʿah Imams' unique perfection.[35] Also, many Ṣūfī authorities[36] and heroic figures of the past like Alexander the Great were retroactively considered to have embodied *al-insān al-kāmil.*[37] Thus the purported androgyny and universality of this concept may be useful in envisioning complimentary possibilities between genders.[38]

However, from these considerations to the claim of universal immutability for this doctrine requires a huge leap of essentializing imagination and entails epistemological violence. For example, consider Lumbard's words: "The doctrine of Universal Man is, by virtue of the fact that it is a traditional doctrine, immutable and eternal."[39] In his circular reasoning this doctrine is traditional because it is immutable and eternal, and it is immutable and eternal because it is traditional. The cultural history of this doctrine, the process by which it was constructed, archived, classified, and deployed is entirely overlooked. The flaw of this doctrine goes deeper than erroneous assumptions of its pre-existence, it is put forth as the arbiter of problematics of embodied and gendered subjectivities. Nasr argues that the Universal Perfect Man is the transcendental androgynous archetype of a "paradisal state" in which the chaos of the gendered subjectivities is collapsed into wholeness. However, as I have argued elsewhere, in the discourse of the Ṣūfīs this ideological doctrine assumes the masculine to be its default gender, implementing, institutionalizing, and authorizing male privilege and

33. Sells 1994, 93.

34. See Anonymous 2018.

35. Amir-Moezzi 1994.

36. For example, Rūmī considered Shams-e Tabrīzī, his spiritual master, to be "the total exemplar of the Universal Perfect Man." Nasr 1972, 58n2.

37. Alexander was identified as the person noted in the Qurʾān as the "Possessor of the Two Horns." He is considered to have reached "the pinnacle of mystical and cosmic apotheosis as the 'perfect person' (*al-insān al-kāmil*) in his legendary journey," which resembles Prophet Muḥammad's night journey (*miʿrāj*) into heaven. See Renard 2001, 622.

38. This potential is lost due to the patriarchal self-same imaginary that structures Ṣūfī discourses and reduces this concept to no more than a poetic fiction. See Tourage 2013, 9–10.

39. Lumbard 2009, 265.

masculine supremacy.[40] There are of course many female mystics such as Rābiʿa al-ʿAdawiyya al-Ḳaysiyya, who are often brought up in discussions of a positive view of women in Ṣūfism. However, through the structuration of the masculine imaginary's narcissistic logic exceptional female mystics take on the male gender, an idea that Perennialists themselves admit is "absurd."[41] In the discourse of the Ṣūfīs, the recurrent abstract deployments of this historical concept signify only the masculine. Despite its cultural history, the violence of its short-sightedness in regard to erasing gender differences, the long stretch of imagination required to connect it to previous Ṣūfī saints and to the Prophet himself, and despite the fact that some Ṣūfī authorities after Ibn ʿArabī contradicted him in this regard,[42] this doctrine is still considered to be universal, immutable, and eternal!

Rūmī and the Overlooked Passages of His *Masnavi*

Like their modern interlocutors such as Schuon and Nasr, premodern Ṣūfī authorities were gendered and embodied subjects. Their mystical output and experiences, far from being universal or timeless, had a specific epistemic genealogy and were shaped by their specific historical contingencies and cultural imperatives. For example, the mystical concepts of Jalāl al-Dīn Rūmī, one of the greatest mystics of the Perso-Islamic world and a favorite poet of contemporary America, are products of a specific process of meaning production. His mystical insights have been expounded in many studies with still room left for many more to come. Long before Rūmī's immense popularity in translation, Chittick considered his message to be "so universal" and "his use of imagery drawn from sources common to all human experience" to be "so liberal" that inherent drawbacks of translations and his references to less familiar Islamic teachings are easily overcome.[43] Chittick's statement indicates that my choice of Rūmī and his *Masnavi* is not incidental. Rūmī's magnum opus, the *Masnavi* is unique in the high regards and immense influence it continues to exert since its inception.[44] In more than 25,000 verses of poetry he moves in a non-linear way from recording his mystical experiences and qurʾānic commentary to everyday events and folk and bawdy tales.

40. Tourage 2007, 165–181; Tourage 2013, 7–9.
41. Tourage 2013, 7–9.
42. Lumbard 2009, 264–265.
43. Chittick 1983, 9.
44. All citations are from the Nicholson edition of the *Masnavi* (Persian spelling used here); see Rūmī 1925–1940. Citations are indicated by book number followed by line number in the text. All translations are mine.

Overlooked Passages in the *Masnavi*

There are the overlooked passages in the *Masnavi* where we find the evidence of, to use contemporary parlance, common racist, sexist, homophobic, and anti-Semitic passages?[45] For example there are passages where Jews are called (ignoble) dogs (1:769) with no courage (1:3971) or knowledge of God. (1:484) They are bent on bringing dark shame on (true) religion. (2:2859) The heart without the light of God is narrow and dark like the soul of the Jew. (2:3130) They are accursed (6:967), fanatically angry (6:958) and are left without guidance of God because they turned away the Messiah (6:445). We can also consider the tale of a Hindu slave, the religious, "racial," and socially inferior dark-skinned other, who transgresses the social boundaries of his time by expressing his secret love for his master's daughter. As a result, his master tricks him into being repeatedly and violently raped by a boorish man – who Rūmī informs us had a huge penis like that of a donkey – over the course of the night amid the celebratory drumming and clapping of the master's family (6:249–321).[46]

Examples of Rūmī's sexism are found in many passages in the *Masnavi* that portray women in an unfavorable light. Rūmī writes that women function as the reminders of the feminine nature of the carnal soul. They are the externalized embodiments of the evils of the carnal soul. He likens the world to a powerful female sorcerer, a "stinking old hag who has potent spells." The unraveling of her sorcery is not a task the commoners are capable of: "If (men's) intellect could loose her knots / God would have not sent the prophets" (4:3196–3197).[47] A similar stance is repeated in another passage where Rūmī informs the (male) reader that "She (the world) is a stinking old hag who by much flattery / displays herself like a young bride" (6:318). He goes on to warn the reader not to be deceived by her rosy cheeks and not to taste her poisonous drink. In one tale, this ugly old hag bewitches a noble prince

45. For a survey of racism in classical Persian literature, see Southgate 1984. Needless to say, we must apply these terms to premodern contexts cautiously. However, to the extent that Ṣūfī authorities and their interlocutors claim universality for their relevance and mystical ideas, and to the extent that this paper aims to upset constructed boundaries that separate modern and premodern subjects, I am justified in applying these descriptive terms to premodern contexts. For a similar treatment, see Sadiyya Shaikh (2012) where she notes that by excusing premodern Ṣūfīs' gendered shortcomings, modern scholars confine the study of Ṣūfism to "a web of symbolic sexism." She has subjected Ibn ʿArabī to a rigorous feminist critique without holding him "hostage to contemporary sensibilities." See Shaikh, 2012.

46. For a discussion of this tale, see Tourage 2007, 178–179.

47. This passage is a reference to the verses from the Qurʾān: "Say: I seek refuge with the Lord of the Dawn, ... From the mischief of those who blow on knots." (Q 113:1 and 4) "Blowing on knots" is a reference to a form of witchcraft practiced by women.

so that he abandons his bride and wedding. She is also referred to as "a black devil," a "ninety-year old hag with a rotten vagina" (4:3148, 49). He writes: "Know that the husband is intellect (*ʿaql*) and woman (the wife) is greed and avarice" (1:2903). If a woman picks up a sword and charges in battle, she does not break the ranks of the enemy, her hand trembles and she causes a "pitiful situation." With this preamble he continues to warn men that their intellect should be "male" and their "ugly carnal soul" female and powerless because women are "inclined towards scent and color" (5:2459–2466). Women worshiping color and scent is repeated in another passage of the *Masnavi* (5:4082). Women use crying as a snare to trap their husbands (1:2394). Their dreams are less than that of a man on account of the deficiency of their intellect and weakness of their soul, which are reflections of their deficient bodies that uncontrollably menstruate (6:4320). Their bodies, like their cunningness and their sexual urges, are uncontrollable. When menstruating, they are like infants who have no control over their bodily discharges and fluids; just like the "vile" and "polluted" persons, they may soil the ground upon which men pray (2:3424).

The *Masnavi* contains tales such as the one about the high station of a Ṣūfī master, which is truly a reward for his patience with an abusive, monstrous wife (6:2115–2157). A few other cautionary tales warn men of women's cunningness (4:3544–3557, and 6:4449–4537) with the conclusion that, "The deception of women has no end," (6:4475) a reference to the qurʾānic tale of Joseph in which he is seduced by his master's wife.[48] In addition to viewing women as inherently deficient, the representations of women in the *Masnavi* reflect their negative contribution to the biblical narrative of humanity, from Adam's fall from high heavens because of a woman (6:4470, 6:2799 and 6:2796–2797), and Noah's wife undermining his prophetic efforts (6:4472–4474), to Cain killing Abel for the sake of a woman (6:4471), and Joseph falling from grace because of a woman (6:2801).

The negative view of women as bodily and intellectually deficient did not prevent Muslim male mystics such as Rūmī from appropriating the female biological function of birthing and nursing as the analogy of the divinely-inspired creative process of composing mystical writings. Gendering mystical creativity as feminine is an appropriation because the machination of patri-

48. According to the Qurʾān Joseph's unnamed master was a dignitary of Egypt who upon finding out the slyness of his wife tells her: "Your cunning is enormous." (Q 12:24) This statement by an angry man about his wife in a very specific context is often generalized to all women and taken as an indication of women's innate cunningness, as is the case in the *Masnavi*. For a survey of the exegetical approaches to this verse in major Sunnī commentaries, from traditionalists and rationalists to modernists and fundamentalists, see Stowasser 1994, 50–56.

archal masculine imaginary ensured it to be disempowering for women who embody this process of creative reproduction. In fact, as the above negative examples demonstrate, no effort of imagination was spared to differentiate the feminine (and all its attending properties such as birthing and nursing) as a mystical category from its cultural/biological correlate, the woman. Similarly, male and masculine were produced, presumed and authorized as the only ontologically self-sufficient gender in order to successfully resolve the anxiety over multiplicity of gendered and embodied subjectivities (for example, through imaginary constructs such as the Universal Perfect Man).[49]

The Function of the Penis

Related to the patriarchal negative representations of women as inherently evil and bodily and intellectually deficient is the male-centered mysticism of Rūmī that revolves around the function of the penis. In one passage Rūmī analogizes the mystic's creative impulse as men's physical prowess in combat. He writes that beard and testicles do not make a man, since every goat has plenty of beard, and a donkey's penis would have been the king of men (5:3345, 3711). Nevertheless the imagery of erect penis is repeatedly used as an analogy for mystical prowess. For example, beard and mustache do not add to one's manliness when one has a penis that cannot become erect (5:2510–2511). Rūmī takes the potency of a man's erection to sexually enjoying a slave girl as an analogy of a true mystic penetrating the depth of a mystical text:

> These words are like a beautiful bride. What love or affection will a beautiful slave girl have for someone who buys her in order to sell her again? Since the only pleasure such a trader has is in selling the girl, he is impotent. When he buys a girl only to sell her, he does not have the manliness to be buying her for himself.[50]

Linking the intellectual and spiritual prowess of a male mystic to the penetrating function of the erect penis is repeated almost obsessively in many passages of the *Masnavi*. We read about a man whose ignorance is the cause for calling him effeminate like a hermaphrodite (*mukhannath*) who has both male and female genitals, hiding his penis from women and his vagina from men (6:1425–1427). A military general interrupts his sexual intercourse with a beautiful slave girl he is transporting in order to kill an attacking lion. The

49. See Tourage 2013.
50. Rūmī 1330/1951, 111.

brave general returns to the slave girl's bedside, after slaying the ferocious lion, with his penis still erect "like the horn of a rhino" (5:3848–93). In the same story the "manliness" of the general we are told pales in comparison with the "true manliness" of the king who forgives him for his sexual transgression, even though the king loses his erection after hearing the rustling noise of a mouse just as he is about to engage in sexual intercourse with the same slave girl (5:3848–4031).

In the cautionary tale of a slave girl who had trained the donkey of her mistress to engage in sexual intercourse with her (5:1333–1429) it is the "prancing" of the donkey's available penis that excites the girl's sexual urges (5:3715). Rūmī tells us that the girl would slide a gourd over the penis of the donkey to prevent it from fully penetrating her vagina and injuring her during intercourse. The mistress of the house becomes sexually excited and jealous when she finds out that her slave girl is satisfying her sexual urges with the donkey, sends her away and engages in the sexual act with the donkey herself. However, she dies in the process because in her excitement she does not notice the protective function of the gourd. Rūmī's important lesson in this story is that a true Ṣūfī master is like the slave girl and esoteric secrets are like a donkey's erect penis. One cannot become a master simply by observing. Incomplete knowledge of secrets is lethal just like incomplete mastery of the use of the donkey's penis without a gourd. In another tale the penis of a male prankster sitting among females in a religious gathering is linked to the miraculous function of Moses' staff (5:3337). Rūmī also likens his own admiration for his predecessor Bāyazīd Basṭāmī (d. ca. 875) to the desirous bemoaning of a woman who sighed when witnessing donkeys engaged in sexual intercourse, wistfully saying: "If intercourse is what these donkeys do / (then in comparison) these husbands (of ours) must be shitting on our vaginas!" (5:3392).

Making Sense of the *Masnavi*'s Overlooked Passages

Using Jacques Lacan's theory of signification I have argued that in the passages noted above Rūmī utilizes elements of his culture to highlight the locatedness of the subject (human subject or the subject of mystical discourse). They are employed in the midst of a celebrated mystical text to foster transformation of the subject. They indicate that mystical concepts are not restricted to lofty abstract doctrines (such as the Universal Perfect Man). If Rūmī is a great mystic it is because he turns these culturally contingent resources on themselves to foster the unsettling of the self-grounded claims of autonomy, coherence, and completion. Thus rigid boundaries of what constitutes "mystical" subject must be expanded. Here we can add that using jokes and other elements of "low" culture for explicating mystical/philosophical concepts is not an invention of postmodern pop-star philosophers like Slavoj Žižek.[51] Rūmī saw traces of high mystical experiences in the lowest parts of his popular culture and exploited them to his advantage. In this sense the boundaries of high and low culture too are disputable. Moreover, since jokes have discernable roots in the unconscious, as Freud reminds us, Rūmī's unique use of his cultural elements also indicates his own locatedness and the limitations of his mystical imagination, which will be discussed below.

Lacanian Psychoanalysis

Psychoanalysis does not get a favorable reception in Ṣūfī studies. For example, in his hasty evaluation Joseph Massad dismisses European-trained Arab psychoanalysts focusing on "Islam" as narcissistic Europeanized Arabs facing failed prospects of the project of Europeanization.[52] However, more nuanced studies have taken the historical link between psychoanalytical writings and Muslim cultures and mysticism more seriously by revealing a mutually transformative relationship between the two. For example, in her recent book *The Arabic Freud: Psychoanalysis and Islam in Modern Egypt*, Omnia El Shakry unsettles the assumptions of incommensurability between psychoanalysis and Islam. She writes about a "creative encounter of ethical engagement" between psychoanalysis and Islam.[53] She has shown that the new science of self in twentieth-century Egypt was not capitulation to European hegemony, nor was it based in dichotomies of modern or traditional, Western or non-Western. Along the same lines but in a non-Arab context, Gohar Homayounpour's writing on clinical psychoanalysis in Iran refutes claims of an Islamic resistance to psychoanalysis. Homayounpour argues that claims of an Islamic resistance to psychoanalysis is not tenable. Fully aware of the significance of cultural differences, she observes that psychoanalysis was "transplanted" to Iran, but it surely found "a very fertile ground within the Iranian culture.[54] Several studies have discussed the relevance of Lacanian psychoanalysis to studying various aspects of Ṣūfism.[55] Ian Almond has argued that the echoes of Ibn 'Arabi's explanation of the unknowable Divine Essence can be found in the Lacanian concept of the Re-

51. Žižek 2014.
52. Massad 2015, 279.
53. El Shakry 2017, 2.
54. Homayounpour 2012, xxvii.
55. For example, see Ewing 1997; Parker and Siddiqui 2019.

al.[56] In the context of Persian mystical poetry, which contains the bulk of the Islamic tradition of mystical poetry, Michael Glünz has pointed out the relevance of Lacan to premodern Persian poetry, and more recently Claudia Yaghoobi has studied transgression in Persian Ṣūfism through Lacan's concept of "*jouissance*."[57]

Why Lacan?

Lacan's theoretical work is rooted in European medieval theology.[58] He is unique in engaging medieval literature and philosophy to the point that he is described as a "medievalist."[59] More importantly, it is certain features of Lacan's theory that make his work relevant to the study of Ṣūfism. A salient example is his concept of the Real, which, as Michael Sells and James Webb have hinted, has uncanny similarities with the "unseen" in the Islamic context.[60] The Real is a mode of psychical organization that is outside of language, marked by a radical indeterminacy, and inassimilable to any process of symbolization.[61] It is a truth claim defining an unknowable register that requires an act of faith.[62] In this sense it parallels the world of the "unseen" in the Islamic context. The Real might even have the necessary elasticity to be a possible alternative to the academic use of theologically loaded terms like God or Allah.[63] Another relevant feature of Lacan's theory is his formulation of desire, which is rooted in his reading of premodern texts, emphasizing their significance for contemporary concerns with subjectivity.[64] His linguistic turn to Freud puts language and desire at the heart of his theory. In the Freudian model social taboos and moral constraints repress unfulfillable desires in the unconscious, which then resurface when they bypass the censorship of the superego and emerge in condensed, displaced, and symbolic forms, for example, in dreams. In the process they become distorted images of what they were. Therefore they cannot be recognized except through careful interpretation and analysis as symptoms of something buried deep in the unconscious.

56. Almond 2004.
57. Glünz 1995; Yaghoobi 2017.
58. Beattie 2013.
59. Labbie 2006, 4.
60. Sells and Webb 1995.
61. Evans 1996, 160.
62. Beattie 2013, 16.
63. This is similar to proposed terms "unknowable" or "unnameable" by Russel McCutcheon to make an inclusive academic language relevant to its historical and cultural context as well as to nontheistic religious discourses. See McCutcheon 2013.
64. Labbie 2006, 6.

Lacan's semiotic reworking of Freud's psychoanalysis is useful for the studies of mystical texts.[65] This is particularly relevant to studies of Ṣūfism, where communication of esoteric secrets – or safeguarding against the persecution of Ṣūfīs – is the main concern. Similar to the Freudian formulation of repressed desires giving rise to the process of symptoms production, hidden esoteric secrets cannot remain absolutely hidden, nor can they be openly divulged. They are expressed in mystical language using condensed symbols or metaphors intelligible only to the initiates. Like desires, esoteric secrets too are essentially incompatible with language; they can never be fully articulated in language. Therefore like dreams, jokes, symptoms, or slips of tongue, the divulged forms of secrets are only partial manifestations of their repressed content; their full articulations are indefinitely deferred. This is articulated in semiotic terms as the "lack" of a definite referent in the process of signification. In the context of the study of Ṣūfī texts this means that something of the secret is present in mystical language, but full articulation of it eludes language forever.

Lack and Its Promises (and Perils)

In the Freudian model lack is articulated as a state of radical dependency and disempowerment in the core of our being, most glaringly manifested in our vulnerable state as infants. This original lack of control and vulnerability in infancy on an individual level parallels the original chaos and fragmentation on a cultural level. Articulated in semiotic terms, lack refers to the absence of the signified, that is the guarantor of the stability of meaning, in the process of signification. Lack is the name of the tension intrinsic to the mystical projects of articulating the unknowable Real/the unseen. Put differently, lack describes "openness" in our being, an openness that is "a key to both the creativity and vulnerability of human beings."[66] In other words, lack conditions the openness of the creative processes where we get volumes of mystical work and poetry attempting to express the unknowable Real, the Signified.[67] On the other hand lack also brings about vulnerability because the Real remains unknowable. Just as in response to our original unformed state at birth we establish a semblance of the unity of our ego through narcissistic fantasies of power, mastery, and control, on a discursive level we cover our insecurities and the originary lack by producing closed structures, like religious formations and mystical discourses. Lack is therefore both cause and obstacle.

65. See Wolfson 2005.
66. Dicenso 1999, 47.
67. Tourage 2007, 45.

The same lack that propels Rūmī to compose thousands of lines of poetry and mystical speech alluding to what cannot be fully expressed in language also prompts him to obscure his own locatedness. He is clear in his emphasis on the irreducibility of lack, that the inner meanings are not reducible to external forms. Yet he considers his work and himself to be above such cultural constructions – a claim that the Qur'ān does not even accord to the Prophet himself.[68] Not too dissimilar to the Qur'ān, he describes his *Masnavi* with such lofty terms as: "The greatest creed and the most luminous of the holy laws, as well as the most manifest of proofs of God."[69] Claims of the divine origins of the *Masnavi* are supported by its later appellation "the Qur'ān in Persian language." As the sample of the passages quoted above show, the *Masnavi* itself provides ample evidence that, of course, Rūmī never transcended his cultural context. Considering these and many other passages through the prism of theories of gender it becomes clear that in the androcentric context of the *Masnavi* it is the male experience that is privileged and prioritized. Rūmī's mystical discourse structures the supremacy of male and the masculine in all arrangements of signification, which when considering the function of the penis can be described as "phallocentric esotericism."[70] The feminine turns out to be no more than a secondary and derivative disavowed foundation of the masculine, and the female "the ontologically dependent gender and inessential other, never represented as a subject reflecting on her own being."[71] Positive images of women in Islamic sources and history are not rare, but through the self-same operations of masculinist imaginary the few exceptional women (often too exceptional for any other woman to emulate) assume male gender value and become honorary men.

Rūmī along with other premodern Muslim male mystics may be forgiven for their short-sightedness in regard to socially-historically constructed categories that we take for granted. We may spare them the expectation of transcending their androcentric cultural context (even though they claimed to have traversed the depth of the human soul and mapped the heavens above). However, to uncritically privilege records of their mystical experiences over the evidence of their inevitable locatedness in specific cultural contexts is to deny them their humanity in the first place. More relevant to the subject of this chapter, this is also to privilege certain epistemologies as the final arbiter of the "truth" of Ṣūfism (and by extension, of Islam). For example, Nasr views gender differences between males and females as

68. Rubin 2003, 447.
69. Rūmī 2004, 3.
70. Tourage 2007, 149.
71. Tourage 2013.

a "primordial polarization."[72] Essentializing gender relations as a "profound metaphysical relationship" between sexes, he asserts that since God is the Creator, "whatever ensues from the distinction between the two sexes must be related to His Wisdom and Providence." Distinctions between the sexes are therefore not socially-historically constructed according to Nasr, but "essential to the meaning of the human state."[73] Nasr's words are indicative of a discourse that says more about the process of producing the subject of his discussion than any pre-existing primordial state.[74] Any critique of the hegemonic trajectory of this discourse is dismissed as a product of secular modernism and "alien" to the Islamic world view.[75] Even when this critique is based on evidence from the Qurʾān and *ḥadīth*, it is considered to be a rejection of revelation: "they are rooted in mental habits that developed in a secular universe that rejects the centrality of revelation, if not its very veracity."[76]

The effects of such vitriol resistance on contemporary considerations of gender, subjectivity, and power in studies of Ṣūfism could be gauged from the following personal experience. Years ago as a PhD candidate I reviewed a book on the topic of the Shīʿī approach to Ṣūfism and spiritual wayfaring, a compilation of the teachings of the great Shīʿī scholar Sayyid Muḥammad Ḥusayn Ṭabāṭabāʾī (d. 1981), edited by his student, another great scholar in his own right, Sayyid Muḥammad Ḥusayn Ḥusaynī Tehranī, and translated by another scholar Moḥammad Faghfoory (with a forward by Seyyed Hossein Nasr).[77] Nasr's forward, the translator's notes and the editor's introduction provide an informative who-is-who of the greatest masters of Shīʿī esoteric sciences of recent centuries, noting their teachings and their exemplary lives. In my review I made an observation that a "gender-sensitive reading" of this book would find it problematic that not one woman is to be found among the Shīʿī scholars of the past few centuries noted in this book. In what became a "dialogue" published by the same journal, the translator complained and adamantly refuted my review by concluding that "the socio-cultural construction of gender and class" in Ṣūfism should not be understood "through the lenses of feminist theories formulated in secular, non-Islamic, pseudo-socialist Western intellectual circles."[78] Fagh-

72. Nasr 1987, 48.

73. Nasr 1987, 48.

74. For a discussion of "discourse" and "practices that systematically form the objects of which they speak," see Foucault 2005, 53–54.

75. See for example, Murata 1992, 4.

76. Lumbard 2009, 68.

77. Ṭabāṭabāʾī 2003.

78. Faghfoory and Tourage 2007, 141.

foory's comment is typical of the way any contemporary critique of their position is dismissed by labeling it with what seems to be the nastiest terms in academia: feminist, secular, non-Islamic, Orientalist, and Western. Here we can add the fifth point to the limitations imposed on the study of Ṣūfism: proponents of Perennialism consider their own works to be above all critique, above all cultural residue and contextual sediments, and themselves to stand outside the limitations of time and contingencies of space. If we add the theological and apologetic trajectory of the post-9/11 studies of "true Islam" to this self-aggrandizing stance, the result is a hegemonic discourse that forecloses the possibility of critical or alternative modes of knowledge production.[79]

Concluding Remarks

Despite similarities with religious philosophies, Lacan's model of inquiry is not concerned with the theological status of the Real. His goal of upsetting reified universals, however, overlaps with that of Ṣūfī authorities like Rūmī. Instead of positing abstract universals to cover over the lack or deal with the trauma and crisis, they both aim to universalize the subject's capacity for transformation by bringing the subject to accept her location within her cultural context. That is to say, instead of the impossible task of knowing oneself the subject must unknow herself. Articulated in clinical terms, the goal of Lacanian intervention is not to produce a well-adjusted subject living a successful happy social life: "Analysis can have as its goal only the advent of true speech and the subject's realisation of his history in its relation to a future."[80] In a semiotic sense the subject can be the subject of a mystical text, the esoteric secrets whose inevitable location within the limitation of language and culture must be acknowledged before any transformative possibilities could follow. Like the unfulfilled desires in the Lacanian model that can never be satisfied, concealed secrets can never be fully known or revealed. They only partially appear in distorted forms. To put this in Ṣūfī terms, the truth/secrets are always veiled. Like signifiers that never refer to the signified but to other signifiers in an unending chain of signification,[81] the veils will never be lifted, only replaced by other veils. The truth of a mystical text like the *Masnavi* therefore never consists in its representational form, but insists in the process of signification. The content of secrecy,

79. For an informative discussion of post-9/11 apologetic studies, which are dedicated to defending "true Islam" as "minimalist, interior, peaceful, and apolitical," see Merchant 2013, 203.

80. Lacan 1977, 249.

81. Lacan 1966, 502.

however we attempt to define it (definite meaning or the Universal Truth for example) is not the point here, the indications of its symbolic displacement are.

Thus, a creative encounter between Lacanian psychoanalysis and Ṣūfism, or with Rūmī's work at least, would not be about revealing in a "new agey" fashion some easy steps to personal fulfillment, happiness or love; nor is it to put forth culturally constructed categories such as Tradition or the Universal Man as the panacea for our modern condition. Even if there are pre-existing esoteric secrets, the Universal Truth (or the Real of the unconscious) not bound by limitations of culture and language, the mystic's access to them is always already mediated through his particular cultural structures.[82] For example, the genealogy of concepts such as Universal Man shows that the process of their production is rooted in their specific historical and cultural imperatives. It is no surprise that Ṣūfī mystics hardly considered the mystical claims of other Ṣūfīs as authentic. Studies by scholars of Ṣūfism do not make this implicit, but many of the Ṣūfīs and sages were mostly concerned with cataloguing other Ṣūfīs' claims and rejecting those they considered to be false Ṣūfīs, adding volumes to the genre of heresiography and intra-faith polemics.[83] Rūmī himself often attacks false Ṣūfīs with the most vulgar and derogatory terms.

A feature of Lacan's theoretical writings shared by Rūmī's mystical works is that they both undermine their own critical positions by demonstrating ideological tendencies that arise from a lack of self-reflexivity. For example, Rūmī was fully aware that language in general, and Persian mystical poetry with all its sophistication in particular, can only hint at the inner content of mystical experiences. To put it in semiotic terms, Rūmī's work clearly indicated that signifiers lack intrinsic significance, it is their deployment in specific cultural contexts that charged them with significance. Yet, while fully aware of the signifying limitation of reified cultural systems and working to disrupt them, Rūmī considers his own work to be a timeless, divinely revealed scripture, not just similar, but equal to the Qur'ān.[84] If we hold his *Masnavi* to his own standards it is his claim of being God's mouthpiece that deserves our suspicion, not his use of vulgar words and bawdy tales. Similarly, Lacan's critique of the phallocentric system of signification is predicated upon positing a symbolic configuration that he designates as the phallus. It is the concealment of the phallus that militates against totalizing metanarratives of universality by conditioning the indefinite deferral of closure in

82. Katz 1992.
83. Algar 2018.
84. Tourage 2007, 34.

the process of signification. Nevertheless, Lacan maintains that the phallus is the privileged signifier that has no signified,[85] effectively elevating it to the level of a transcendental signifier and endorsing the very phallocentric system he purports to critique.[86] Therefore it would be a mistake to consider either Lacan's or Rūmī's works as impartial, which brings us to conclude that neither postmodern theories nor some premodern historical moment can be the privileged neutral epistemic site of meaning production.

Contrary to the opinions of his future commentators who dismissed the passages quoted above as the products of the failing mind of an aging mystic, Rūmī did not consider them as "obscene," or "vulgar" (*mustahjan*).[87] These seemingly "un-mystical" passages provide a good case for studying the instability of the subject of Ṣūfism by pointing to the tension inherent in the very definition of what is "mystical." They demonstrate that religious writings in general and mystical writing in particular are not fixed abstract enterprises. Even within a particular religious tradition mystical experiences cannot be framed in a monolithic way, because their abstract subjects emerge within a symbolic matrix of mutable cultural terms that are irreducible to specific regimes of knowledge production. Dismissing the generic approaches to the variety of phenomenological studies of mystical experiences, Moshe Idel writes: "When studying the religious writings we do not witness fixed systems, clear-cut theologies or frozen techniques, whose essence can be easily determined, but living structures and proclivities for moving in a certain direction, or directions, rather than crystallized static entities."[88] In the case of Rūmī, his precepts have been interpreted through and under the enormous influence of the theosophic system of Ibn ʿArabī.[89]

In comparing Lacan and Rūmī's concerns with the process of the construction of the subject we must be cognizant of the interplay of sameness and difference. Their overlap does not make them identical, but it does problematize the dichotomizing dialectics that, akin to a simplistic Clash of Civilizations thesis, situate postmodern theories as the antithesis of the subject of Ṣūfism. The goal is not to erase the epistemological differences between the two, nor to apply a priori the concepts of the one to the concerns of the other, or to over-generalize the conclusions. My goal has been to disrupt the dialectical logic of contraries that mark many studies of Ṣūfism. That is, to transform these two seemingly antithetical discourses to dialogi-

85. Lacan 1977, 288.

86. For a critiques of Lacan's concept of the phallus, see Fuss 1989, 6–12.

87. See Tourage 2007, 11.

88. Idel 2002, 19.

89. For example, Ibn 'Arabi's concept of "the Creative Feminine" was read into the works of Rūmī under the immense influence of Ibn 'Arabi's theosophy. See Furuzanfar 1367/1990, 3.103.

cal pairs that share similar if not the same concerns with subjectivity and the interrogation of metanarratives of universality. The result is alternative ways of conceiving subjectivities while unsettling presumptions of a need for maintaining an epistemological other, against which scholars of Ṣūfism (the Perennialists, the Orientalists, fundamentalists or modernists) can conveniently consolidate the parameters of their own ideological positions.

The stability of such doctrines as the Universal Perfect Man, Tradition or Perennial Truth – or projects of returning to an imaginary Golden Age/primordial state, or holding out for a messianic apocalyptic future – is contingent upon assuming an existential crisis at the core of modernity, which can only be contained by constructing rigid epistemological fortifications. It is these neatly fabricated dividing walls that allow for the construction of binaries like premodern-modern, secular-religious, liberal secularists-religious dogmatists, progressive-traditionalist. This is not to deny the "crisis" of modernity, but to dispute that it is quintessentially modern or destructive. Crisis, also known as tension, lack, alienation or split of the subject, is at the core of subjectivity. It is, paradoxically, the condition of and the impediment to the process of meaning production and subject formation. The need for building such othering walls may arise from a number of different concerns, for example, it may be rooted in attempts at gaining a measure of autonomy and authenticity in differential relations of power – we can think of Spivak's "strategic essentialism" in a post-colonial context here.[90] But policing these walls points to the way some modern scholarly studies of Ṣūfism authorize and institutionalize their own closed modalities of knowledge production. Conversations between post-modern theories and Ṣūfism rupture the neat surface of these divisive walls by countering claims of wholeness, impartiality, stability, and universality of their subject matter. These creative conversations can also question the common theses that doubt Muslims' full assimilation into the modern world; or the ones arguing that problems of the Islamic world are caused by too abrupt, forceful, and superficial exposure to modernity. What these interactions also demonstrate is that one should not be compelled to defend conversations between Ṣūfism and psychoanalysis against charges of capitulation to secular liberalism, cultural imperialism, or neo-colonial Orientalism. We can argue that mystics of the past, particularly Ṣūfīs, intuited well what postmodern theorists formulated later.

90. Strategic Essentialism suggests that while we accept that "in principle" there are no essential identities, for specific political reasons "in practice" we "act as if there were." See Ray 2009, 110.

Bibliography

Algar, H. 2018. "Impostors, Antinomians and Pseudo-Sufis: Cataloguing the Miscreants." *Journal of Islamic Studies* 29.1: 25–47.

Almond, I. 2004. *Sufism and Deconstruction: A Comparative Study of Derrida and Ibn 'Arabi.* London and New York.

Amir-Moezzi, M. A. 1994. *The Divine Guide in Early Shi'ism: The Sources of Esotericism in Islam.* Translated by D. Steight. Albany, NY.

Anonymous. 2018. "A woman has the absolute right to voice her frustrations against a Prophet. Sit. Down." *The Fatal Feminist*, March 18. https://thefatalfeminist.com/2018/03/18/a-woman-has-the-absolute-right-to-voice-her-frustrations-against-a-prophet-sit-down/.

Beattie, T. 2013. *Theology After Postmodernity: Driving the Void – A Lacanian Reading of Thomas Aquinas.* Oxford.

Boroujerdi, M. 1996. *Iranian Intellectuals and the West: The Tormented Triumph of Nativism.* Syracuse.

Burkhardt, T. 2008. *Introduction to Sufi Doctrine.* Bloomington, IN.

Chittick, W. C. 1983. *The Sufi Path of Love: The Spiritual Teachings of Rumi.* Albany.

———. 2005. *The Sufi Doctrine of Rumi.* Bloomington, IN.

Dicenso, J. 1999. *The Other Freud: Religion, Culture and Psychoanalysis.* London.

El Shakry, O. 2017. *The Arabic Freud: Psychoanalysis and Islam in Modern Egypt.* Princeton.

Ernst, Carl W. 1997. *Sufism: An Introduction to the Mystical Dimension of Islam.* Boulder, CO.

Evans, D. 1996. *An Introductory Dictionary of Lacanian Psychoanalysis.* New York.

Ewing, K. 1997. *Arguing Sainthood: Modernity, Psychoanalysis and Islam.* Durham.

Faghfoory, M, and M. Tourage. 2007. "A Dialogue." *The American Journal of Islamic Social Sciences* 24.1:140–143.

Foucault, M. 2005. *The Archeology of Knowledge.* Abingdon.

Freud, S. 1953–1974. *The Standard Edition of the Complete Psychological Works of Sigmund Freud.* Translated by J. Strachey. 24 vols. London.

Furuzanfar, B. 1367/1990. *Sharh-e Masnavi.* 3 vols. Tehran.

Fuss, D. 1989. *Essentially Speaking: Feminism, Nature and Difference.* New York.

Glünz, M. 1995. "The Sword, the Pen and the Phallus: Metaphors and Metonymies of Male Power and Creativity in Medieval Persian Poetry." *Edebiyat* 6:223–243.

Homayounpour, G. 2012. *Doing Psychoanalysis in Tehran.* Cambridge, MA.

Hodgson, M. G. S. 1974. *The Venture of Islam: Conscience and History in a World Civilization. Vol. One, The Classical Age of Islam*. Chicago and London.

Idel, M. 2002. "'Unio Mystica' as a Criterion: Some Observations on 'Hegelian' Phenomenologies of Mysticism." *Journal for the Study of Religions and Ideologies* 1:19–41.

Izutsu, T. 1983. *A Comparative Study of Key Philosophical Concepts*. Berkeley.

Katz, S. T. 1992. "Mystical Speech and Mystical Meaning." In *Mysticism and Language*, edited by S. T. Katz, 3–41. New York.

Knight, M. M. 2017. *Why I am a Salafi*. Berkeley.

Kugle, S. A. 2006. *Rebel Between Spirit and Law: Ahmad Zarruq, Sainthood, and Authority in Islam*. Bloomington.

——. 2007. *Sufis and Saints' Bodies: Mysticism, Corporeality, and Sacred Power in Islam*. Chapel Hill.

Labbie, E. F. 2006. *Lacan's Medievalism*. Minneapolis.

Lacan, J. 1966. *Écrits*. Paris.

——. 1977. *Écrits: A Selection*. Translated by A. Sheridan. New York.

Lipton, G. A. 2018. *Rethinking Ibn 'Arabi*. Oxford.

——. 2011. "Secular Sufism: Neoliberalism, Ethnoracism, and the Reformation of the Muslim Other." *The Muslim World* 101.1:427–440.

——. 2017. "De-Semitizing Ibn ʿArabi: Aryanism and the Schuonian Discourse of Religious Authenticity." *Numen* 64:258–293.

Lumbard, J. E. B. 2009. "The Decline of Knowledge and the Rise of Ideology in the Modern Islamic World." In *Islam, Fundamentalism, and the Betrayal of Tradition: Essays by Western Muslim Scholars*, edited by J. E. B. Lumbard, 39–77. Bloomington.

McCutcheon, R. T. 2013. "Naming The Unnameable? Theological Language and the Academic Study of Religion." In *Theory and Method in the Study of Religion: Twenty Five Years On*, edited by A. Hughes, 87–99. Leiden.

Merchant, Y. 2013. "Taking A Critical Turn: Reflections on Islamic Studies and the Relevance of John Wansbrough." In *Theory and Method in the Study of Religion: Twenty Five Years On*, edited by A. Hughes, 203–207. Leiden.

Massad, J. 2015. A. *Islam in Liberalism*. Chicago. Mirsepassi, A. 2011. *Political Islam, Iran, and the Enlightenment: Philosophies of Hope and Despair*. Cambridge.

——. 2017. *Transnationalism in Iranian Political Thought: The Life and Time of Ahmad Fardid*. Cambridge.

Mishra, P. 2016. "Jordan Peterson and Fascist Mysticism." *The New York Review of Books*, December. http://www.nybooks.com/daily/2018/03/19/jordan-peterson-and-fascist-mysticism/.

Murata, S. 1992. *The Tao of Islam: A Sourcebook on Gender Relations in Islamic Thought*. Albany.
Nasr, S. H. 1972. *Sufi Essays*. Albany.
——. 1987. *Traditional Islam in the Modern World*. London.
——. 2003. *A Young Muslim's Guide to the Modern World*. Chicago.
Parker, I., and S. Siddiqui. 2019. *Islamic Psychoanalysis and Psychoanalytic Islam*. New York.
Peterson, J. B. 2018. *12 Rules for Life: An Antidote to Chaos*. Toronto.
Ray, S. 2009. *Gayatri Chakravorty Spivak: In Other Words*. Oxford.
Rubin, U. 2003. "Muhammad." *Encyclopaedia of the Qur'an*.
Renard, J. 2001. "Alexander." *Encyclopaedia of the Qur'an*.
Rūmī, J. 1925–1940. *The Mathnawi of Jalalu'ddin Rūmī*. 8 vols. Edited and translated by R. A. Nicholson. London.
——. 1330 (1951). *Kitab-i Fihi ma Fihi*. Edited by B. Furuzanfar. Tehran.
——. 2004. *The Masnavi: Book One*. Translated by J. Mojaddedi. Oxford.
Sedgwick, M. 2004. *Against the Modern World: Traditionalism and the Secret Intellectual History of the Twentieth Century*. Oxford.
Sells, M. A. 1994. *Mystical Languages of Unsaying*. Chicago.
Sells, M. A., and J. Webb. 1995. "Lacan and Bion: Psychoanalysis and the Mystical Language of Unsaying." *Theory and Psychology* 5.2:195–215.
Shaikh, S. 2012. *Sufi Narratives of Intimacy: Ibn 'Arabi, Gender, and Sexuality*. Chapel Hill.
Schimmel, A. 1975. *Mystical Dimensions of Islam*. Chapel Hill.
Southgate, M. 1984. "The Negative Images of Blacks in Some Medieval Iranian Writings." *Iranian Studies* 17.1:3–36.
Stowasser, B. F. 1994. *Women in the Qur'an, Traditions, and Interpretations*. New York.
Ṭabāṭabāʾī, S. M. H. 2003. *Kernel of the Kernel, Concerning the Wayfaring and Spiritual Journey of the People of Intellect: A Shi'i Approach to Sufism*. Edited by S. M. H. Husayni Tehrani. Translated by M. H. Faghfoory. New York.
Tourage, M. 2007. *Rūmī and the Hermeneutics of Eroticism*. Leiden.
——. 2013. "Performing Belief and Reviving Islam: Prominent (White Male) Converts in Muslim Revival Conventions." *Performing Islam* 2.1:207–226.
Varisco, D. M. 2007. *Reading Orientalism: Said and the Unsaid*. Seattle.
Wolfson, E. R. 2005. *Language, Eros, Being: Kabbalistic Hermeneutics and Poetics*. NewYork.
Yaghoobi, C. 2017. *Subjectivity in Attar*. West Lafayett, IN.
Žižek, S. 2014. *Zizek's Jokes: Did you Hear the One About Hegel and Negation?* Edited by Audun Mortensen. Cambridge, MA.

12

Lost Orientalism, Lost Orient, and Lost Orientals: An Overview[1]

Majid Daneshgar

Orientalism Phobia and Its Consequences

Saidean Legacy

LET US BE HONEST and ask how many scholars of Islam are today able to read the main Islamic languages of Arabic, Persian (old, middle, and/or modern), Ottoman Turkish, Malay (Jawi), and Urdu, as practiced by hundreds of Orientalists during the eighteenth and nineteenth centuries? It is too naïve to say that all of those multilingual Orientalists were puppets of a Royal Court that wished to enslave Muslims. Today, using discourse analysis, with the aid of a third party's knowledge and expertise (for example, a research assistant), to complete an ethnographical and anthropological project is the top priority of a large number of professors and researchers of Islamic studies. In the best-case scenario, Christian-Muslim relationship dialogue is emphasized, in the light of historical and textual analysis, in order to stop the so-called blasphemy and violence that is still active. Yet such advocates of Christian-Muslim relations in the West tend to avoid calling themselves "Orientalist." I also think that "Orientalist" is no longer a true title to be ascribed to a scholar of Islam, because there are, at present, very few scholars like William Jones (d. 1794), Arthur Lumley Davids (d. 1832), Arthur Henry Bleeck (d. 1877), among others, who were proficient in various Islamic languages. However, the "Orientalist" critical function and philological expertise should not stop.

It would be rehashing earlier literature to say how much Muslims have critiqued Orientalists.[2] Their (mis)understanding of Orientalism pervaded the Muslim world. Many Muslims thought that the first and foremost goal behind "Orientalists' exploring the Orient" was/is to expand their politi-

1. I thank Deutsche Forschungsgemeinschaft (DFG) (Projekt number 415543504) for providing me with this opportunity to write this chapter.

2. E.g. Daneshgar 2019.

cal, economic, and cultural influence over the Orient. This is why a large number of Muslims usually view the Western study of Islam as a tireless, purposeful, and constant imperial endeavor aimed at ruling Muslims.[3]

One may wonder when such an "anti-Orientalist" approach was *systematically* added into Muslim literature? I would say that this approach emerged in academic discourse after Edward W. Said's (d. 2003) *Orientalism*.[4]

Although *Orientalism* was influential and timely, the number of errors found throughout its pages could fill several thick books. Certainly, Said was able, on the basis of Foucauldian discourse, to shed light on how knowledge gave Europeans, both physically and mentally, ruling power over "Arabs," but he failed to classify Europeans as various groups. He did not notice that a large number of Europeans were amazed by Islamic traditions and the chanting of poems for the sake of Islam and Muḥammad. He ignored that Muslims were ambivalent about Orientalists. Some admired them, some criticized them. Iranian and Malay scholars were appreciative of Theodor Nöldeke's (d. 1930) studies on qurʾānic chronological orders,[5] and there were Egyptian thinkers and religious figures who clearly distinguished between a European colonial officer and a European scholar.[6] Recent critical works have blamed him for not consulting more accurate and comprehensive literature from the East and the West. One may well be surprised to see that Said's book, addressing both Europeans and Orientals, does not include references produced in the Orient by Orientals, in oriental or Islamic languages, who were, according to Said, under European dominance. He was also pretty selective, as he displayed only his own Orient (the Arab world) through the lens of a particular clique of Orientalists. Besides historical and methodological inconsistencies, he, as someone who had seemingly lived in the past, presented the root of Orientalism as an ancient imaginary, a mental, and later political, interest of Europeans whose main opponents were Orientals, Saracens, Arabs, and Muslims.

Linking "Saracens" with "Muslims" and "Arabs" is itself seductive. In a large corpus of earlier literature, not only by Said but also by Muslims themselves, Saracens, Arabs, and/or Muslims were *mistakenly* displayed as poor, inferior people who were surrounded by occidental vampires hungry for the scantily-clad oriental woman who would sing and dance for them.

3. E.g. Alvīrī 1393/2014.

4. Said 1978.

5. Saḥāb 1938; Atjeh 1952.

6. For example, Egyptian commentator and thinker Ṭanṭāwī Jawharī (d. 1940) divided Europeans into three groups, including (a) Christian missionaries; (b) scientists and intellectuals; and (c) colonial officers, orientalists, and political rivals of the Muslims. For more, see Daneshgar 2017.

According to Said and advocates of his *Orientalism*, Europe found its sexual, physical, and mental health and happiness in the Orient. For some reason, however, the reverse of this process never ever happened!

Said's definition of the "Orient" is both a mischaracterization and dangerous. Reducing the Orient as "the Holy Land," "Palestine," "Egypt," or say, "the Arab world" – his homeland – and the Orientalists as the scholars of the only "Arab-Islamic World" (that is, *al-mustaʿribūn* not *al-mustashriqūn*),[7] meant that he ignored other Asian countries as a part of the Orient. For Said, Persia, India, Ottoman Turkey (minus its Arabian parts), Malaya, China, and Japan, the countries and nations which had regularly been presented as part of the Orient in medieval and classical works, maps, paintings and studies, were simply not important. He failed to show that *mustaʿribūn* and *ʿulamāʾ al-mashriqiyyāt* are not similar. The first one, according to the early twentieth-century Arab scholars, refers to the scholars and experts of the Arab world and its Islamic civilization, while the latter refers to non-Arabic as well as non-Islamic language and sciences of the Orient, too.[8] In addition, this is despite the fact that these places were not only colonized by Muslims, but their citizens were also part of colonial armies.[9] Putting aside the Muslims' invasion of Europe and North Africa soon after the death of the Prophet of Islam, Edward Said could simply ignore how, for example, Nāder Shah of Persia (r. 1736–1747) invaded India, leading to a savage massacre as well as massive plundering.[10] For Said (in his *Orientalism*) and his acolytes, however, colonialism, imperialism, plundering, and exploitation could be done by Europeans.

Consequences

Less Critical Studies

Reputable Western non-Muslim scholars of Islam – with whom I have had personal discussions – prefer not to be known as "Orientalists." They do not wish to carry the Saidean label of "Orientalist" whose investigation of the Orient, according to Muslims, largely derived from lust rather than scholarly passion. So, it seems wise for them to detach themselves from the textual and philological legacy of earlier Western scholars of Islam (namely, Orientalists). This may be one of the reasons why they tend to produce less critical and more apologetic works.

7. See Kurd ʿAlī 1948, 347–362.
8. Kurd ʿAlī 1948, 347.
9. Nishihara 2005, 241–253.
10. Said failed to notice, or mention, that Nāder Shah is hailed as a hero in Iran, where his commemorative statue, tomb, and museum are situated.

As someone who grew up, studied and worked in Shīʿī and Sunnī, and Western contexts, I can understand why some of these Western scholars of Islam produce less critical work. One reason could be due to the desire to counteract political demagogues, religious authorities, and Islamophobic think tanks. I do agree that the "Islamophobia" could to a large extent make lay people and international news agencies pessimistic towards Islam. However, I always wonder if Islamophobia could be stopped through a normative and prescriptive reading and interpretation of Islam and Islamic studies. Being uncritical of the past will likely not help us to be critical of our present. In other words, it should be almost impossible to be critical of current political and cultural situations, while our approach to the past becomes less critical.

Massimo Campanini, for example, has tirelessly dedicated his time to the study of Islam, but in so doing he has (re-)produced propagative and apologetic studies. We see this in his recent endeavor to promote debate on a "philosophical" reading of qurʾānic exegesis.[11] Despite having an intriguing title, *Philosophical Perspectives on Modern Qurʾanic Exegesis*, the content of his book largely presents an apologetic study of qurʾānic interpretations. The author, impressed by Hasan Hanafi, takes Islam for granted and does not raise philosophical questions, beginning with "Why and How," about the origin and formative period of Islam and Islamic interpretation of the Qurʾān. Given the main accountability of Campanini, as a scholar interested in philosophy, one wonders why he did not raise questions about the origin, validity, philosophy, and development of Islamic teachings before opening a philosophical discourse on interpreting the Qurʾān? In Campanini's opinion, reading Islam critically and through the lens of history will not be helpful as its conclusions might upset the beliefs of one billion Muslims. For him and many others, we should accept Islam as what it is and not make Muslims digress by questioning their belief and past. Campanini views *Muḥammad: His Life Based on the Earliest Sources* by Martin Lings (d. 2005), later known as Abū Bakr Sirāj al-Dīn, as more accurate than the works and statements of more critical scholars, such as Andrew Rippin (d. 2016). For instance, Campanini writes,

> Obviously, Lings read Muhammad's life through the eyes of the believer, and clearly he considered the traditional Islamic sources reliable. Andrew Rippin called Lings' work 'utter mythology,' but Rippin belongs to the sceptical school of Wansbrough.[12]

11. Campanini 2016.
12. Campanini 2016, 18–19.

Although Campanini is not an advocate of Lings, his emphasis is rather on the rejection of Rippin's "skepticism." Unlike Campanini, I do not see skepticism as the result of a Saidean "Orientalism" project, but part of an academic endeavor to shed light on the past. Campanini becomes even more apologetic when he ignores recent epigraphical and archeological findings, among others, proving the existence of "Judeo-Christian" literature and tradition in the Arabian Peninsula before and during the establishment of Islam. As such he, along with critics of Orientalism in the Muslim academy, echoes that

> Many Orientalists (like Wansbrough and his school or recently Luxenberg, Reynolds and others) argue for a strict dependence on the Qurʾān from Judeo-Christian sources, thus minimizing or rather denying Qurʾānic and Islamic 'originality'. A great ideological bias against Islam is at work here, I believe.[13]

This is despite the fact that Campanini himself does not approach the "originality" of Islam and Islamic formative sources.[14]

Forgotten Orientalists

Another issue is the marginalization of works written by Christian scholars of Islam in the nineteenth century. For example, Rev. S. Baring-Gould's (d. 1924) important work on biblical figures, *Legends of the Patriarchs and Prophets and Other Old Testament Characters*, is largely ignored. This is in spite of the fact that, although his understanding of biblical figures is to a large extent indebted to Muslim scholars, including Abū Jaʿfar Muḥammad b. Jarīr al-Ṭabarī (d. ca. 311/923), both Muslim and non-Muslim scholars of biblical, post-biblical, Islamic, and interreligious studies do not use it.[15] As such, there are plenty of eighteenth and particularly nineteenth century works on Islam written by European scholars that are ignored for no other reason than they were produced during the colonial period and are pejoratively labeled as "Orientalist."

In this regard, the widely cited article by Matthew E. Falagas and his colleagues contends that,

> The Islamic state was formed in 622 C.E., when the Prophet moved from Mecca to Medina. Within a century after his death (632 C.E.) a large part of the planet, from southern Europe throughout North Africa to Central Asia and on to India, was controlled by

13. Campanini 2016, 55.
14. See my review of Campanini's book, Daneshgar 2018a.
15. Baring-Gould 1884.

> and/or influenced by the new Arabic-Muslim Empire. In 711 C.E., Arab Muslims invaded southern Spain and a center of flourishing civilization (al-Andalus) was created. Another center emerged in Baghdad from the Abbasids, who ruled part of the Islamic world during a historic period later characterized as the "Golden Age" (~750 to 1258 C.E.).[16]

It is no surprise to see that the majority of citations to their article belong to Muslim scholars across the world, who took the "Islamic golden age" for granted. Recently, Aaron W. Hughes has opened up a new discussion in order to criticize current religious studies programs whose backbone, despite a lack of awareness, has been shaped by scholarly works produced before the twentieth century. According to him, a large quantity of research by Muslim and non-Muslim scholars has failed to notice that the Islamic Golden Age – a term which is widely and frequently used by Muslim traditionalists, nationalists, and propagandists – is not a historical but a modern trope invented by German-Jewish scholars in the nineteenth century. According to Hughes, the German Hebraist, Franz Delitzsch (d. 1890) "coined the term 'golden age' to refer to Muslim Spain."[17] Although Hughes' statement requires further evidence to arrive at firm answers, he invites scholars to put this notion "under the analytic microscope."[18]

If we continue to ignore this eighteenth- and nineteenth-century literature, the historical tradition of "studying the Orient" by Europeans will soon be forgotten. Regardless of their approach to Islam and Muslim communities, to what extent are we aware of their precise investigation of Oriental sources and communities? There are a few scholarly works which comprehensively address how and under what circumstances the masterpiece of the Persian poet, Saʿdī Shīrāzī's (d. ca. 690/1292) *Golestān* (the Rose Garden), or the treatise of Ikhwān al-Saffāʾ (the Brethren of Purity) were expertly translated in English and Urdu, for example, in the Fort William College and other institutes in India in the nineteenth century.[19] Of course, available evidence shows that imperial organizations were responsible for this translation project in the Indian subcontinent. However, due to current excessive (and superficial) engagement with colonial and "post"-colonial theories, we almost ignore how the mechanism of translation, its distribution, readers' groups, and so on and so forth, was accomplished.

16. Falagas 2006, 1581–1586.
17. Hughes 2018, 21.
18. Hughes 2018, 1.
19. A few examples are found in the Otago University Special Collections, New Zealand. See Daneshgar and Kerr 2017.

Claiming that "Orientalism" was, is, and will be a viable undertaking practiced by Western nations and scholars, even after they were "kicked out" of the Muslim nations, however, has led many to overlook just how Orientalists learned about "Islam," and produced knowledge on it.

In line with some Muslim commentators and reformists, Islamic studies is seen as a hostile and faithless Euro-centric product that revolves around the names of Ignác Goldziher (d. 1921) and Theodor Nöldeke up to John Wansbrough (d. 2002), Patricia Crone (d. 2015), Andrew Rippin (d. 2016), and Gerald Hawting (b. 1944), among others.

Unsurprisingly, Muslim and apologist reading of Western Islamic studies has been selective and incomplete, and functions largely as a response to the so-called *Orientalist study of Islam*. The most obvious example is the work by the Pakistani chemist, Muzaffar Iqbal, someone much impressed by Said. For him, most works, if not all, by Western scholars are inherited from European colonial officers and Orientalists. This is why he, in response to the efforts of Western scholars in general and their *Encyclopaedia of the Qurʾān* (*EQ*) in particular, has produced a so-called *Integrated Encyclopedia of the Qurʾān* (*IEQ*). To answer the question "are there works similar to *IEQ*?" Iqbal says:

> There is no reference work on the Qurʾān in [the] English language that takes, as its foundational premise, the Muslim belief that the Qurʾān is a revealed text. The two extant encyclopedias (Brill's six volume *Encyclopaedia of the Qurʾān* [2001–2005] and the single volume, 772-page work published by Routledge, *The Qurʾān: an Encyclopedia* [2005]) have been rejected by Muslim scholars as works steeped in neo-Orientalism. [20]

Although *IEQ* is significantly selective, and as Andrew Rippin says, largely Sunnī- and Ashʿarī-centric, the editor claims that it is "a reference work that excludes references to those sources which do not believe in the Divine authorship for the Qurʾān and this gives *IEQ* its uniqueness."[21] However, Iqbal nowhere mentions who exactly these "Muslims" are who rejected Western encyclopedias. Indeed, Brill's *EQ* has been systematically translated largely

20. A brief answer to such questions are found in the *IEQ* homepage, too: http://www.iequran.com/faq.php.

21. Ibid. He also says, "Non-Muslim academic scholars have yet another dilemma when approaching the Qurʾān. They cannot commit themselves to any position about the Divine origin of the Qurʾān; their professional obligation is to maintain a certain detachment from the object of their study." Iqbal 2008, 539.

by a group of young scholars in Iran who considered it a main source for the study of Islam.[22] Today, Indonesian and Turkish scholars have become more interested in Brill's *EQ*.

Intra-Orientalism

As previously mentioned, *Orientalism* or *al-istishrāq* is globally and largely known as the product of a non-Muslim reading of the "[Arab] Islamic World" and producing knowledge about it. This is the second issue addressed in this chapter, and deals with intra-reading of the Orient, that is, "intra-Orientalism." This term displays the way Arabs, Persians, and Turks, and citizens in the heartland of Islam viewed their Islamic and non-Islamic *mashriq* (Orient), that is to say "Muslim *mashriqiyyāt*."[23]

As has been the case with "Orientalism," Muslims' knowledge of and production of knowledge on the West, Occidentalism (*maghribiyyāt*) has been hidden under the canopy of political sentiments, and anti-Christian and anti-European/Western – largely known as "Occidentosis" – that contrasts Muslims' Islamic and national values with Western civilization. The works by Jalāl Āl-e Aḥmad (d. 1969) "Gharb-zadegī" ("Occidentosis: A Plague from the West") and Abul Hasan Ali Hasani Nadwi (d. 1999) "Islamiyyat aur Maghribiyyat" were pioneer sources which systematically drew modern studies on the West towards a harsh and pessimistic perspective. For instance, Nadwi says that "among the Muslim countries confronted with western thought and values India had the distinction of taking a first stand against the West."[24] However, we should admit that the Muslims' knowledge of their occident, *maghribiyyāt*, due to their willingness to engage and compete with the West over a long time, is much better than their *mashriqyyāt*.

Archives suggest that Islamic scientific literature in general, and medical and philosophical traditions in particular, were largely based on the first phase of "Greek-Egyptian" translation into Arabic during the Umayyad period.[25] This continued until the second phase of the translation movement during the Abbasid period, when the Mesopotamians and various groups of Arabs, non-Arabs, and Muslims not only translated fundamental sources but also edited, revised, and critiqued what had already been produced in their

22. See Daneshgar, 2016, 367–385.

23. *Istishrāq* and *mashriqiyyāt* can be used for "Orientalism" interchangeably. However, as the first one (*istishrāq*) is largely known as Western reading of the Orient, the second one (*mashriqiyyāt*) is used here to highlight Muslims' reading of their own Islamic and non-Islamic Orient. See: Kurd ʿAlī, 1922.

24. Nadwi 1983, 18.

25. Salim Khan 2008, 11–12.

occident. Nonetheless, this notion soon became entwined with anti-Christianity in the medieval era, and, therefore, whatever occidental, or originally occidental, works Muslims wanted to read could have been viewed, at the outset, negatively.

Mashriqiyyāt

Allow me to explore how the "Orient," beyond its Euro-centric and Arabo-Turko-Persianate Islamic-centric definitions, has been ignored in the Islamic literature. In so doing, manuscripts long neglected by scholars on account of their lack of philological expertise and familiarity with other cultures will play an instrumental role.

Today, many scholarly works on *tafsīr*, *kalām*, *taṣawwuf*, and so on, are based on printed edition works. The recent academic digital trend (digital Islamic studies) seeks to reform this approach by encouraging scholars to (re-)examine manuscripts from other sources. Yet, it has largely failed to put available manuscripts under "an analytic microscope." It fails to account, for example, how different copies of manuscripts can be systematically and deliberately censored by scribes, rulers, and authorities. This means that readers often remain ignorant of what the *actual* source was.[26]

The application of manuscripts to the study of Islam is still in its infancy. In the Western academy it is selective, and in the Muslim academy, indigenous. Scholars in the West only examine the sources that are largely related to their major research field. For example, their projects on classical Islamic philosophy and theology are done by means of philosophical-theological manuscripts and they do not, often, consider supplementary manuscripts of *tafsīr*, *ʿulūm al-gharība*, *ḥadīth*, etc., in spite of the fact that classical Muslim thinkers displayed their opinions through various interconnected exegetical, theological, philosophical, and medical works, among others. Muslims, on the contrary, tend to study homegrown manuscripts. For instance, Persian manuscripts of any classical category in Islam are chiefly/largely reviewed in Iran or by Iranian scholars, Ottoman-Turkish sources mainly in Turkey or by Turks, and Malay-Jawi sources in Malaysia, Singapore, and Indonesia by Malays. One may wonder, for example, how many, Persian [Shīʿī] Qurʾān commentaries are studied by Muslim scholars in India, Pakistan, Malaysia, Turkey or, to move a bit westward, in Egypt and Sudan.

Given this misreading of Oriental sources, scholarly attempts to find an answer for the relationship between the non-Islamic languages of Chinese, Japanese, and Indian with Muslims in Iran, Arabia, Malay-Indonesia, and vice versa, are still bare.

26. Daneshgar 2018b.

Missed Ethical Knowledge

Our knowledge of sexual intercourse and ethics in Islam is scarce, tradition-based, and largely Arabo-Persia-centric.[27] This is despite the fact that Islamic sexual treatises were produced in pluralistic societies like China and India, among others, where Muslims were/are part of a larger community. As will be shown, these Muslim authors were proficient in the non-Islamic languages of their own nations, so they were able to produce Islamic works according to other traditions. Indeed, an "intra-translation" movement evolved among Muslims in non-major Islamic lands.

Modern literature on Islamic sexual ethics, like that of Kecia Ali, whose Islamic allusions are mostly Arabo-Sunnī-centric, builds a wall between the readers' so-called inherent belief and practice, and desire. Ali's emphasis on "sexual ethics" is mainly based on Islamic scriptures, while the readers' understanding of her work on *sexual ethics and intercourse* in Islam is legalistic and beyond reality-discussion. According to Ali, citing Ibn Hajar, "*zina*; *liwat*; having intercourse with livestock; having anal intercourse with a female stranger; tribadism, which is a woman doing with a woman something resembling what a man would do with her; and a husband having intercourse with his wife's corpse"[28] are all forbidden in Islam. Through the lens of Islamic law, this is accurate. However, it is also theoretical and assumes that every Islamic legal restriction applies to the real lives of all Muslims.

Another work similar to that of Kecia Ali is the one compiled by Abdullah R. Muhametov and Laila-Olga But, entitled "Love and Sex in Islam."[29] They view sexual intercourse through the lens of al-Ghazālī (d. ca. 1111) as well as apologetic traditional figures whose main concern was whether having intercourse with a woman toward *qibla*, in the nude, etc. contradicts Muḥammad's teachings, or not. Readers of such works rarely find an opportunity to view sexual ethics in Islam beyond the confines of Islamic law, and to see how other Orientals including, for example, non-Muslim Indians have contributed to the development of Islamic culture and rituals. It is apparent that there is little difference between insiders' and outsiders' perspectives when scholars only view Islamic ethical knowledge through Islamic scriptures, rather than exploring other literary works that have influences Islamic discussions and rituals. Actually, such *fiqhī*-based literature, promoted by globally-known scholars, in its best-case scenario has led readers astray from seeking the "real" Muslim perception and feeling of sexual

27. However, a few Malay scholars became interested in sexual intercourse debates in Malay literature.

28. Ali 2006, 97.

29. Muhametov and But 2013.

intercourse. A review of Islamic manuscripts, which I have been engaging with for several years, suggests that prominent Muslim thinkers, writers, and religious figures used and/or promoted different types of visual and literary sources on sexual intercourse whose production and distribution were strictly forbidden in Islamic law. According to these works, the *others*' culture, coming from India or China, not only affected their approach towards sexual relationships, but also allowed them to clearly and publicly disagree with Islamic jurists and jurisprudence. The sexual teachings exhibited, reflecting on their imagination and desires, were in contrast to those of Islamic law. Most illustrated works in this category clearly explained various forms of sexual intercourse in contrast to those listed by Ibn Hajar (cited by Kecia Ali).

An example is a widely read Persian book entitled *Ladhdhat al-Nisāʾ* (On the Pleasure of Women), which was apparently based on the erotic Indian story of *Koka Shastra/Shastar;* it shows how Muslims (either rulers or servants) sought their feelings beyond the walls of mosque. Available copies of this treatise were translated by the famous mystic, writer, and translator of the fourteenth century, Ḍiyāʾ al-Dīn Nakhshabī (d. ca. 751/1350), sometimes referred to as Bakhshī, who also translated the Persian version of the "Tales of the Parrot" (*Ṭūṭī-nāmeh*). He begins his work with (fl.1),

> whoever is ignorant of the various aspects of intercourse with young and beautiful women is like an ape whose knowledge about nutmeg is merely gained through eating it
>
> agar kasī az ʿilm-e īn resāla ʿārī, az zanān-e javān-e khūb ṣūrat ke be-dast-e ū oftad ū rā hamān qadr naṣīb bovad ke būzīna rā jouz-e hindī be-dast āyad.

Most of the extant manuscripts contain ten chapters, which include illustrations (miniature paintings) showing various types of sexual intercourse. They depict forbidden (*ḥarām*) images, among other things, the simultaneous intercourse of a man with two women, a woman having intercourse with an animal resembling a bear, and two men engaged in anal sex.[30] As discussed in my previous works, subsequent copies of these manuscripts were widely censored and *Ladhdhat al-Nisāʾ* was transformed into a pure medical/ethical treatise without any allusion to naked depictions and explanations. This censorship not only caused scholars to forget their past, but also to forget how their past was interconnected with non-Muslim Indian ethical and sexual issues.

Other works inspired by Indo-Chinese culture were ignored by scholars,

30. See Daneshgar 2018.

too. For instance, the Persian manuscript, MSR-38, entitled *Khiyāl-e Fallāḥ* (the Dream/Imagination of Fallāḥ) preserved in the Alexander Turnbull Library at the National Library of New Zealand, Wellington, was translated and edited by Muḥammad Fallāḥ Ṣāliḥ Ḥusayn al-Kūlālī. According to Muḥammad Fallāḥ, he translated this tale from the Sanskrit Book of Hind (*az ketāb-e Hend-e Sahns Keret*),[31] when he was encouraged to do so by his interlocutors (namely, literary figures) who were all impressed with its poetic, metaphorical and ethical aspects. As such, they called the texts *ʿarūs-e Hend* (the bride of India).

It is true that Islamic teachings, based on the Qurʾān and *ḥadīth*, are replete with ethical advice. However, modern studies do not show that the Muslims' ethical progress in society was, indeed, relevant to non-Islamic sources compiled in non-Islamic-centric contexts.

Forgotten Orientals in the Heartland of Islam

This is a recent academic trend in Islamic studies through which scholars – beyond the so-called colonialism framework – pay more attention to Muslim communities in other parts of Asia. A great addition to this development is the recent work by Kristian Petersen on "Interpreting Islam in China," which stimulates readers to learn about the history of Islam, the Qurʾān and the Arabic language among East Asian Muslims. Such studies have the potential to fill a huge gap, as they tell us how Muslim communities outside the Arabo-Persianate world developed and continued their activities up to the present day. However, we still do not know how these communities and their study of Islam, Qurʾān, and *tafsīr* affected the mainstream (Sunnī and Shīʿī) of the Middle East. Although Petersen's work highlights the roots of the influence of Arabic Islam in East Asia, of which our knowledge is limited, it still presents a one-way street towards the propagation of Arabo-Persian sources beyond the borders of the core land of Islam.

Some decades earlier, Peter G. Riddell was among the first scholars to comprehensively assess the connection between the Arab's development of Islam throughout the Middle East and Egypt and that of the Malay-Indonesian World. He highlighted how Muḥammad ʿAbduh (d. 1905) and his modern interpretation of Islam shaped the reformist thought of Malay scholars. Nonetheless, it is not yet known whether Malay-Indonesian Muslims, coming from a pluralistic context (Chinese/Indian/Buddhist/Hindu), affected Islam in its core land. The large body of works dealing with Islam in the East separated its inhabitants, for example, Chinese and Malay-Indonesian Muslims, from their non-Islamic surroundings. One may wonder how the

31. Also Hindavi [Sanskrit].

hundreds of Chinese and Malay-Indonesian scholars who resided in Egypt and Ottoman Turkey as well as Mecca and Medina had influenced the reading of Islam of Arabs, Persians, and Turks.[32] Historical sources suggest that Shaykh Muḥammad bin ʿUmar Nawawī al-Jāwī al-Bantānī (d. 1314/1898), the famous Indonesian commentator of the Qurʾān in the nineteenth century, spent considerable time teaching and promoting Islam in Mecca, where he was chosen as the Imam and had his own circle of students and followers. Due to his importance, he was called "ʿĀlim al-Ḥijāz" (Gifted Scholar of Mecca).[33] He came from a Southeast Asian background, where non-Muslims and Muslims used to live together, to live in the less-pluralistic context of Arabia. He produced a commentary on the Qurʾān entitled "Marāḥ Labīd li-Kashf Maʿnā al-Qurʾān al-Majīd" in two volumes, which has been widely read and accepted by other Islamic nations. Most *tafsīrī* studies in the West are silent about the contribution of this commentary on the later generation of exegetical works produced by Arabs and Persians. This is despite the fact that scholarly references to this commentary have been seen in Persian, Arabic, and Urdu literature.

The importance of manuscript studies is highlighted again. Scholars of Malay-Indonesian Islam used to visit local libraries in cities such as Jakarta and Kuala Lumpur, or European collections in Leiden, London, Berlin, Paris, or occasionally in Turkey and Egypt. However, one may wonder if Iran, Afghanistan, Pakistan, Tajikistan, among others, may house other Malay manuscripts which have not yet been examined by experts. While searching the Iranian libraries' special collections, I found, to my knowledge, for the first time in the history of Malay Islamic manuscripts, a few but very important Arabic manuscripts with interlinear Javanese translations and commentaries; which were apparently read and kept by a religious family called Sorkheʾī which belonged to the Iranian city of Semnan. This manuscript, split into various treatises, is an ethical and legal source which was read for centuries by Sunnī Muslims. More importantly, this manuscript includes notes in Persian which suggest that Persian Muslims used to read and translate Arabic works into Malay, or there were some Malays who could translate Arabic works into Malay while being inspired by Persian literature. Either way, this finding can add value to the literature of Malay-Indonesian Islam, and answer when and under what circumstances Arab-Persian Muslims interacted with those of Malays, and through what type of religious

32. While the current volume was in production, it came to my attention that an edited volume, *Ottoman-Southeast Asian Relations Sources from the Ottoman Archives*, edited by İsmail Hakkı Kadı and A.C.S. Peacock has been published by Brill.

33. Nawawī al-Jāwī al-Bantānī 1417/1996, *Marāḥ Labīd*, 1:4.

sources they exchanged their literature.[34] Nonetheless, most studies tend to show that interaction was only in one direction, from the Middle East to the Malay-Indonesian world. This is why our Malay Islamic studies are, unsurprisingly, still an Arabo-Sunnī-centric knowledge replete with references to traditional orthodox works.

Lost Orient and Orientals in Qurʾānic Exegetical Studies

The cornerstone of qurʾanic exegetical studies (*tafsīr* studies) has been set in the modern study of Islam by the Hungarian scholar, Ignác Goldziher. He produced the first modern literature of *tafsīr* in the early twentieth century. The obvious point seen across his work(s) is that, for him, non-Muslims in classical and modern Islamic commentaries are only Jews and Christians. This approach has also been developed by other scholars of Islam and *tafsīr*. Hundreds of studies dealing with Islamic commentaries and qurʾānic translations define non-Muslims in Islamic commentaries as either Jews and/or Christians. For example, Walid A. Saleh's focus on a Lebanese scholar, al-Biqāʿī, and his application of the Bible in order to (re-)interpret the Qurʾān, sheds light on the importance of biblical literature for classical Muslims.[35] In addition, Gabriel S. Reynolds' emphasis on the approach of classical exegetical figures (*mufassirūn*) to Jesus' ascension in *sūrat al-Nisāʾ* (Q 4:157–158) lays out various types of agreements and disagreements between classical thinkers on a common point largely related to the Christian tradition.[36]

In addition to qurʾānic references to biblical names/stories, the migration of Muslims, and their second and third generations who reside in the West, is attracting the attention of Islamicists, encouraging them to write on the history of the Muslim and Christian relationship.

Rippin's textbook on *Muslims: Their Religious Beliefs and Practices* highlights the interaction of Arab Muslims with Jews and Christians in their neighboring communities and clans from before the emergence of Islam.[37] Many scholars also approached traditional radical Muslims to see how Ibn Taymiyya (d. ca. 728/1328), who is known as a leading opponent of Christians (as well as Shīʿīs), among others, promoted anti-Christian instructions to mainstream Sunnīs. Debates between Muslim newcomers in the West paved the way for the scholars of Islam to examine the historical relationship between the two religions. Unsurprisingly, one does not expect to see well-written

34. It can be said that the Italian scholar, Alessandro Bausani (d. 1988), was among the last to pay attention to the contribution of Persian in Malay philology.

35. Saleh 2008, 629–654.

36. Reynolds 2009, 237–258.

37. Rippin 2012, introduction.

studies on the role of "other" Orientals who have been in contact with Arab and Persian Muslims (perhaps more than Christian Europeans) for some time, until they become an important factor in contemporary political challenges. This is, however, despite the fact that Muslim commentators of the Qur'ān have alluded to Indians, Chinese, Japanese and other Orientals as "non-Muslims". For instance, the earliest exegetical references to Asians are to be found in one of the first commentaries, *Tafsīr* of Muqātil b. Sulaymān (d. ca. 150/767). To interpret Q 17:104, where the Israelites are told: "Settle down in the land. When the promise about the Hereafter comes along, We will bring you in together as a rabble," he notes the name of a non-Islamic region:

> The Children of Israelites were seventy thousand behind the river in China.[38]

On another occasion, regarding Q 71:28, Muqātil b. Sulaymān mentions the names of India (*al-Hind*) and China (*al-Ṣīn*) alongside those of Qibṭ, Fārs, Sūdān, and others.[39] These can thus be considered the first direct references to the names of other non-Muslim Asian and African regions in qur'ānic commentaries. Other commentaries did not go much further, as their focus was still on Judeo-Christian and biblical material.

However, during the late nineteenth and early twentieth centuries, as a result of various religious and political concerns, the Ottoman Empire under Abdul Hamid II (d. 1918) expanded its relations with various Asian nations, including Japan and China.[40] At the same time, Arab nations, particularly Egypt, hosted archaeologists and scholars who tried to link the so-called great ancient civilizations together. The Egyptians were keen to welcome the Chinese to their country because some eighteenth-century European studies on ancient civilizations had claimed that both the Indian and Chinese civilizations had been shaped by the ancient Egyptians.[41] Furthermore, information found in articles by, for example, Joseph de Guignes and Needham, who hypothesized that China was "an Egyptian colony," was admired by the Egyptians. Some European scholars not only thought that cultural similarities between these two nations existed, but that there were also similarities between their scripts.[42] Thus, finding out more about China would, it was thought, help Egyptians learn more about the history and superiority

38. Muqātil b. Sulaymān.1423/2002, *Tafsīr Muqātil*, 2:554.
39. Muqātil b. Sulaymān.1423/2002, *Tafsīr Muqātil*, 4:452.
40. Karpat 2001, 237.
41. Huet 1717; see also, Haycock, 2016, 133–160.
42. Haycock, 2016, 133–160.

of their own nation. Simultaneously, European scholars and colonial officers produced many works introducing Chinese medicine, philosophy, and religion, and particularly Chinese Buddhist works.[43] Some such works also addressed the relationship between the Christian faith and Buddhism.[44] In such a context, Egyptian scientists were, naturally, influenced by reports, publications, and relations between Muslims and other Asians. The most widely-available source about the Chinese in qurʾānic commentaries is that of Ṭanṭāwī Jawharī (d. 1940), who repeatedly mentions them. However, some years earlier Muḥammad bin Aḥmad al-Iskandarānī (d. 1888) was the first to pay particular attention to this topic in his *tafsīr*. He was a physician as well as a religious scholar, who is sometimes known as the founder of the scientific interpretation of the Qurʾān. All his works include references to the Chinese, Japanese, and other Asian communities. For example, and much earlier than Jawharī, he used different ancient and modern languages, including Chinese and Japanese, along with Tibetan and Tatar, in order to interpret Q 30:22: "And of His signs is the creation of the heavens and the earth and the diversity of your languages and your colors. Indeed in that are signs for those of knowledge."[45] His comments were not limited to ethnicity and languages; using his physiological expertise and his earlier publication on herbs and vegetables and their relation to a healthy soul, mind, and body, he highlighted the role of various spices that grow in different parts of Asia in his second *tafsīrī* work, *Tibyān al-Asrār*. The way he describes the qualities of herbs and their influence on the anatomical structure of human beings is very similar to that found later in Jawharī's *tafsīr*.[46] Al-Iskandarānī also introduces the names of various important geographical places to Arab readers and students, including the Himalayas, when he interprets Q 16:66 and its references to livestock.[47]

Later on, as Johanna Pink has demonstrated, Buddhist literature circulated across Egypt in the nineteenth and twentieth centuries might have well have had an influence on the Egyptians' *tafsīr* production. She outlines the way Tawfīq Ṣidqī (d. 1920), another Egyptian physiologist interested in Islamic debates, discussed that the fig whose name is mentioned in Q 95:1–3 is "the tree of Buddha, the founder of the Buddhist religion whose original truth was corrupted ... considerably because Buddha's teachings were not written down afterwards when the number of his adherents had increased."[48]

43. Strong 1899; Inglis 1916, 587–602.
44. On Buddhism in qurʾānic exegetical discourse see: Pink 2016, 317–338.
45. Al-Iskandarānī 1862, 1:140–141.
46. Jawharī 1935, 24:310–311.
47. Al-Iskandarānī 1882/3, 8–10, 110–111.
48. Pink 2016, 332.

Moreover, Jawharī systematically incorporated recent European findings into his twenty-six-volume commentary on the Qurʾān, and also applied Chinese alphabets and writing styles in his *tafsīr*. He did not limit his references to China, mentioning other Asian societies such as Persia, India, and Malaya. As he wished to raise the profile of and unite Muslims in general and Arabs in particular, he applied Arabic as the superior language, which became more important after the revelation of the Qurʾān. In this regard, he believed that the fluency, style, and calligraphy of the Arabic language was very attractive, and would inspire other communities to learn qurʾānic Arabic. Then, he presented the Arabic and the Chinese translation of Q 112. To support his claims, he asserted that Egyptian culture had a deep influence on the cultures of other societies and ancient Egyptian philosophy shared many things with China (of Confucius), India, and Greece.

These references to non-Islamic Oriental traditions, which greatly affected the development of (modern) qurʾānic exegetical works, have been ignored by the majority of scholars. Simply speaking, scholars did not see any reason to examine how and under what circumstances Chinese literature was introduced to commentators and religious figures in Egypt. The less connection a historical issue has with current political debates, the less interest there is in examining it.

Final Remark: The Neglected Islamic Tradition of Afghanistan

Some important historical sites and regions were already part of a wider civilization, and so they have largely retained their historical titles. For instance, the regions in Afghanistan, which had been a part of Persia, are still seen under the canopy of the Persianate world. This is to some extent true as Afghanistan was historically a large region attached to Persia and was impressed by, and had influence on, other empires. However, one may wonder if Afghanistan is independently studied by scholars, rather than as part of a larger or more historical region.

Also, earlier studies on the Afghans' religion have been conducted either by anthropological historians or scholars of literature, and no one has seriously examined them through the lens of religious and Islamic studies. For example, no qurʾānic exegetical work, trend, or approach emanating from Afghanistan has been introduced to us. This is despite the fact that Kabul University, founded in 1932, and other universities and higher educational centers in Afghanistan, have had qurʾānic sciences programs. Andreas Dürr, who is completing his PhD in anthropology, spent some time in Afghanistan and informed the audience at the DAVO conference in Frankfurt that *Tafsīr al-Jalālay* is the most common classical exegetical work which is still read by Afghan students. He conducted his studies by means of interviews in order to examine "religious education and the discourse about Islamic orthodoxy and local practice in Eastern Afghanistan."

Political discussions revolving around Afghanistan since the late twentieth century limited Afghani Islamic studies to ethnographic and anthropological research and case studies to find an answer to: "what is the root of radicalism?" So, ignorance of the contribution of Afghans and Afghanistan to the formation of Islamic civilization and Islamic studies remains. For instance, to my knowledge, almost all scholarly works on the history of the Qurʾān and *tafsīr* in European languages are silent about earlier famous commentators who were born in Afghanistan. Among them is an influential but obscure scholar, Mawlānī Yaʿqūb Charkhī (d. ca. 851/1447), who was born in the small village of Ghaznī, in what is today Afghanistan. He is the author of the famous Qurʾān commentary, *Tafsīr-e Charkhī*, which in his time was soon translated into various languages: the Chagatai language by Ḥājī Sayyid ʿAtāʾī in 993/1585; Ottoman Turkish by Ghorāb-zāda (d. ca. 1099/1688); and later into Urdu in 2005.[49] The importance of this *tafsīr* becomes clearer as it includes references to important exegetical works, some of which remained unknown for centuries.[50] Afghanistan's Islamic and exegetical schools are still unknown and it is as yet unclear when scholars will pay special attention to its contribution to the development of Islam and the Qurʾān.

The fear of Orientalism and being labelled as "Orientalists" prevent Western scholars of Islam from being critical of history. The reduction of experts of the East to the Arab world, lack of philological expertise as well as unfamiliarity with Muslim and non-Muslim manuscripts, has contributed to the study of Islam being less critical, if not actually apologetic. A large number of scholars have to accept religious/Islamic phenomena as well as teachings in order to avoid being called a "skeptic," whose interest, according to their opponents, lies in criticism of and/or downgrading Muslim culture and civilization.

This chapter, thus, invited readers to re-examine earlier classical and modern literature on the Orient, Orientals, and Orientalism, produced by both Muslim and non-Muslim scholars.

49. Nou-shāhī 1393/2014.
50. Daneshgar (forthcoming).

Bibliography

Ali, K. 2006. *Sexual Ethics and Islam: Feminist Reflections on Qur'an, Hadith and Jurisprudence*. London.

Alvīrī, M. 1393/2014. *Muṭāliʿāt-e Islāmī dar Gharb*. 7th edition. Tehran.

Atjeh, A. B. 1952. *Sejarah al-Qurʾān*. Jakarta.

Baring-Gould. S. 1884. *Legends of the Patriarchs and Prophets and Other Old Testament Characters*. New York.

Campanini, M. 2016. *Philosophical Perspectives on Modern Qur'anic Exegesis Key Paradigms and Concepts*. Sheffield.

Daneshgar, M. 2016. "Western Non-Muslim Qurʾanic Studies in Muslim Academic Contexts." *Islamic Studies Today: Essays in Honor of Andrew Rippin*, edited by M. Daneshgar and W. A. Saleh, 367–385. Leiden.

——. 2017. *Ṭanṭāwī Jawharī and the Qurʾān: Tafsīr and Social Concerns in the Twentieth Century*. London and New York.

——. 2018a. "Philosophical Perspectives on Modern Qur'anic Exegesis Key Paradigms and Concepts, by Massimo Campanini." *Reading Religion*. June 12. http://readingreligion.org/books/philosophical-perspectives-modern-quranic-exegesis.

——. 2018 b. "Censored Manuscripts, Censored Intellects: Can We Trust the Past?" *Mizan*. April 23. http://www.mizanproject.org/censored-manuscripts-censored-intellects/.

——. 2019. *Studying the Qurʾān in the Muslim Academy*. Oxford.

——. forthcoming. "Islamic Exegetical Tradition in Afghanistan."

Daneshgar, M.,and D. Kerr. 2017. *Middle Eastern and Islamic Materials in Special Collections, University of Otago*. Dunedin.

Falagas, M. E. et al. 2006. "Arab Science in the Golden Age (750–1258 CE) and Today." *The FASEB Journal* 20. 10:1581–1586.

Haycock, D. B. 2016. "Ancient Egypt in 17th and 18th Century England." In *The Wisdom of Egypt: Changing Visions Through the Ages*, edited by P. J. Ucko and T. Champion, 2nd edition, 133–160. London.

Huet, P. D. 1717. *The History of the Commerce and Navigation of the Ancients*. London.

Hughes, A. W. 2017. *Shared Identities: Medieval and Modern Imaginings of Judeo-Islam*. Oxford.

Inglis, J. W. 1916. "The Christian Element in Chinese Buddhism." *International Review of Mission* 5.4:587–602.

Iqbal, M. 2008. "Integrated Encyclopedia of the Qur'ān (IEQ): Raison d'être and Project Summary." *Islamic Studies* 47.4:537–543.

al-Iskandarānī. M. A. 1862. *Kashf al-Asrār al-Rabāniyya*. Cairo.

——. 1882/3. *Tibyān al-Asrār*. Damascus.
Jawharī. Ṭ. 1935. *Al-Jawāhir fī Tafsīr al-Qurʾān*. 26 vols. Cairo.
Karpat, K. H. 2001. *The Politicization of Islam: Reconstructing Identity, State, Faith, and Community in the Late Ottoman State*. Oxford.
Kurd ʿAlī. M. 1922. *Gharāʾib al-Gharb*. 2 vols. Kuwait.
——. 1948. "al-Mustaʿribūn min ʿulamā al-Mashriqiyyāt." *Majalla al-Majmaʿ al-ʿilmī al-ʿArabī bi-Dimishq* 23.3:347–362.
Muhametov, A. R. and Laila-Olga But. 2013. *Love and Sex in Islam: The Collection of Fatwas and Articles. Popular Theological Edition*. Bloomington, IN.
Muqātil b. Sulaymān. 1423/2002. *Tafsīr Muqātil*. Beirut.
Nadwi, A. H. A. 1983. *Islamic Studies, Orientalists, and Muslim Scholars*. Translated by M. Ahmad. Lucknow.
Nawawī al-Jāwī al-Bantānī. 1417/1996. *Marāḥ Labīd li-Kashf Maʿnā al-Qurʾān al-Majīd*. Beirut.
Nishihara, D. 2005. "Said, Orientalism, and Japan." *Alif: Journal of Comparative Poetics* 25:241–253.
Nou-shāhī, ʿĀ. 1393/2014. "Charikhī, Yaʿqūb." *Encyclopaedia of the World of Islam*. vol. 11. http://rch.ac.ir/article/Details/7935.
Pink, J. 2016. "The Fig, the Olive, and the Cycles of Prophethood Q 95:1-3 and the Image of History in Early 20th-Century Qurʾanic Exegesis." In *Islamic Studies Today: Essays in Honor of Andrew Rippin*, edited by M. Daneshgar and W. A. Saleh, 317–338. Leiden.
Reynolds, G. S. 2009. "The Muslim Jesus: Dead or Alive?" *Bulletin of the School of Oriental and African Studies* 72. 2:237–258.
Rippin, Andrew. 2012. *Muslims: Their Religious Beliefs and Practices*. Third edition. London and New York.
Ṣahāb, A. 1938. *Farhang-e Khvāvar-shenāsān: Dar Sharḥ-e Ḥāl va Khadamāt-e Dāneshmandān-e Īrān-shenās va Mostashreqīn*. Tehran.
Said, E. W. 1978. *Orientalism*. New York.
Saleh, W. A. "A Fifteenth-century Muslim Hebraist: al-Biqāʿī and His Defense of Using the Bible to Interpret the Qurʾān." *Speculum* 83. 3: 629–654.
Salim Khan. M. 2008. *Islamic Medicine*. New York.
Strong, D. M. 1899. *The Metaphysic of Christianity and Buddhism: A Symphony*. London.

Index